further

01

Hey! We are the foto
We are more
graphy studen
29 different universit
from all over the wor
old blue bus is drive
Bangert. We visit ph
conferences
and we pres
around the b
and exhibitio

ɔus society.

ıan 400 photo-

s studying at

es and schools

d. Our 30 year

n by Christoph

otography festivals,

and workshops—

nt our work in and

s during screenings

s in public spaces.

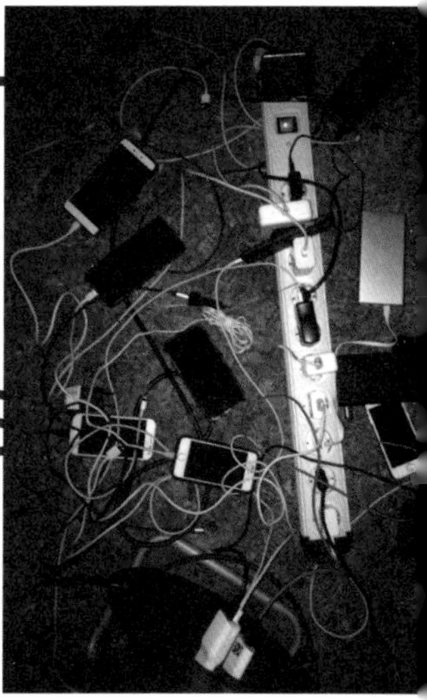

The bus is a photo s
The fotobus proje
on solidarity and
We help each oth
We are a bit like a fa
neys are experimer
They are free of ch
student of photogra

This is made possib
and supporting mer

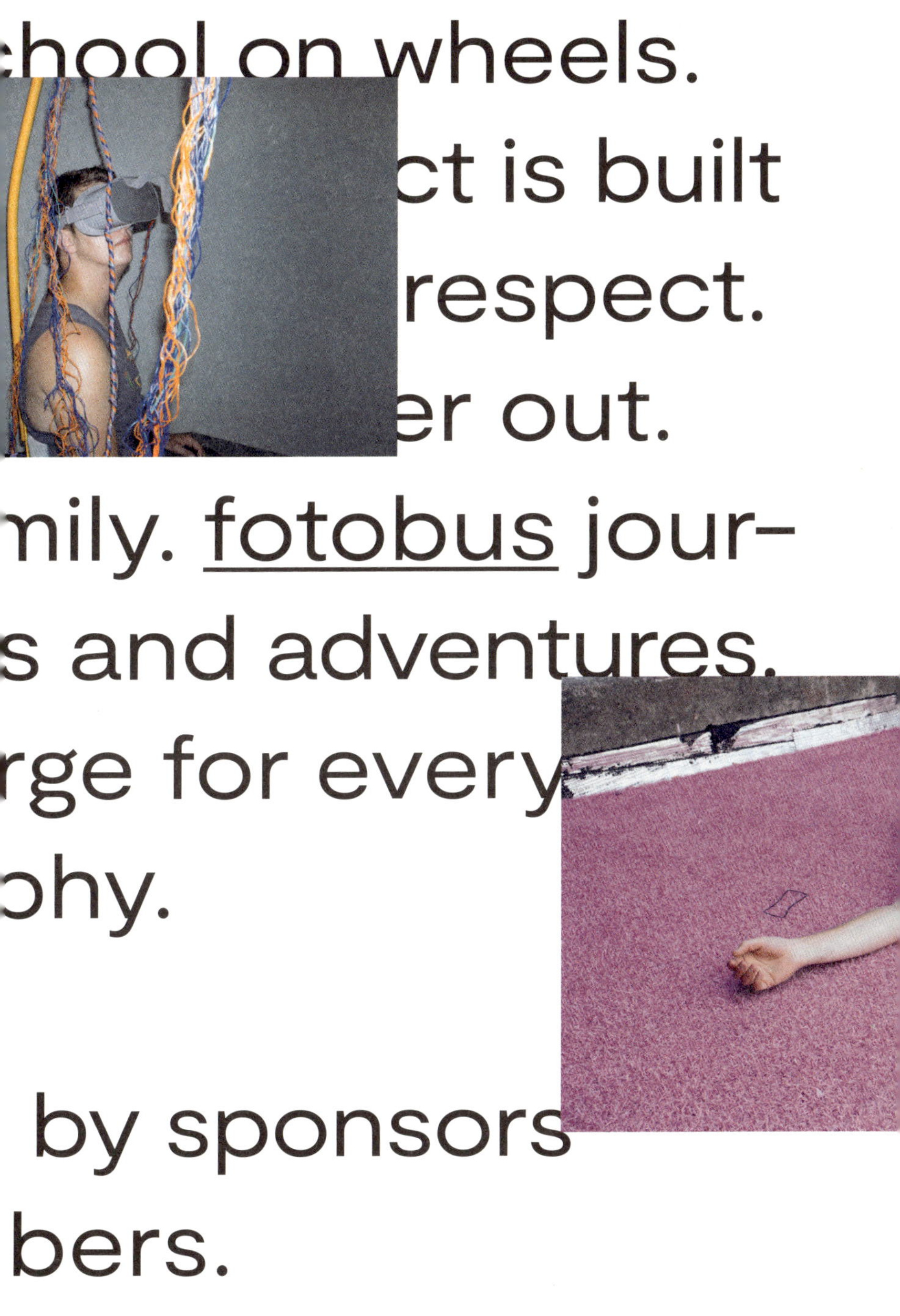

chool on wheels.

ct is built

respect.

er out.

nily. fotobus jour–

s and adventures.

rge for every

phy.

by sponsors

bers.

You are holding the
our annual publicati
in your hands. It sh
works by our memb
senting a cross sec
young engaged ph

By picking up
you are supp
and help us, well, to

ery first issue of

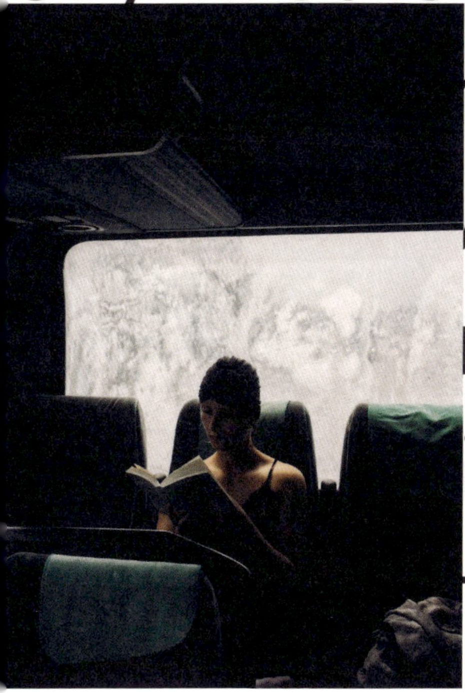

n *further*

ws 34

rs, repre-

ion of

tography

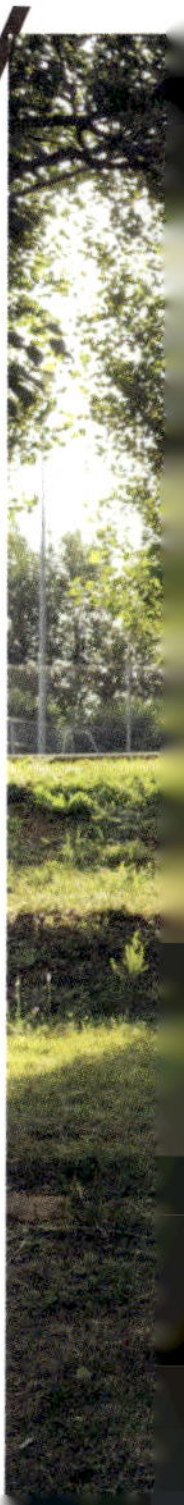

his copy of *further*

rting our activities

go further!

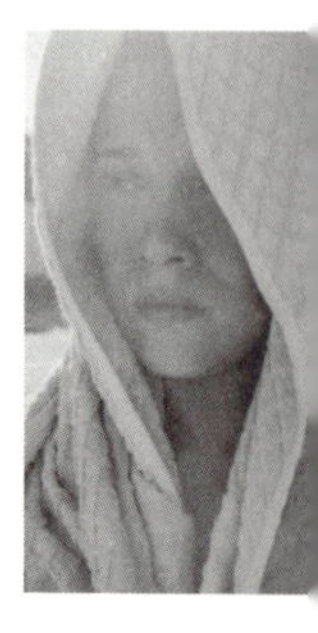

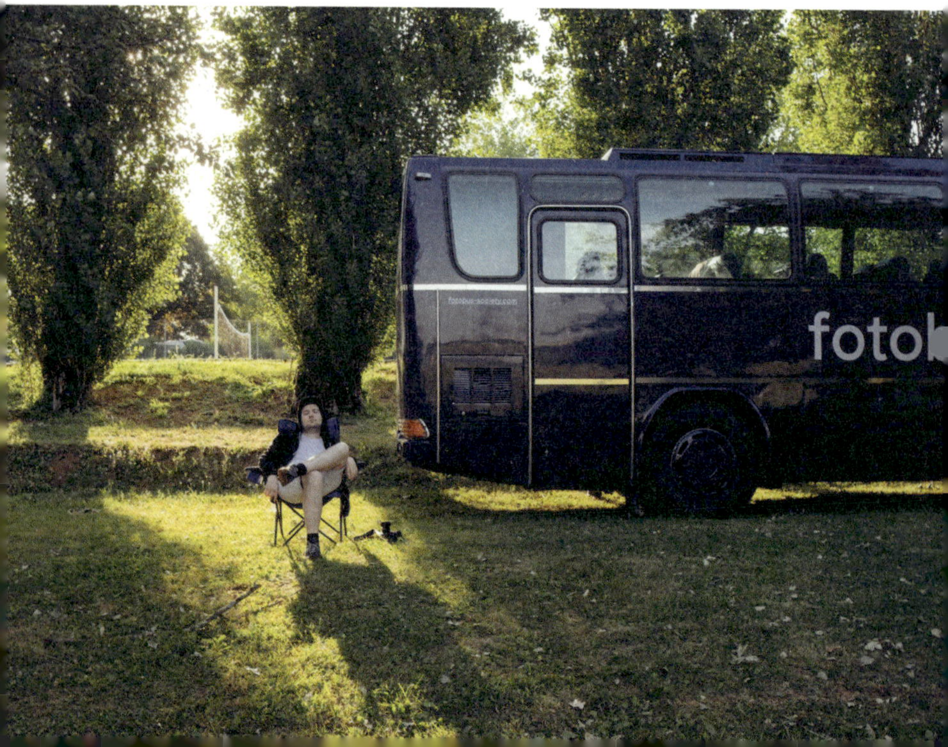

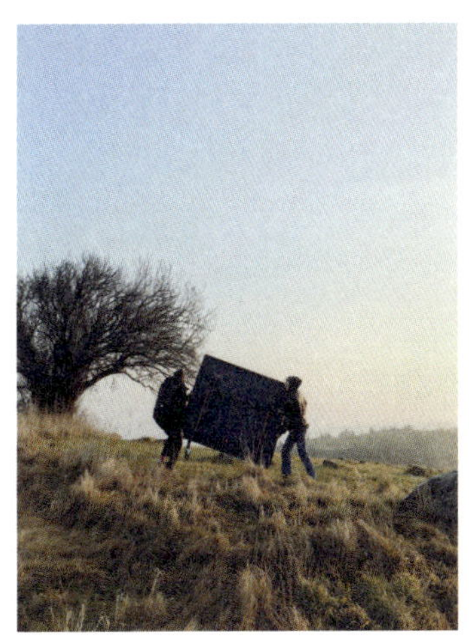

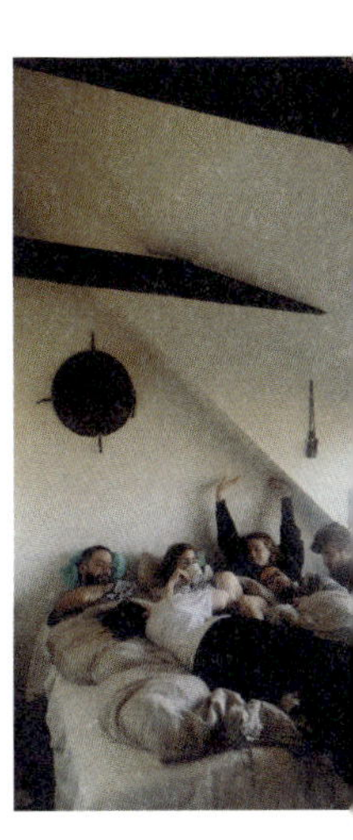

fotobus society

01

The origin of the marksmen's clubs in Germany goes back to civil defense militias in the Middle Ages. Most of them still have strict rules, do not allow female members and represent conservative Christian values. Each club hosts a "Schützen-fest", an annual festival that lasts three days and consists of a church service, parades through the village as well as dances and a competitive shooting of a wooden bird target to elect the annual king.

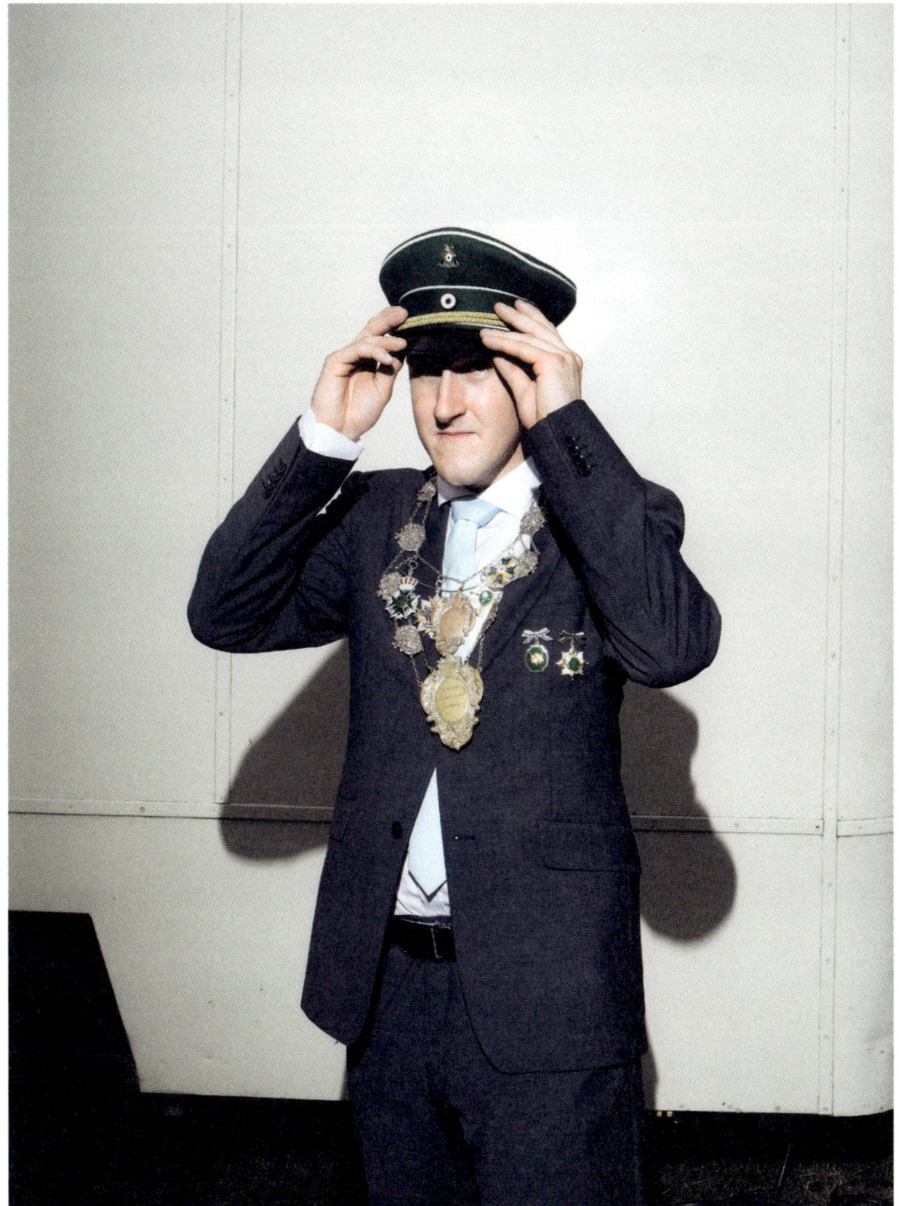

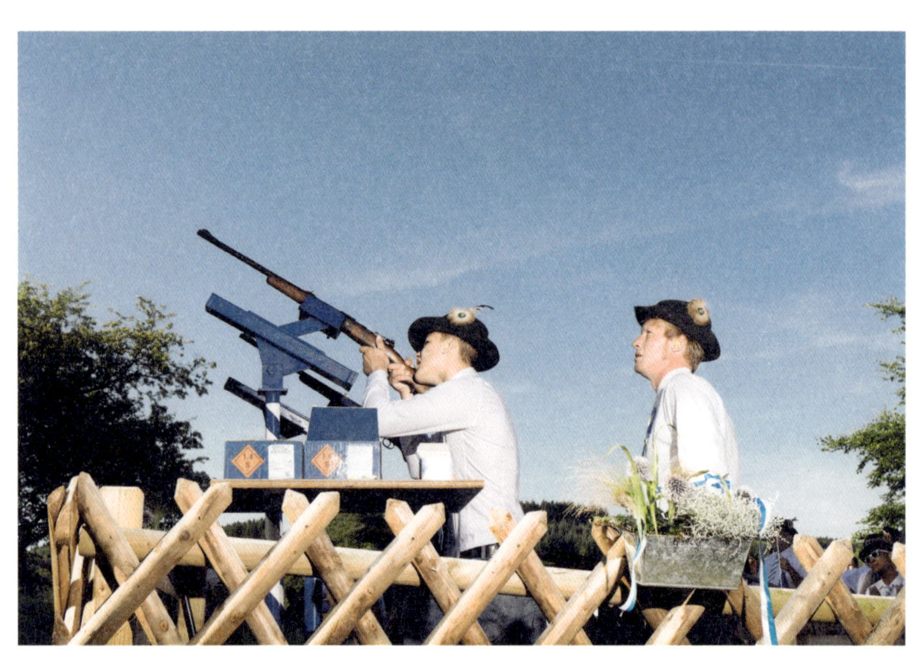

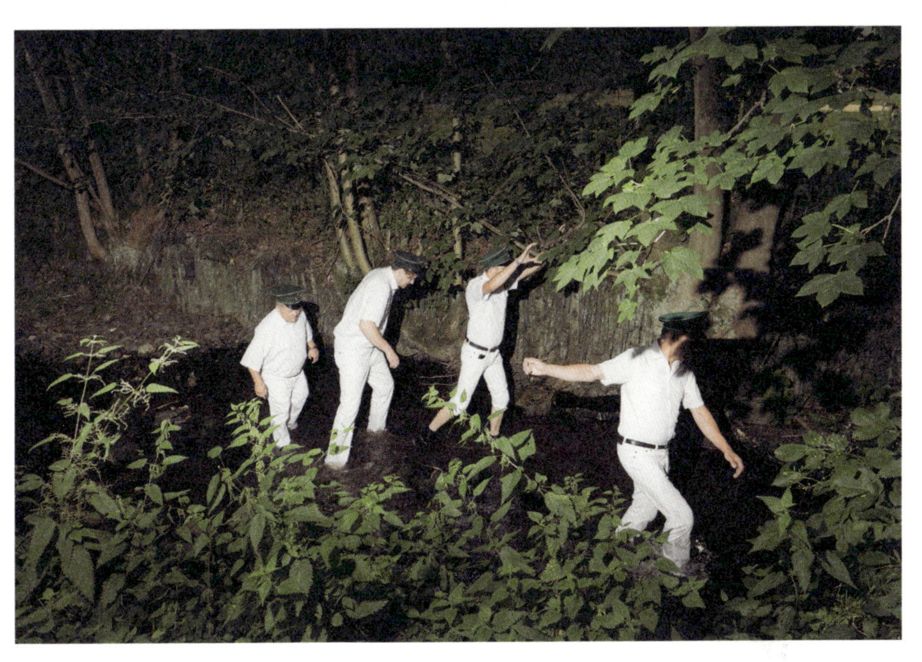

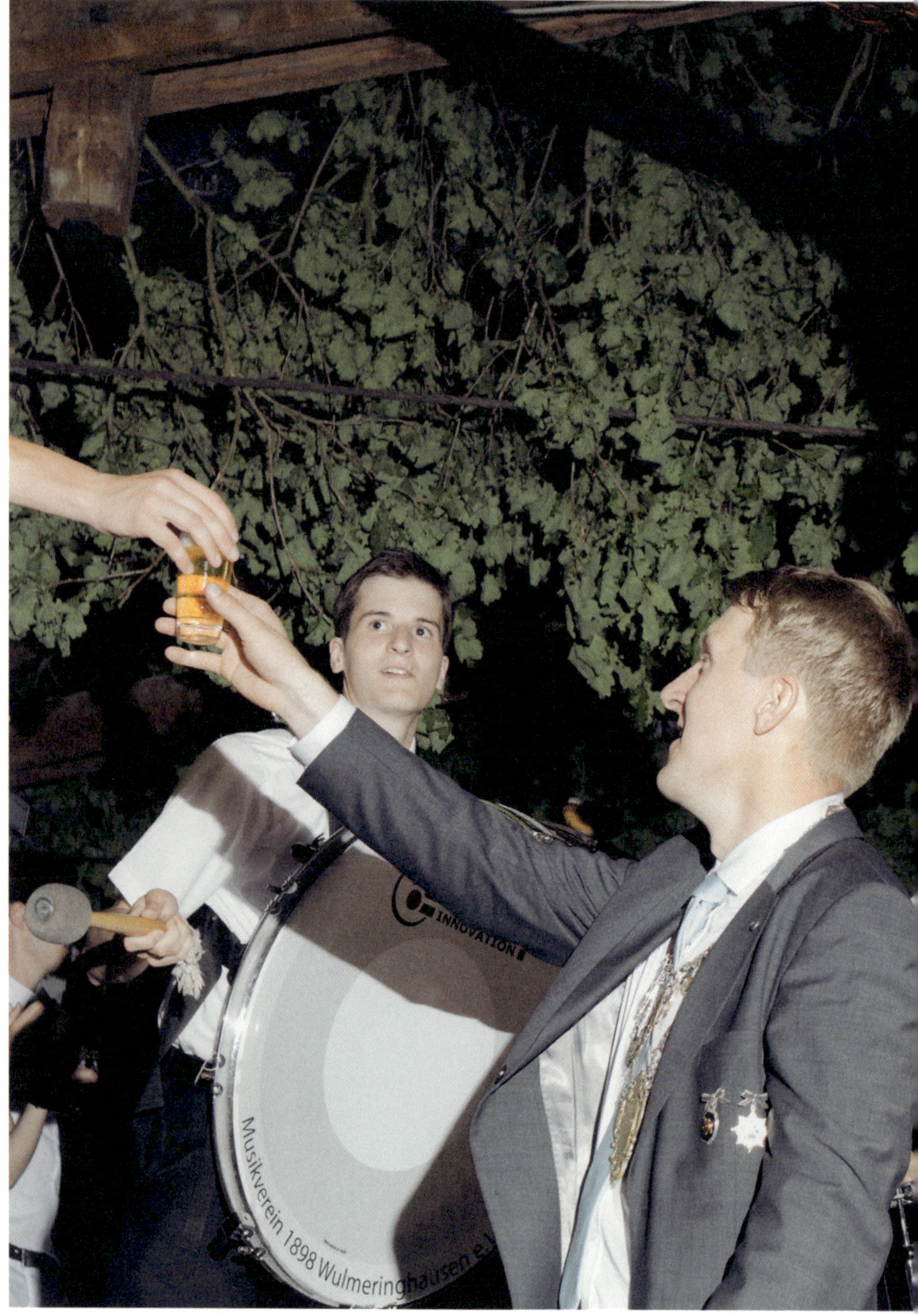
INNOVATION
Musikverein 1898 Wulmeringhausen e.

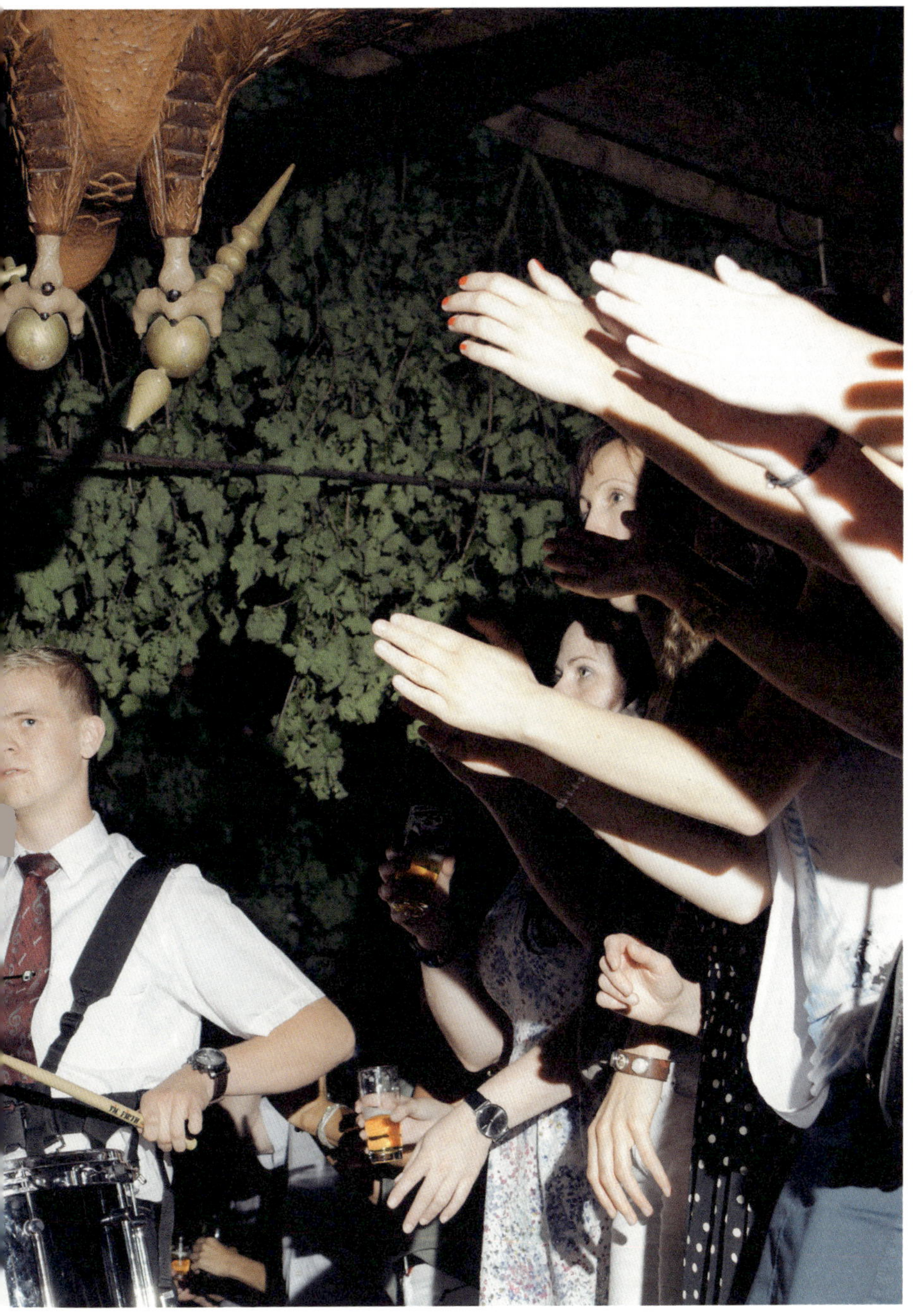

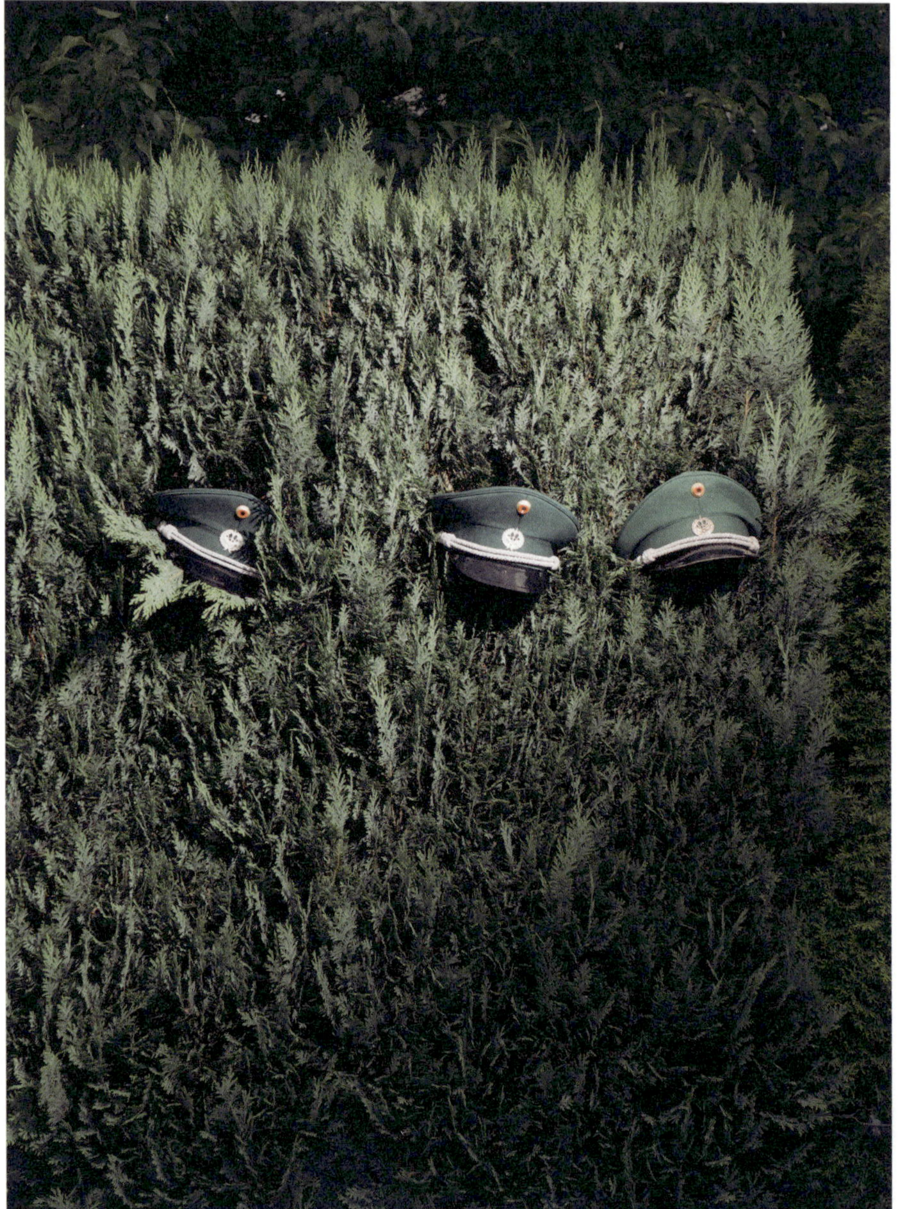

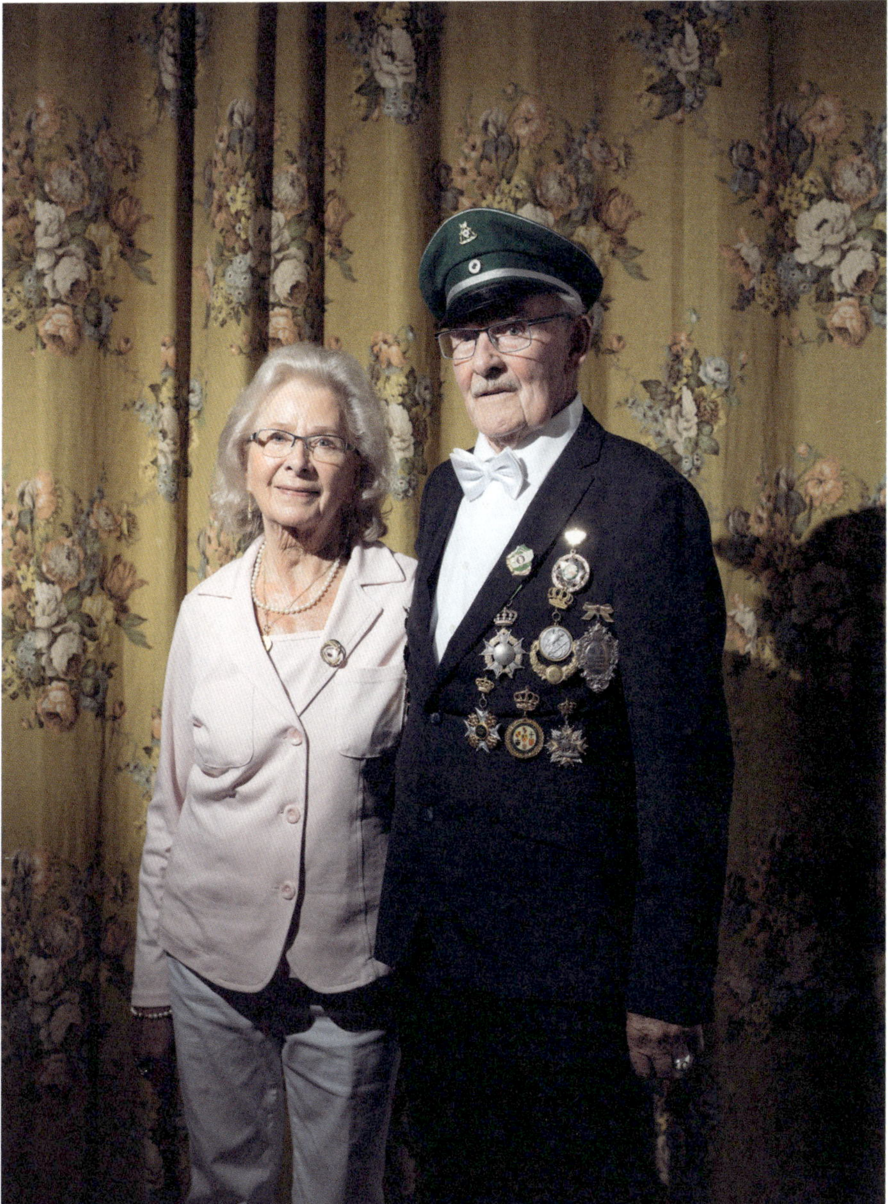

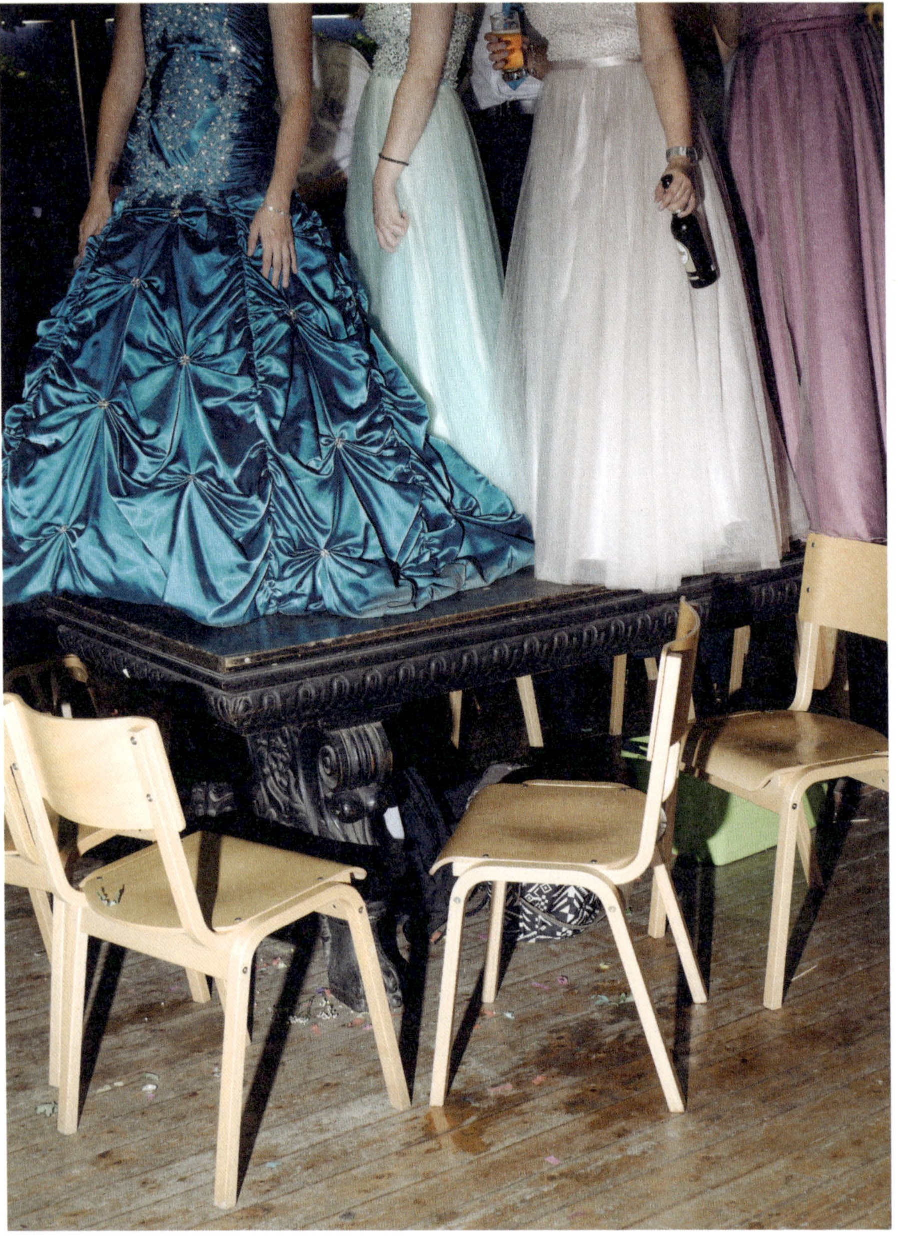

Mafalda Rakoš

I Want To Disappear — Approaching Eating Disorders

02

What does it feel like to be affected? How is this conflict linked to one's own (sexual) identity? Why does controlling one's body help someone to feel "better"? 20 protagonists shared their testimonials, their drawings, texts, sculptures, and pictures to show that eating disorders are never a sign of a lonely or weak person.

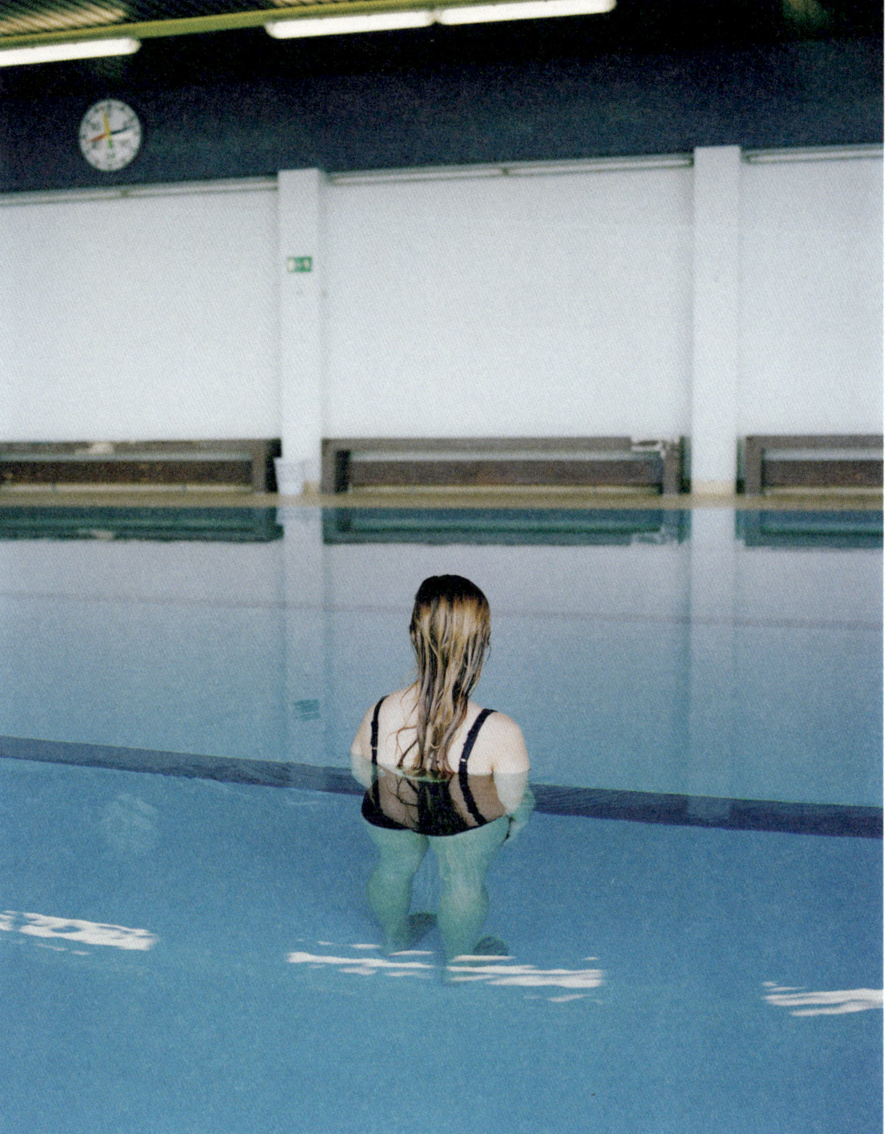

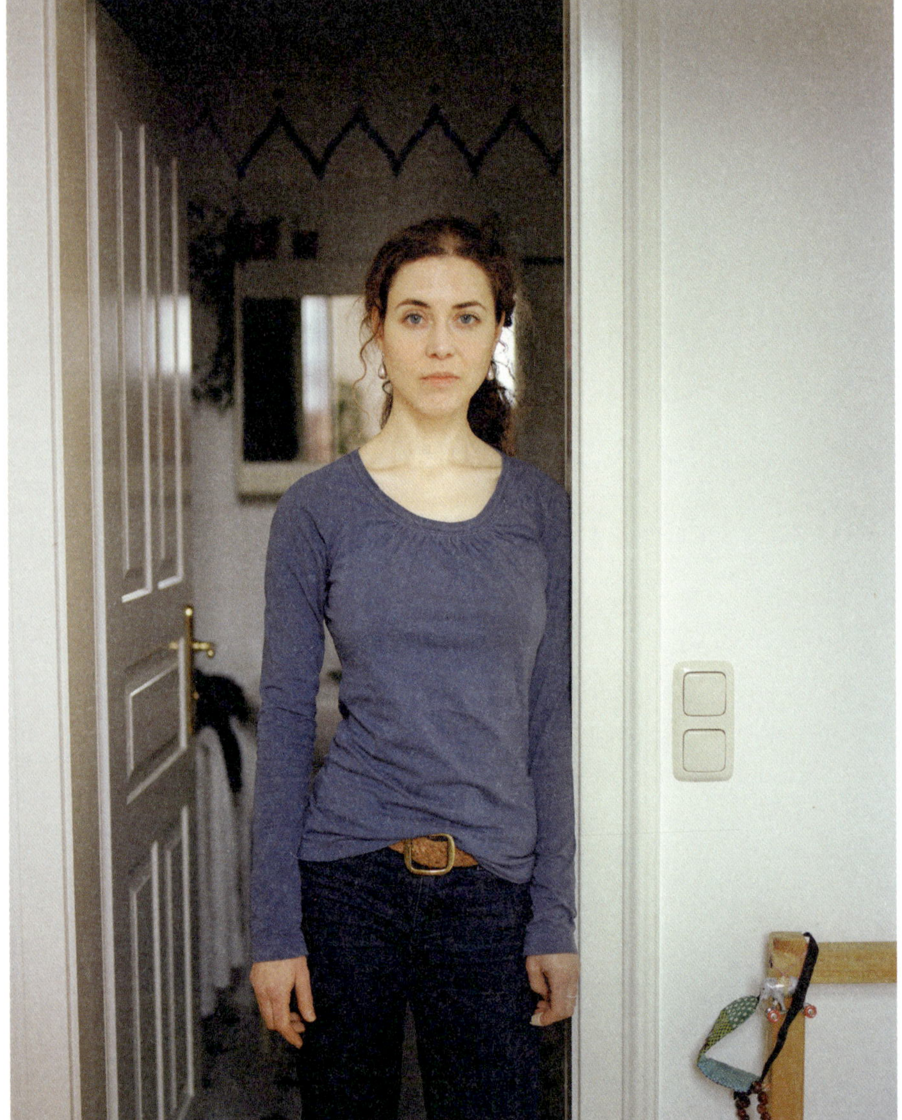

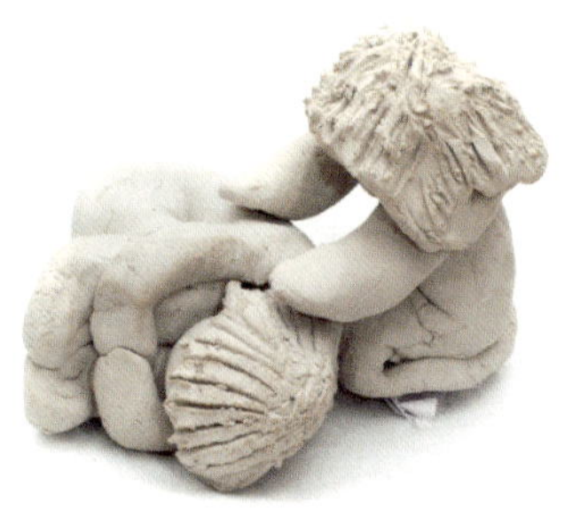

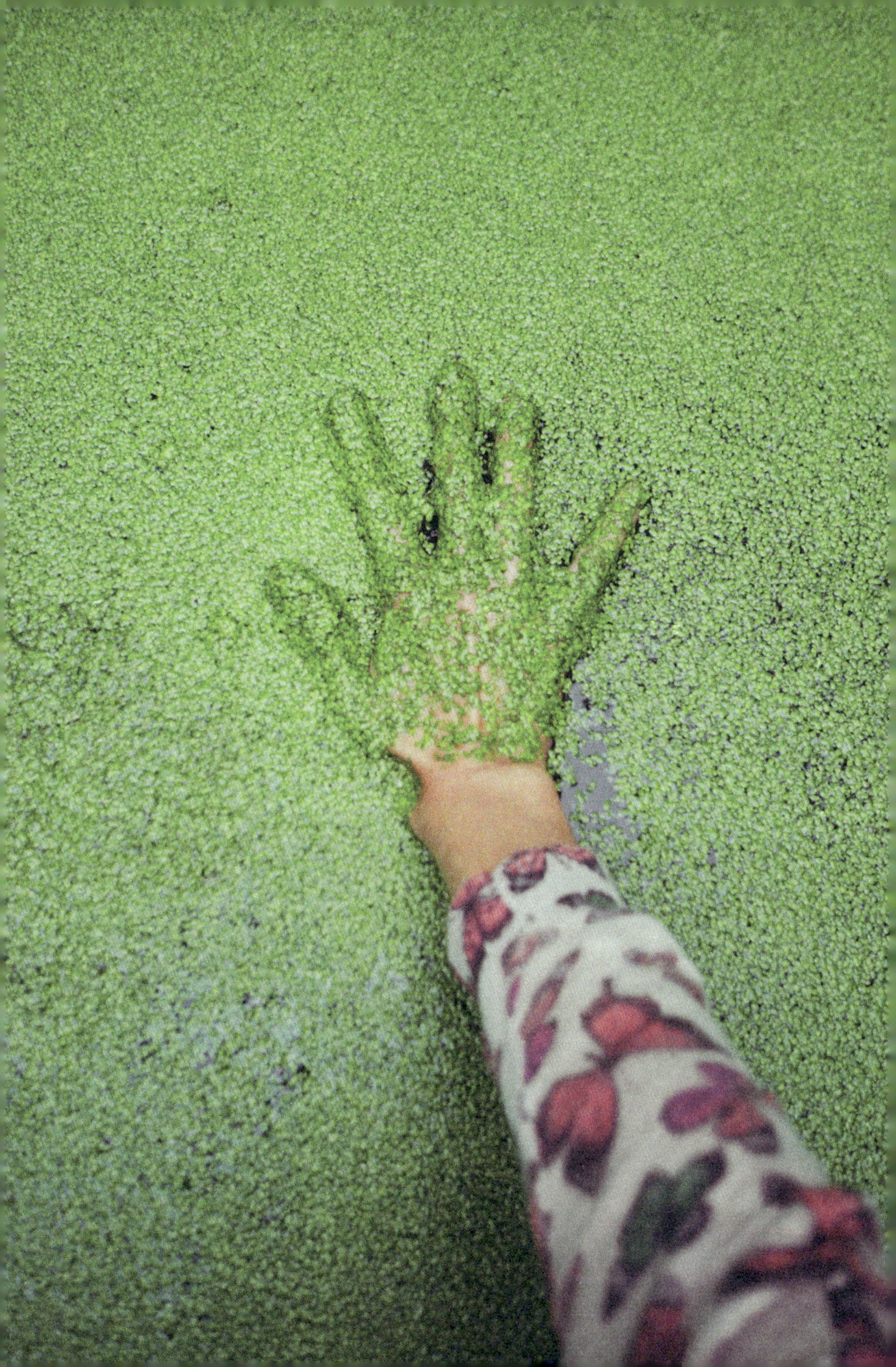

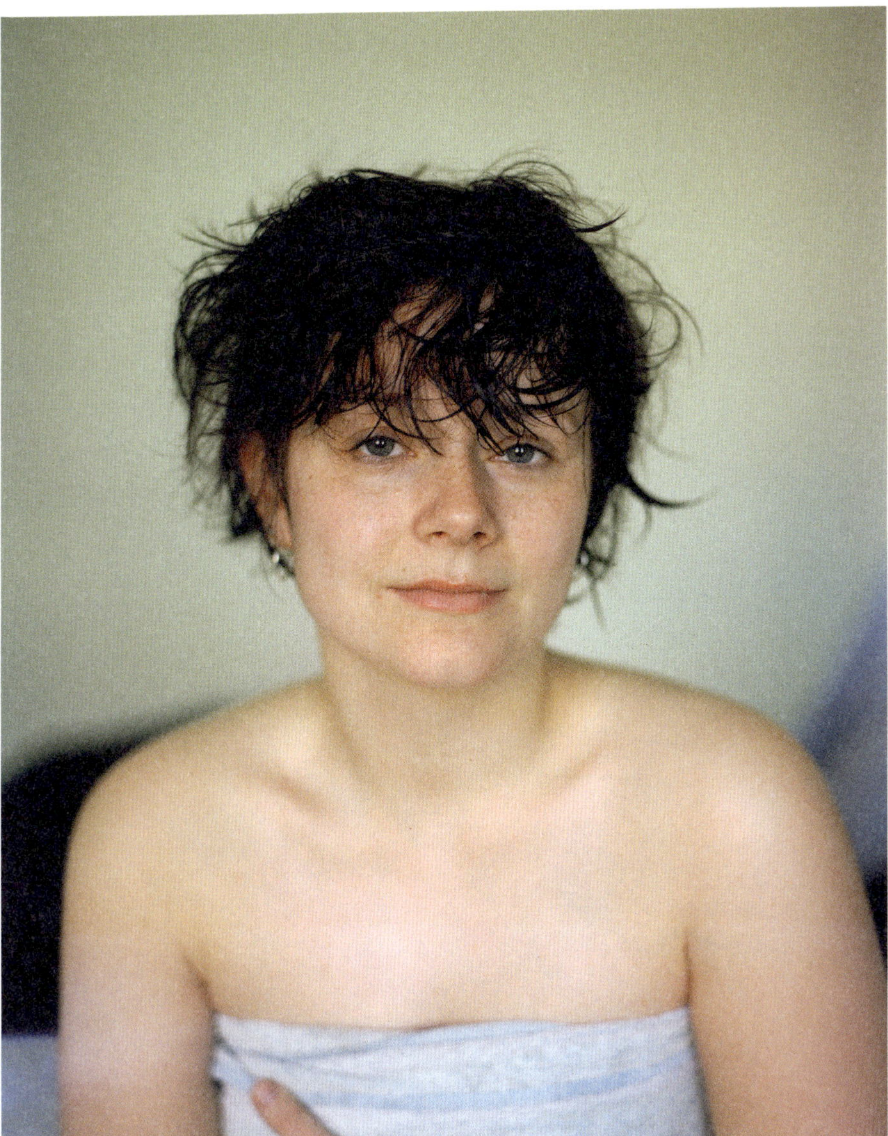

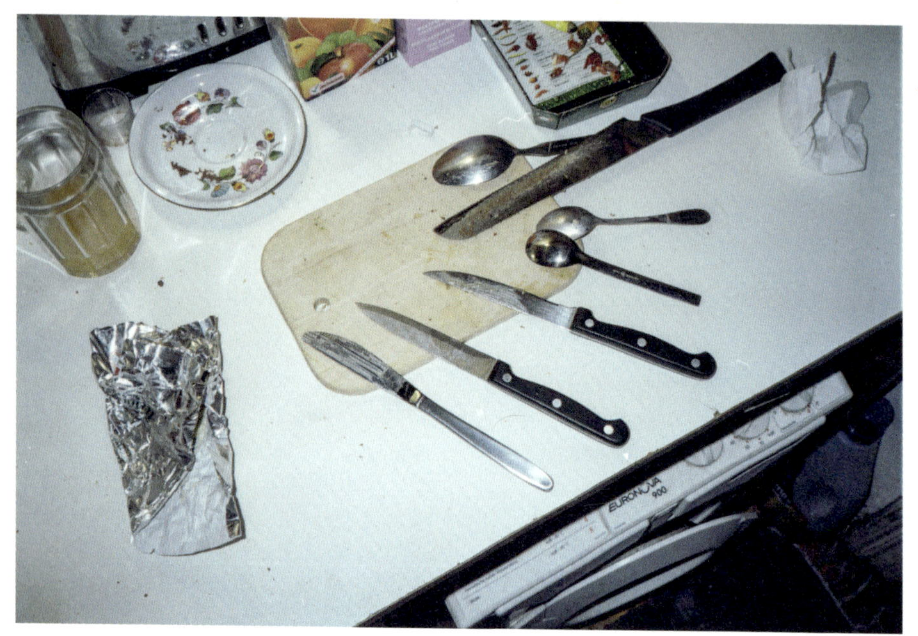
EURONOVA
900

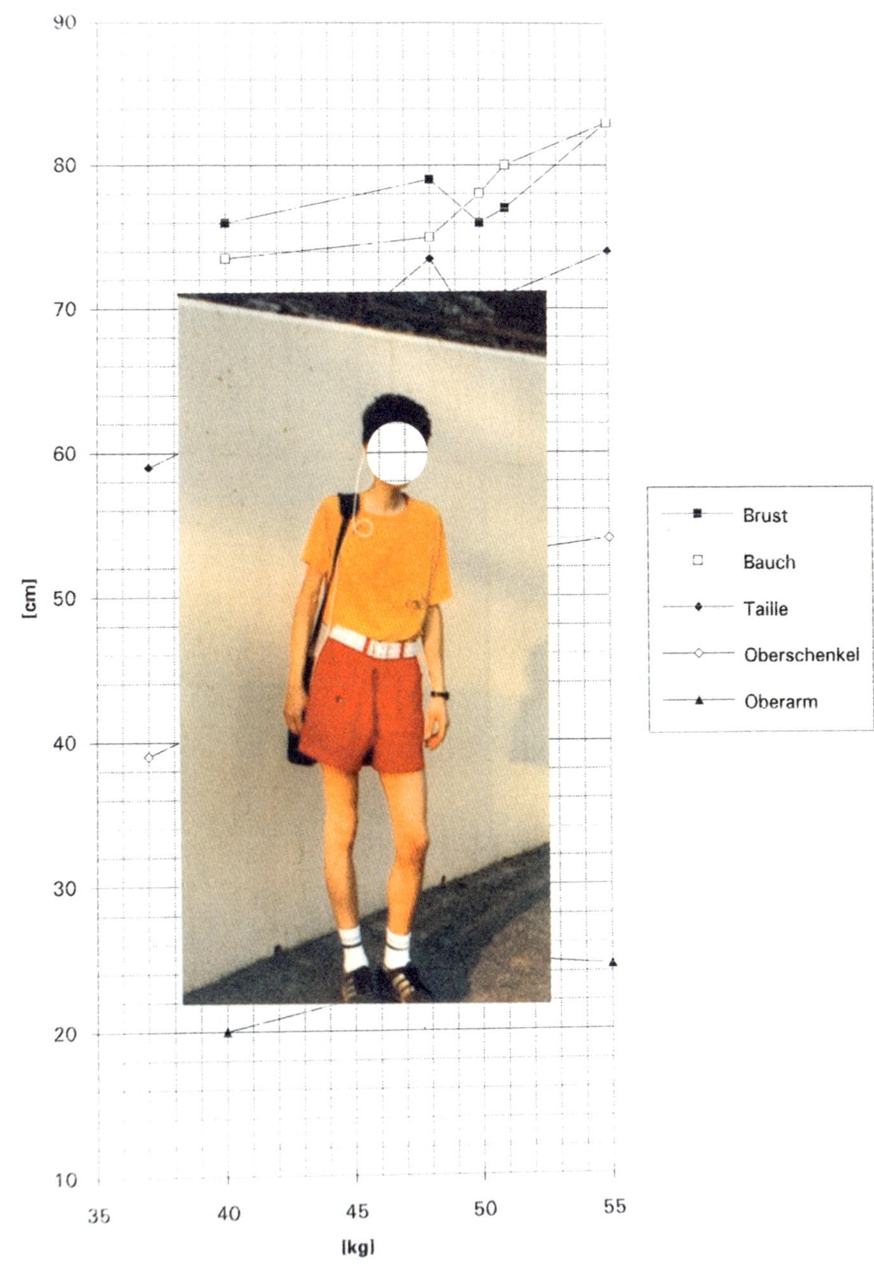

90
80
70
60
50
40
30
20
10
[cm]
35
40
45
50
55
[kg]
Brust
Bauch
Taille
Oberschenkel
Oberarm

03

Every second murder remains unprosecuted in Germany. My sister died on March 2nd, 2018 at the age of 17. Her diaries revealed that she had been sexually abused. Six months earlier, my little half-sister had also reported sexual abuse by her father. There was no investigation.

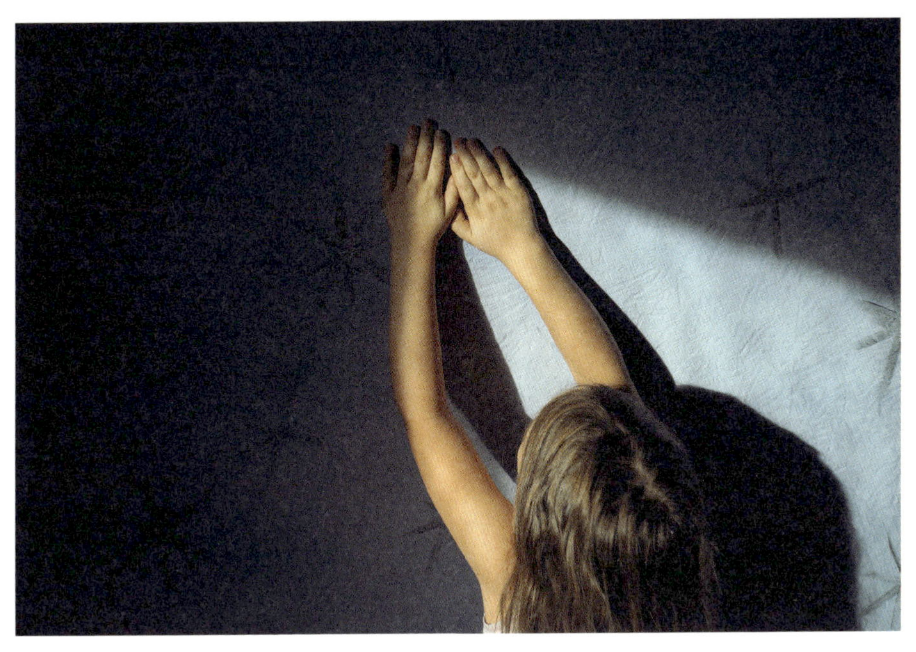

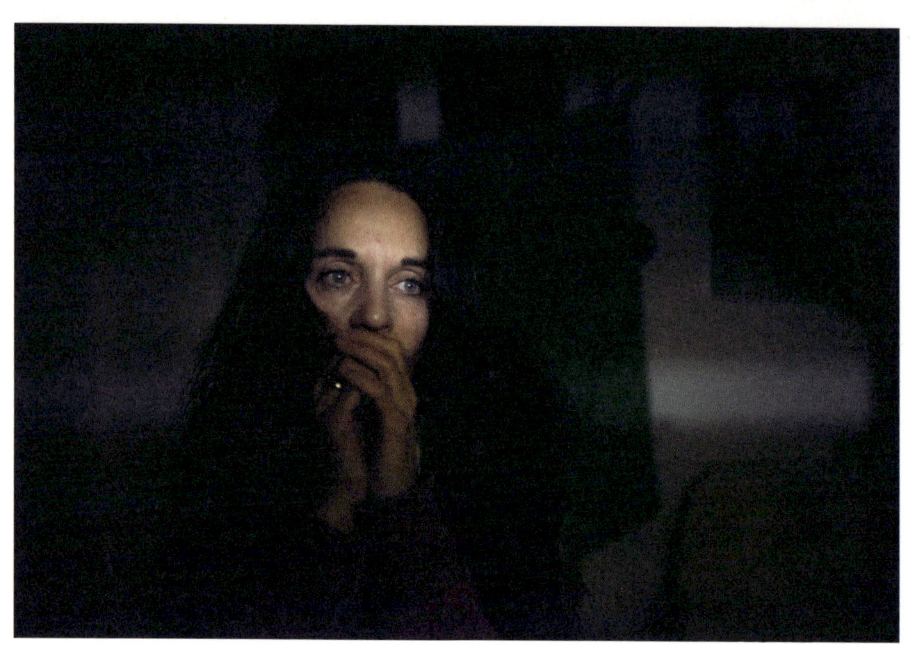

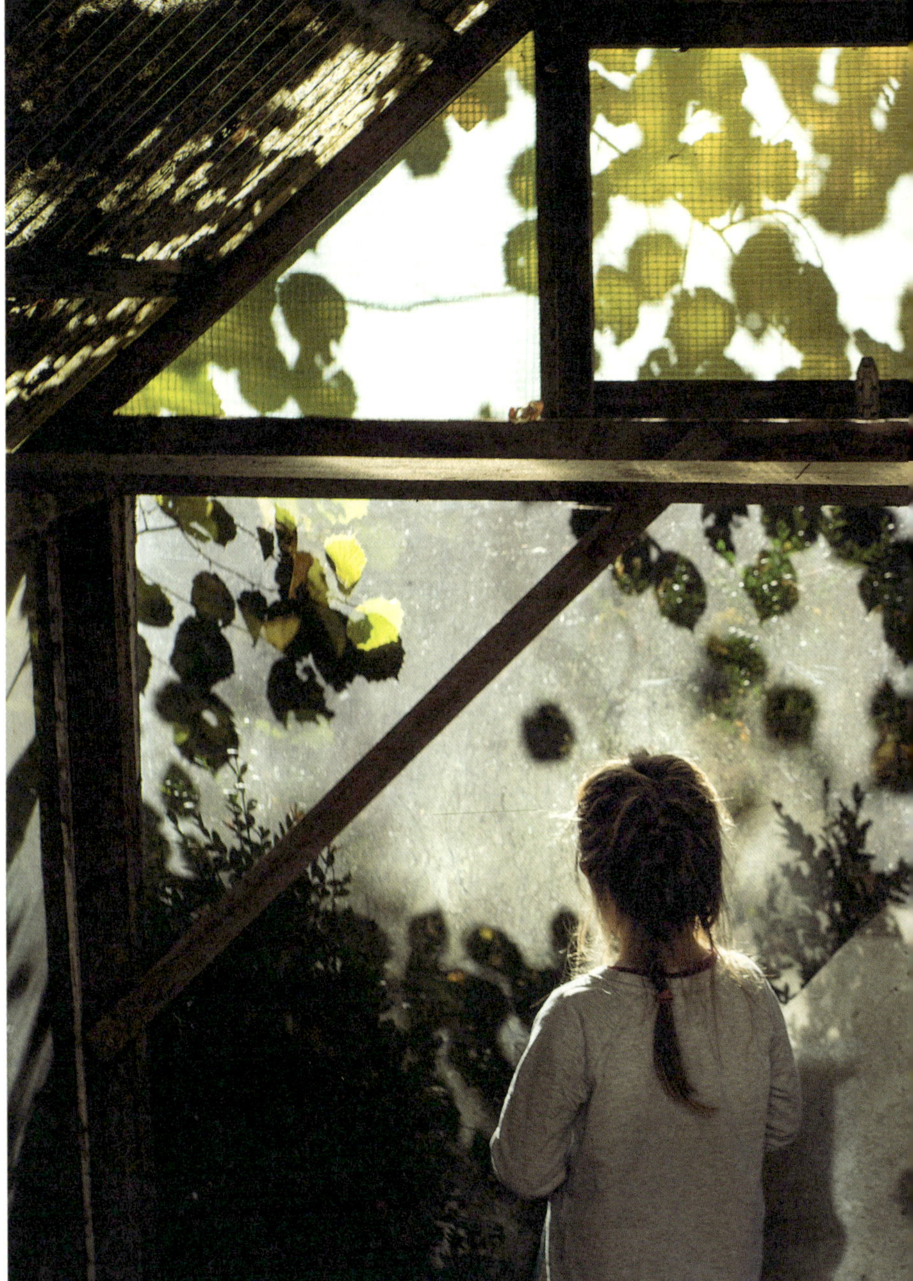

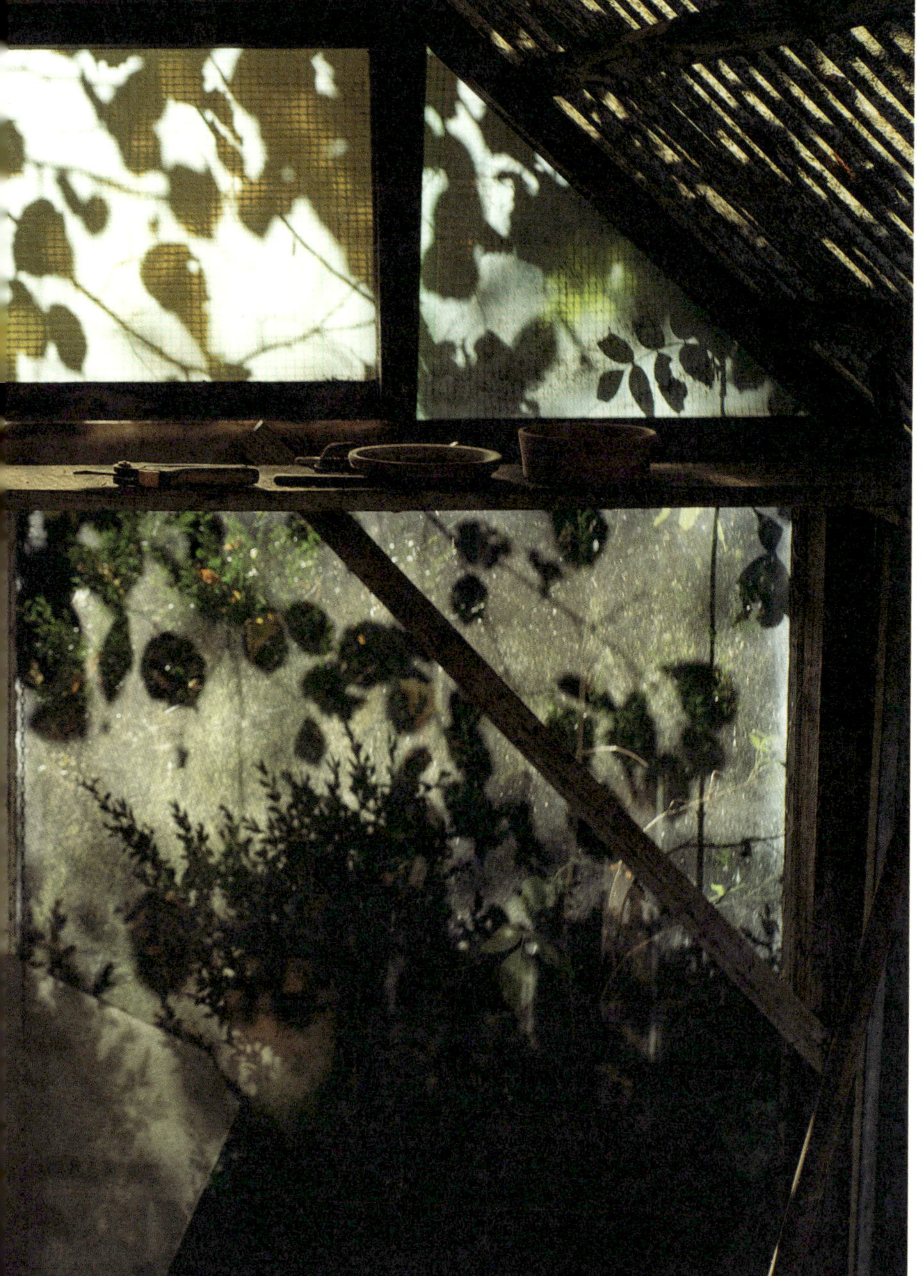

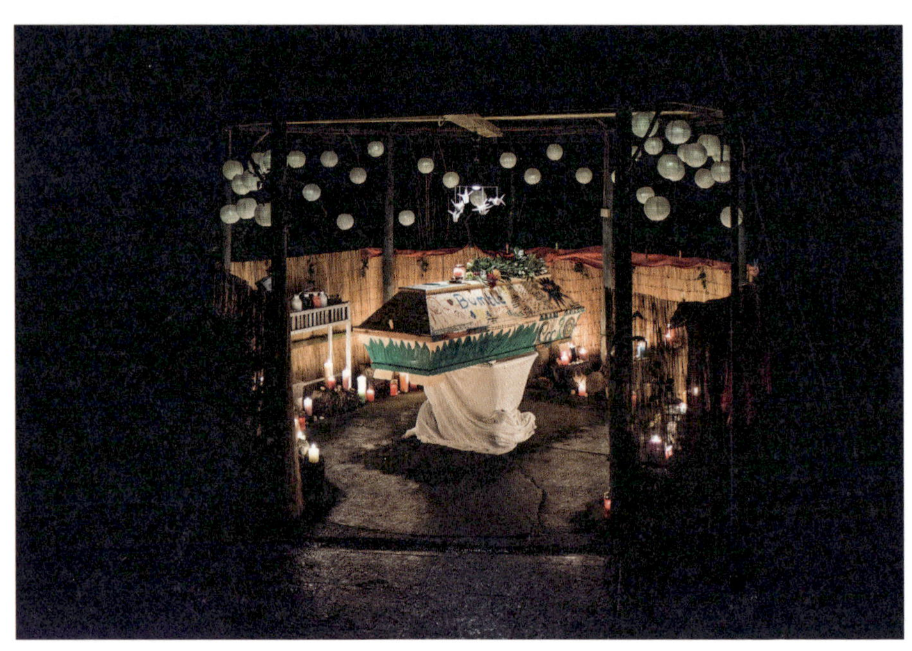

04

People often expect a logical answer for everything that happens around them. The lack of conclusions for certain perceptions creates the possibility of acceptance.

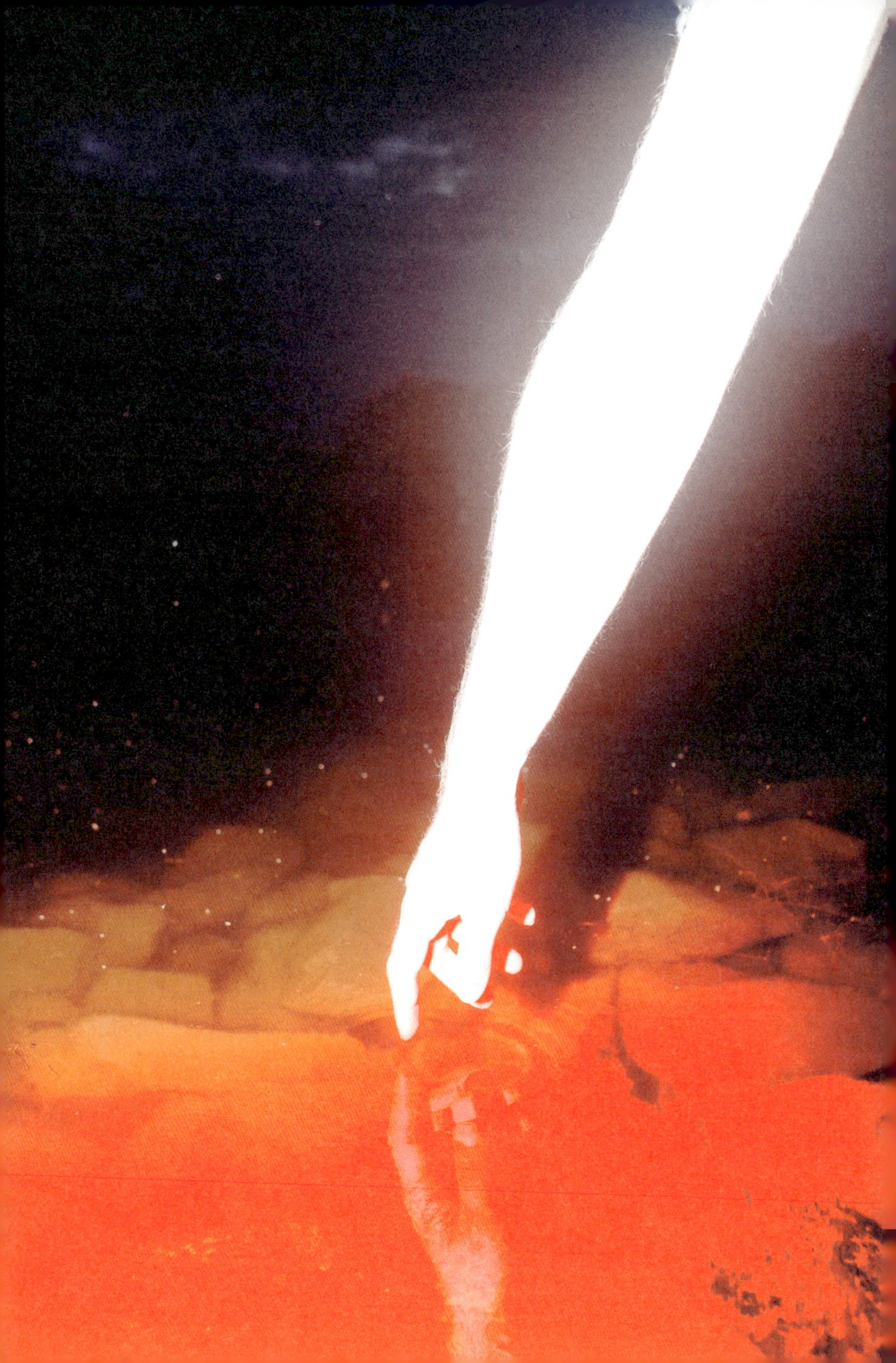

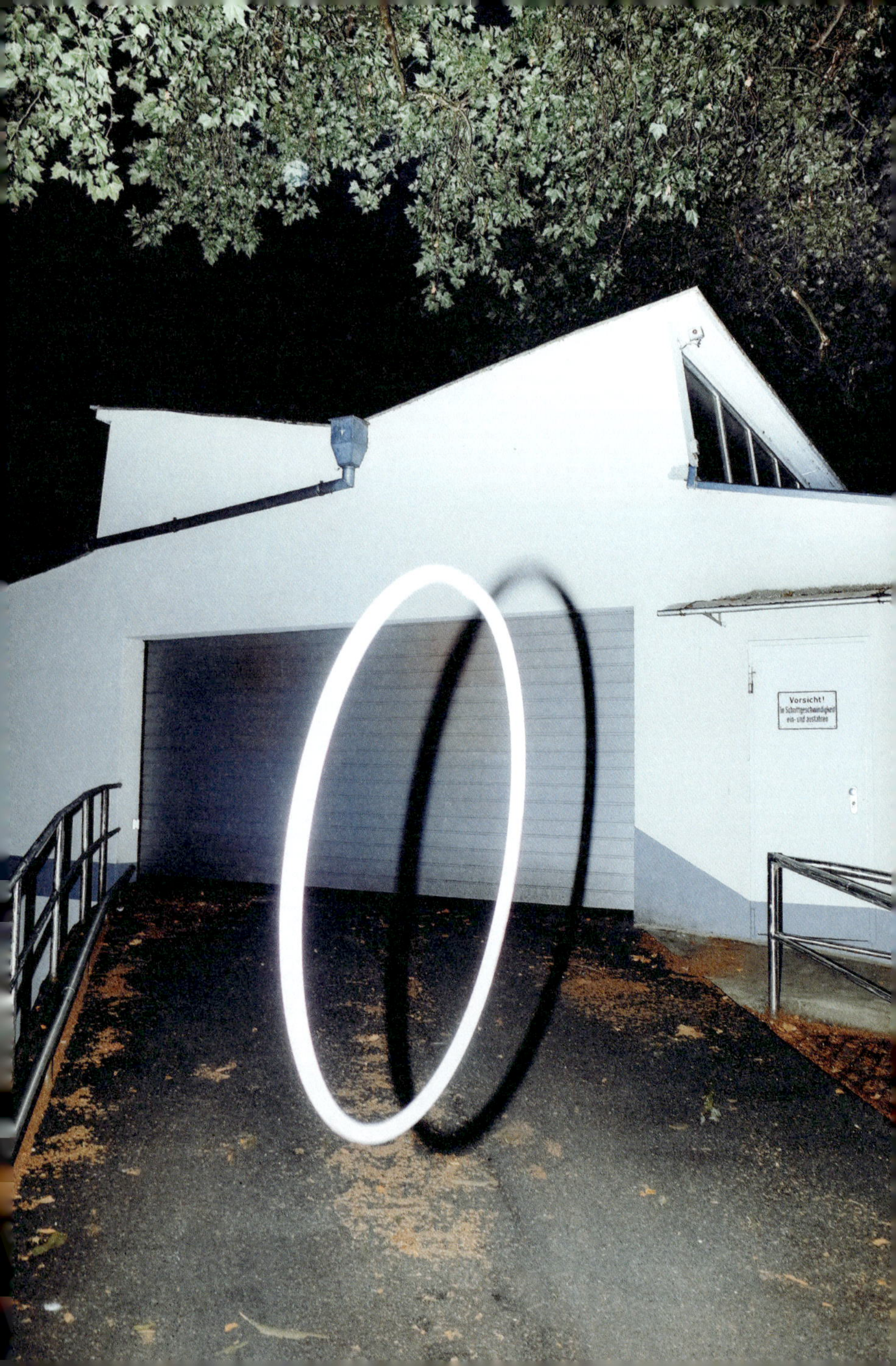
Vorsicht!

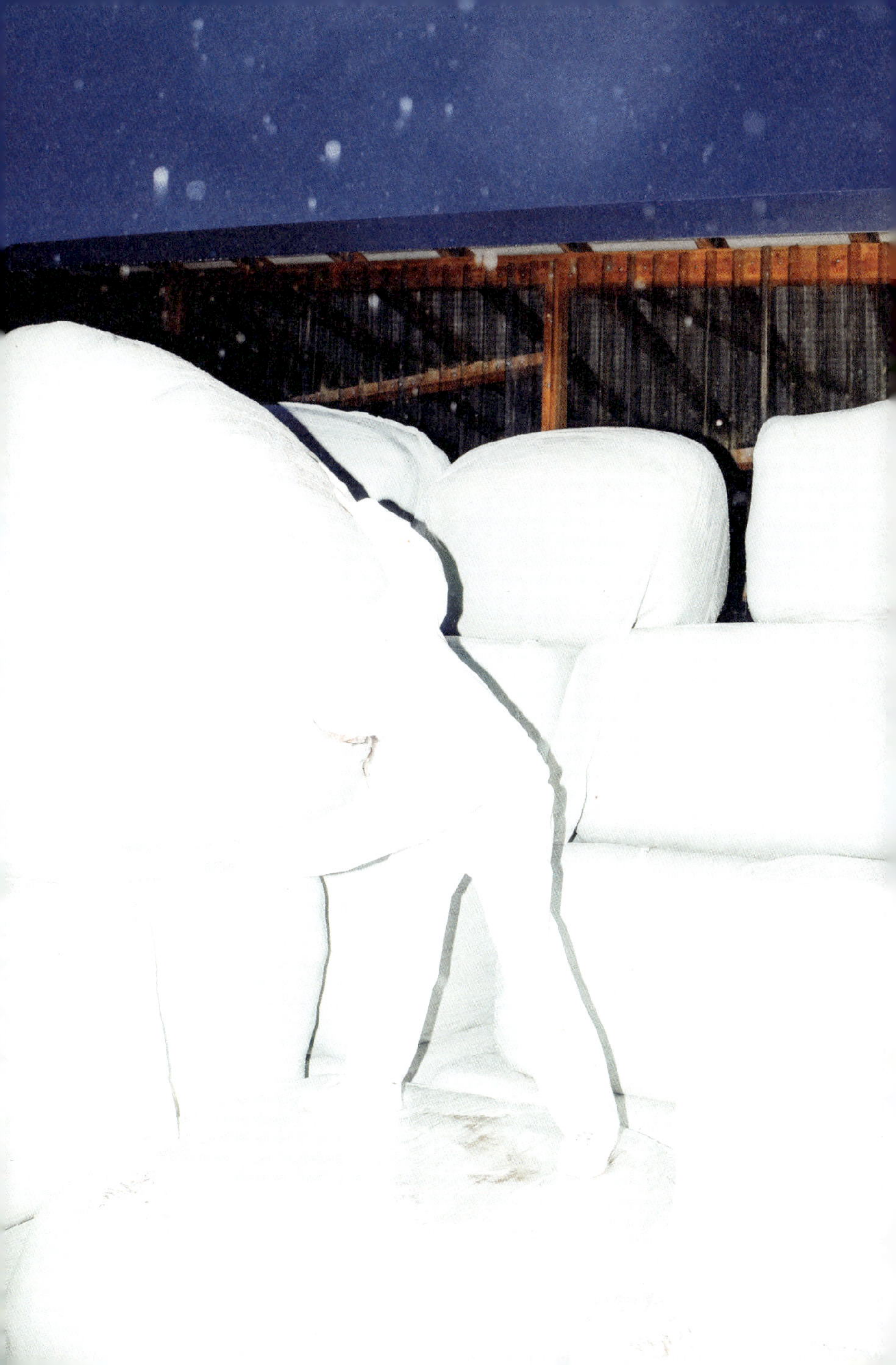

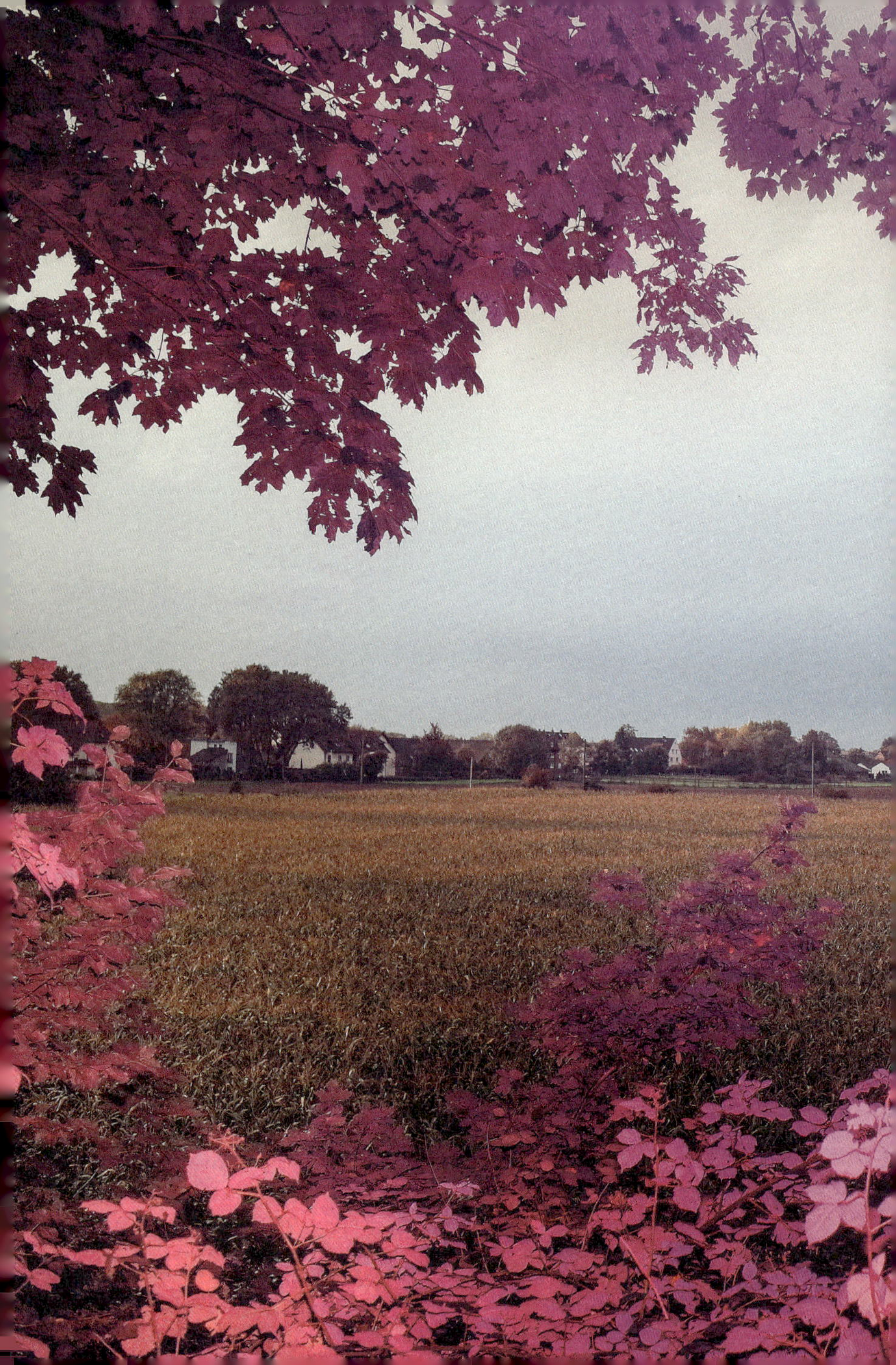

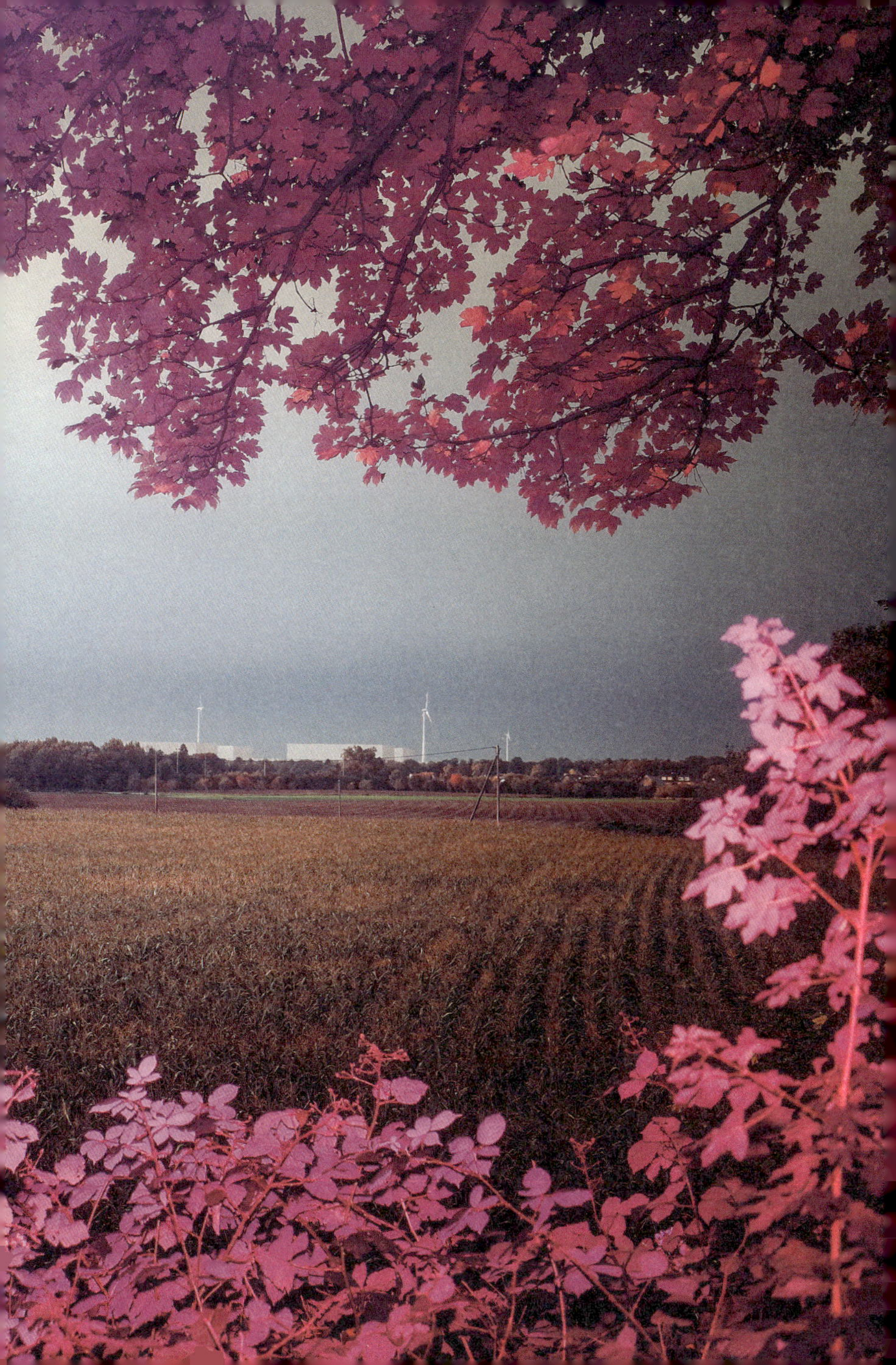

Felix Kleymann

Sexshine State

05

Pornography: trivialized or frowned upon—the depiction of the sexual act divides society, yet sex sells and porn is omnipresent. The industry makes around $13 billion in profit, with up to 200 film scenes being produced each day in California alone. Everyone has access to pornography and everyone has an opinion. But what do we know about the making of porn?

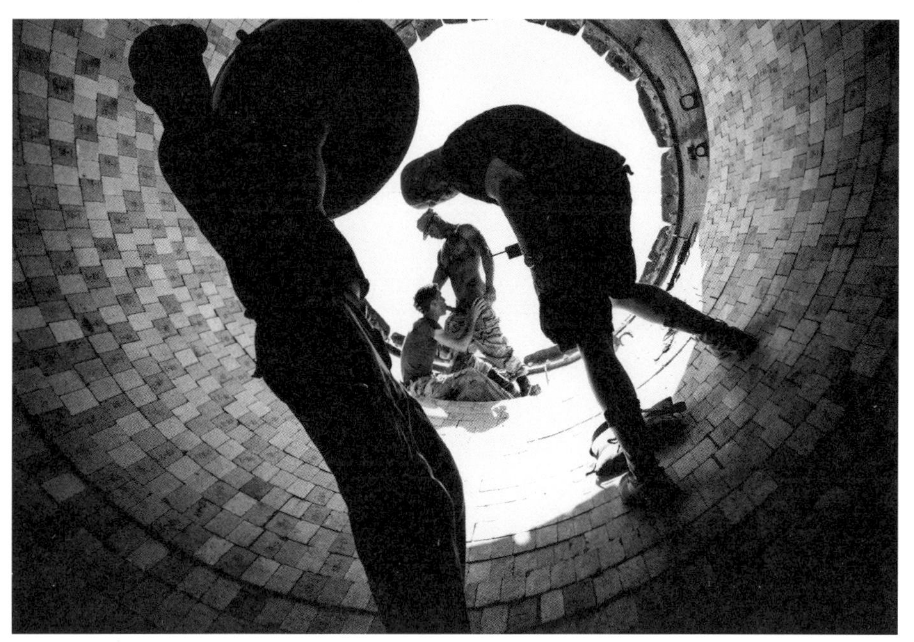

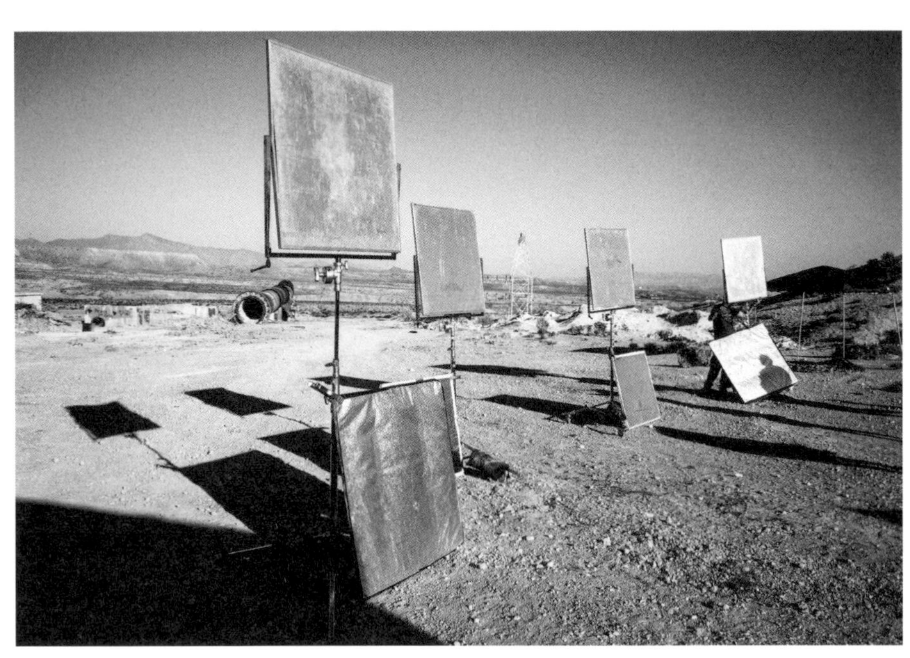

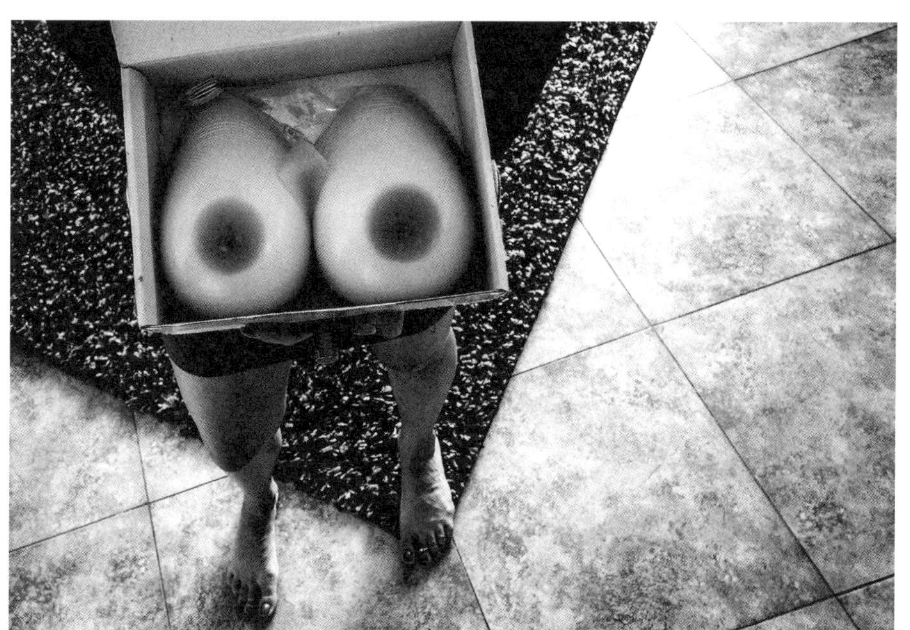

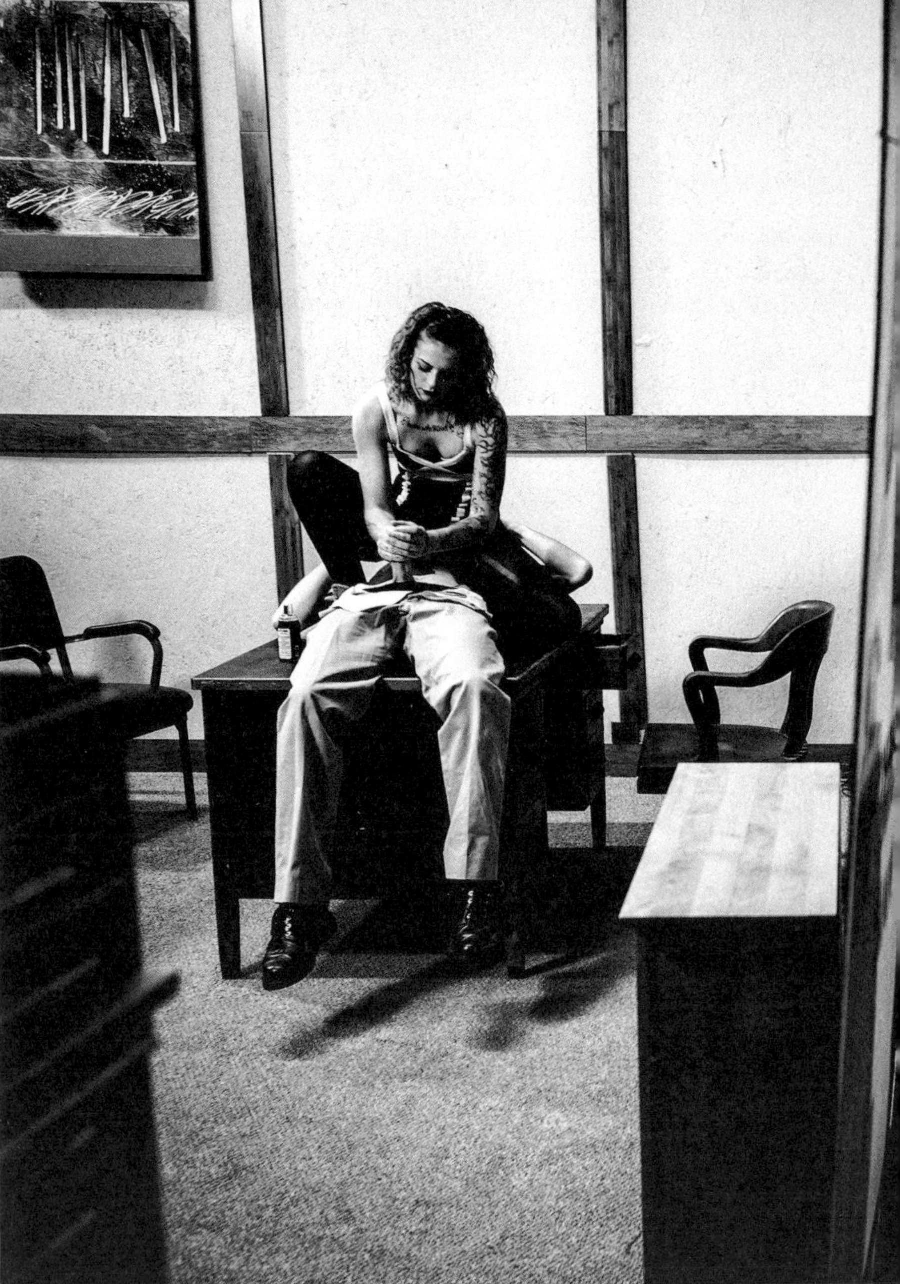

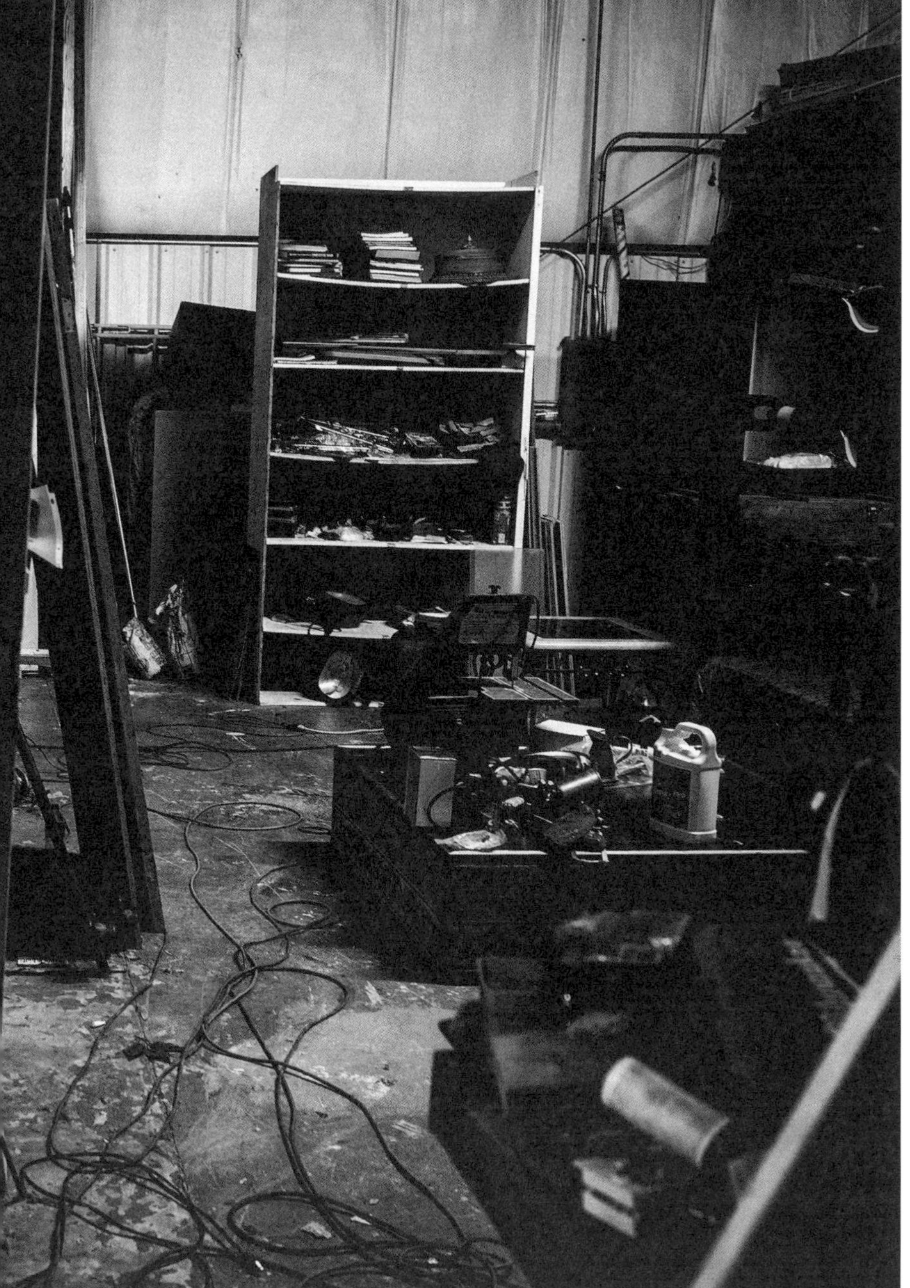

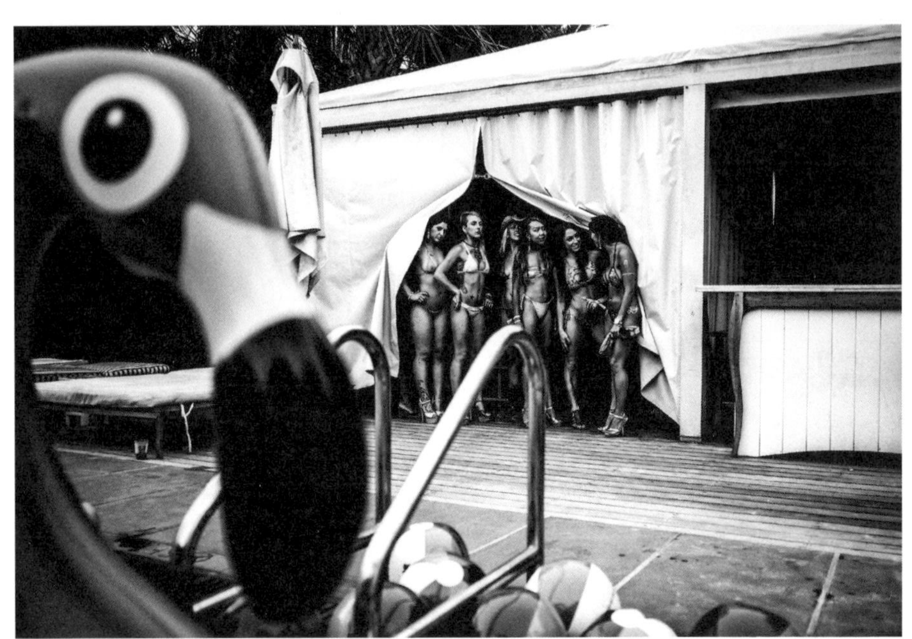

06

Dolls that look like real babies can make their mothers feel loving and caring. Without the dolls being able to respond, they still can be an opportunity for the women to regain control of their feelings, wishes, and needs.

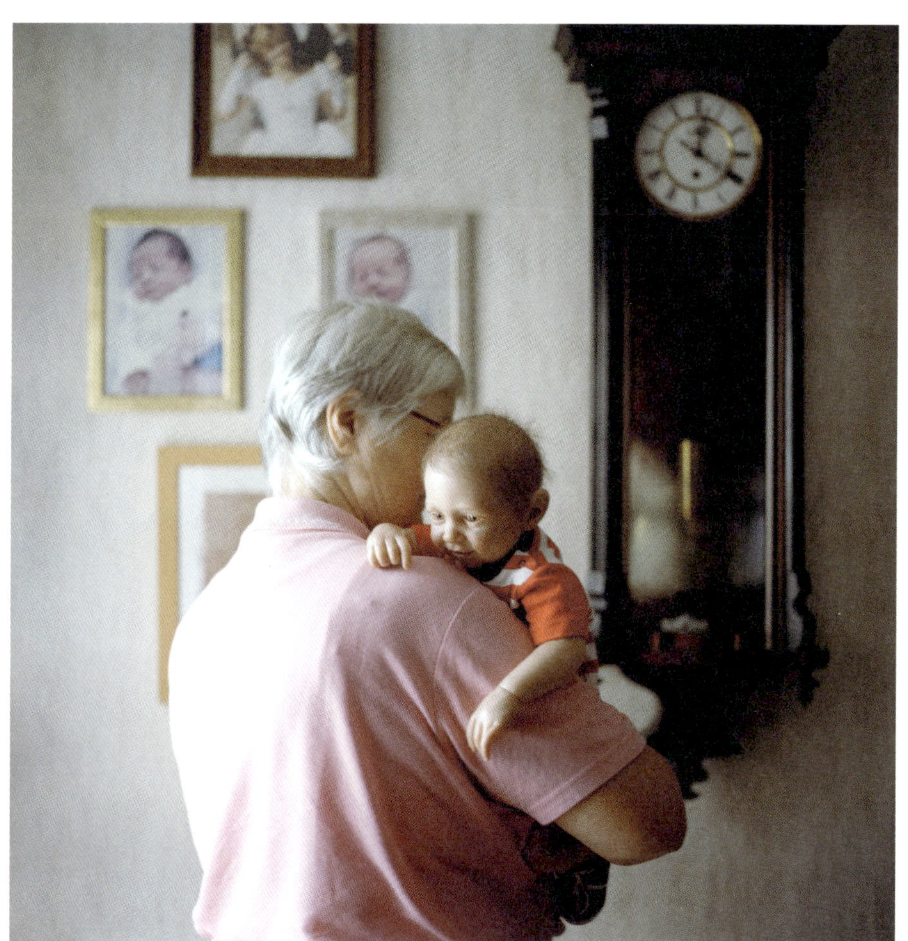

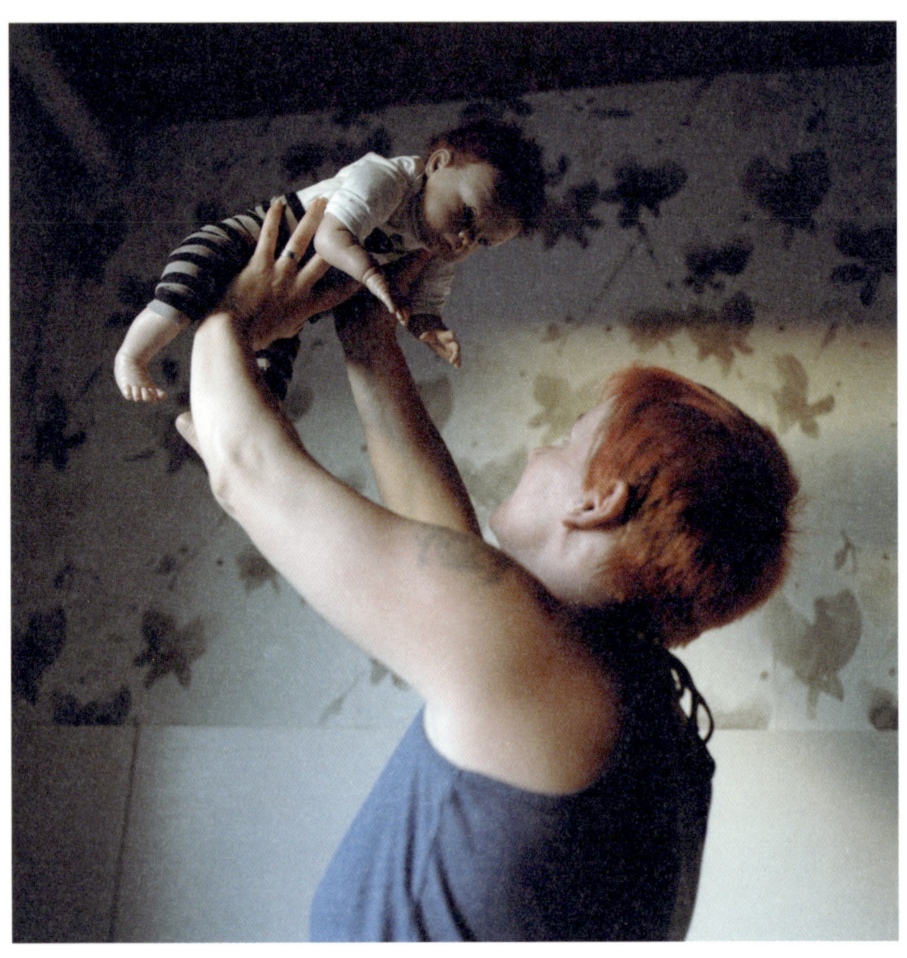

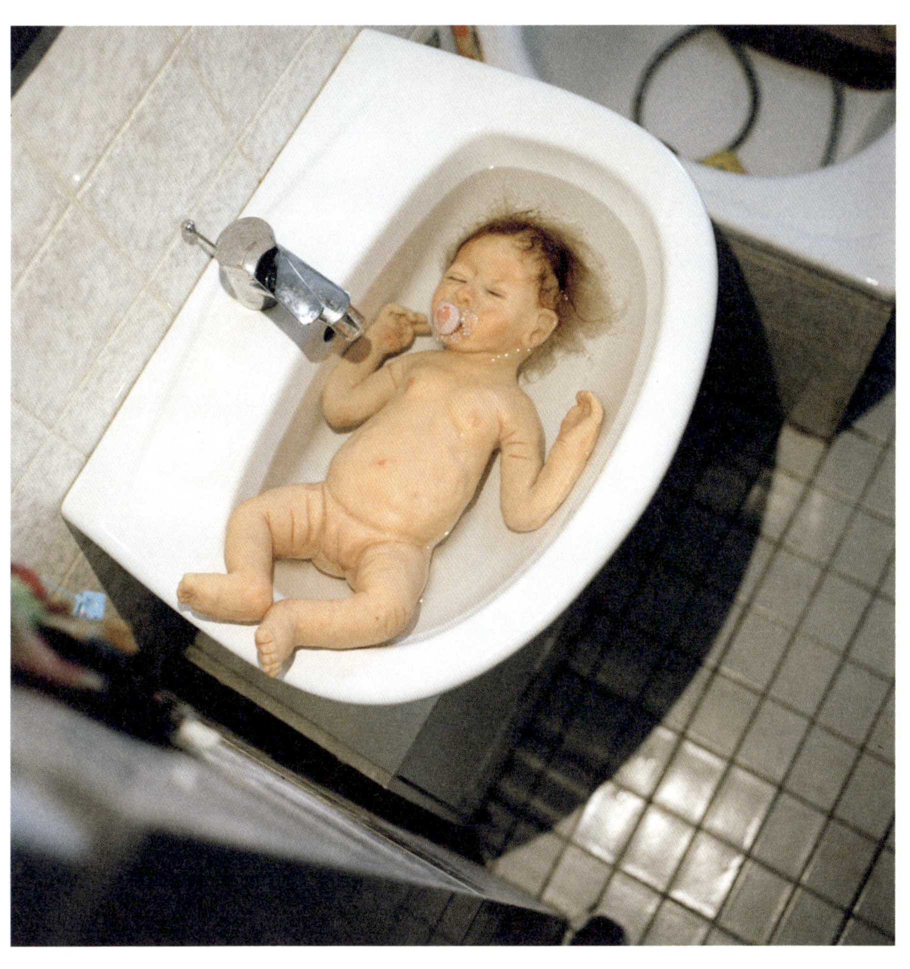

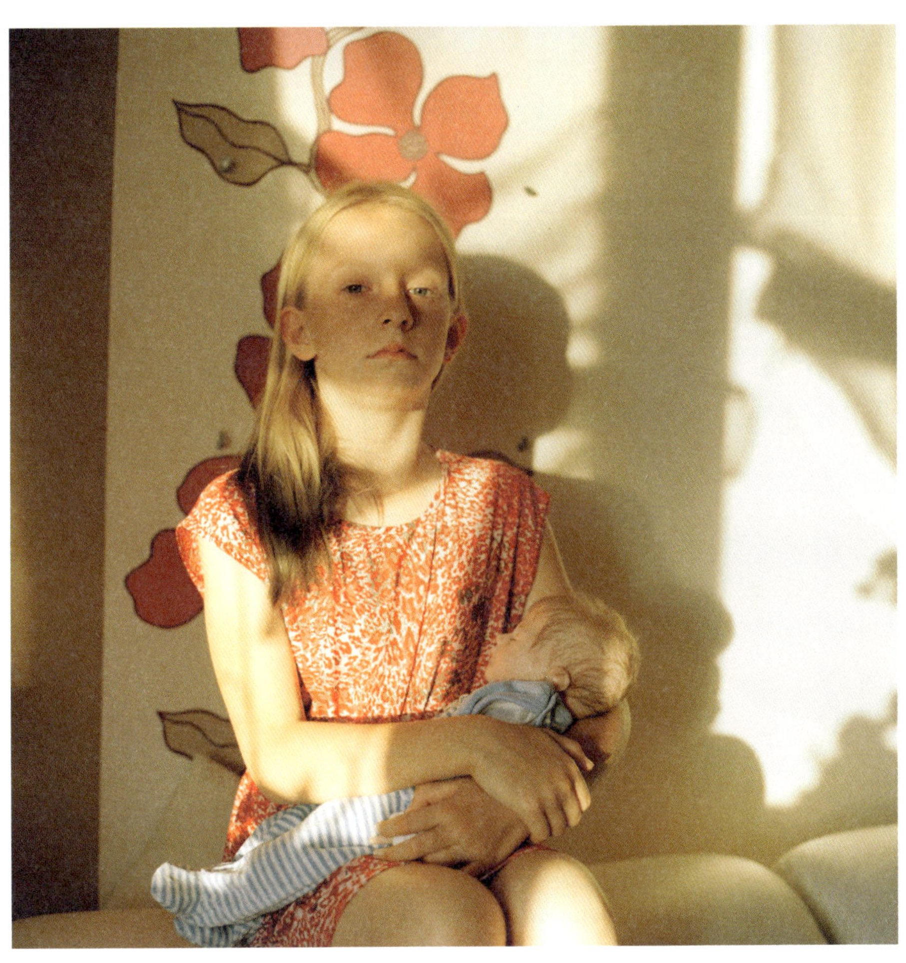

Elias Holzknecht

The New Alpine Landscape

07

Climate change has arrived in the Alpine valleys and the landscape is evolving. The increasing lack of snow is causing major problems for the largest local industry: tourism.
To meet the expectations of millions of tourists, new technologies have been developed to artificially create natural experiences.

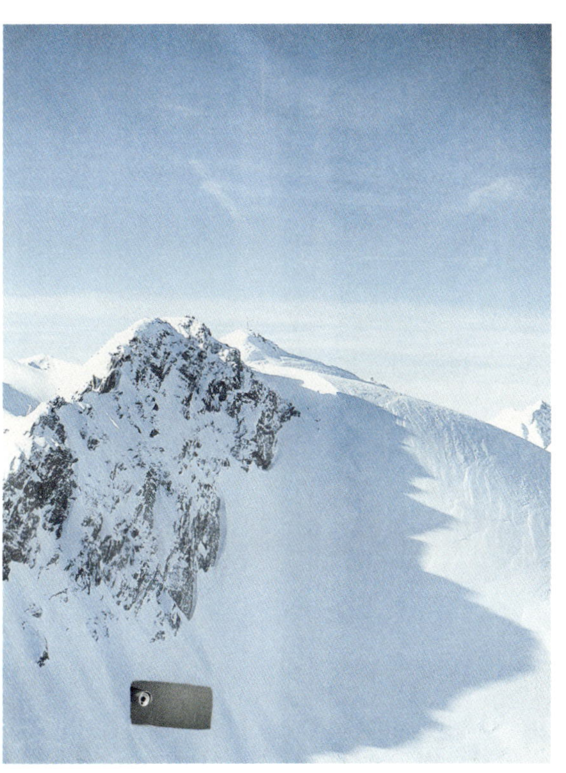

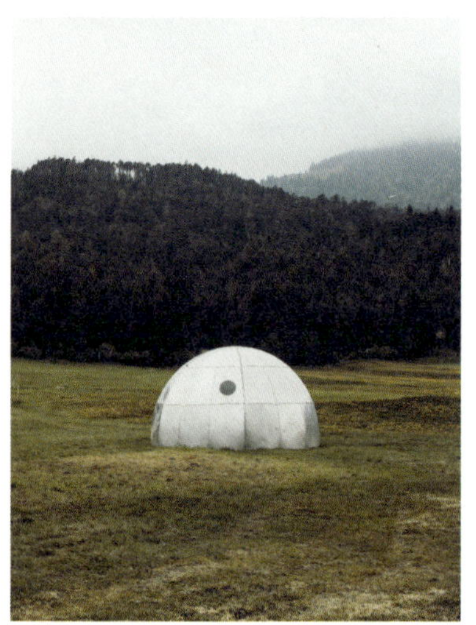

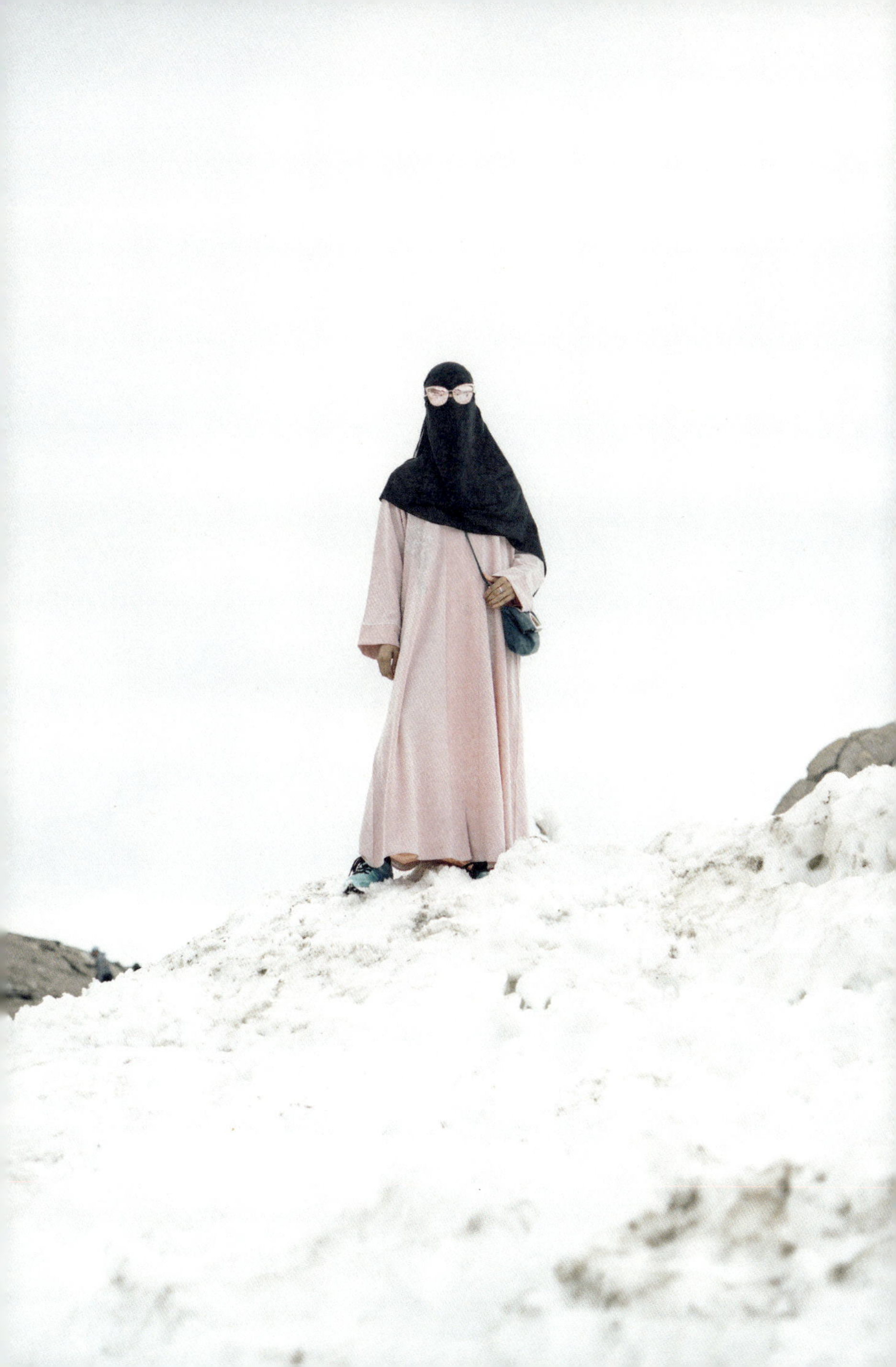

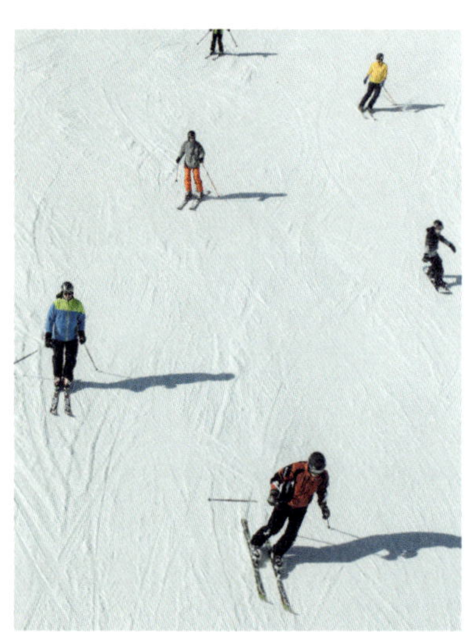

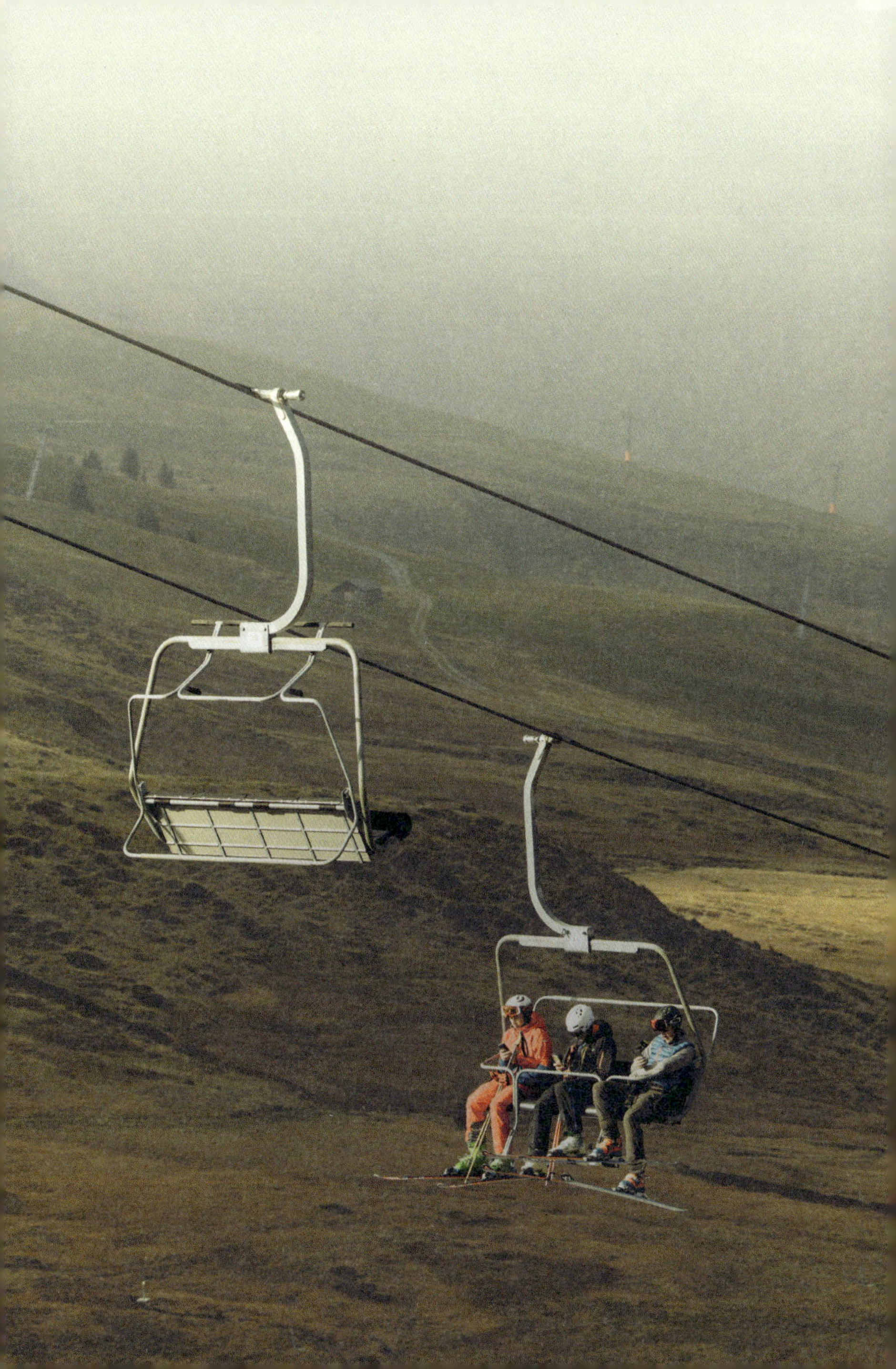

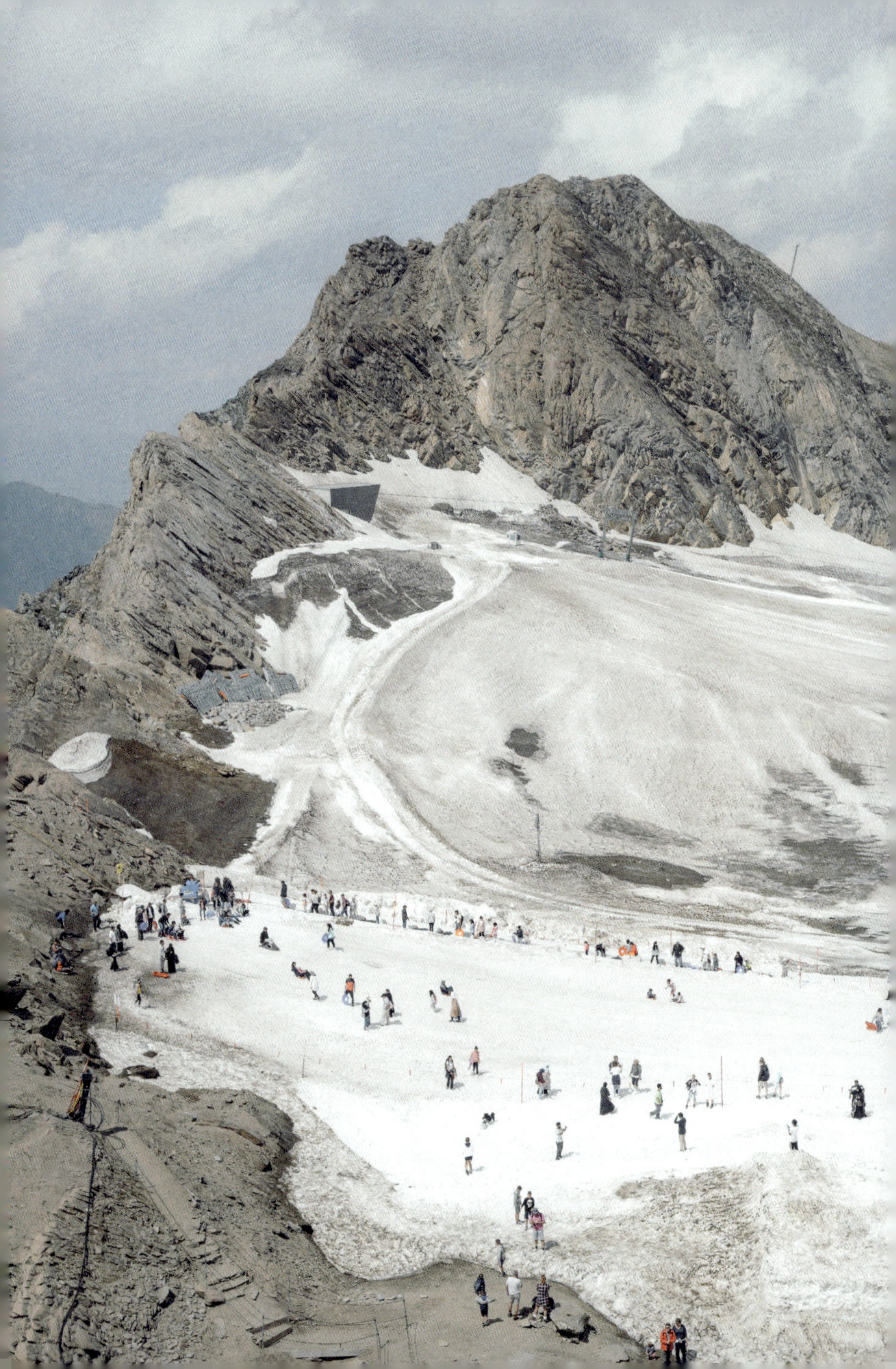

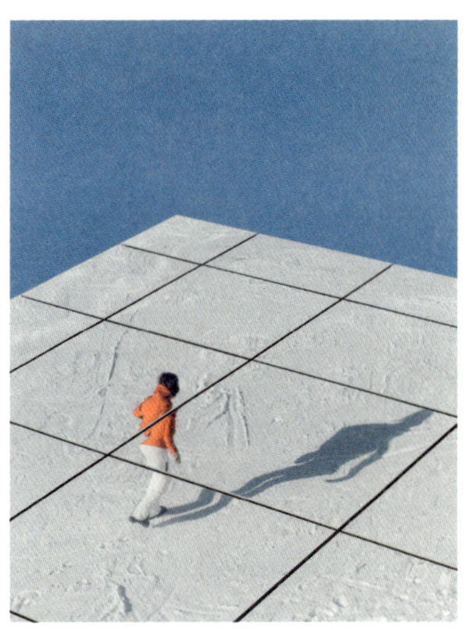

Martin Lamberty

My Friends Got Famous

08

Seven years ago, I took photographs of my friends making music for the first time. In the beginning, it was just the three of them and the band had no name. They went on to call themselves by their surnames: AnnenMayKantereit.

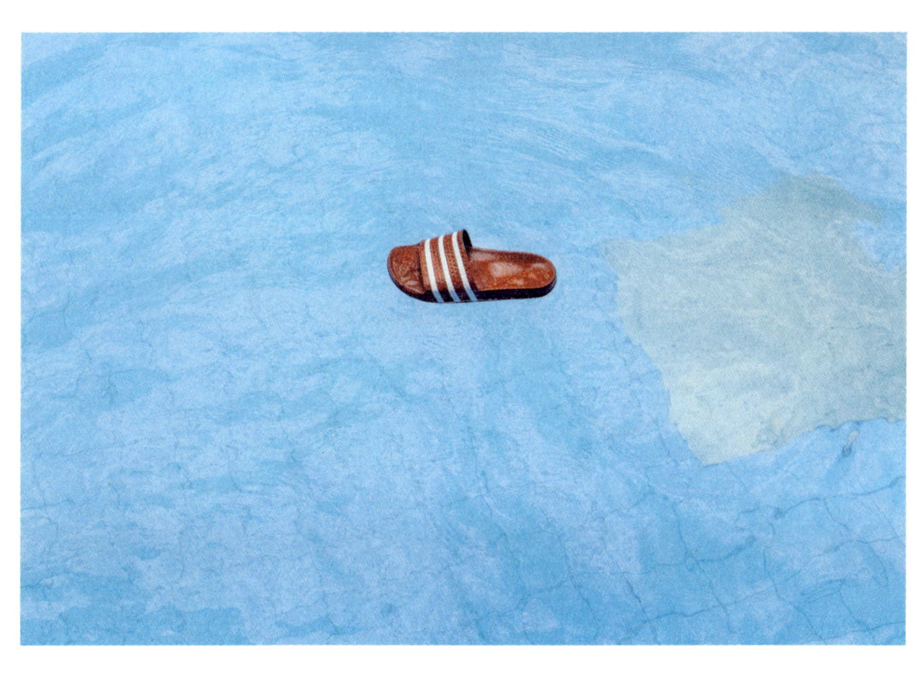

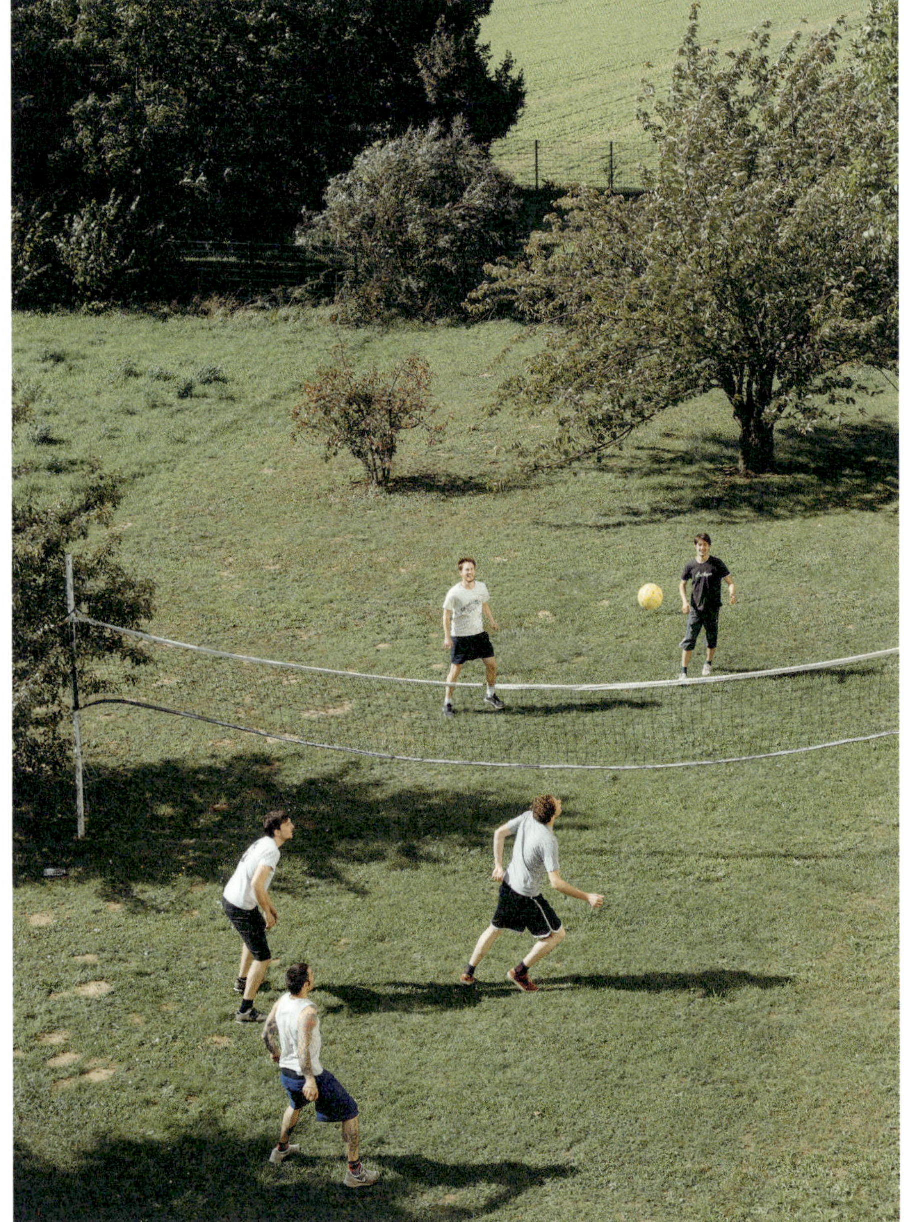

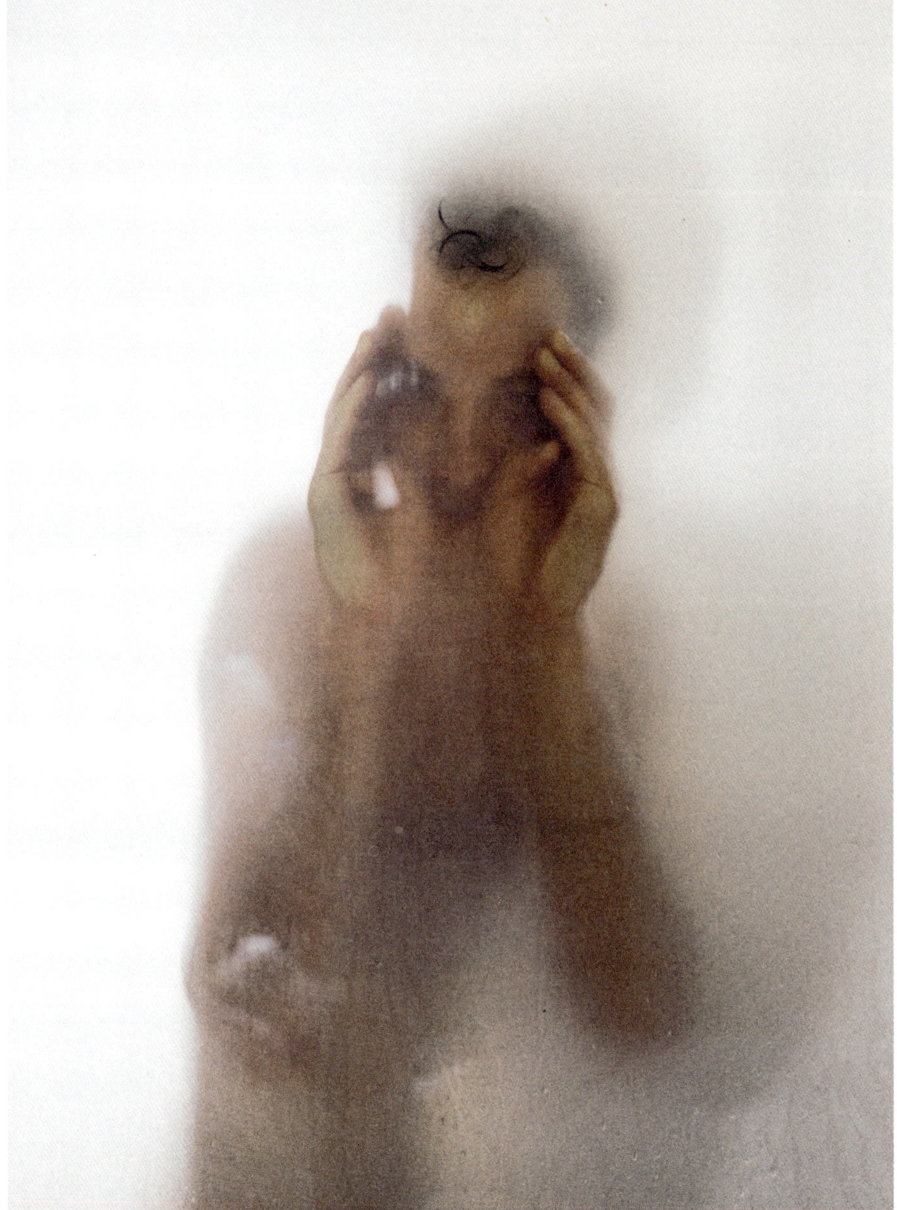

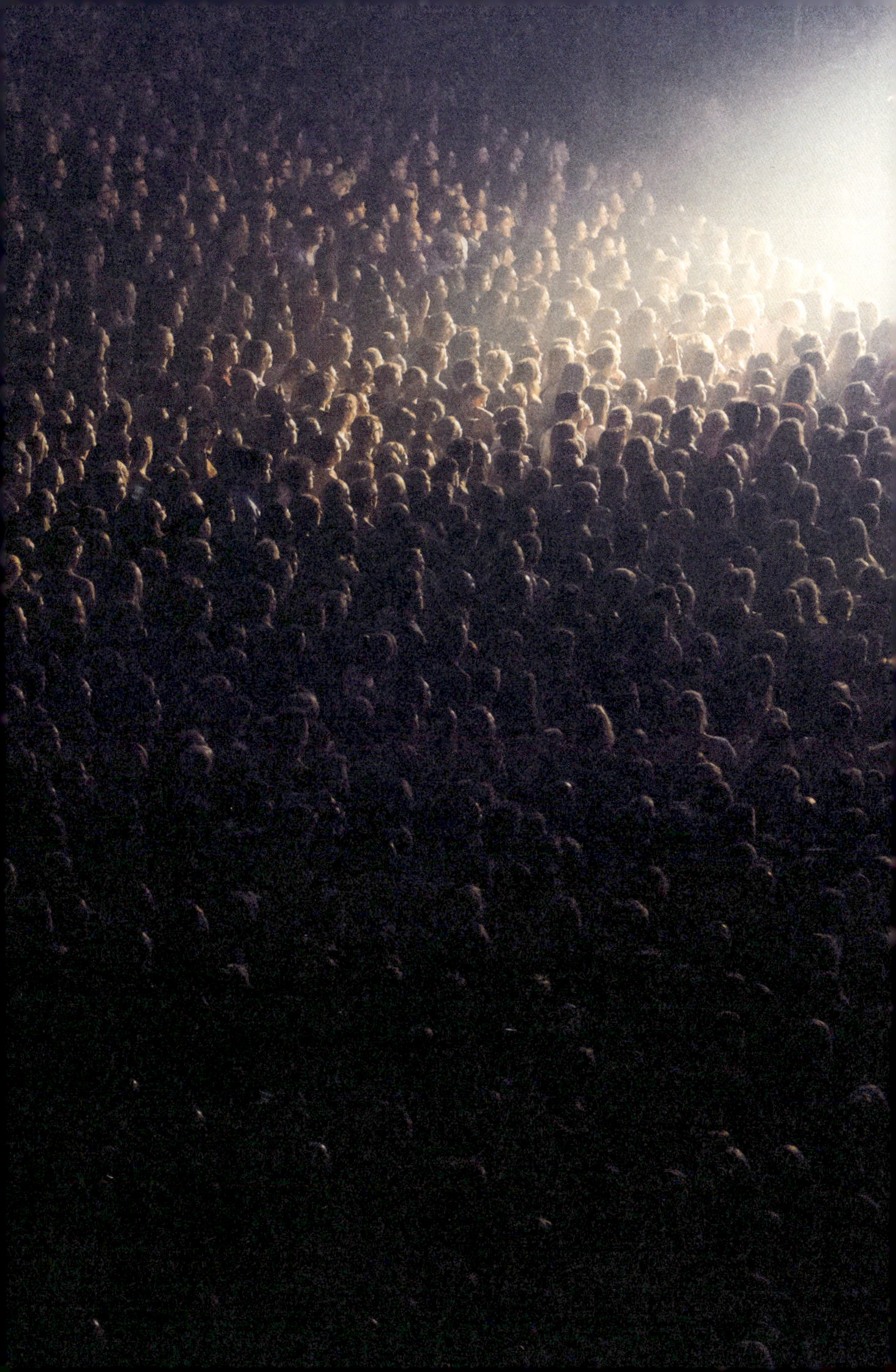

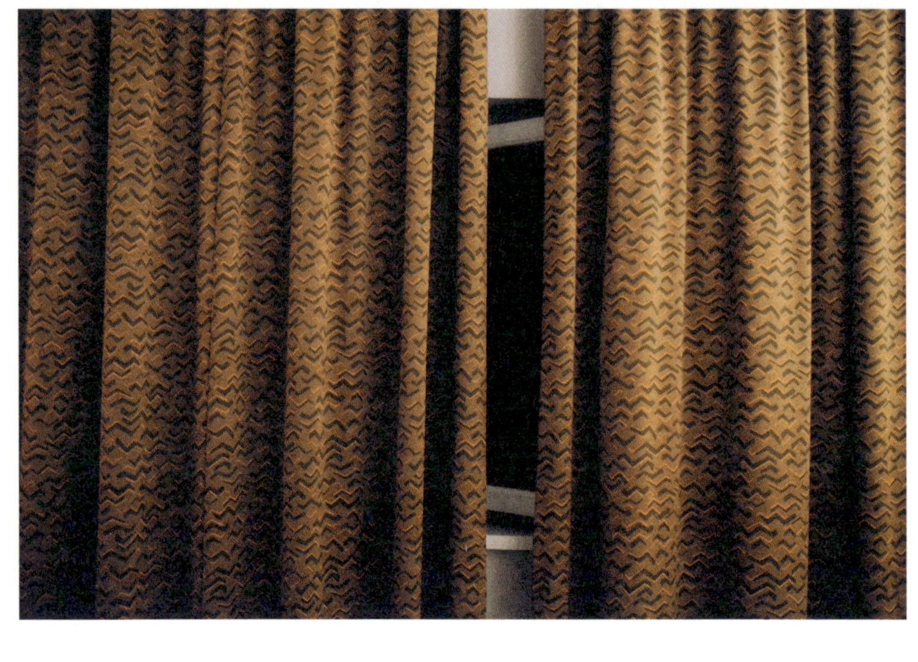

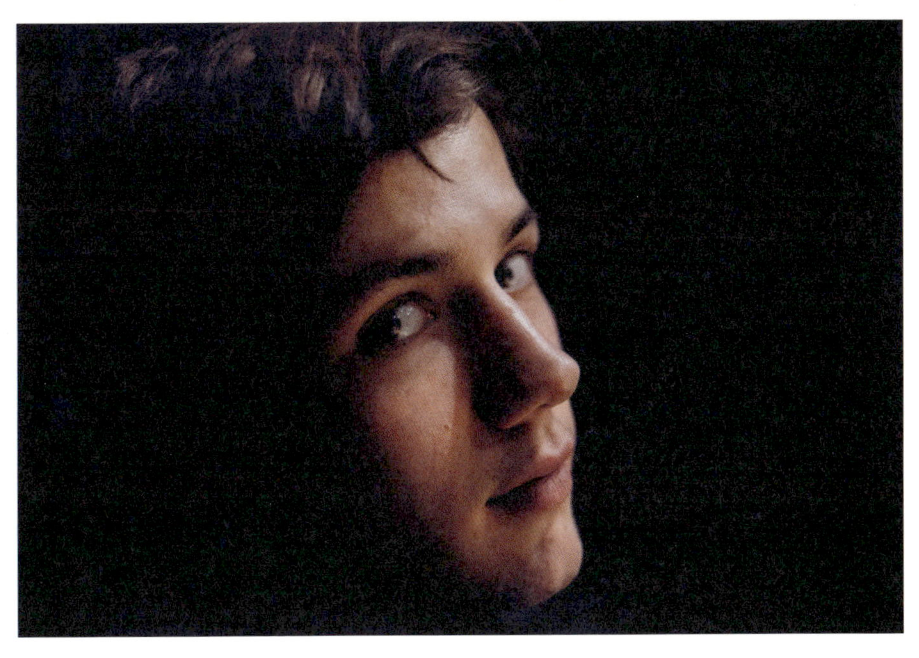

09

Lake Urmia in northwestern Iran, one of the biggest salt lakes on earth, shrank by 80 percent over the last several years. The water left, so did the people: villages are deserted and the struggle for those that stayed is steadily increasing.

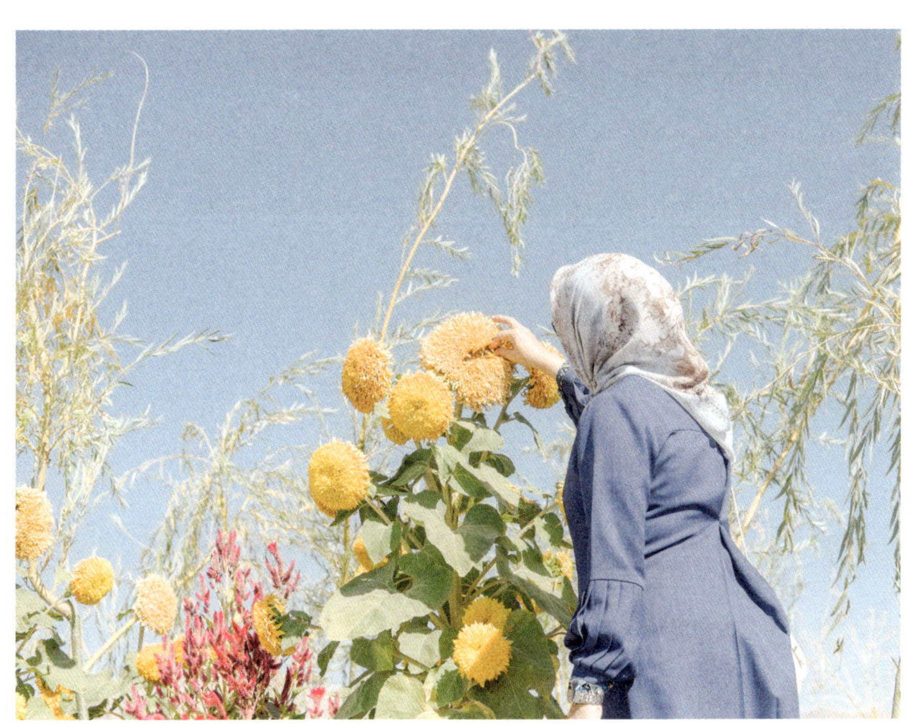

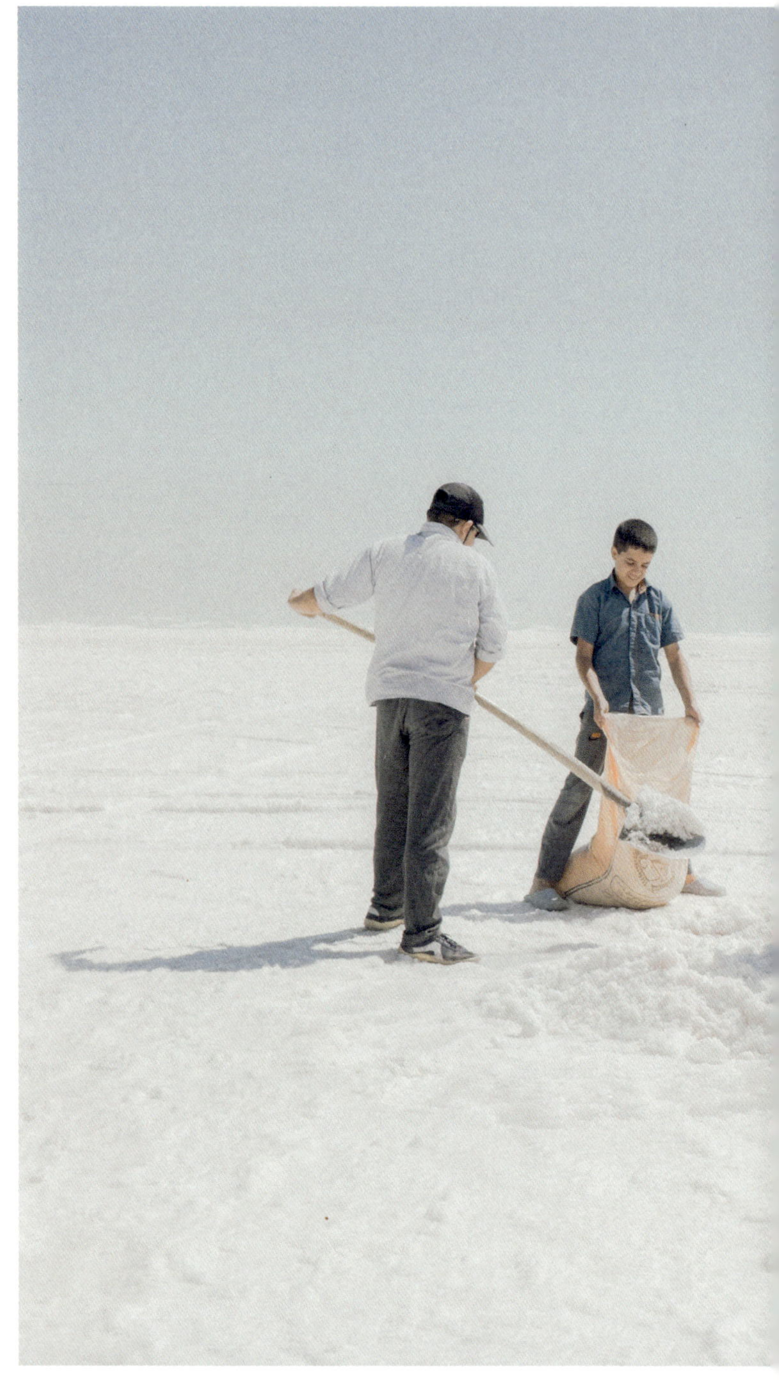

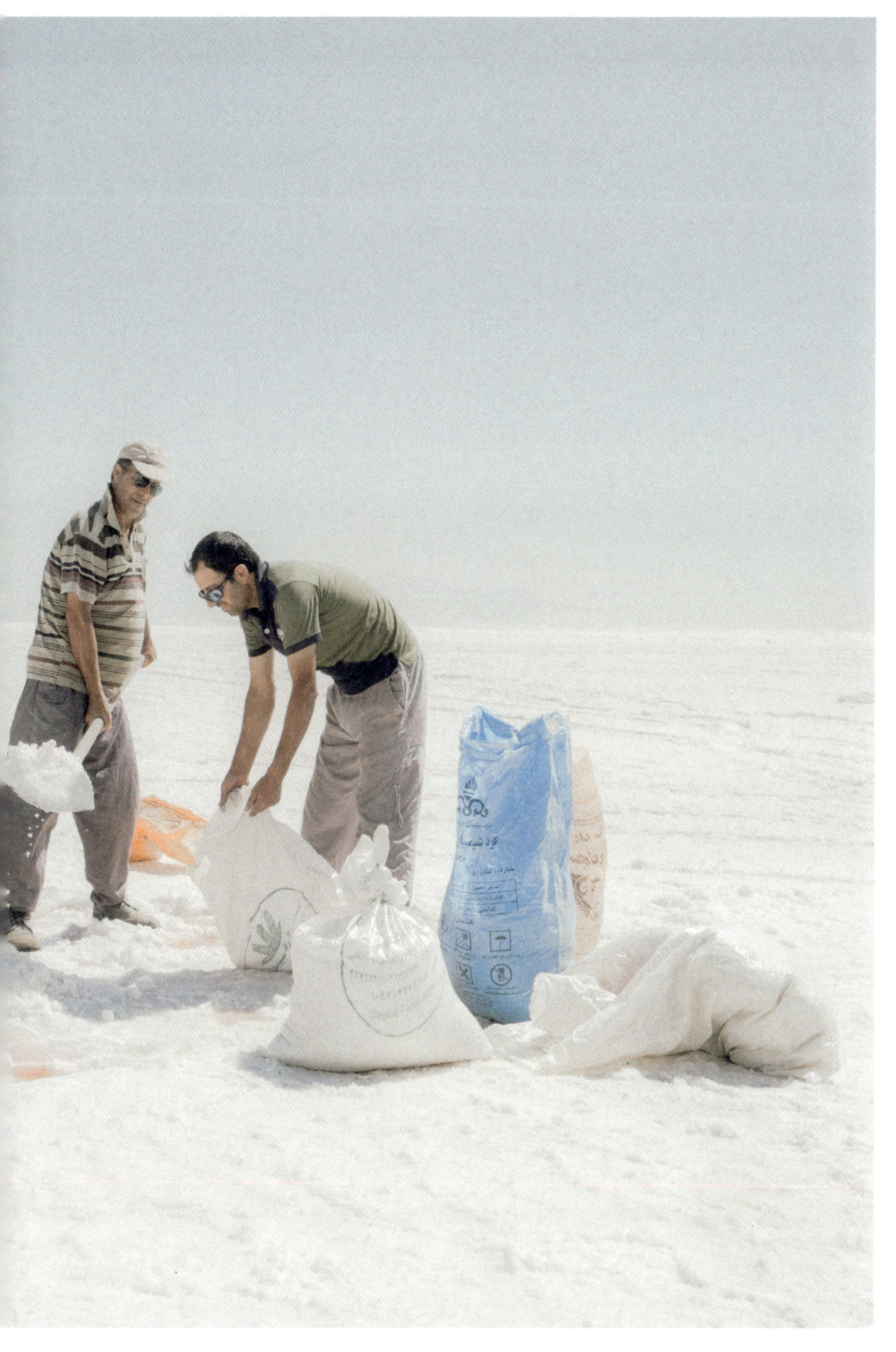

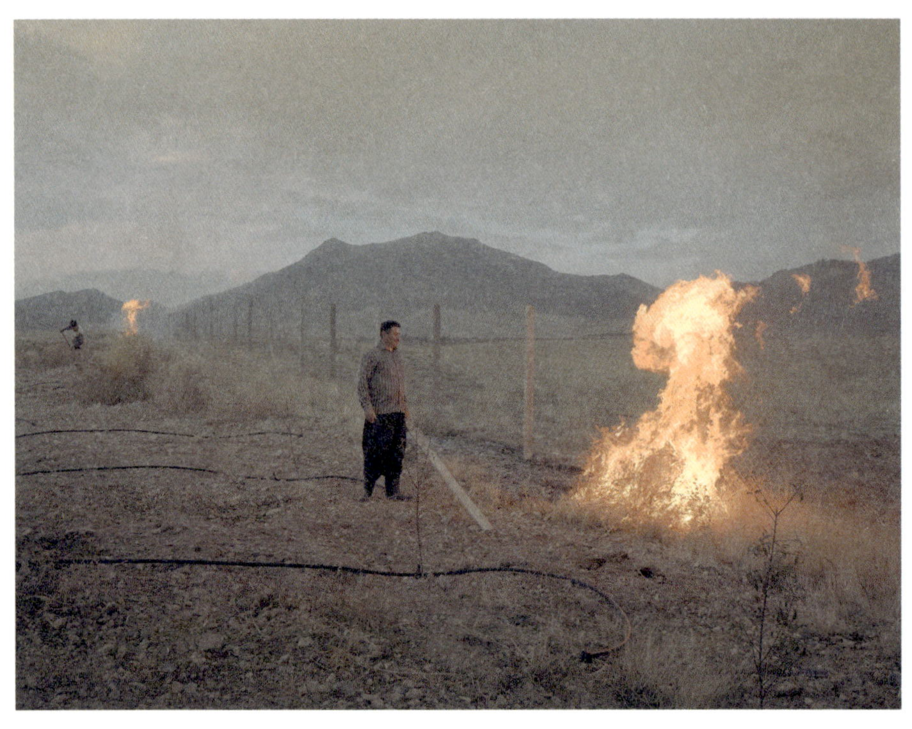

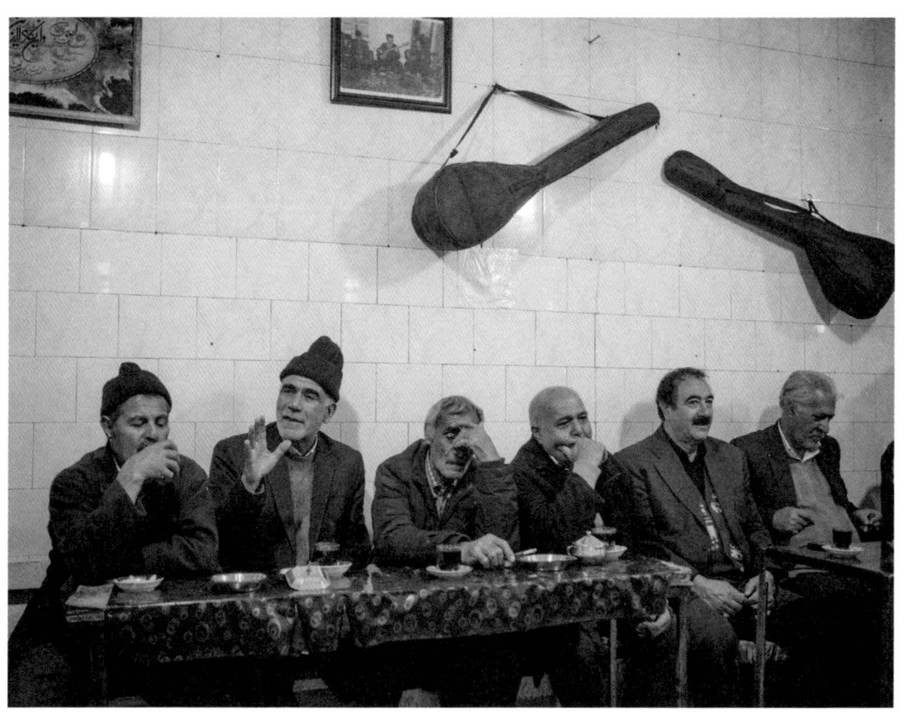

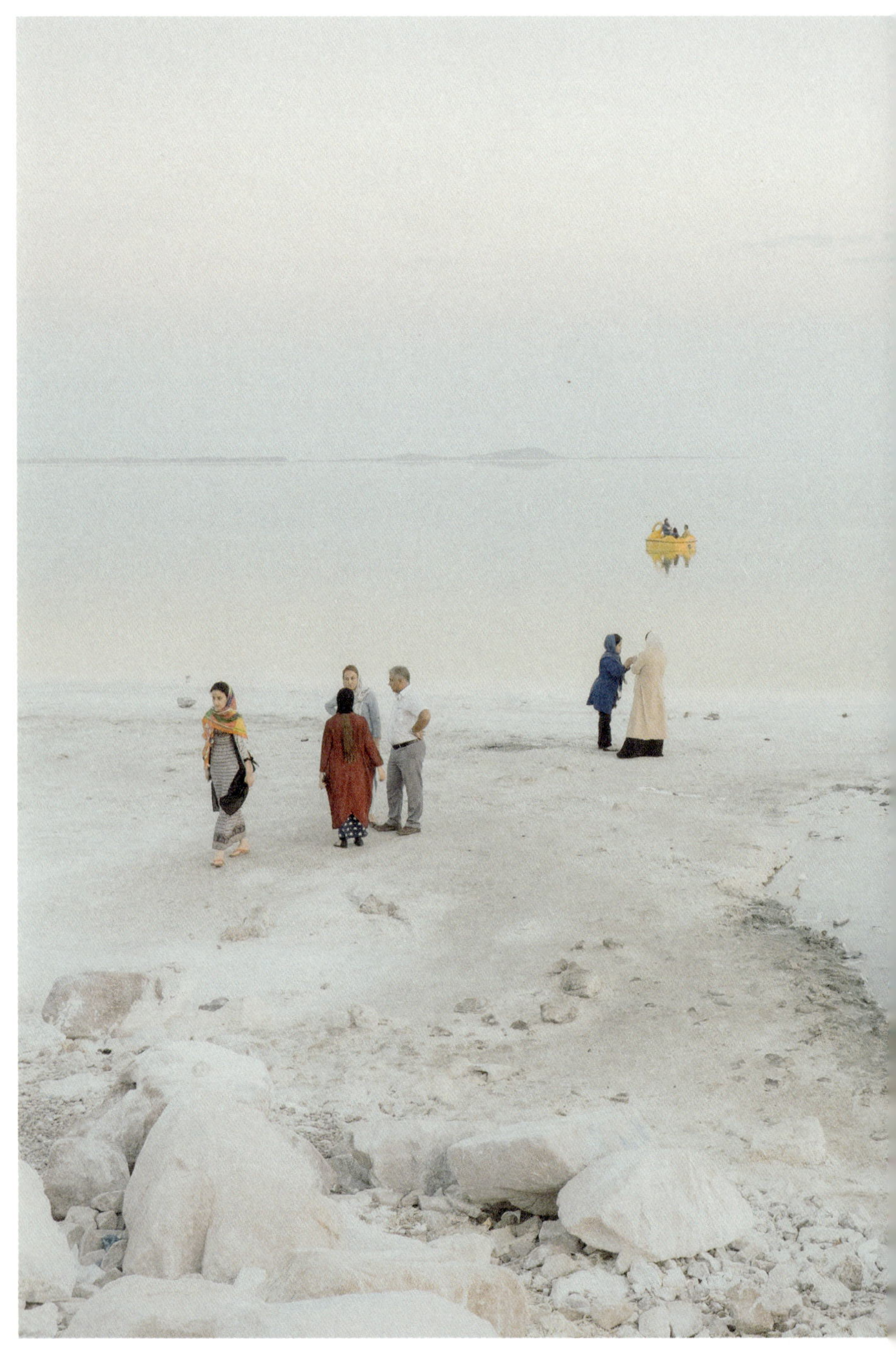

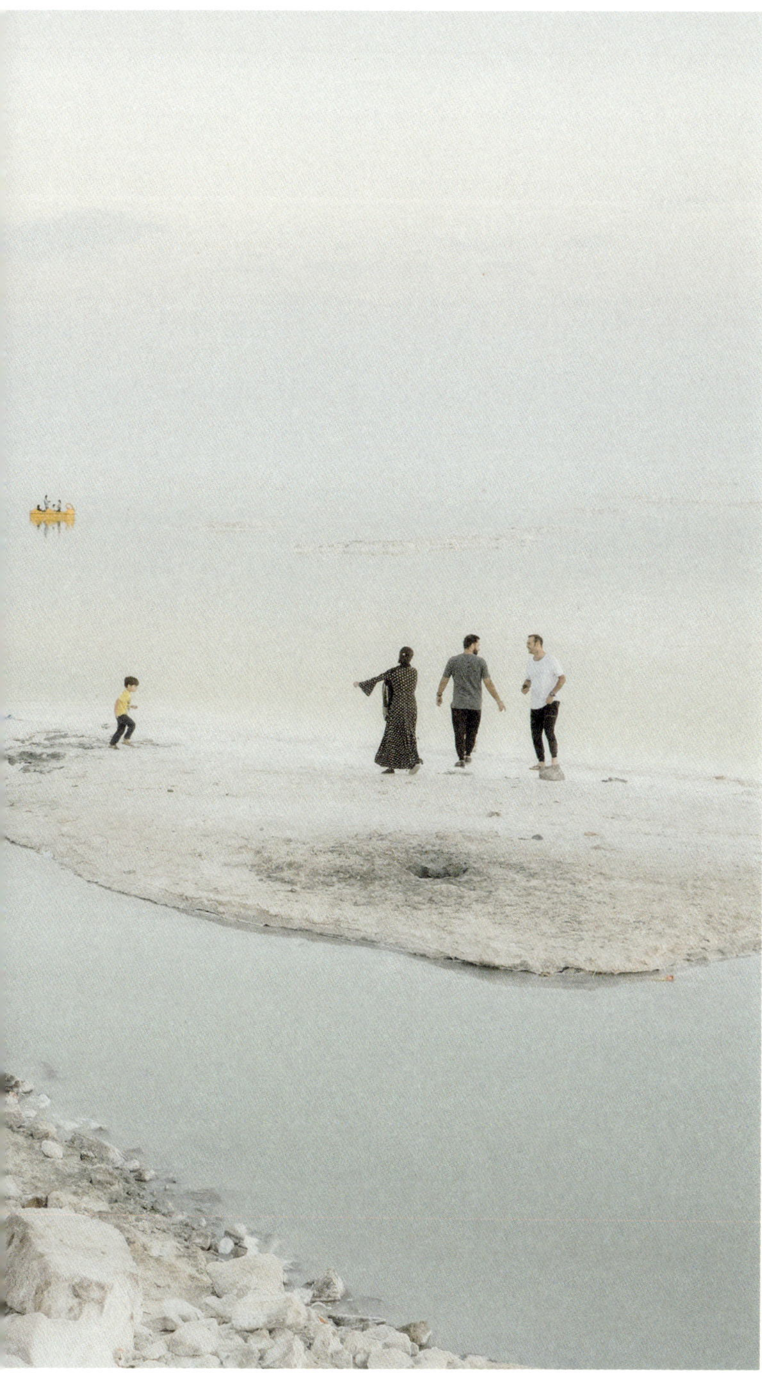

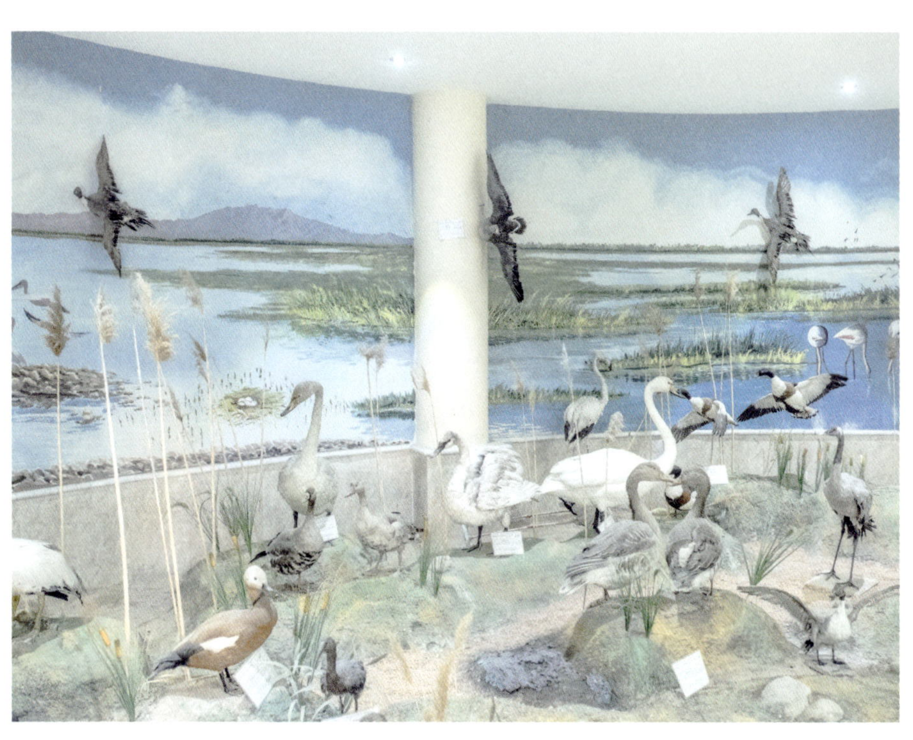

Lucas Bäuml
Lando Hass

Political Hectares

10

Extreme economic differences, racism, uneven chances of education and employment as well as corruption are dividing South African society. 25 years after the end of Apartheid, a small white minority still claims most of the country's land.

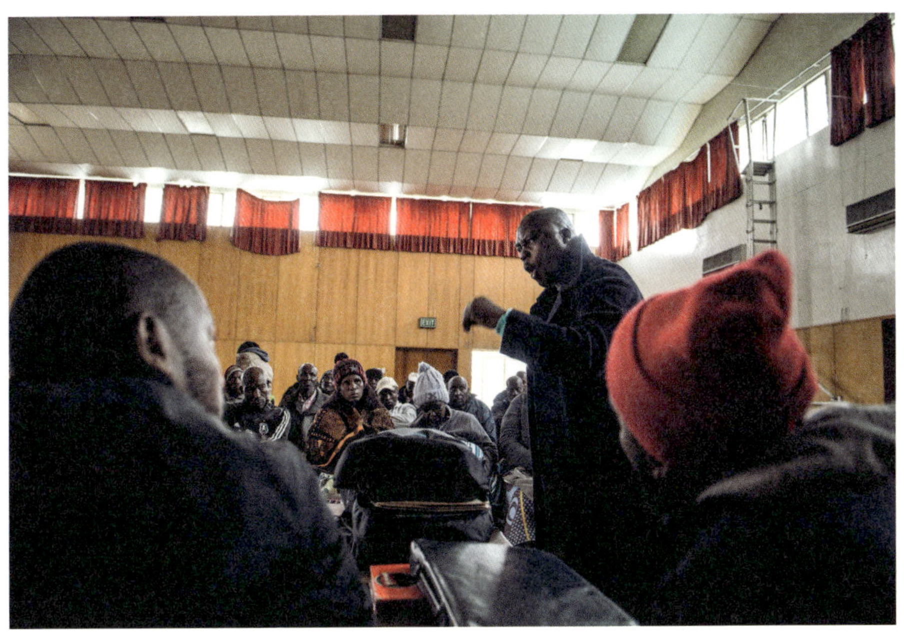
EXIT

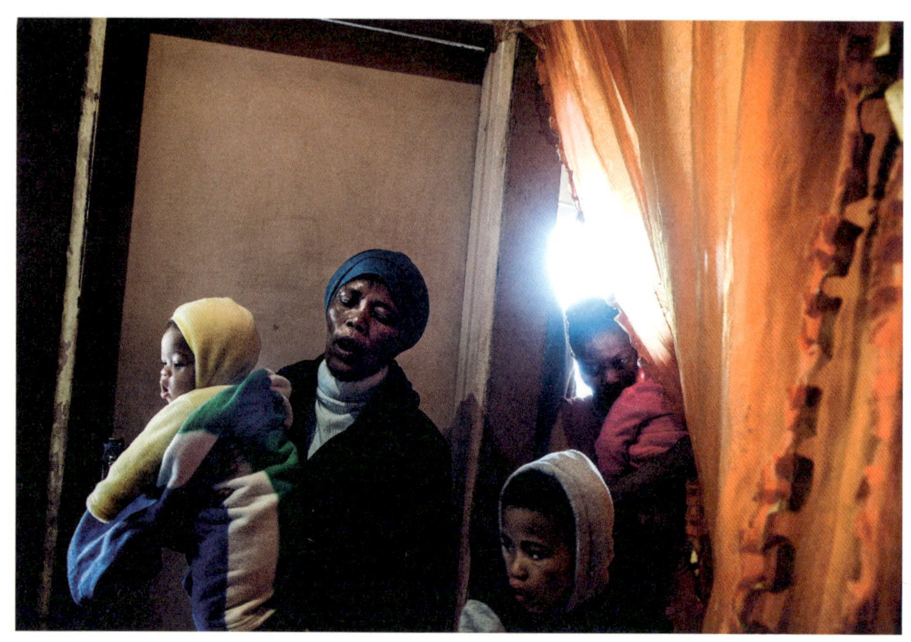

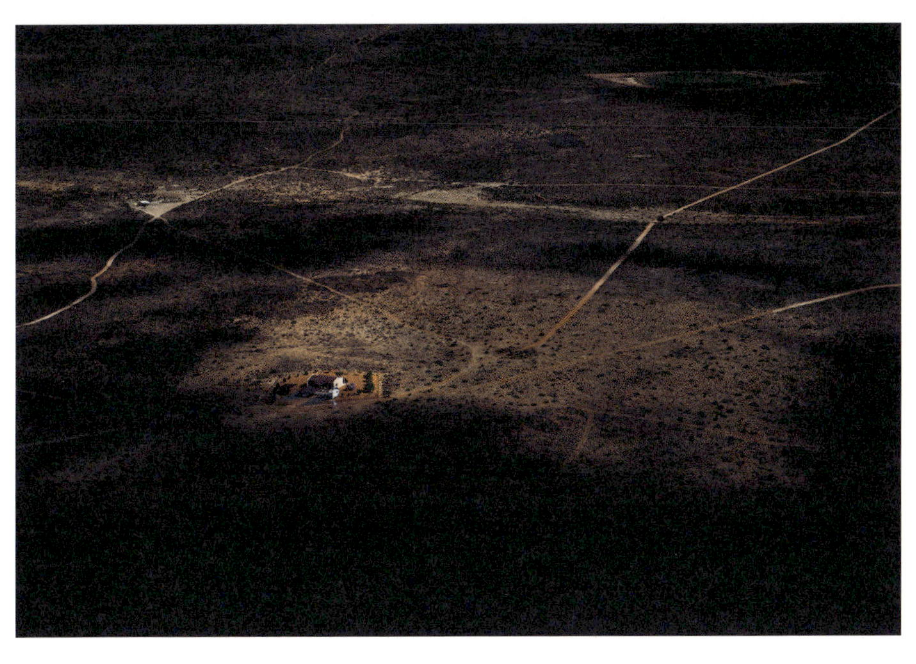

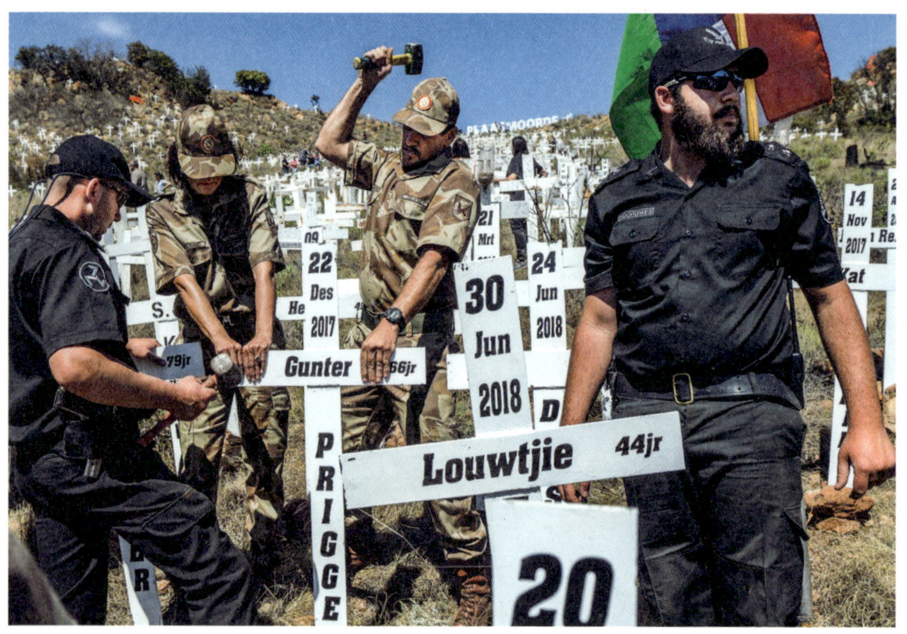
PLAASMOORDE
22
Des
2017
21
Mrt
30
Jun
2018
24
Jun
2018
14
Nov
2017
Kat
79jr
Gunter
66jr
Louwtjie
44jr
PRIGGE
20

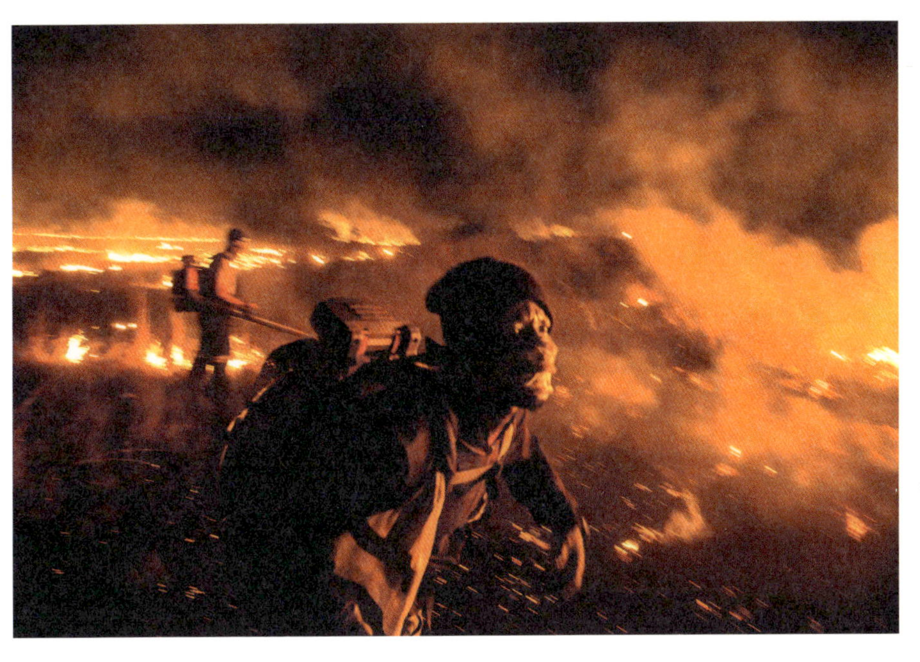

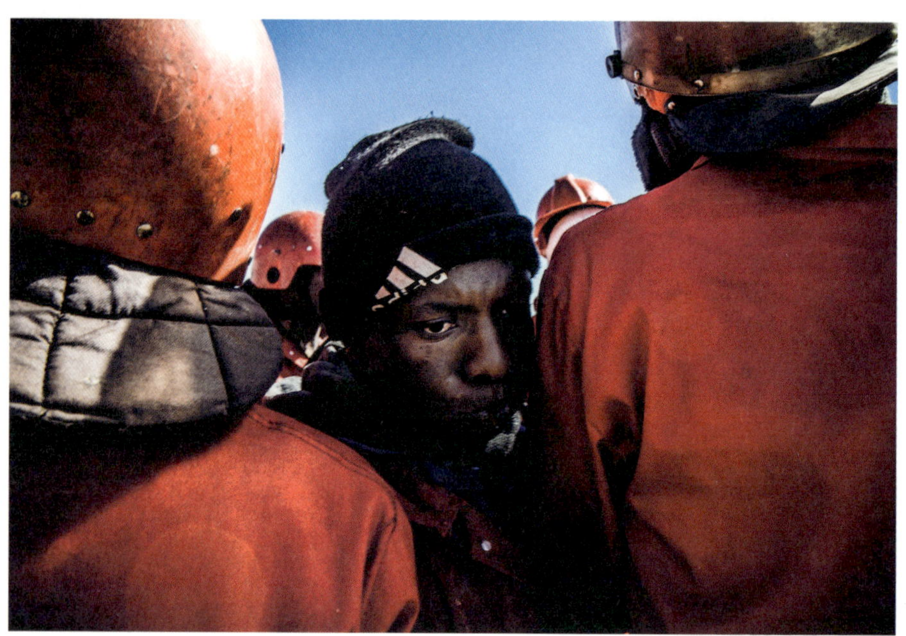

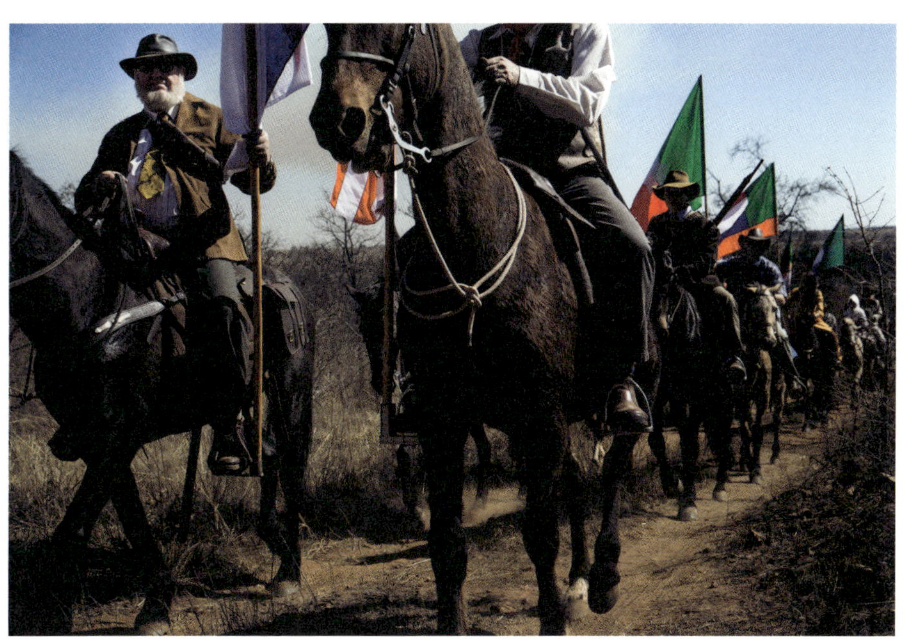

11

The Israeli transgender artist Roey Victoria Heifetz arrived in Berlin in 2012 with great expectations. Confronted with her burgeoning transsexuality, she tries to initiate a social discourse on identity and sexuality with the help of her own art.

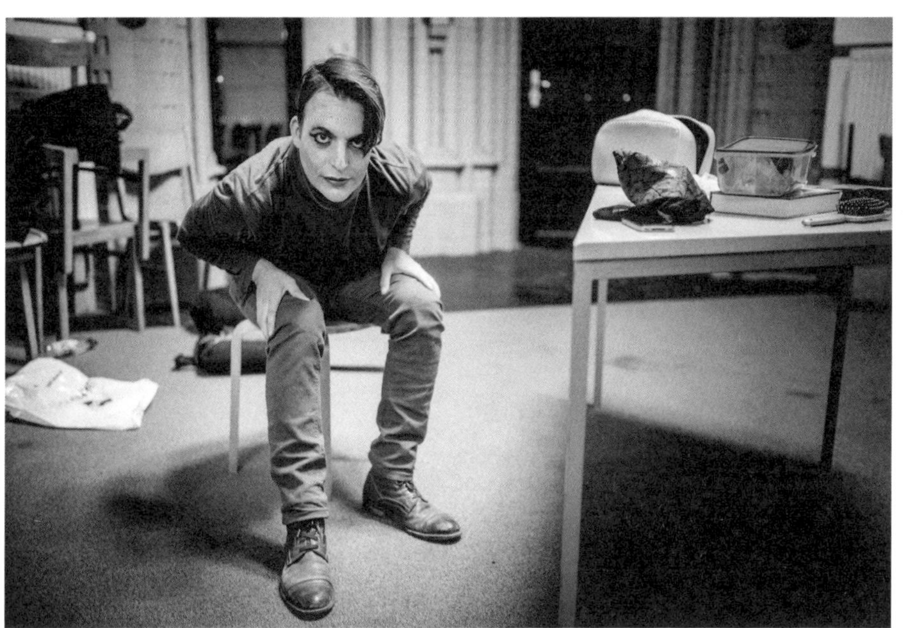

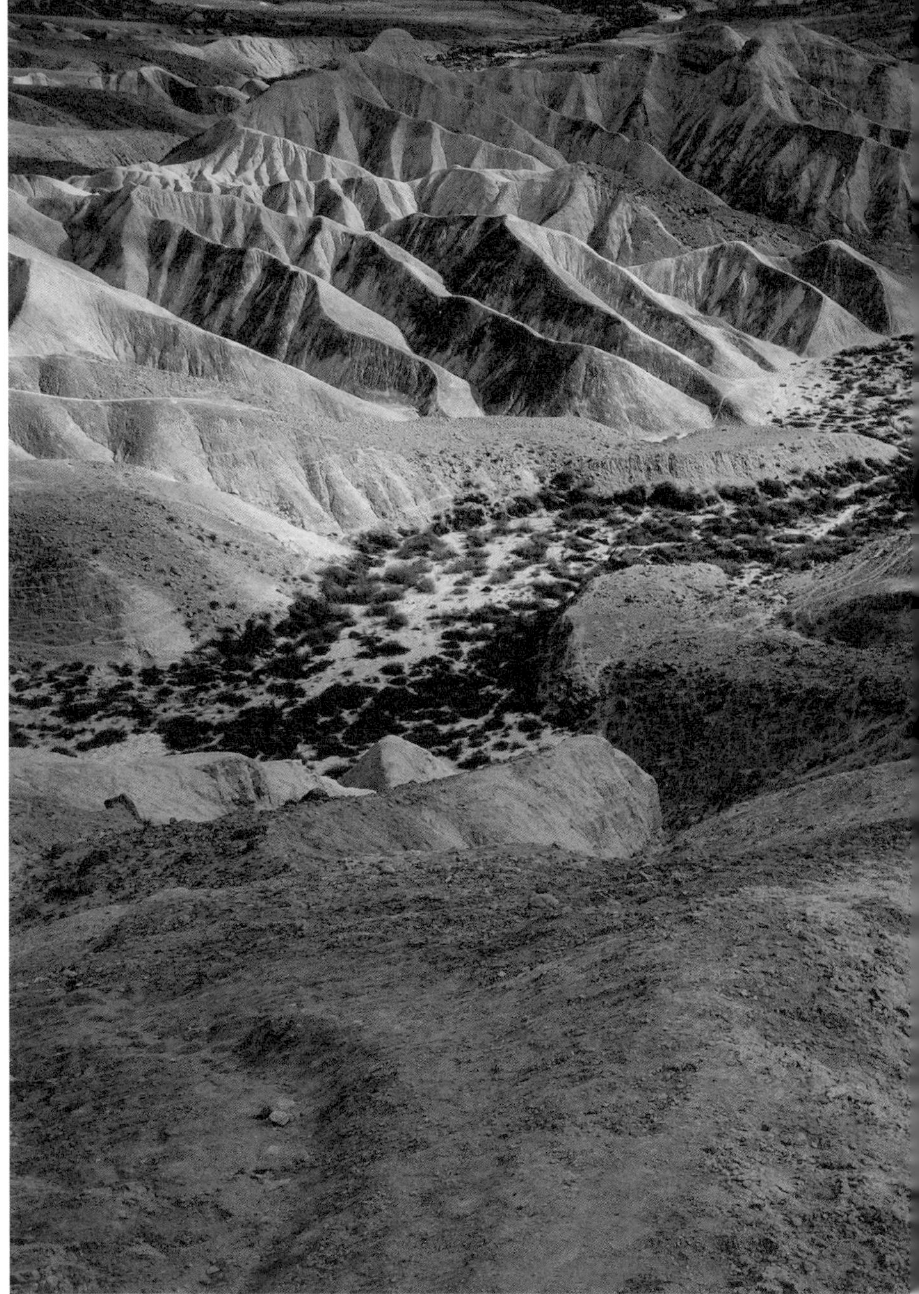

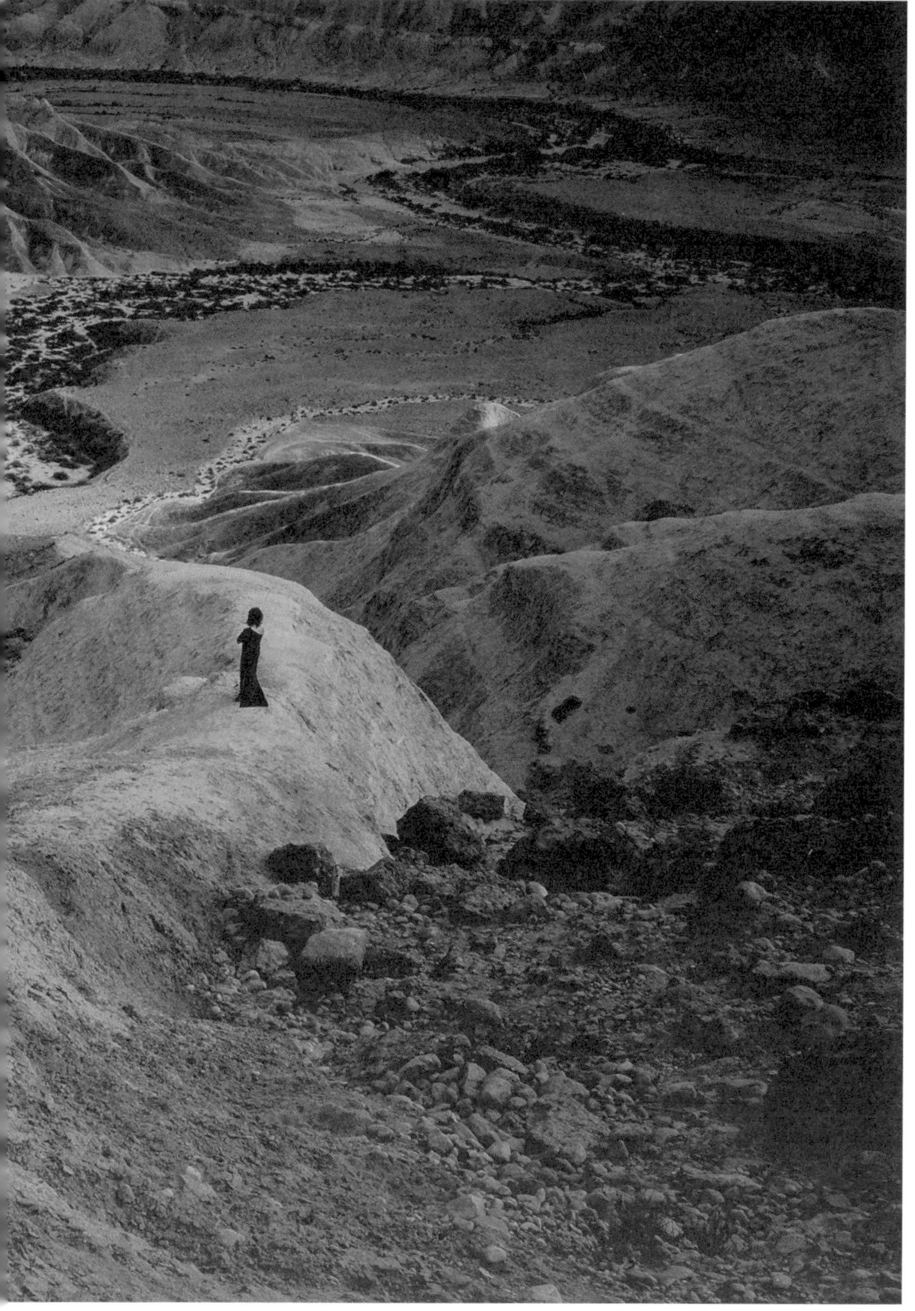

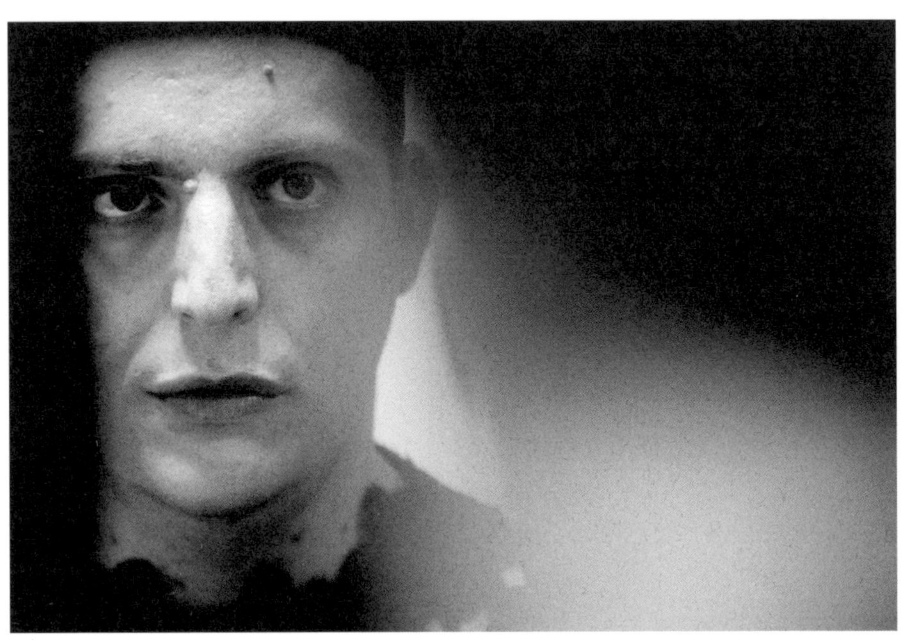

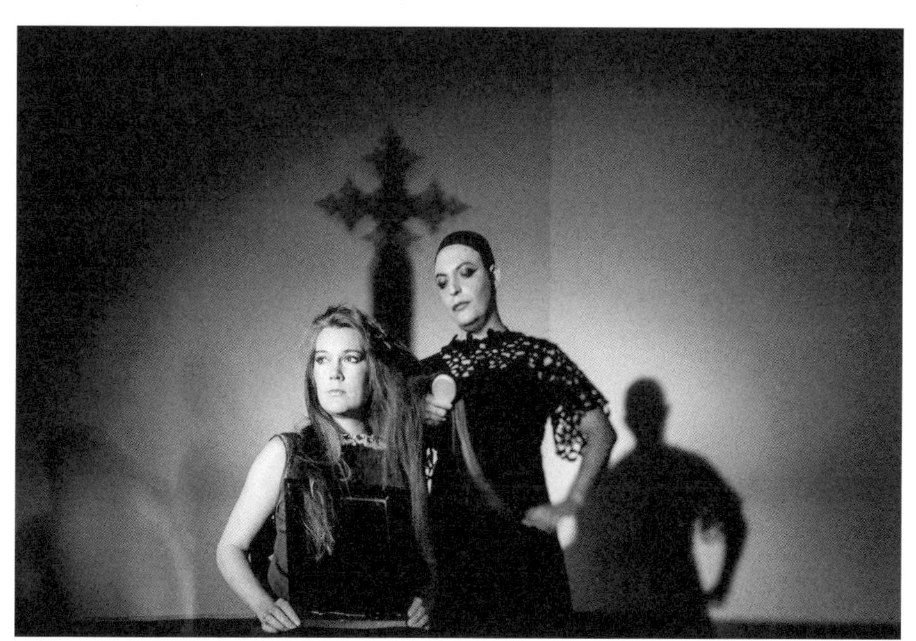

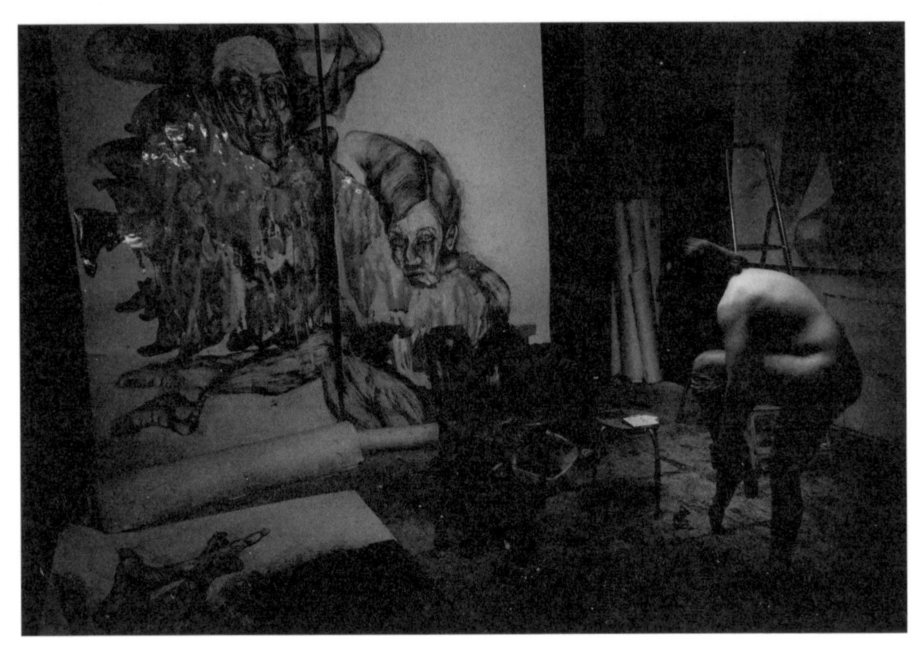

Ole Witt

Help Desk—
Random Acts Of Administration

12

In India everything changes every 50 kilometers—the food, the language, the mentality. The only constant is the condition of the government offices. Indian administration works like traffic: There is no recognizable system, but somehow you get to your destination anyway.

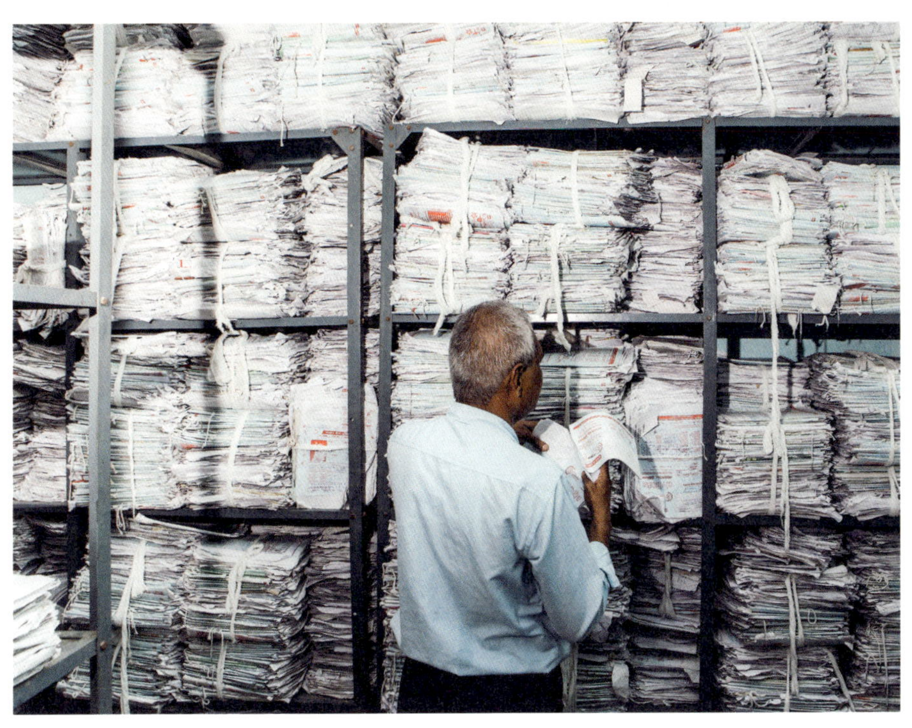

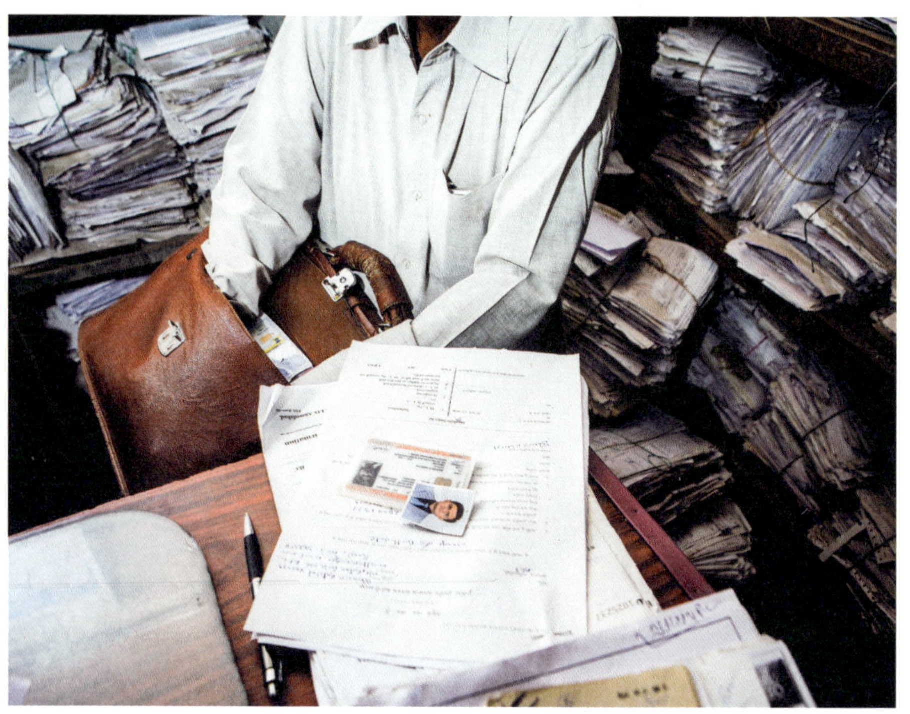

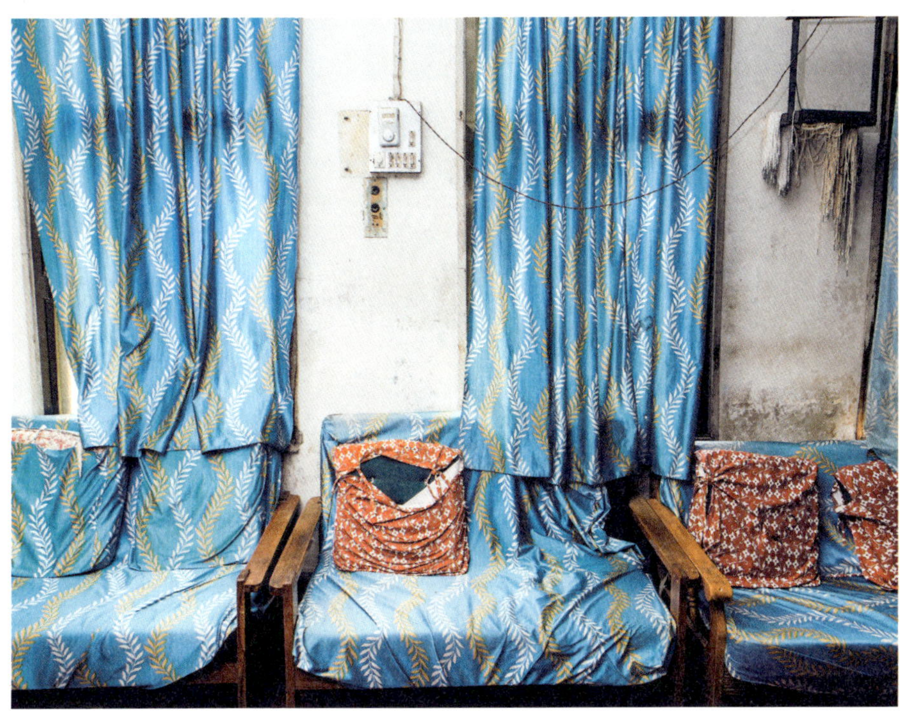

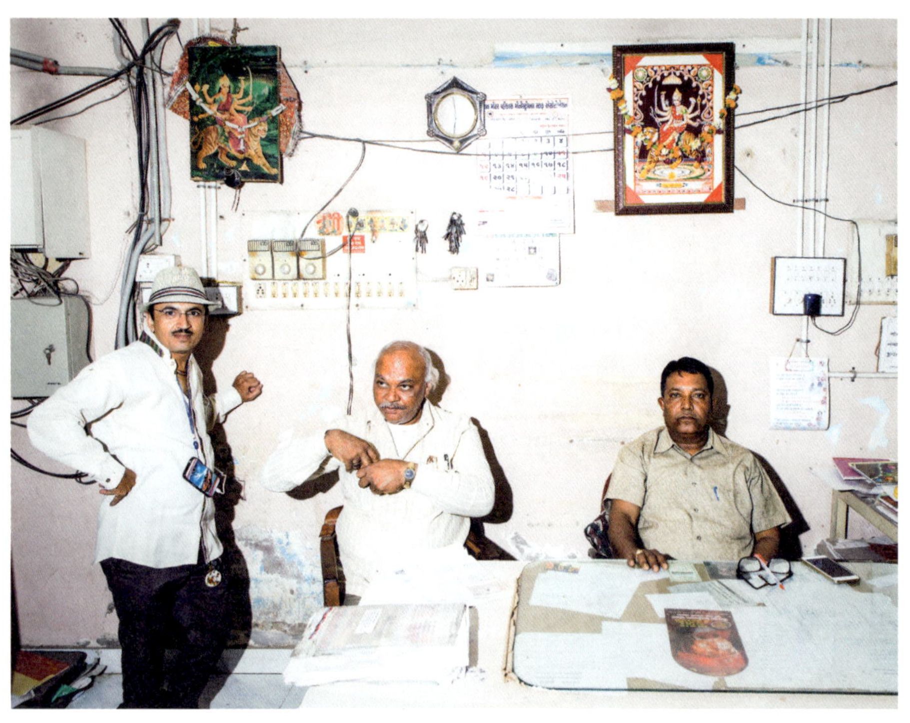

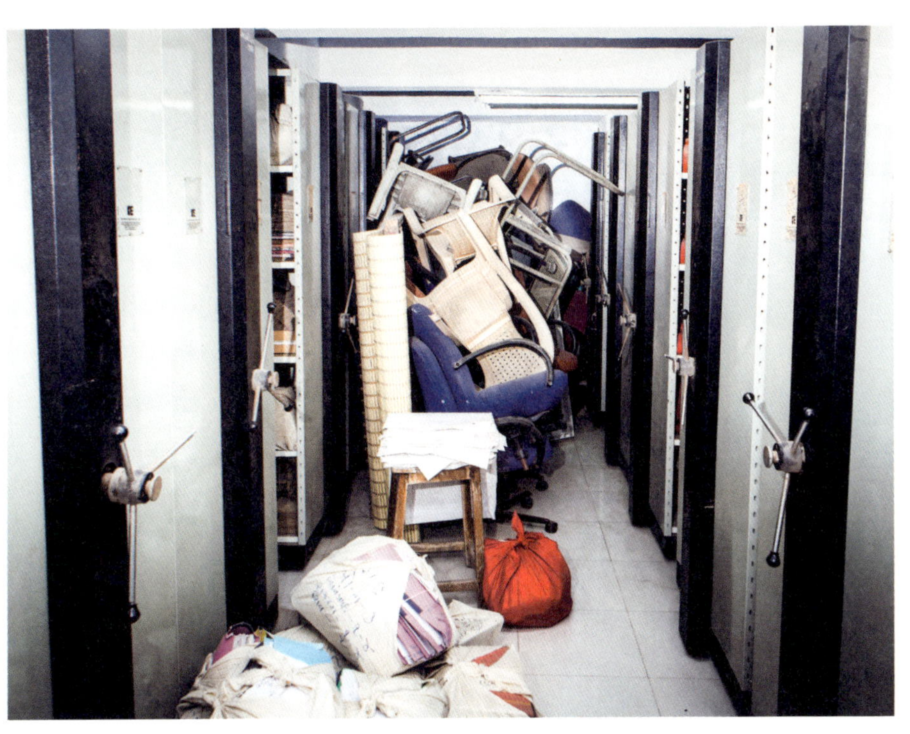

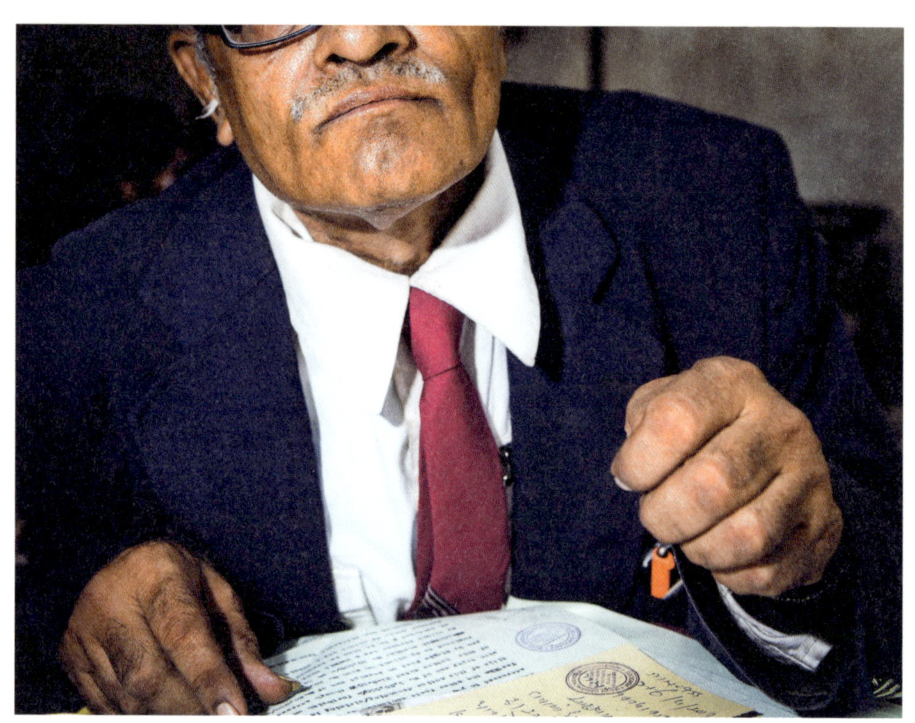

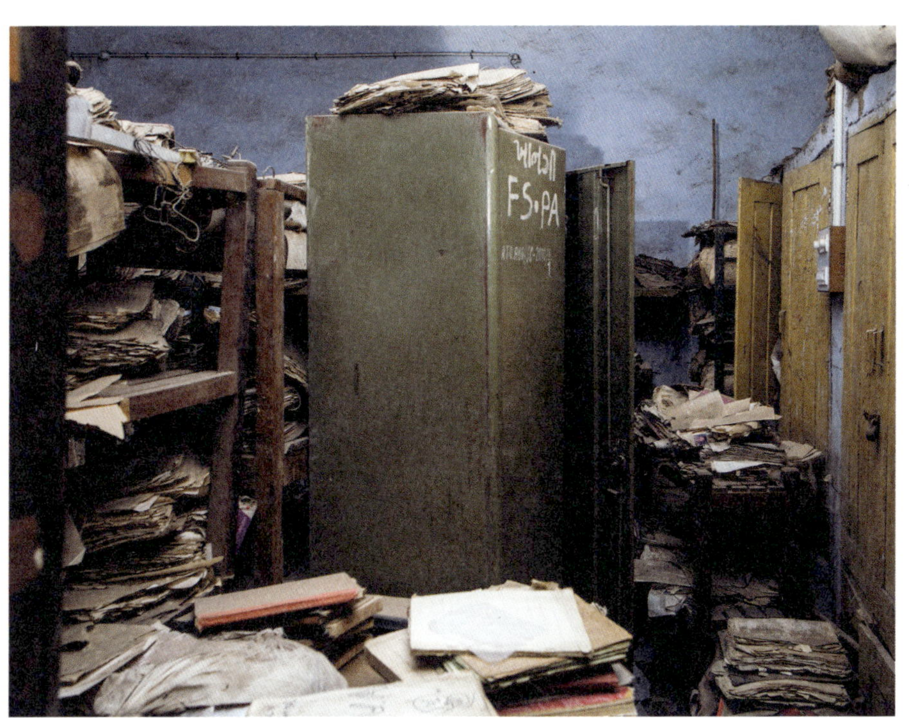

Luise Jakobi

You Can Ask Me Everything

13

In the year 2018, an artificial intelligence was able to maintain a phone call with a human without revealing itself as a technological artefact. This leads to pressing questions regarding the way intelligent machines are used and perceived by society. What lies ahead for the relationship between humans and machines?

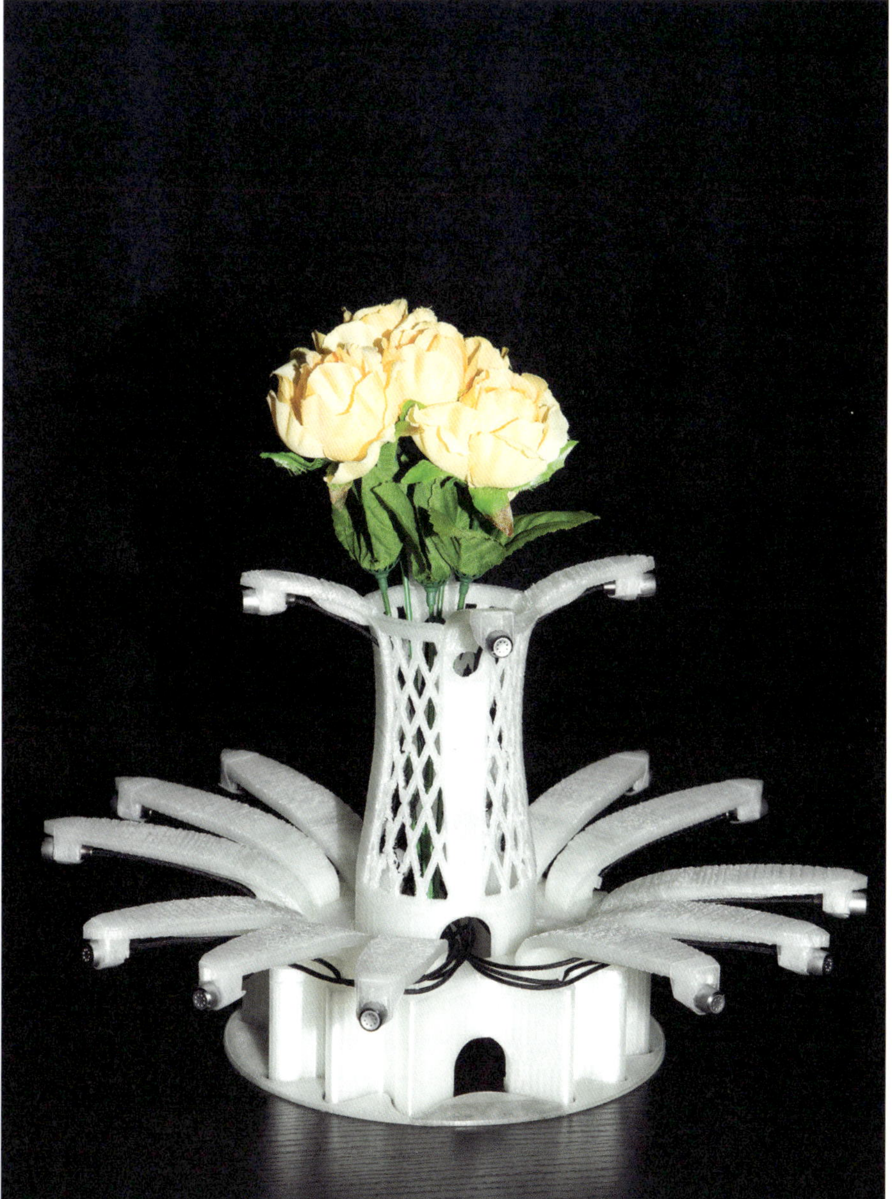

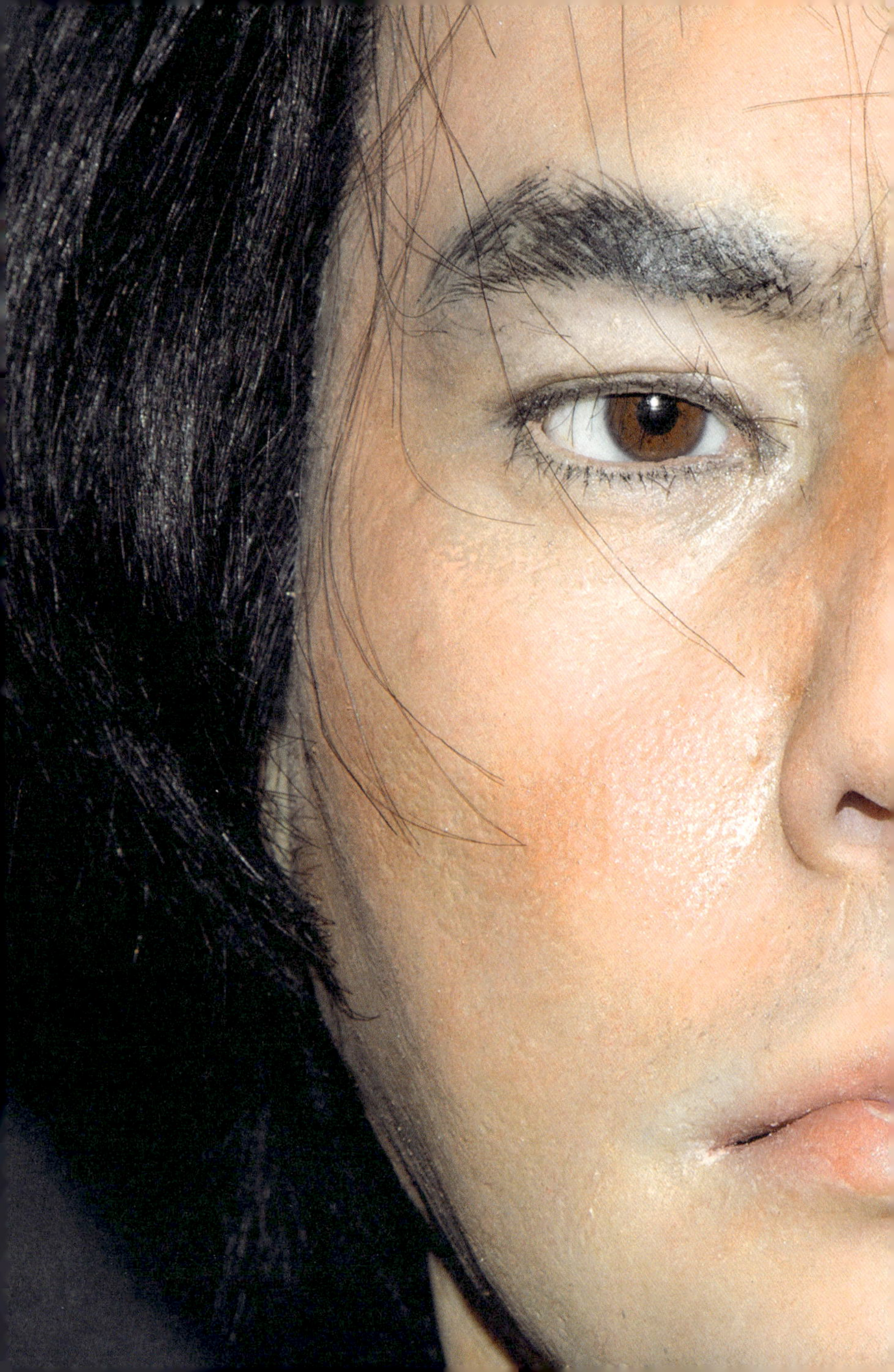

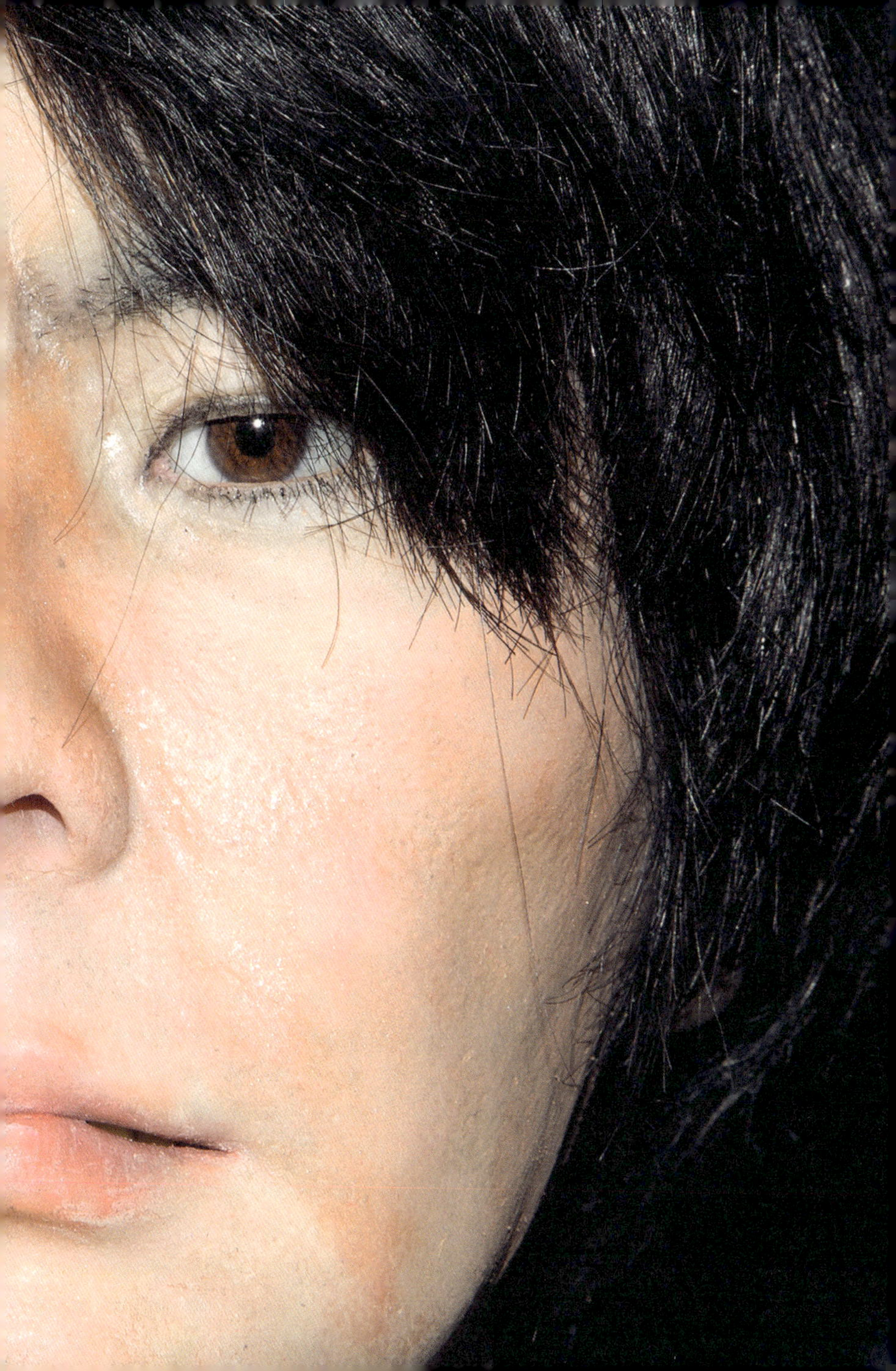

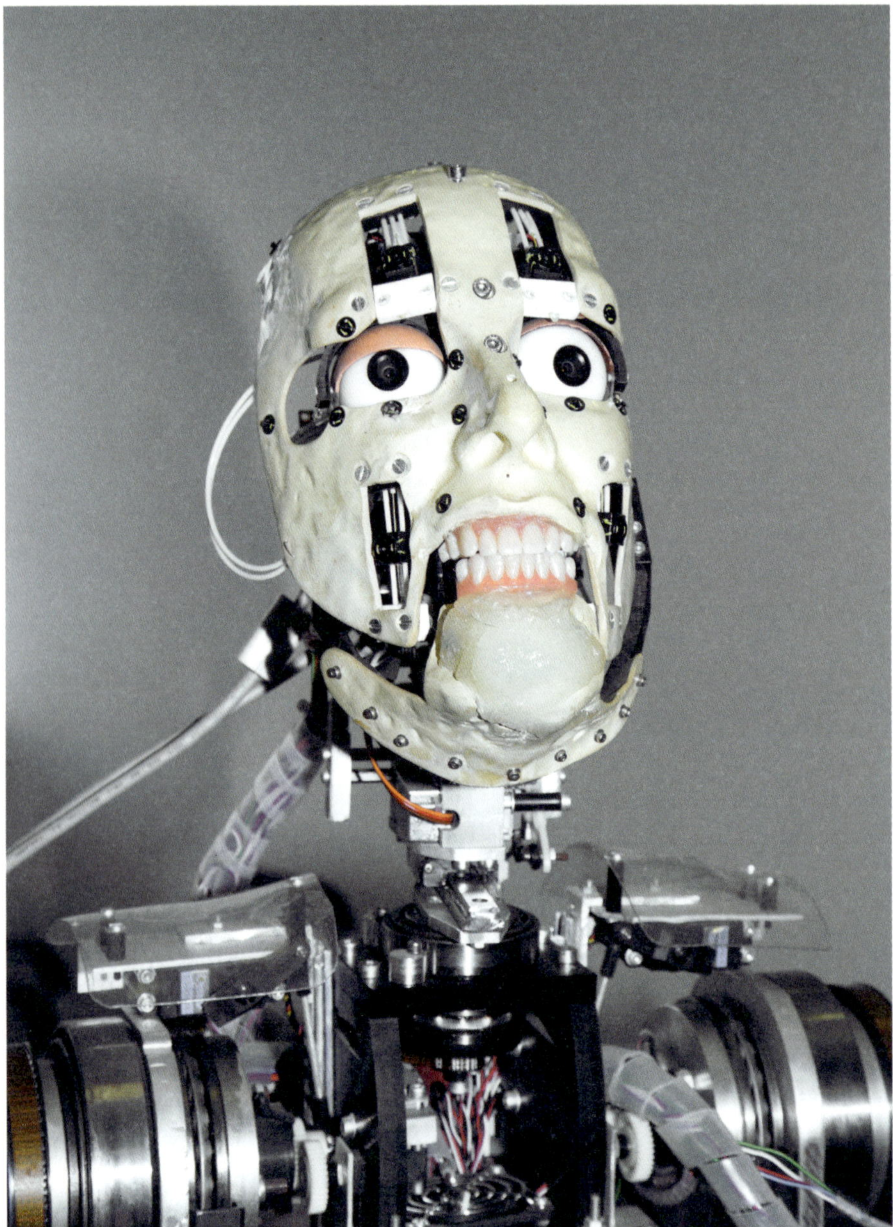

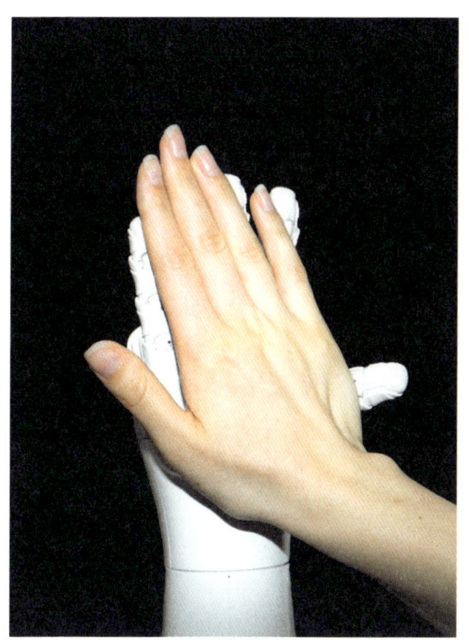

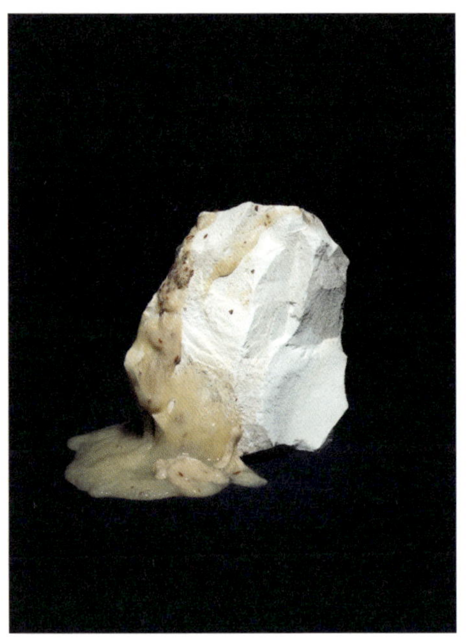

Ronja Hermann

Seepferdchen ohne Kopf

14

My mother died of leukemia at age 28. After 25 years of unexpressed acceptance, I started to wonder what kind of person my mother was, how we spent our short time together and how her absence shaped me growing up.

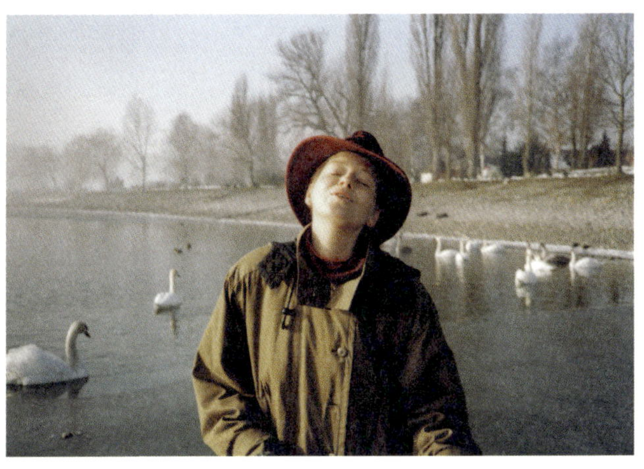

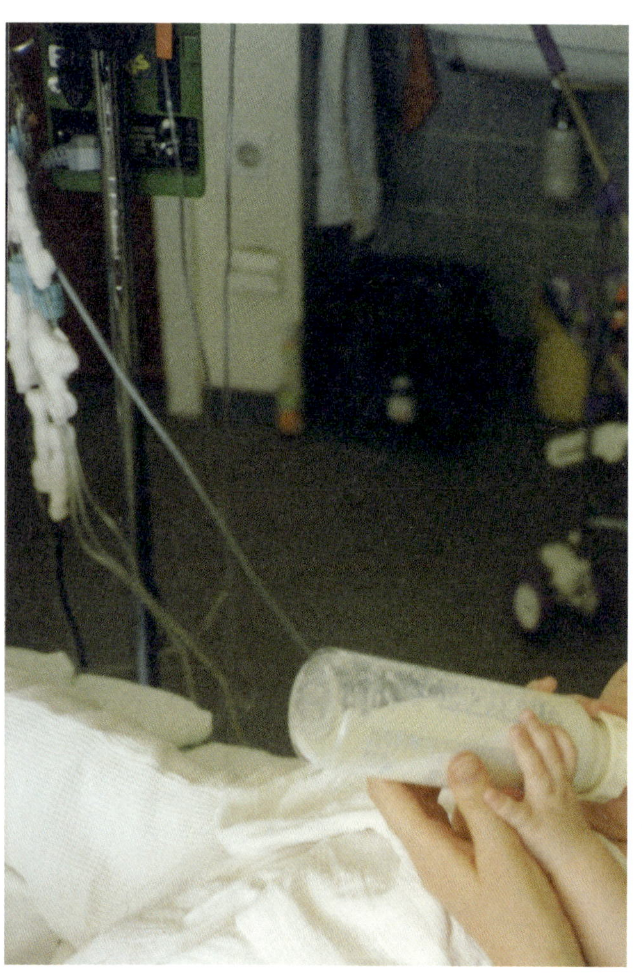

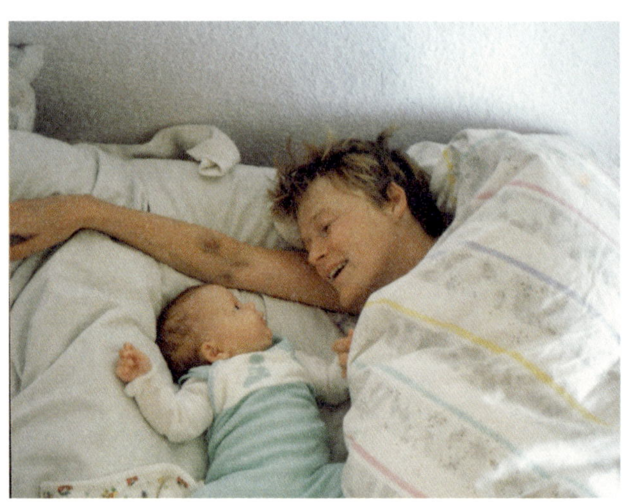

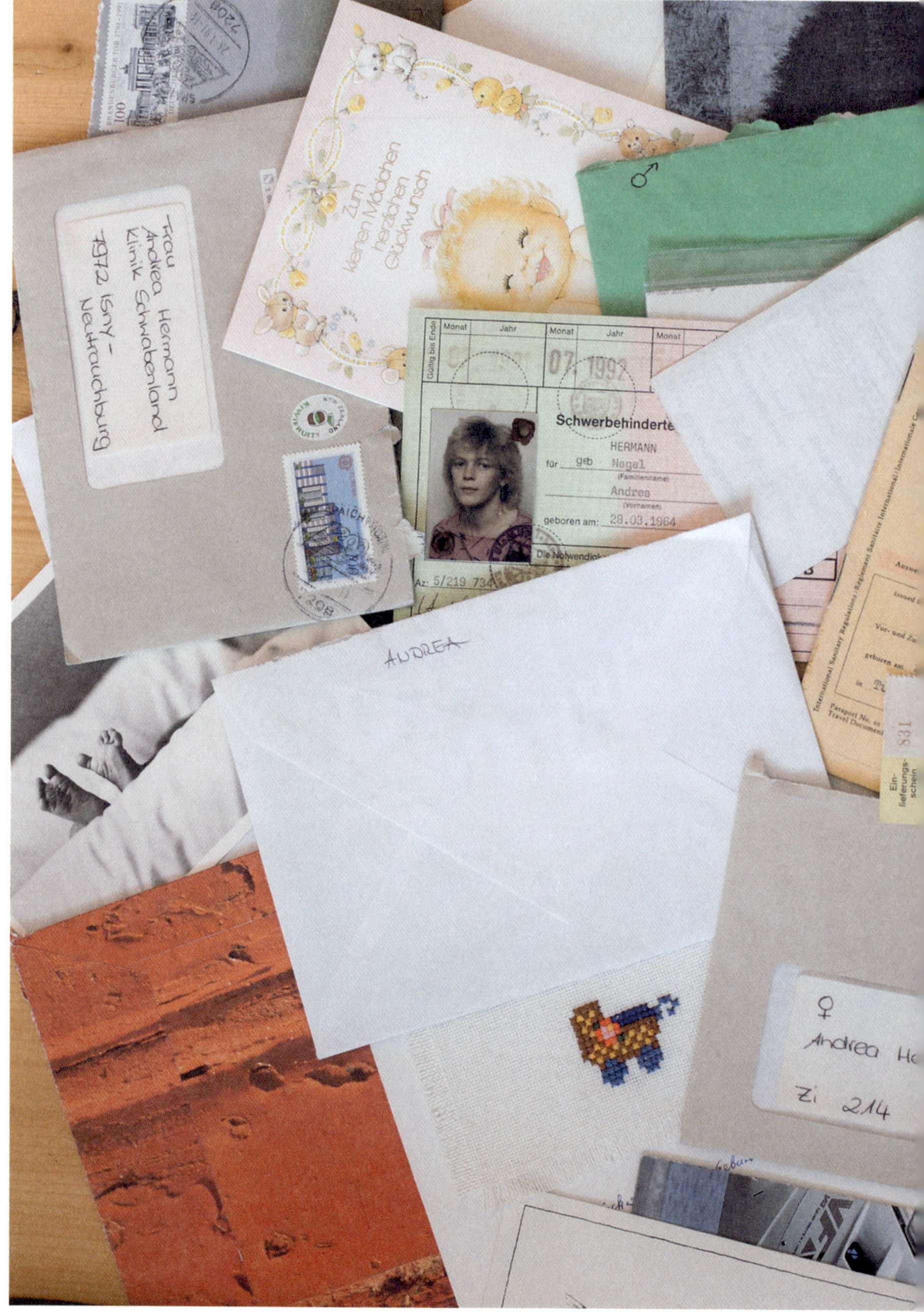

Frau
Andrea Hermann
Klinik Schwabenland
7972 Isny –
Neutrauchburg
Zum
kleinen Mädchen
herzlichen
Glückwunsch
Gültig bis Ende
Monat
Jahr
07. 1992
Schwerbehinderte
HERMANN
für geb Nagel
(Familienname)
Andrea
(Vornamen)
geboren am: 28.03.1964
Die Notwendigk
Az: 5/219 734
ANDREA
Andrea He
Zi 214
Ein-
lieferungs-
schein
831

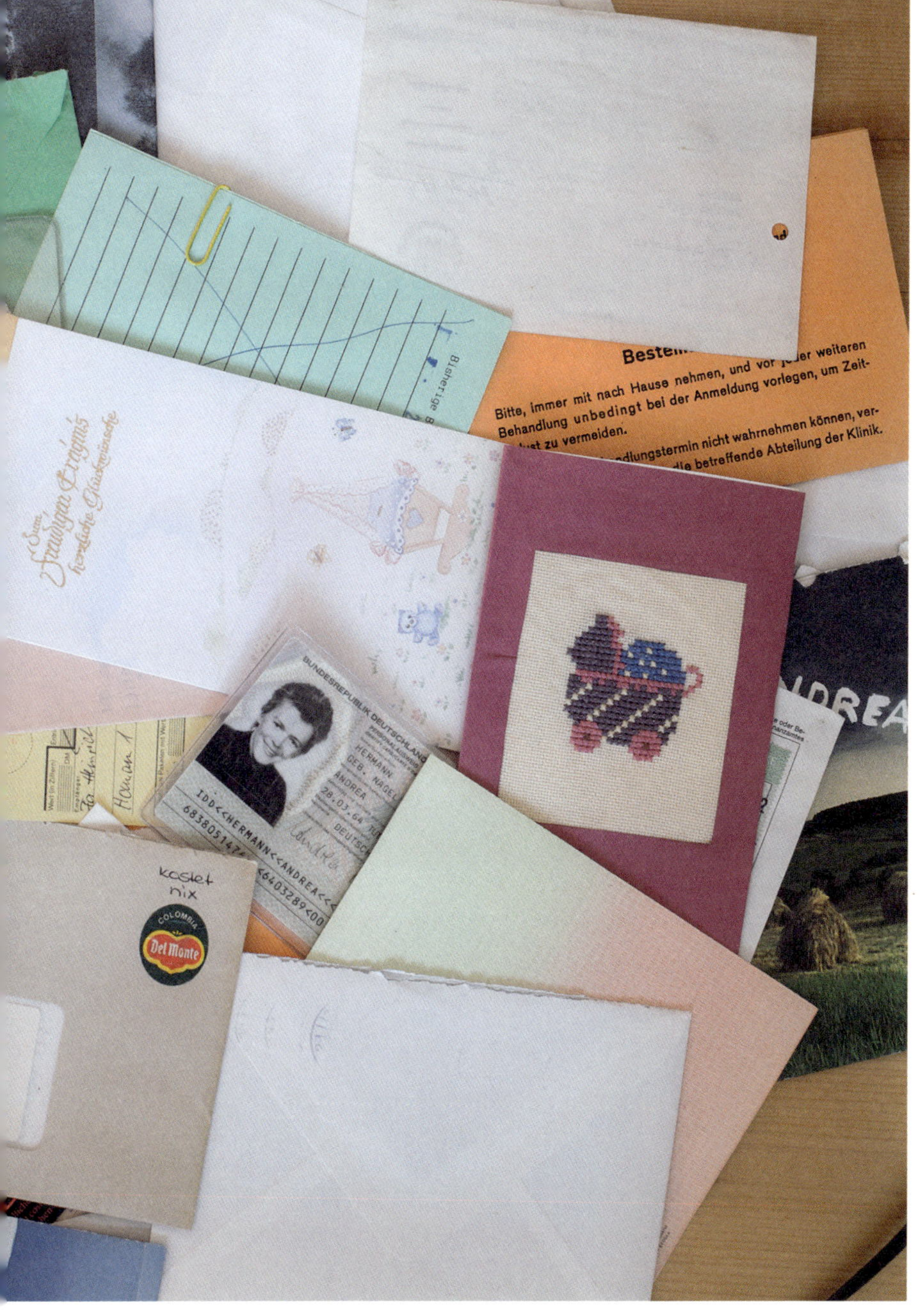

Bitte, immer mit nach Hause nehmen, und vor
Behandlung unbedingt bei der Anmeldung vorlegen, um Zeit-
die betreffende Abteilung der Klinik.
Bisherige
BUNDESREPUBLIK DEUTSCHLAND
HERMANN
GEB. NAGEL
ANDREA
28.03.64
IDD<<HERMANN<<ANDREA<<
kostet
nix
COLOMBIA
Del Monte

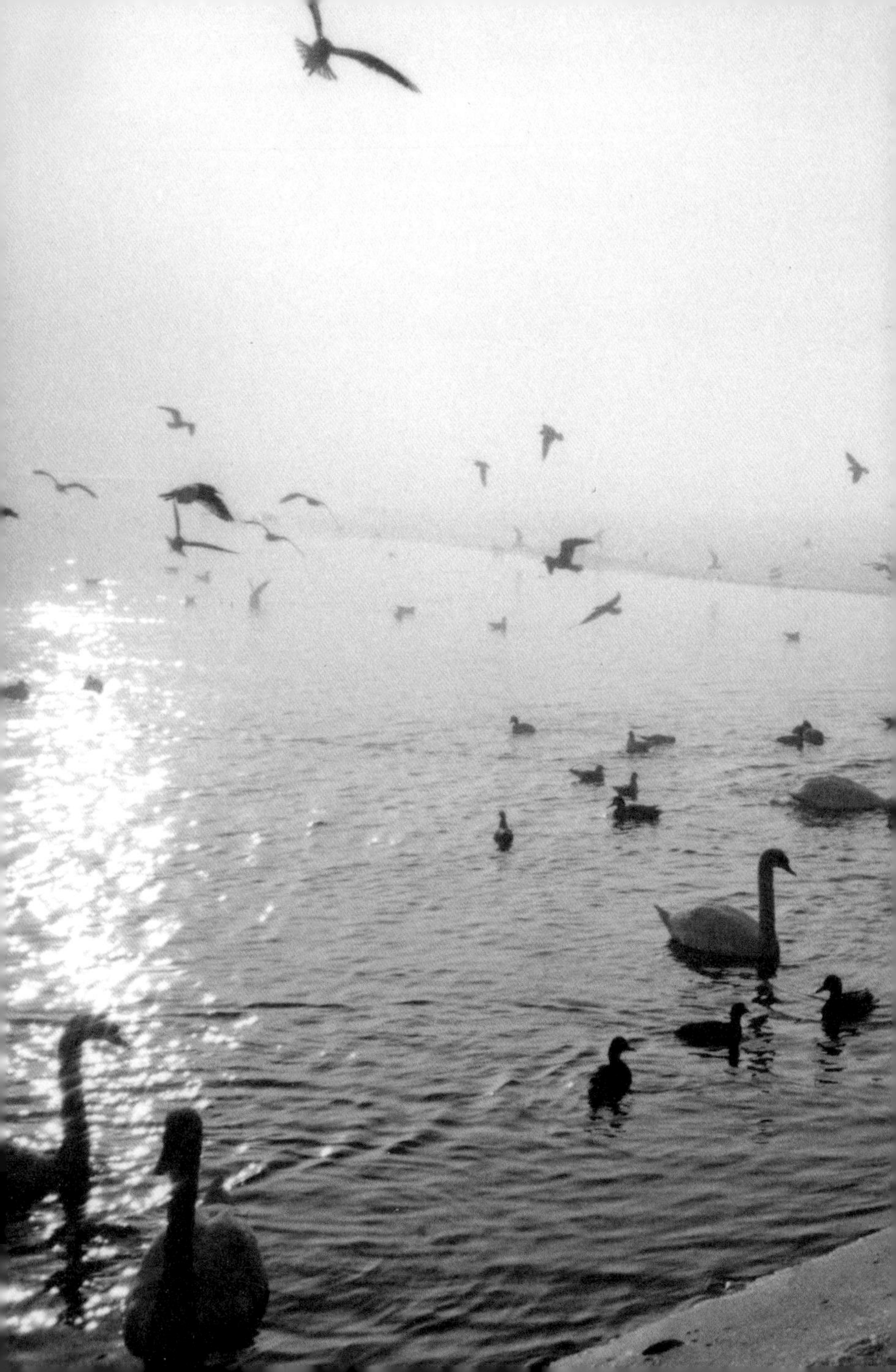

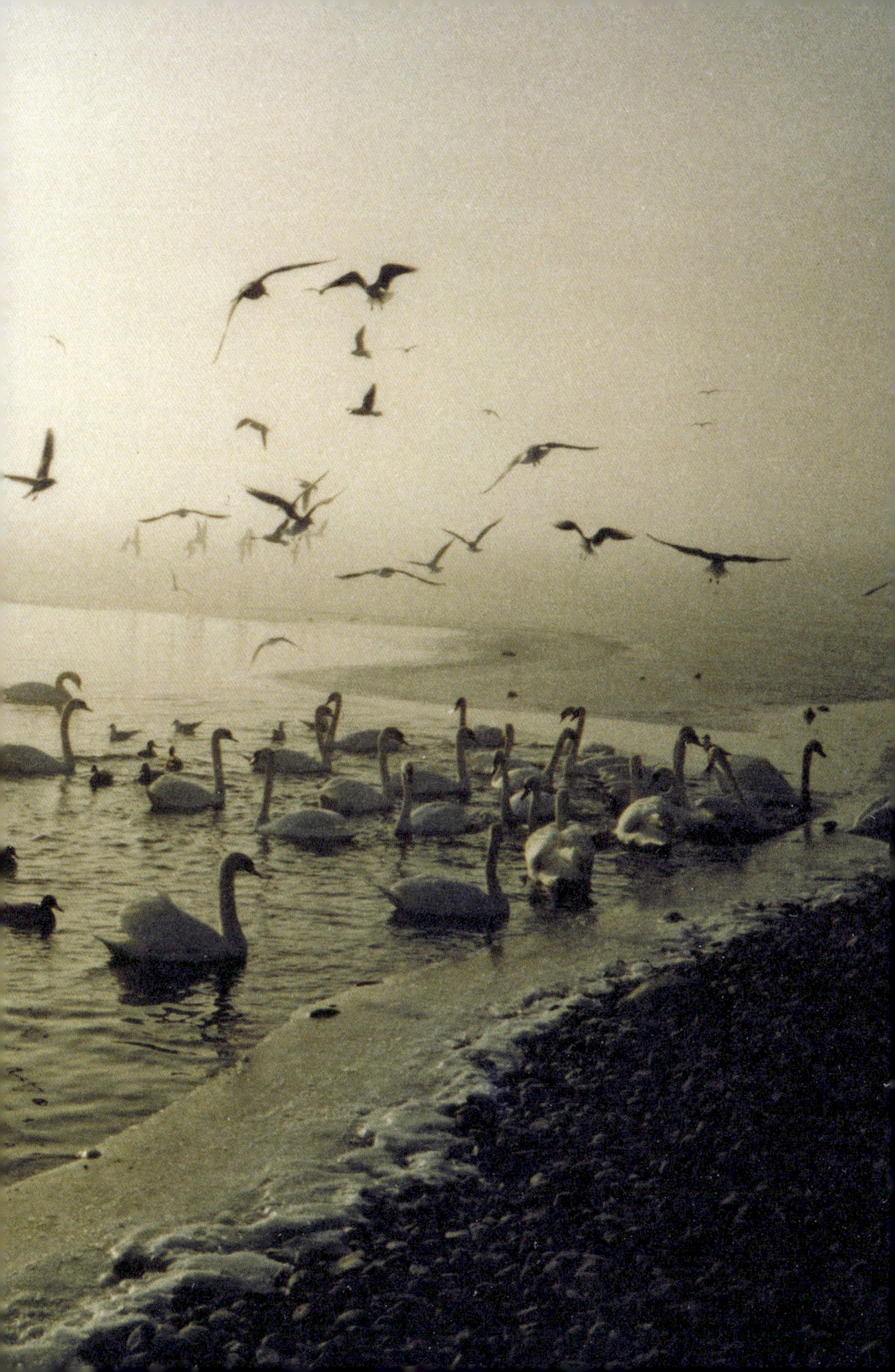

Jann Höfer

Like Wet Cement

15

After 40 years of physical and sexual abuse by sect leader Paul Schäfer, the inhabitants of the former Colonia Dignidad seek their future in tourism. Themed as a German idyll, the small village in Chile avoids having to come to terms with its past.

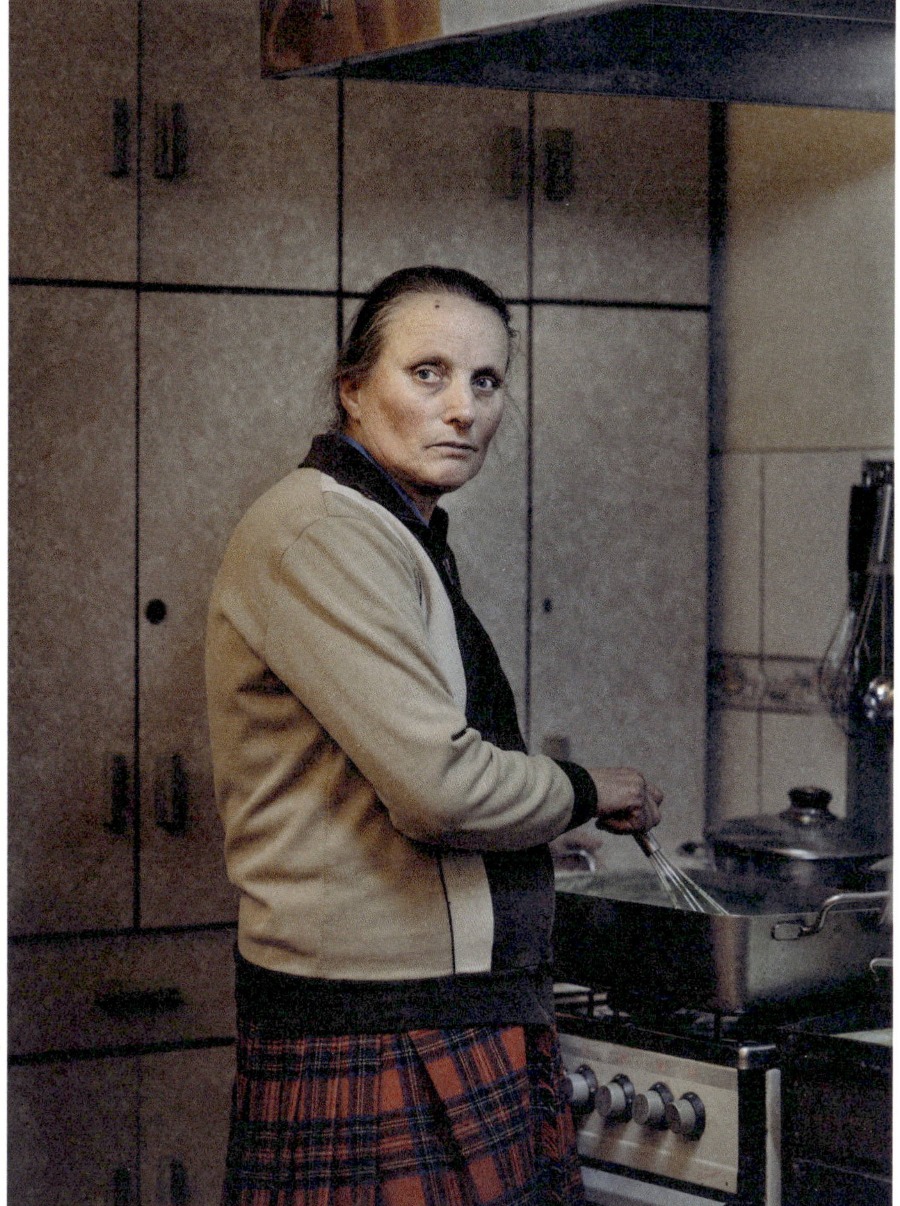

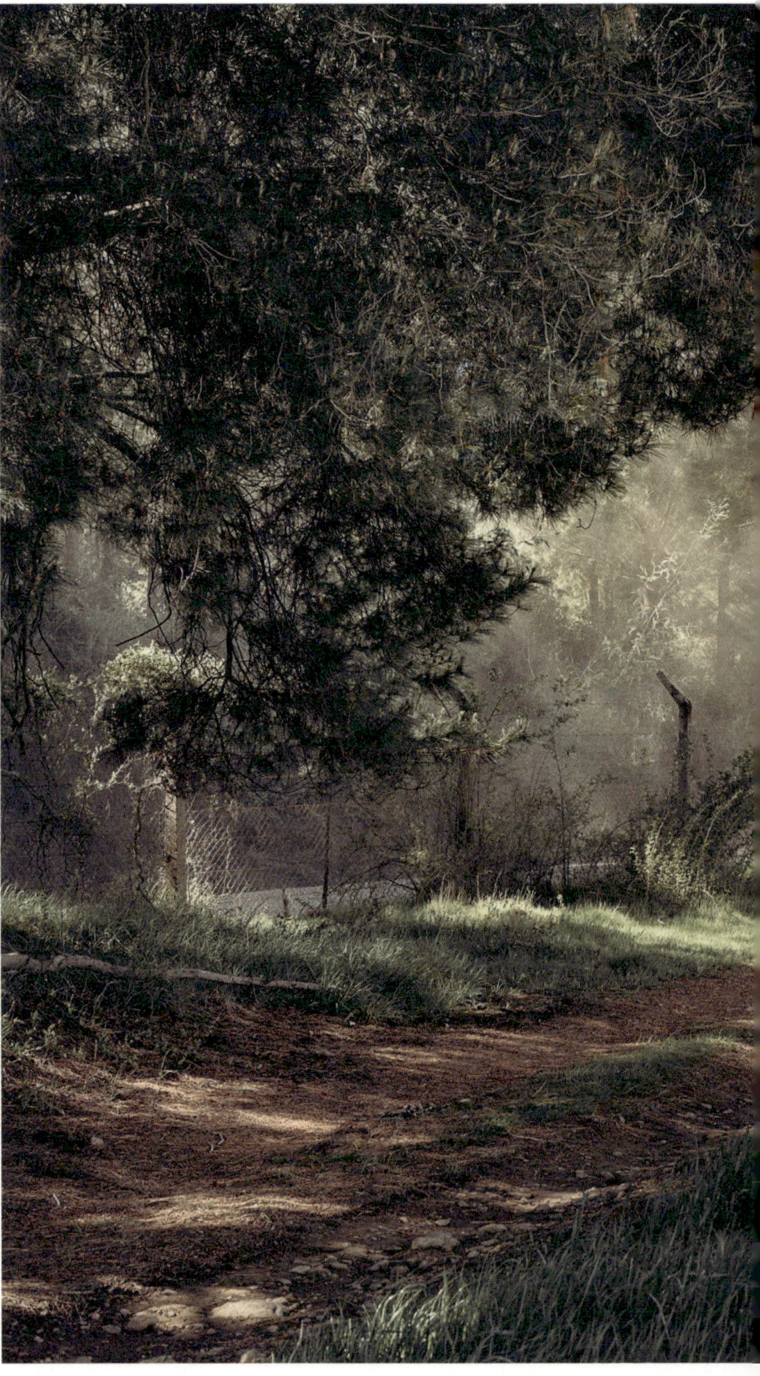

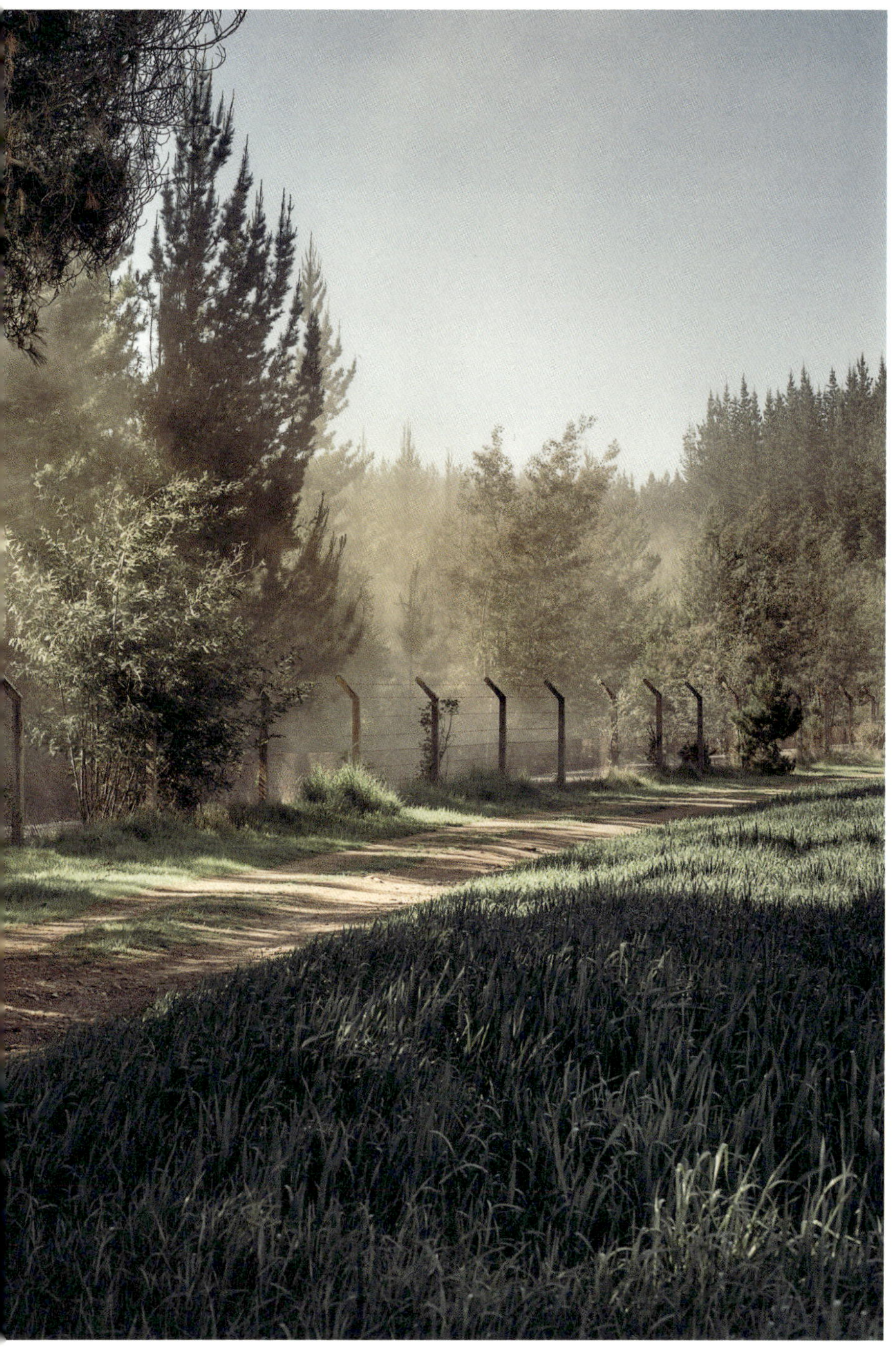

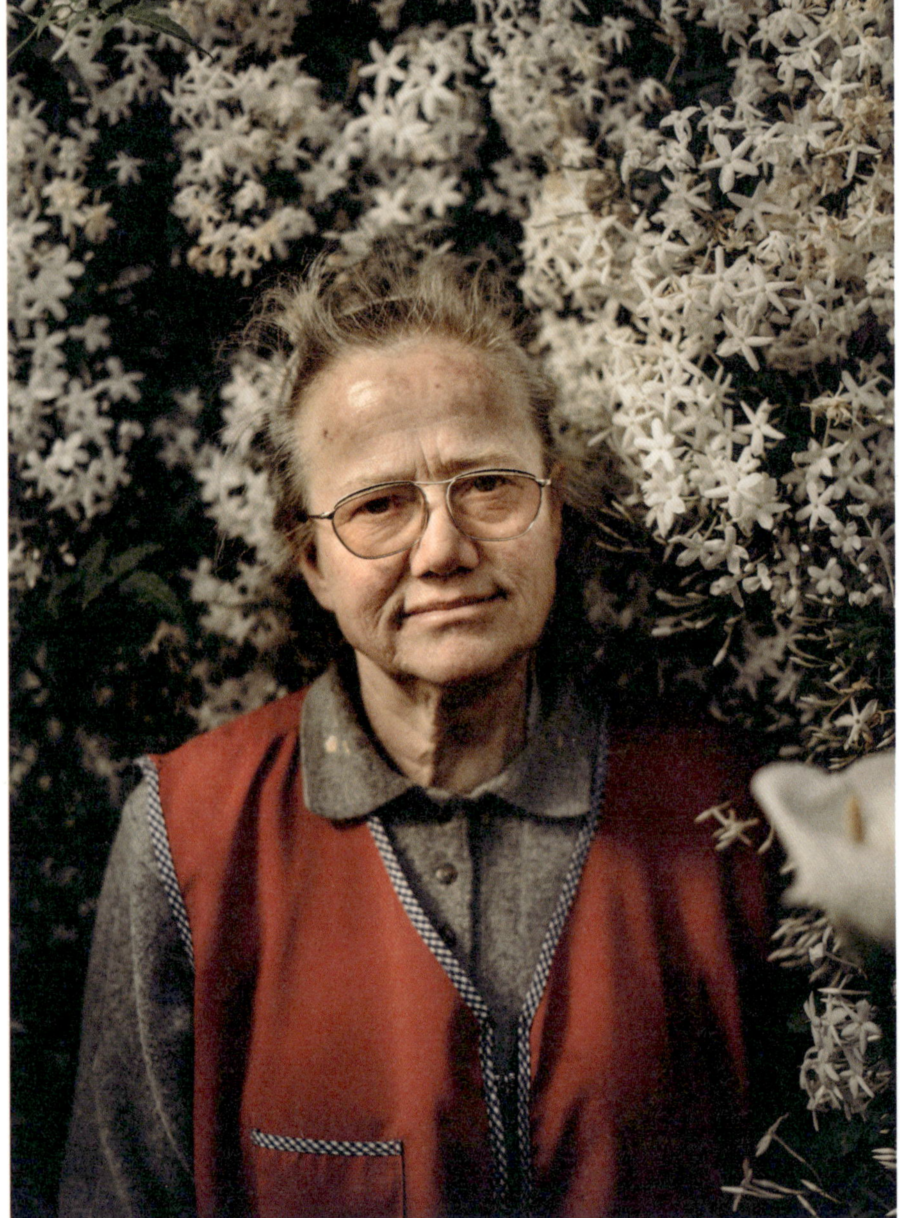

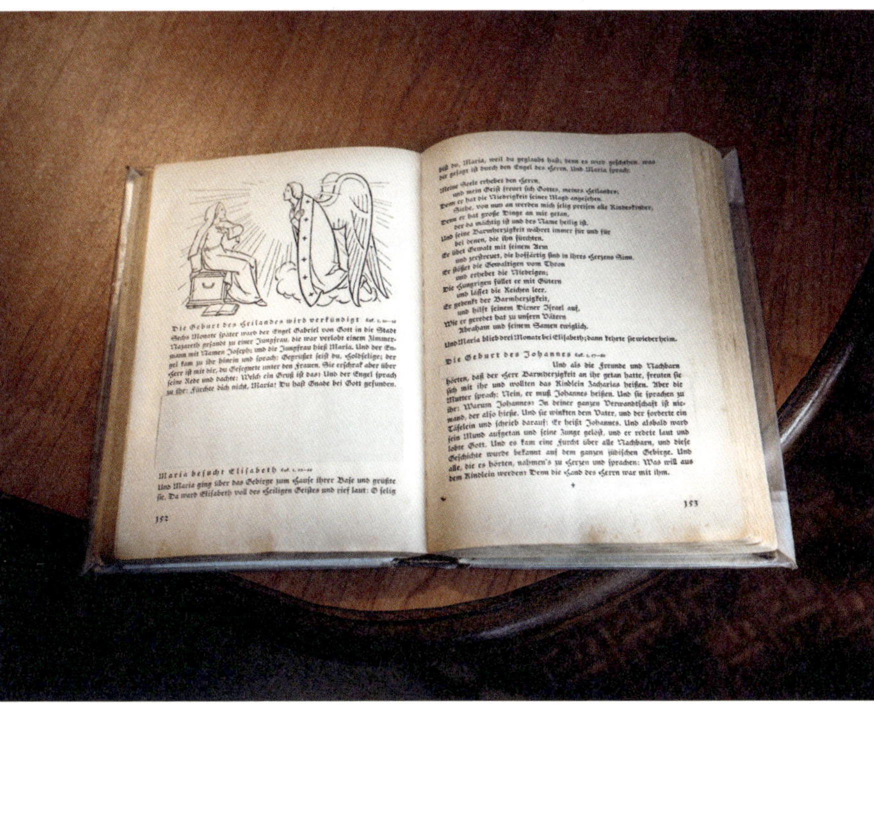

Die Geburt des Heilandes wird verkündigt

Sechs Monate später ward der Engel Gabriel von Gott in die Stadt Nazareth gesandt zu einer Jungfrau, die war verlobt einem Zimmermann mit Namen Joseph; und die Jungfrau hieß Maria. Und der Engel kam zu ihr hinein und sprach: Gegrüßet seist du, Holdselige; der Herr ist mit dir, du Gesegnete unter den Frauen. Sie erschrak aber über seine Rede und dachte: Welch ein Gruß ist das? Und der Engel sprach zu ihr: Fürchte dich nicht, Maria! Du hast Gnade bei Gott gefunden.

Maria besucht Elisabeth

Und Maria ging über das Gebirge zum Hause ihrer Base und grüßte sie. Da ward Elisabeth voll des Heiligen Geistes und rief laut: O selig

352

bist du, Maria, weil du geglaubt hast; denn es wird geschehen, was dir gesagt ist durch den Engel des Herrn. Und Maria sprach:

Meine Seele erhebet den Herrn,
und mein Geist freuet sich Gottes, meines Heilandes;
Denn er hat die Niedrigkeit seiner Magd angesehen.
Siehe, von nun an werden mich selig preisen alle Kindeskinder,
Denn er hat große Dinge an mir getan,
der da mächtig ist und des Name heilig ist.
Und seine Barmherzigkeit währet immer für und für
bei denen, die ihn fürchten.
Er übet Gewalt mit seinem Arm
und zerstreuet, die hoffärtig sind in ihres Herzens Sinn.
Er stößet die Gewaltigen vom Thron
und erhebet die Niedrigen;
Die Hungrigen füllet er mit Gütern
und lässet die Reichen leer.
Er gedenkt der Barmherzigkeit,
und hilft seinem Diener Israel auf,
Wie er geredet hat zu unsern Vätern
Abraham und seinem Samen ewiglich.

Und Maria blieb drei Monate bei Elisabeth; dann kehrte sie wieder heim.

Die Geburt des Johannes

Und als die Freunde und Nachbarn hörten, daß der Herr Barmherzigkeit an ihr getan hatte, freuten sie sich mit ihr und wollten das Kindlein Zacharias heißen. Aber die Mutter sprach: Nein, er muß Johannes heißen. Und sie sprachen zu ihr: Warum Johannes? In deiner ganzen Verwandtschaft ist niemand, der also hieße. Und sie winkten dem Vater, und der forderte ein Täfelein und schrieb darauf: Er heißt Johannes. Und alsbald ward sein Mund aufgetan und seine Zunge gelöst, und er redete laut und lobte Gott. Und es kam eine Furcht über alle Nachbarn, und diese Geschichte wurde bekannt auf dem ganzen jüdischen Gebirge. Und alle, die es hörten, nahmen's zu Herzen und sprachen: Was will aus dem Kindlein werden? Denn die Hand des Herrn war mit ihm.

353

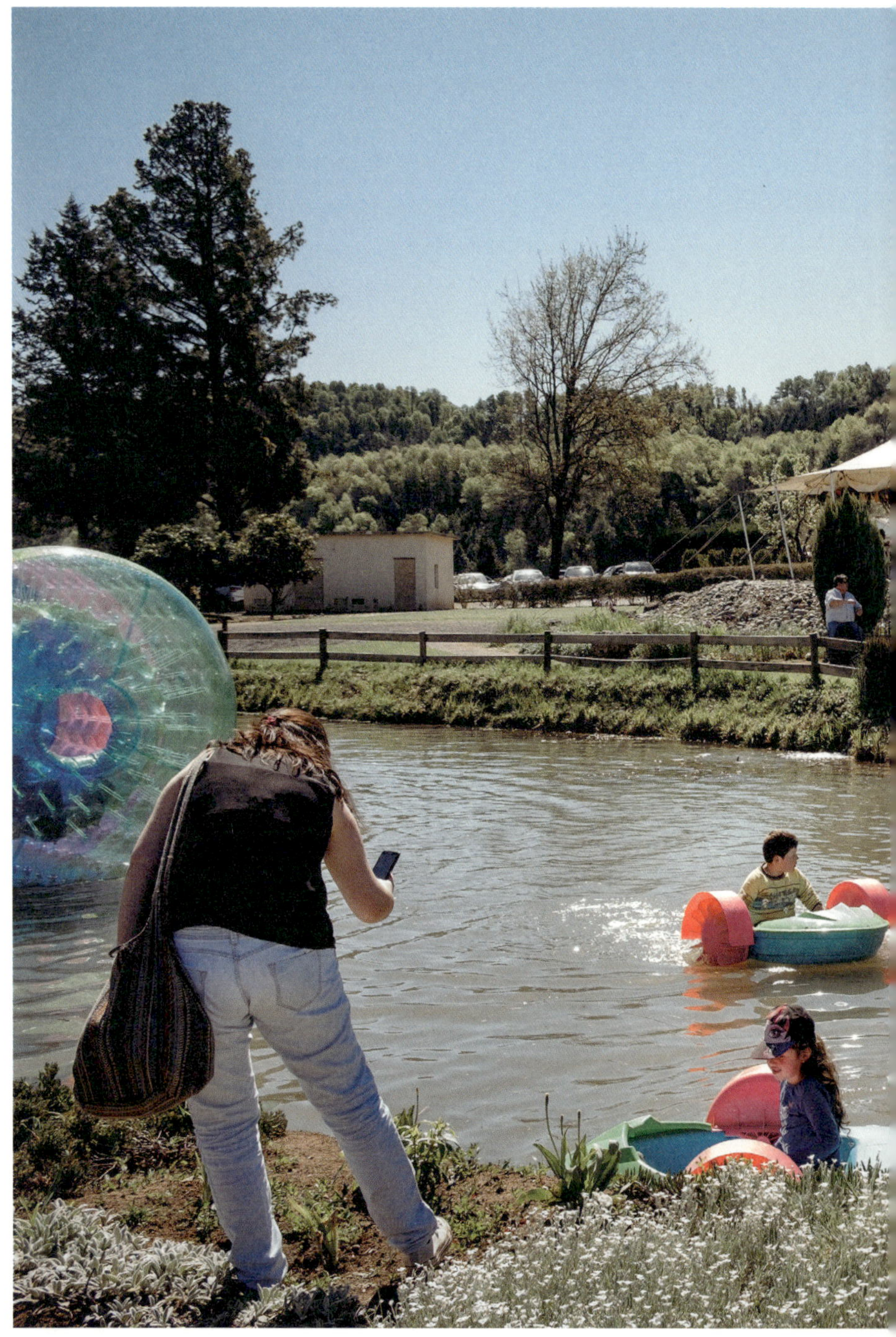

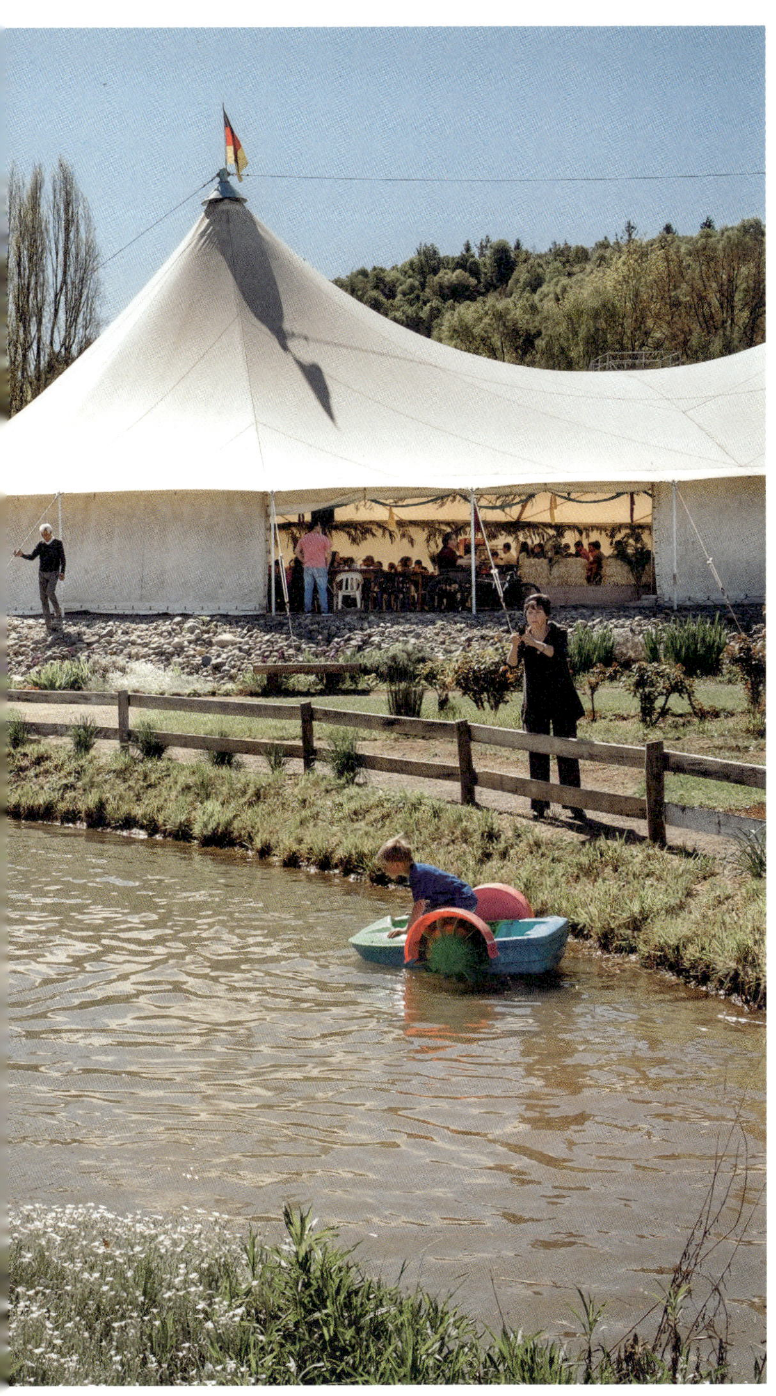

Ingmar Björn Nolting Hinter Fassaden

16

The apartments of the 1970s housing block “Iduna-Zentrum” near Göttingen’s city center were regarded as a prime address for the upper working class. It shares its fate with similar apartment blocks all over Germany: Today, they are home to people on the edge of society and considered to be deprived areas—symbols for a failed city planning utopia.

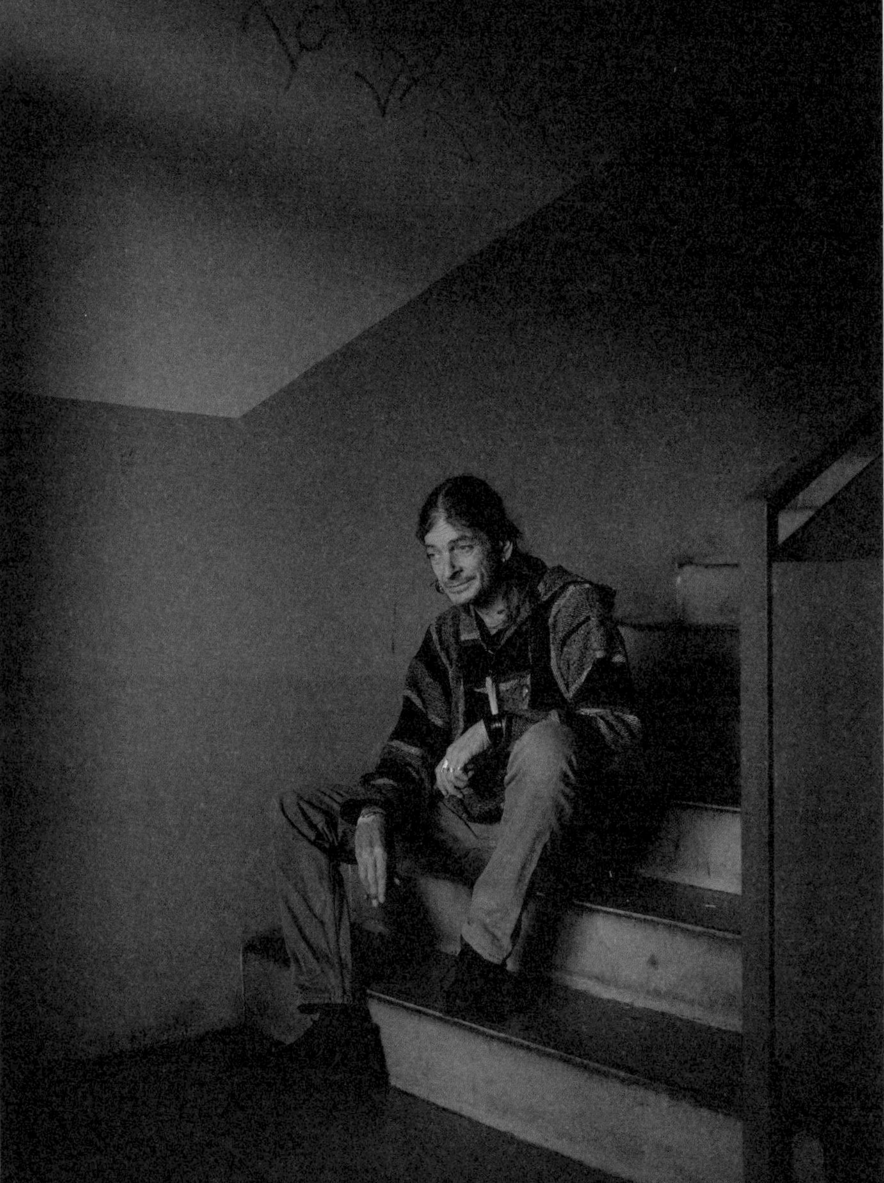

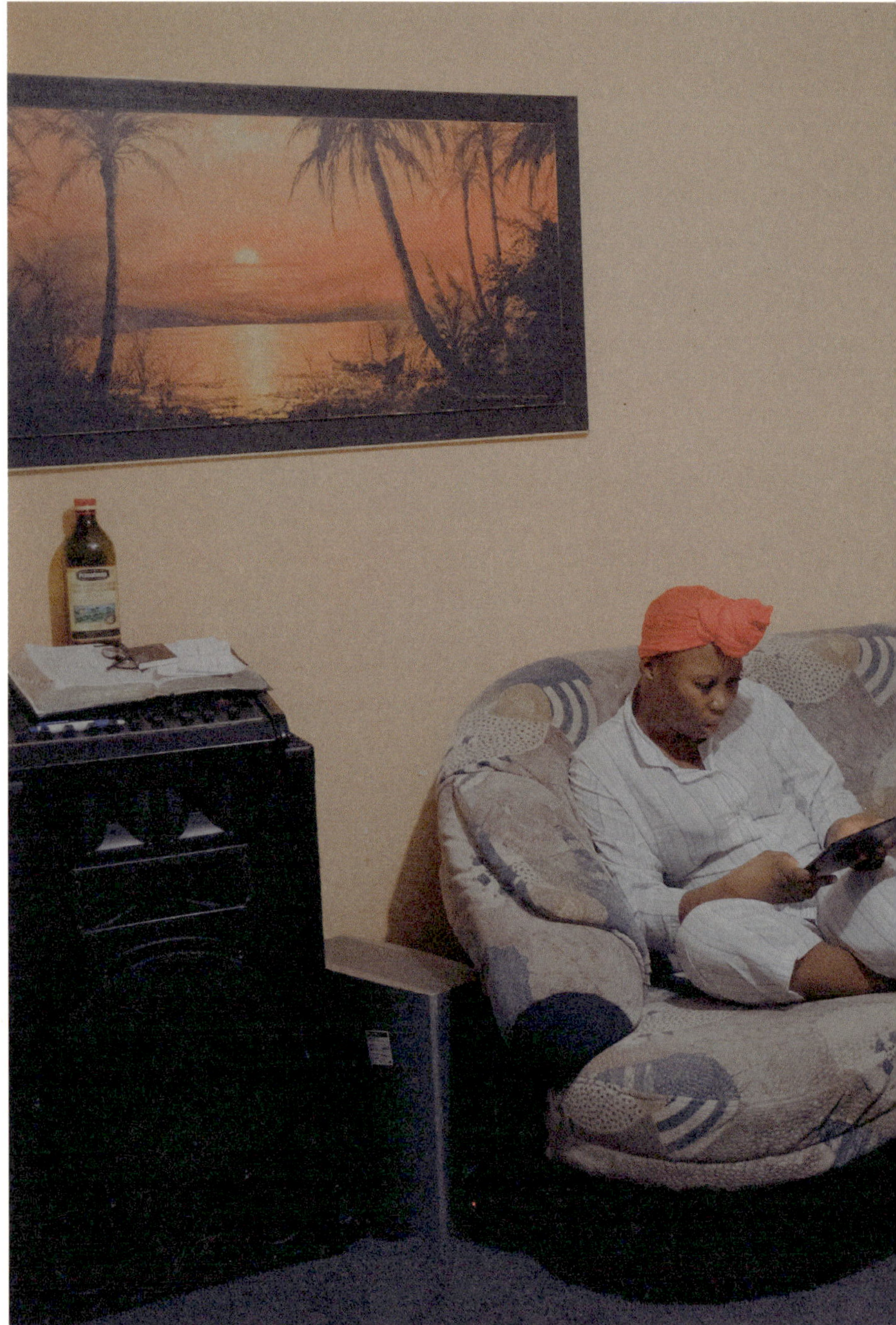

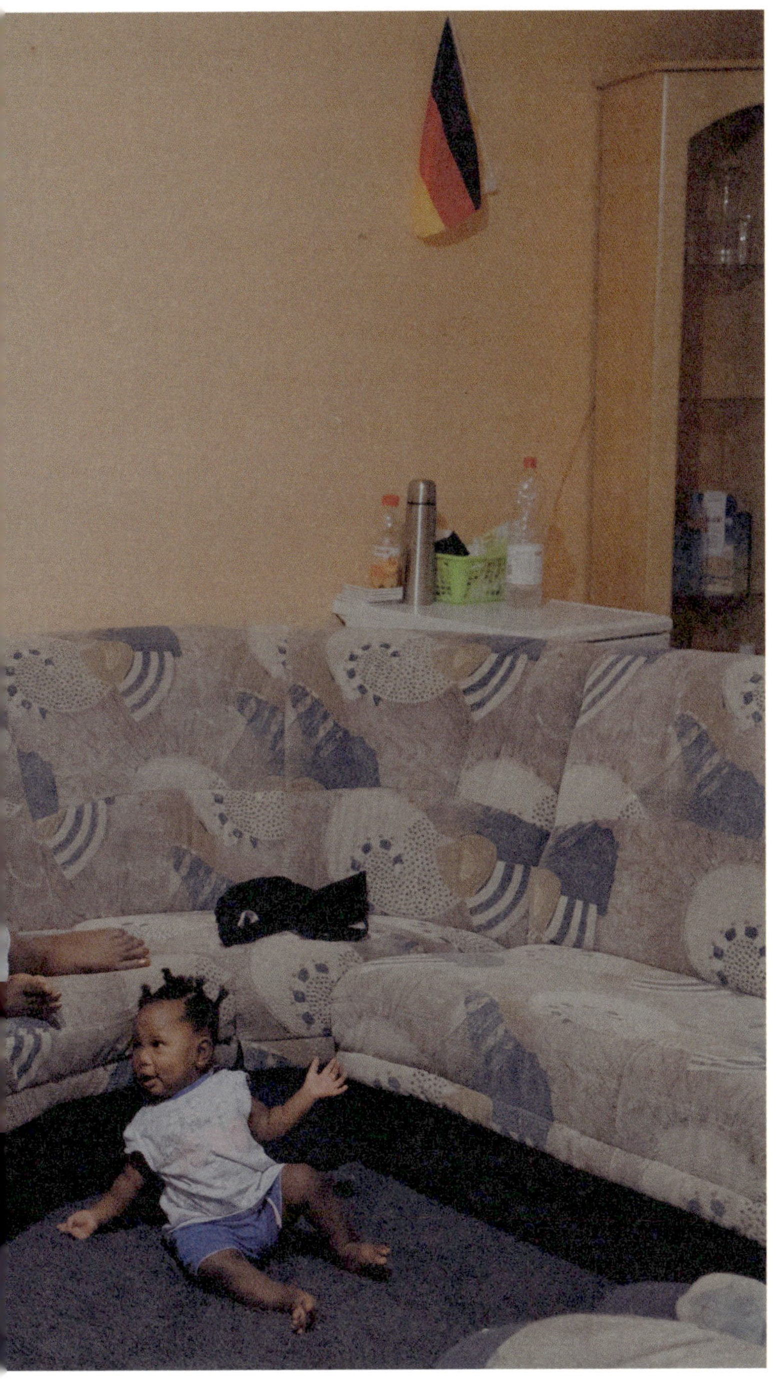

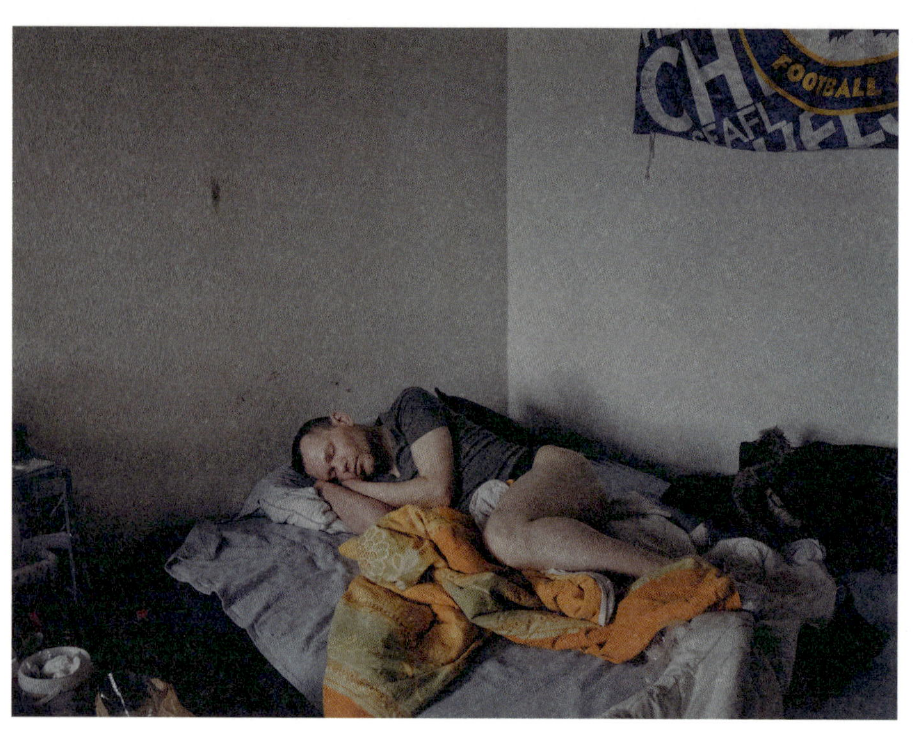
FOOTBALL

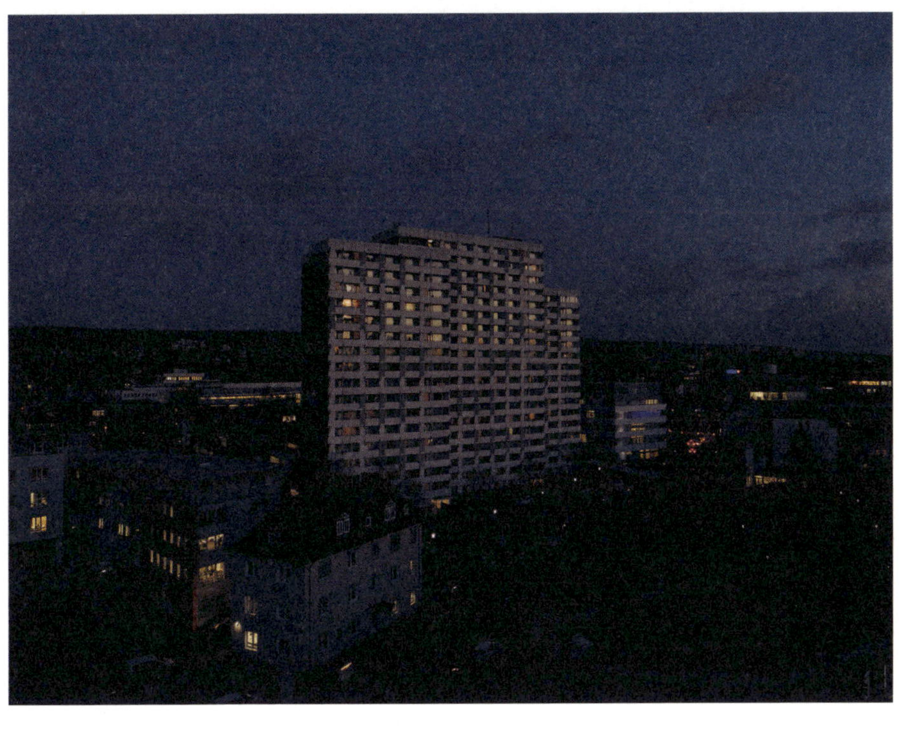

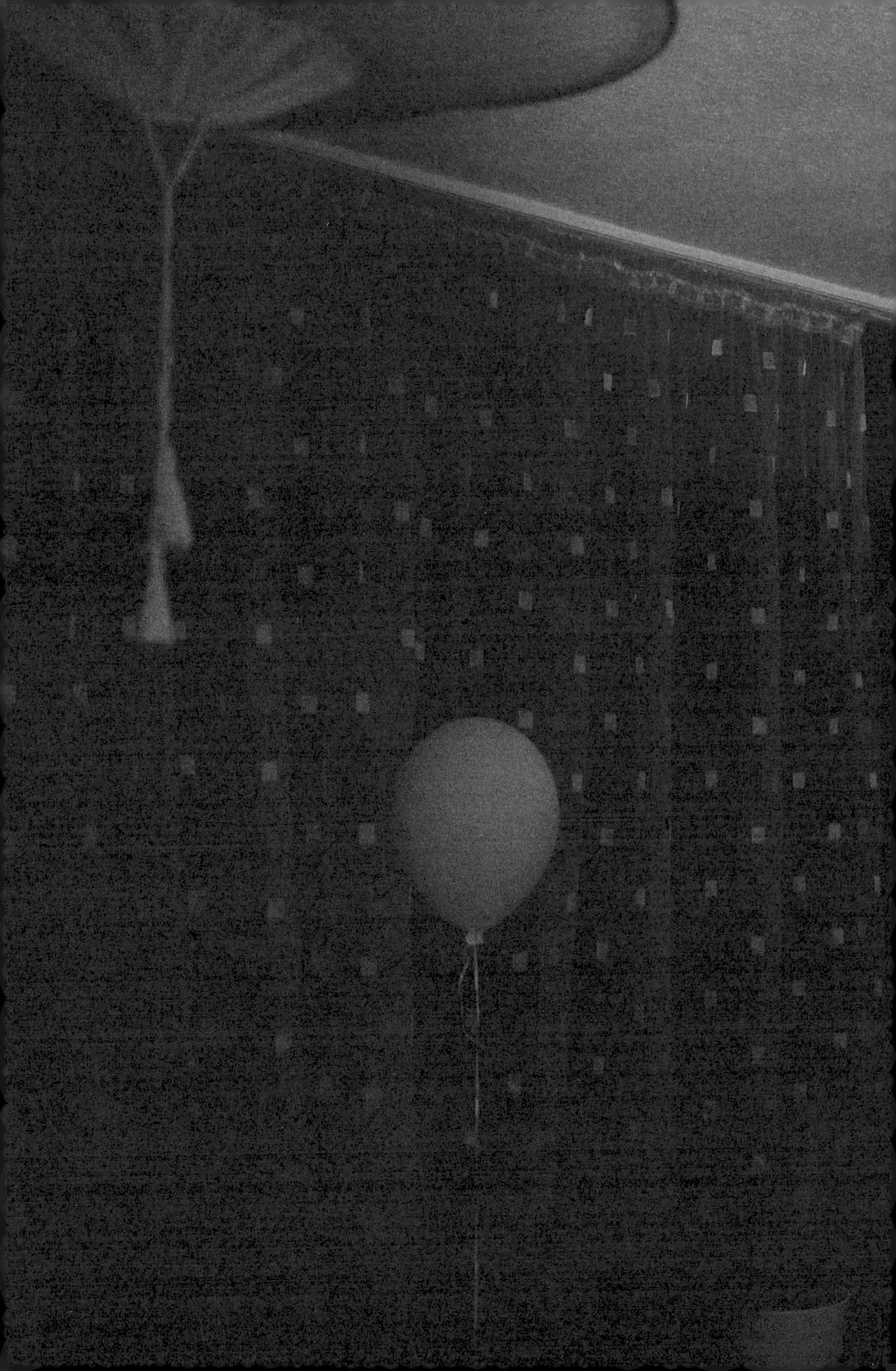

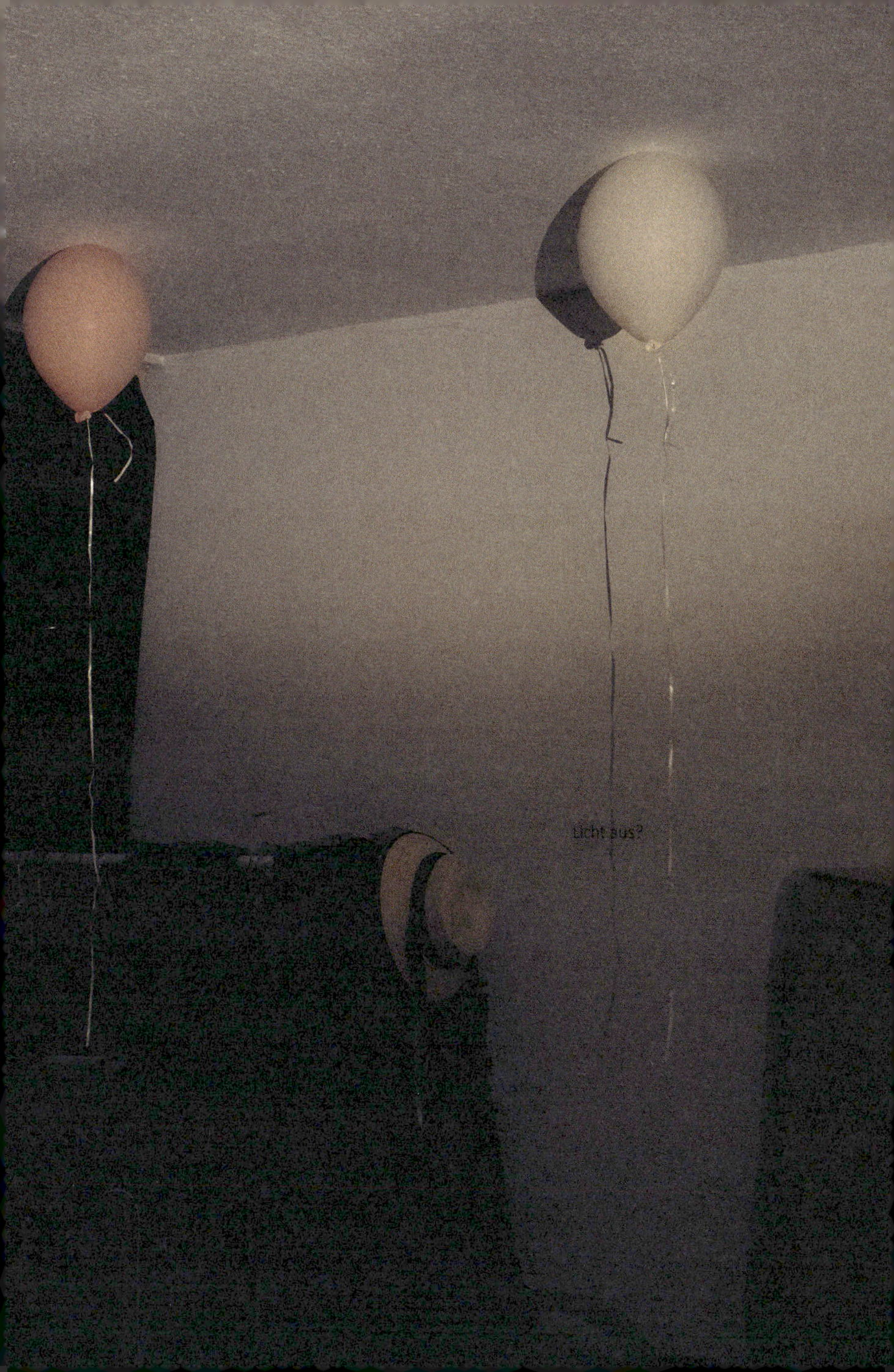

Licht aus?

Kristina Lenz

Meet Me In Cognito, Baby. In Cognito We'll Have Nothing To Hide

17

Photography can be a tool to open doors, lead to new places, enter the world of a stranger. But how authentic are these encounters? How honest is this type of communication?

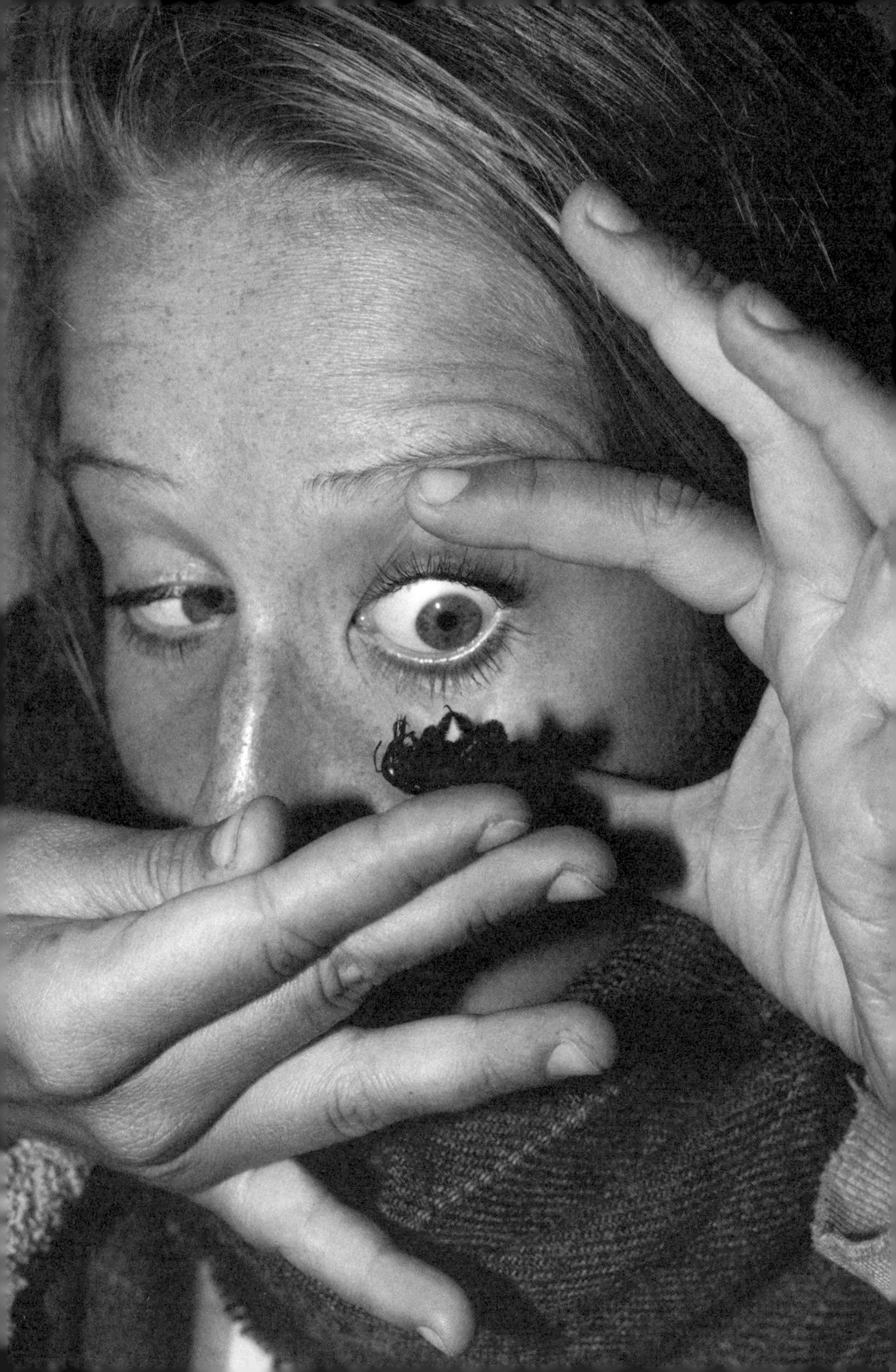

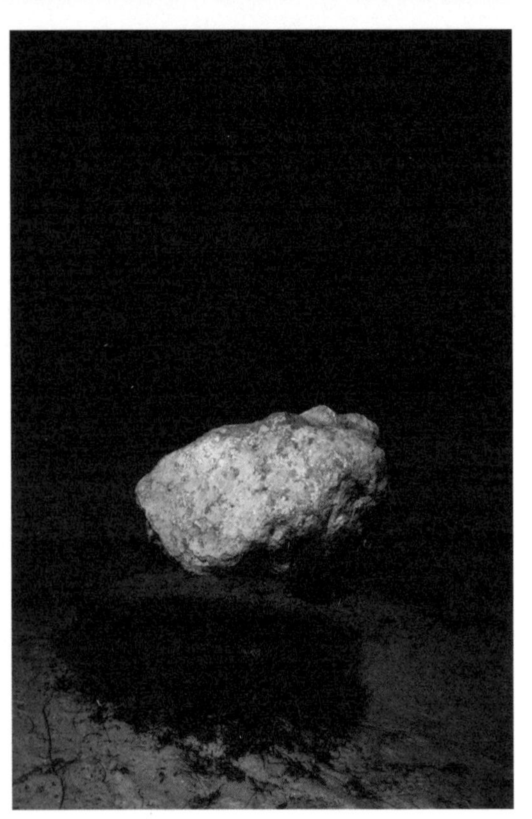

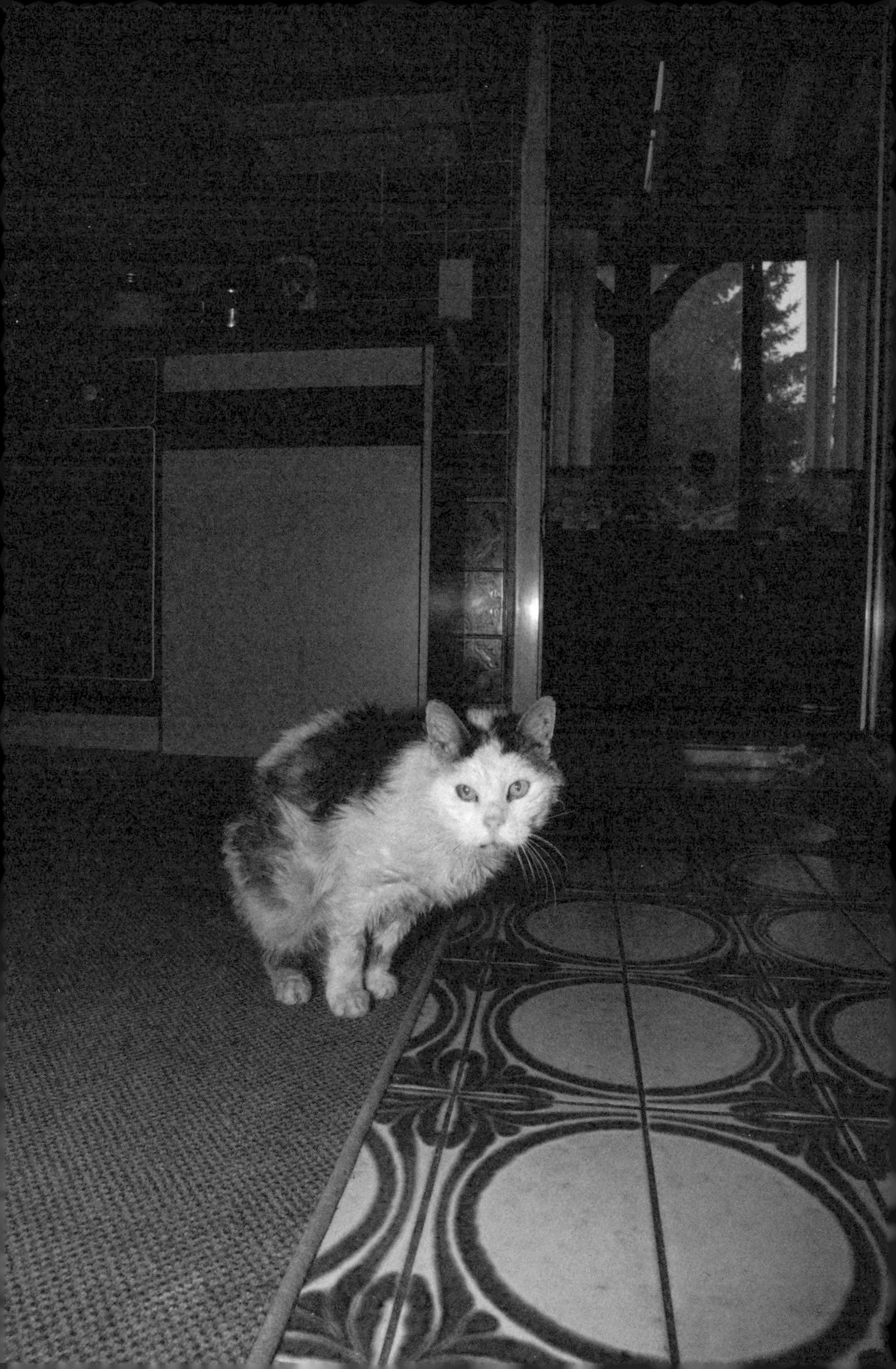

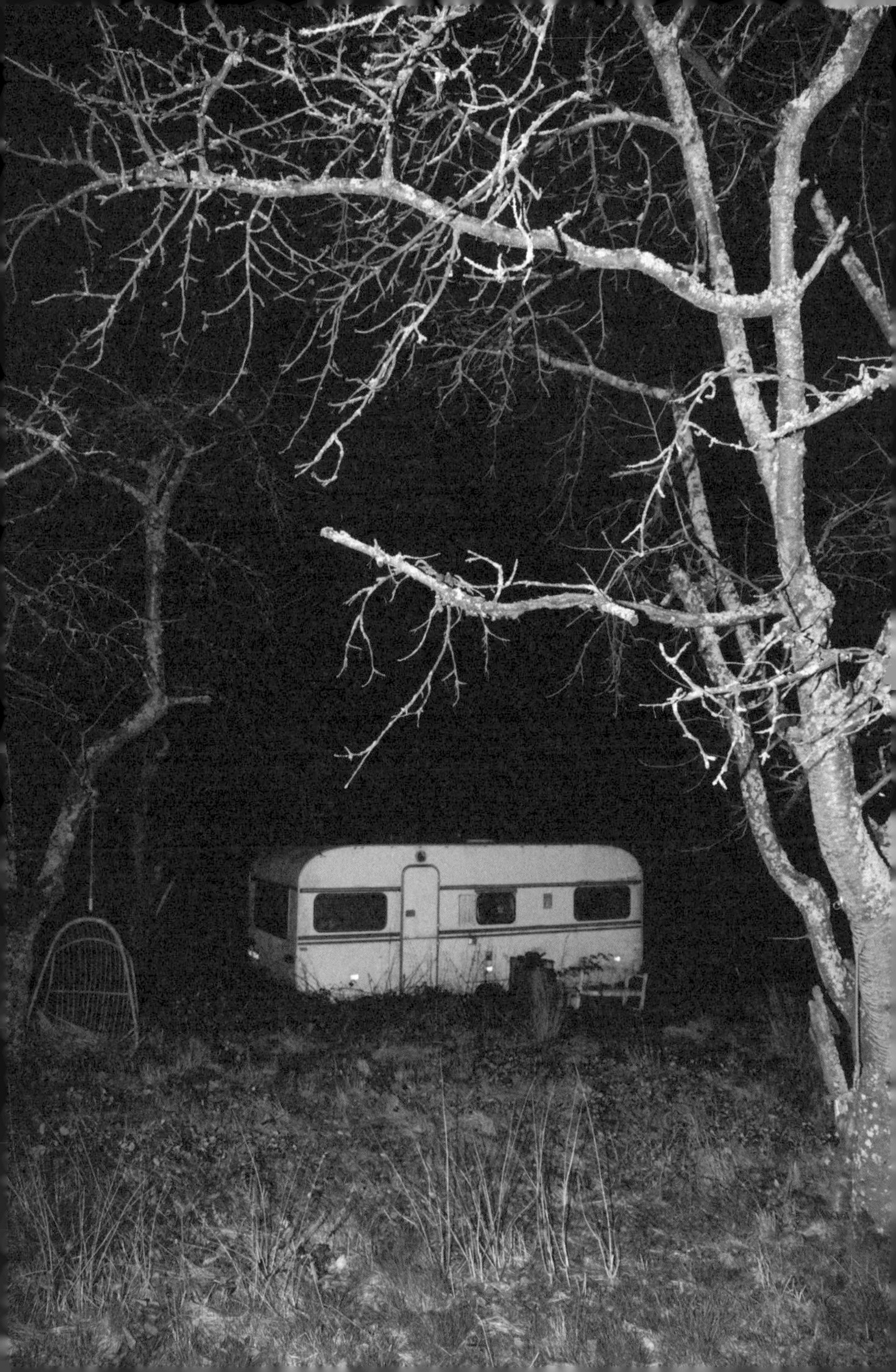

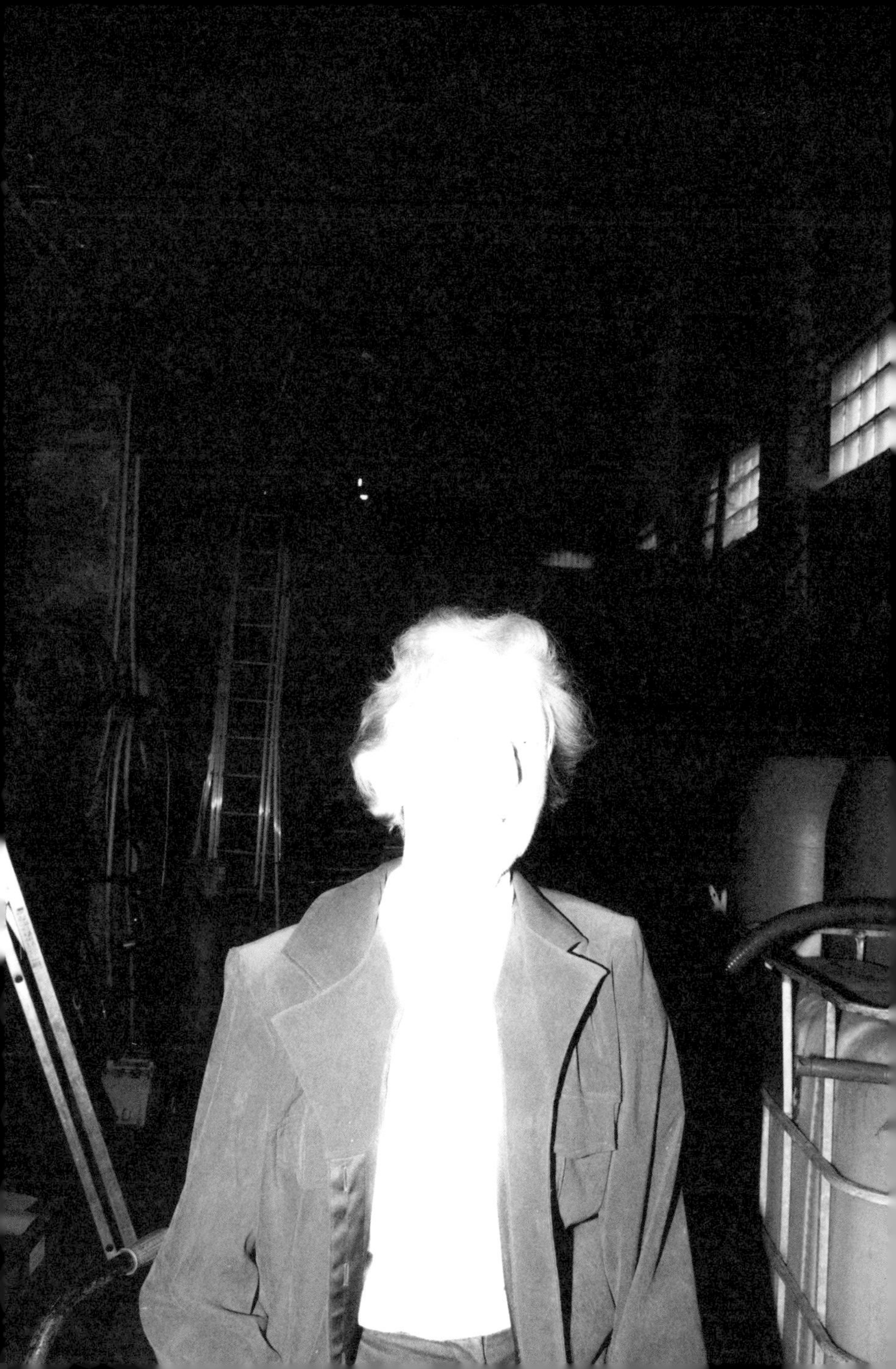

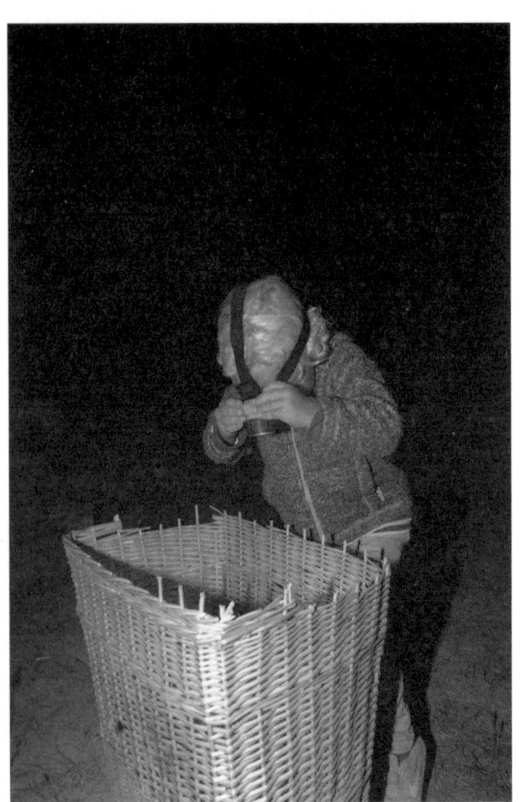

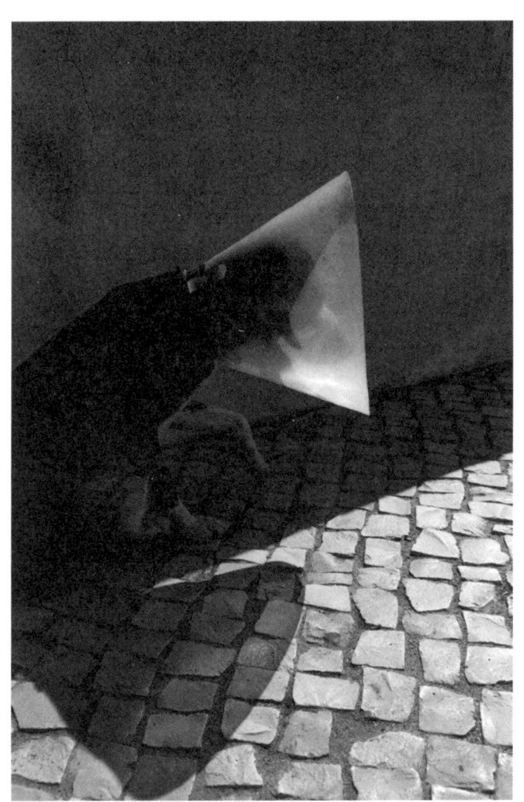

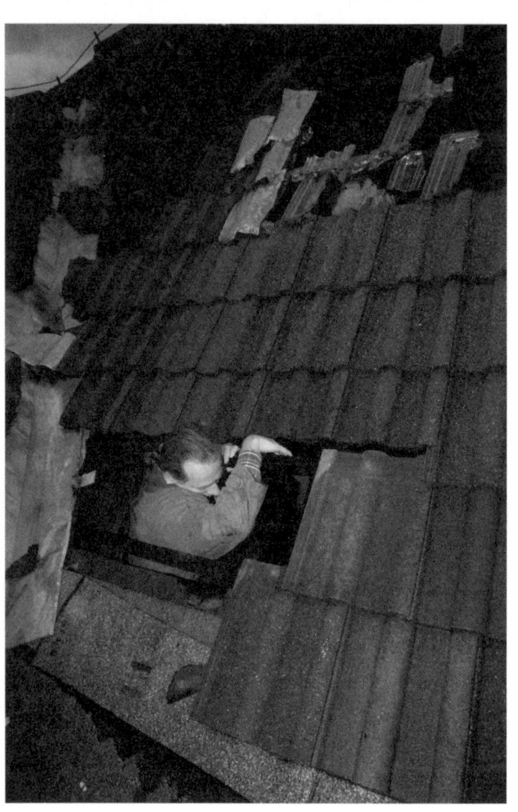

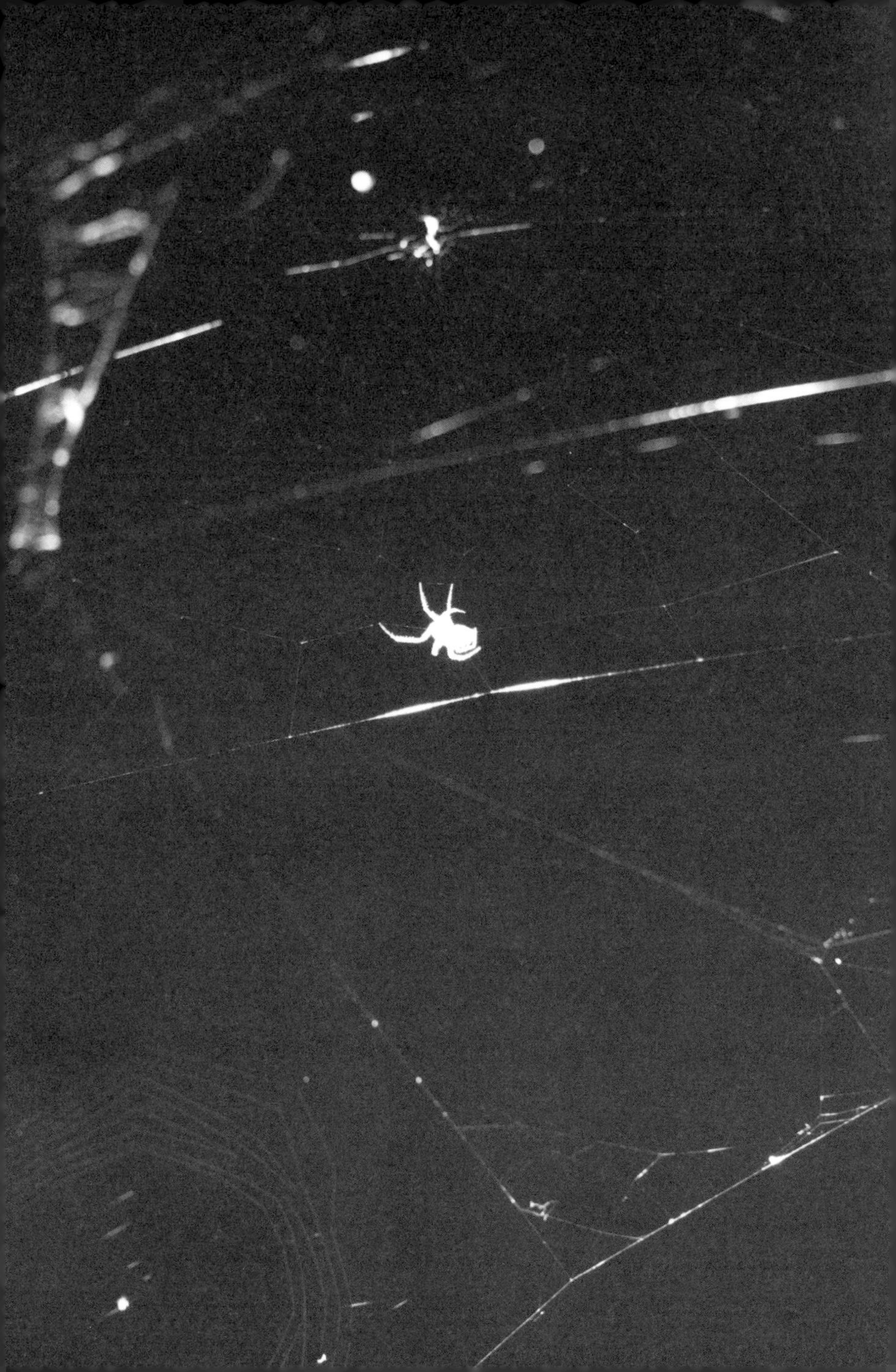

Markus Seibel

Europas Herbst / Europe’s Fall

18

According to the International Organization for Migration, 32,700 refugees died during migration since 2014—roughly 18,000 of them at European borders, making them the deadliest in the world.

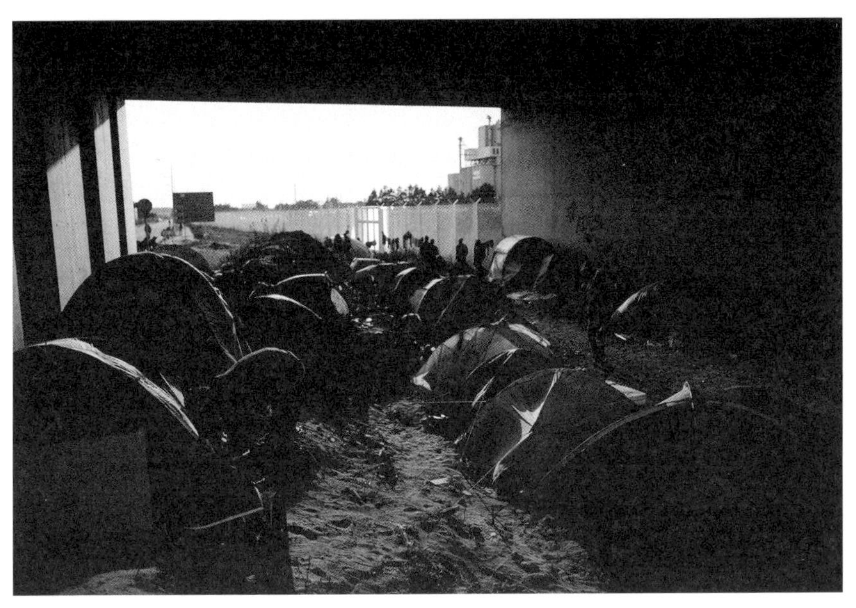

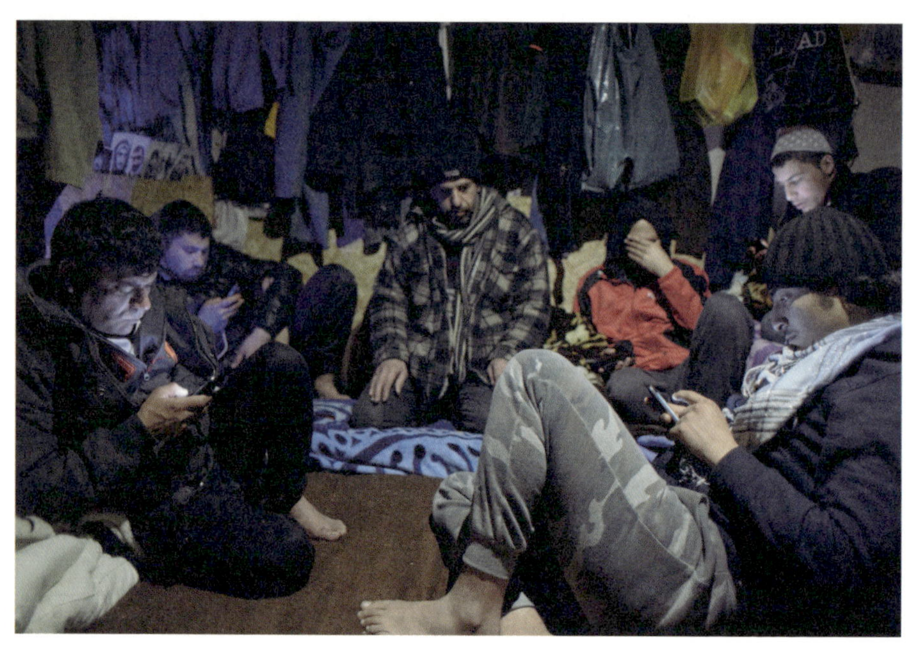

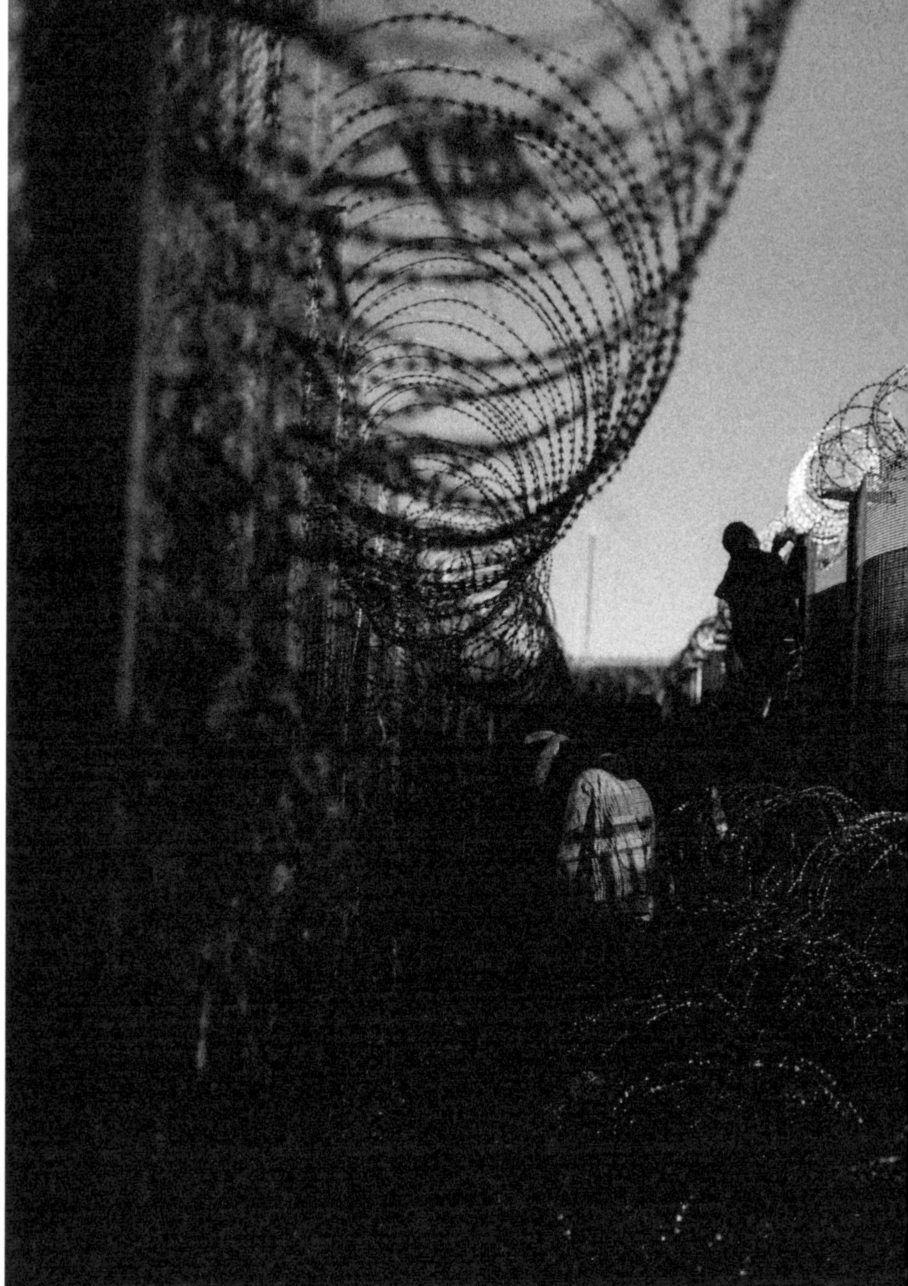

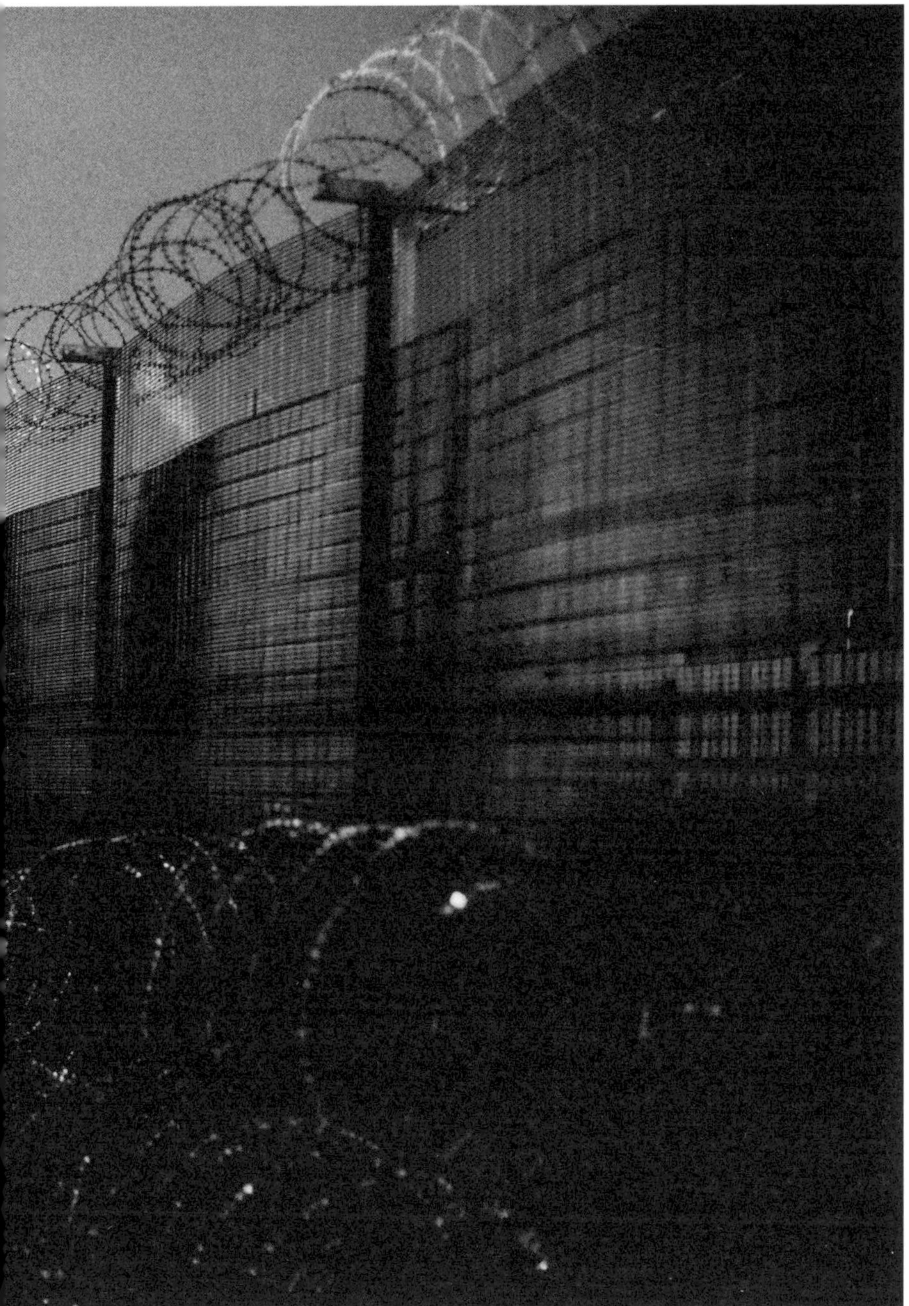

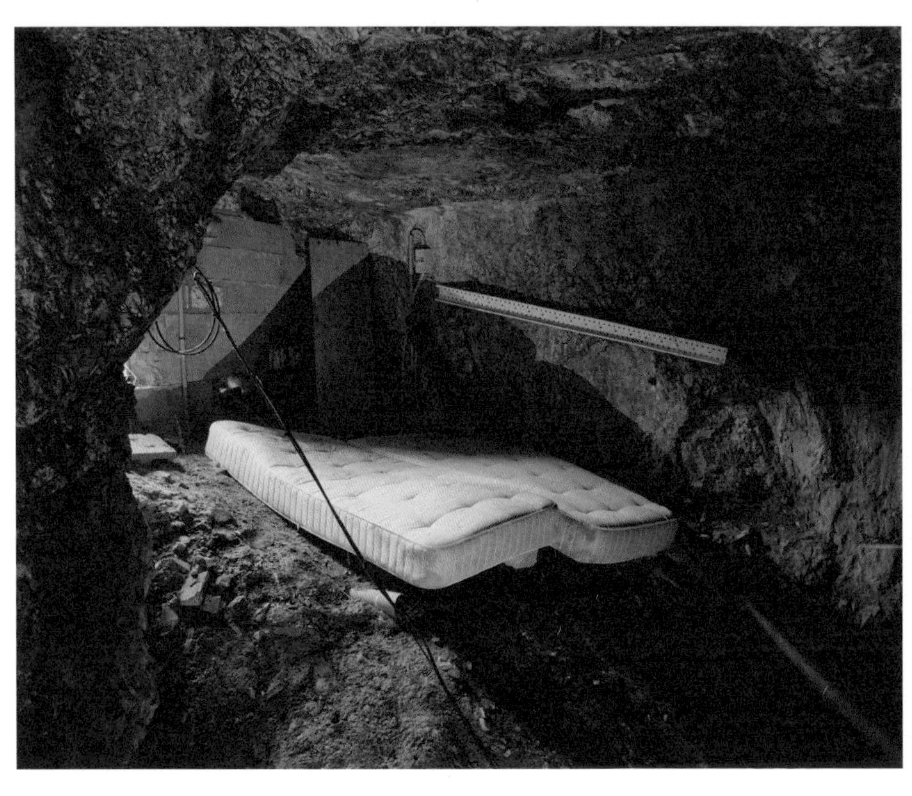

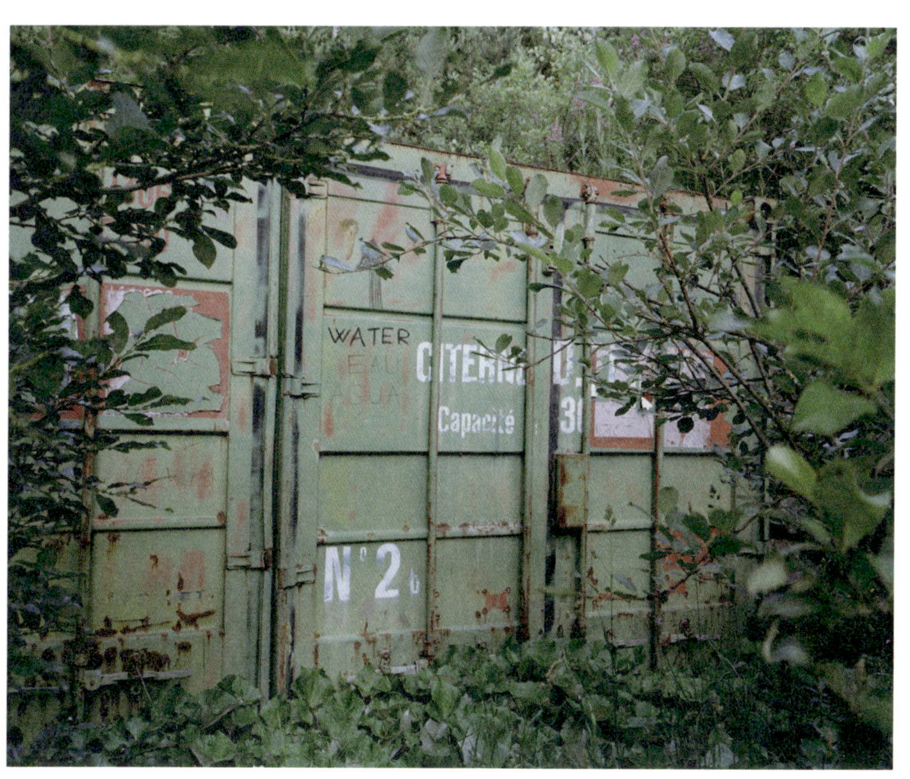
WATER
EAU
AQUA
Capacité
N°2

Elena Fiebig

Avakyan

19

On the Georgian side of the border between Turkey, Georgia, and Armenia lies a remote mountain village of 150 house-holds. There, an Armenian community lives in a parallel world neglected by Georgian society, ruled mainly by women, elderly, and children.

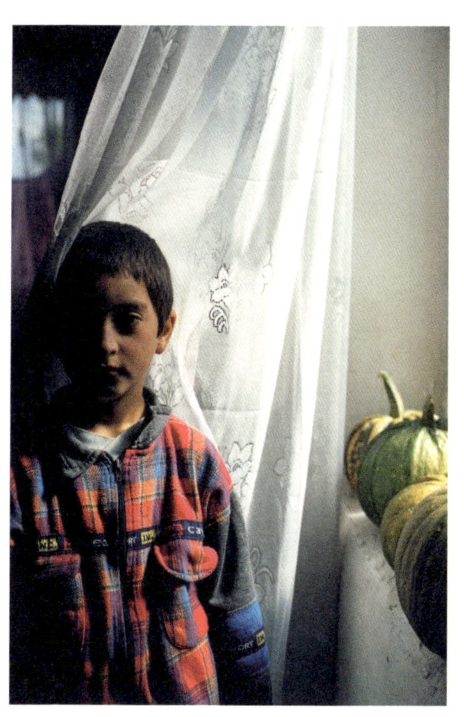

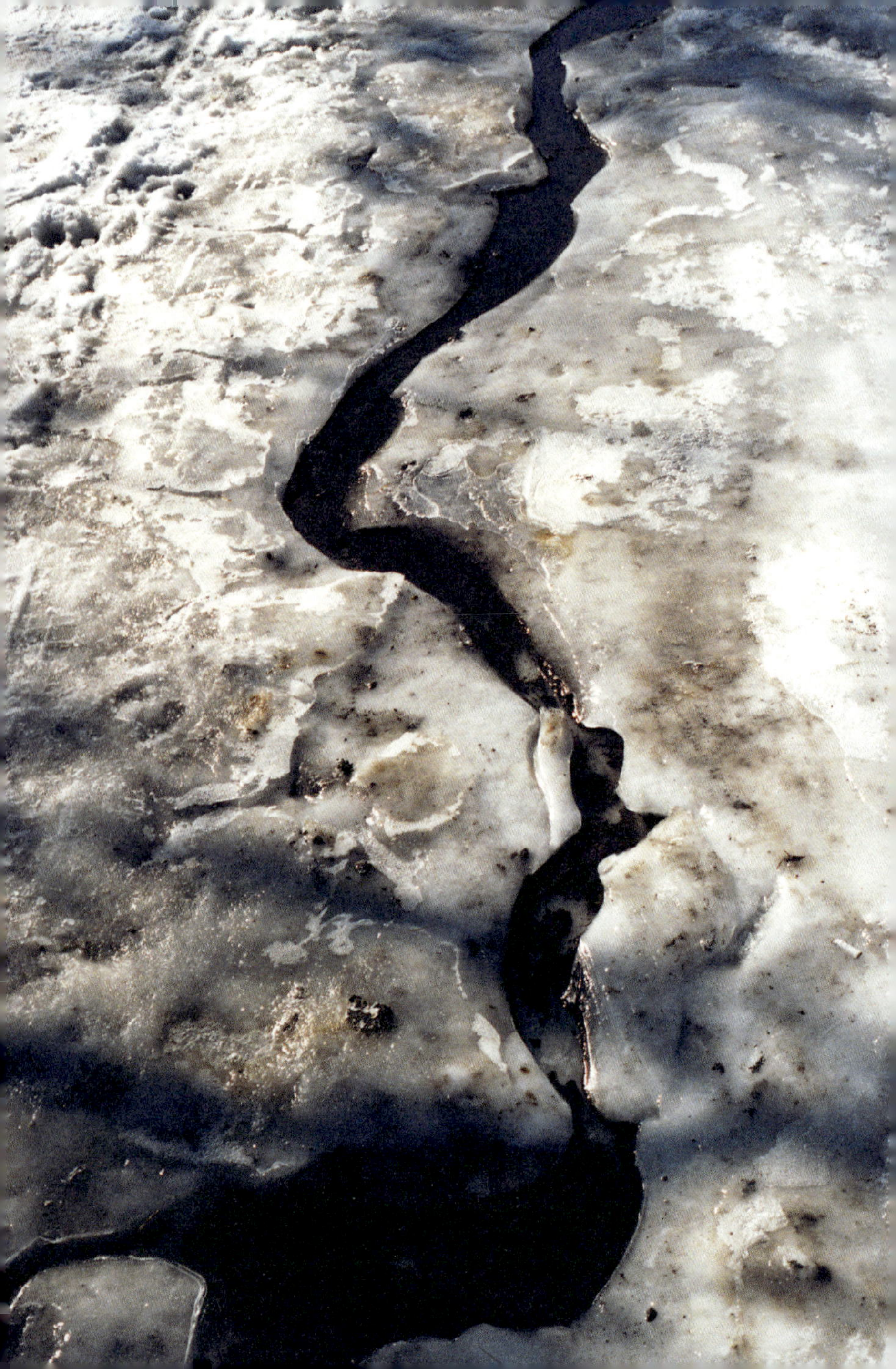

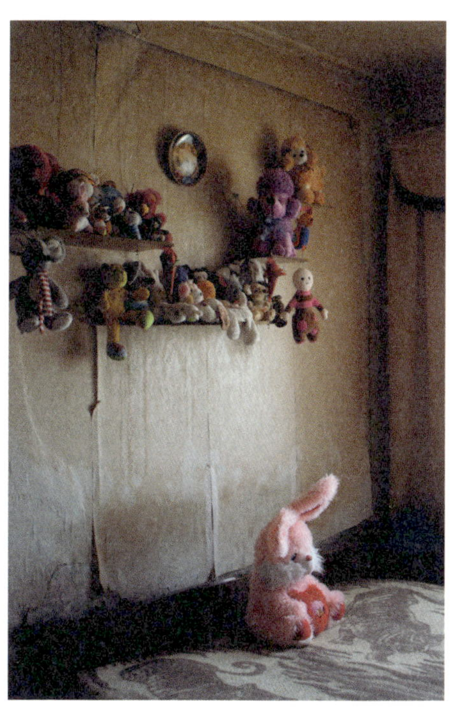

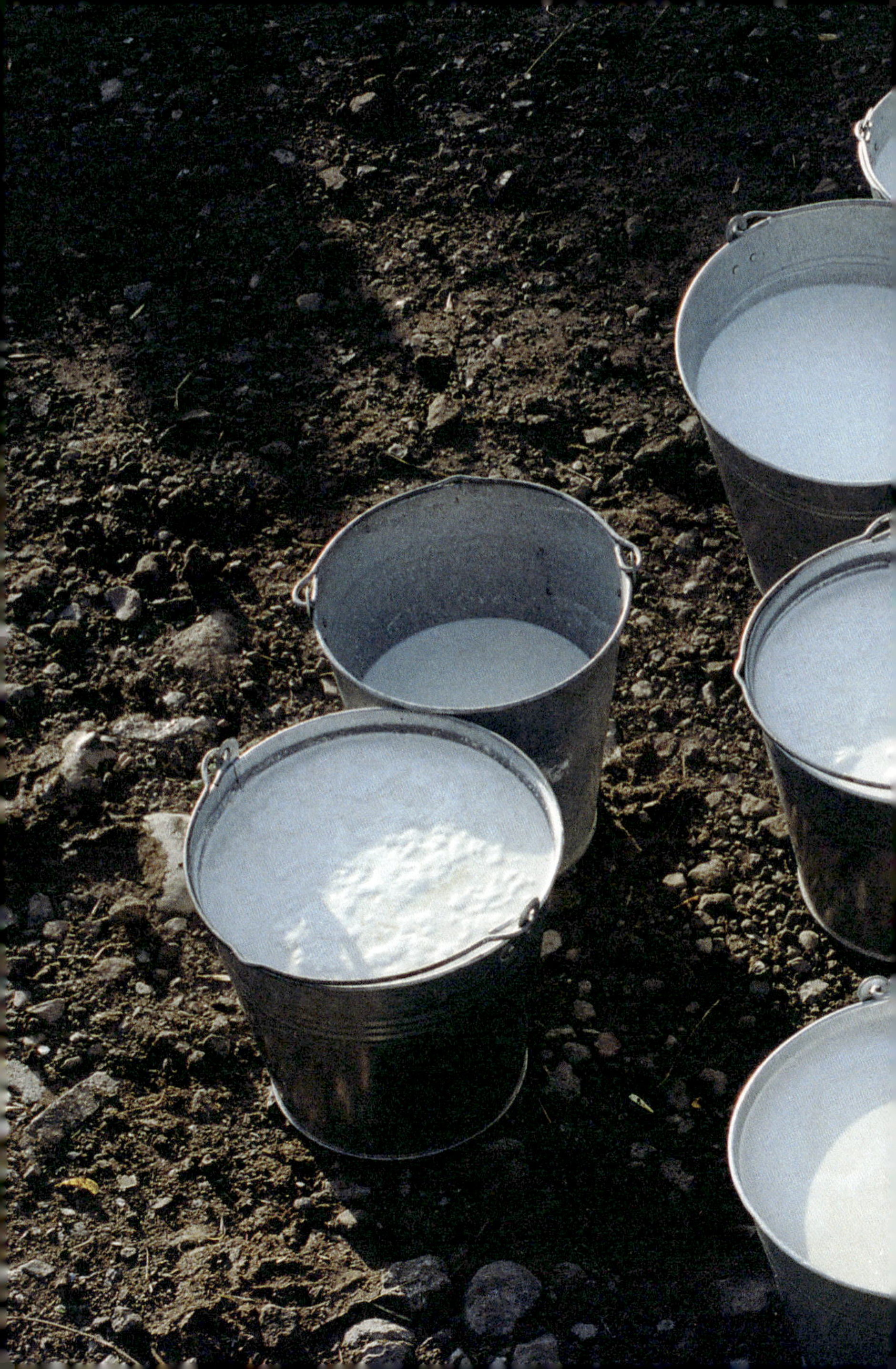

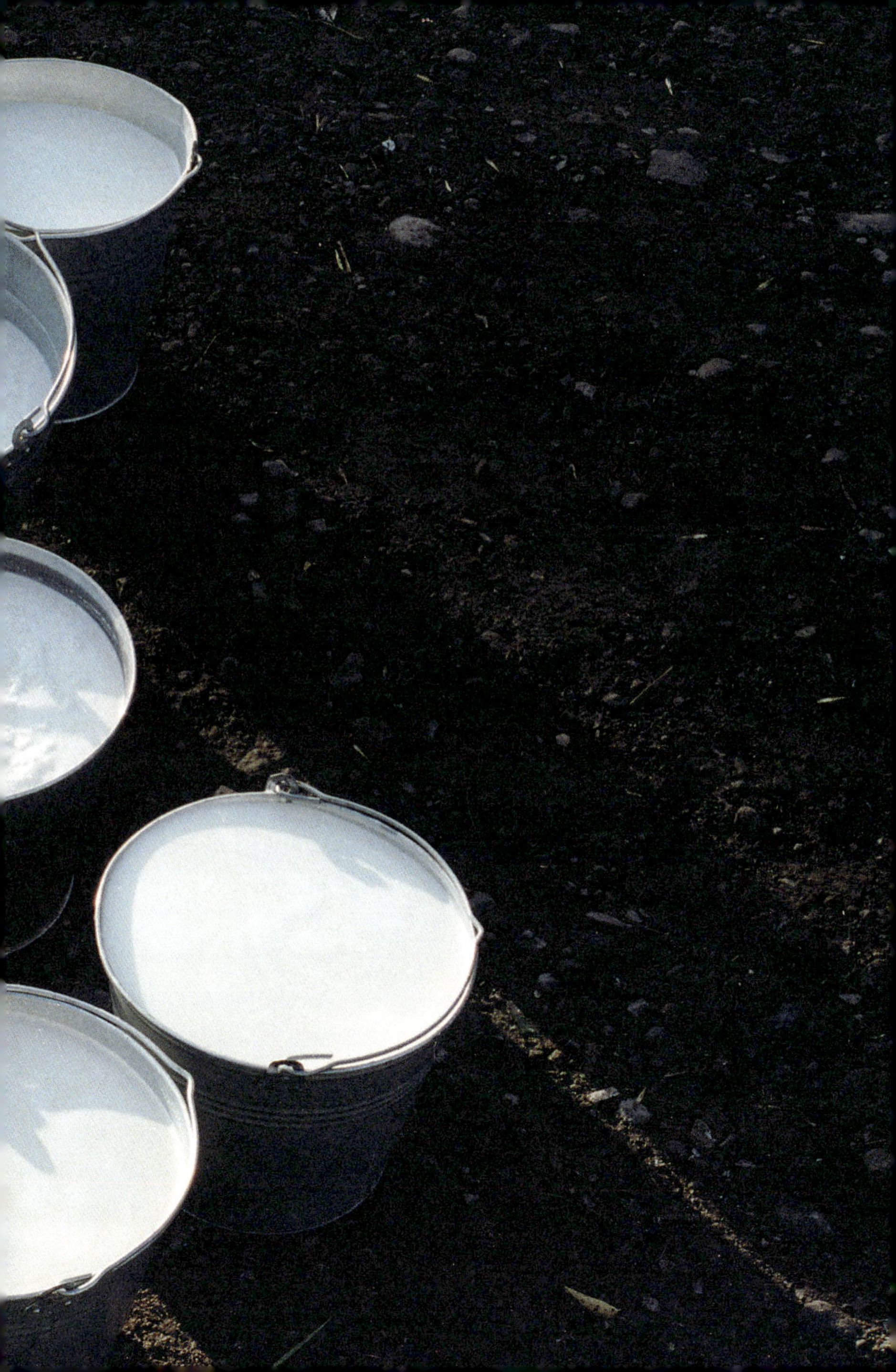

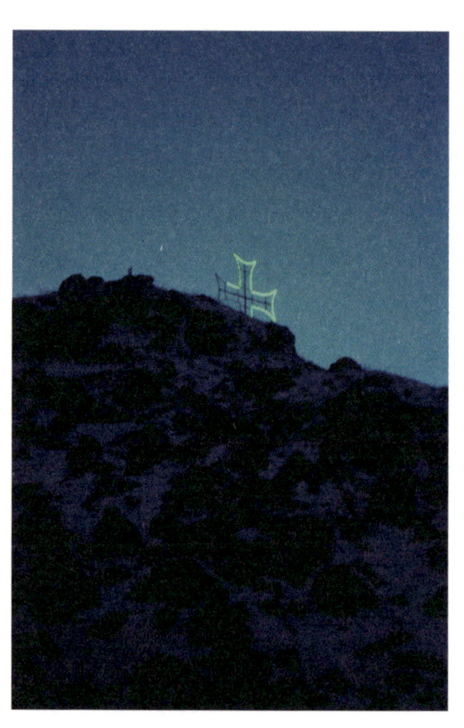

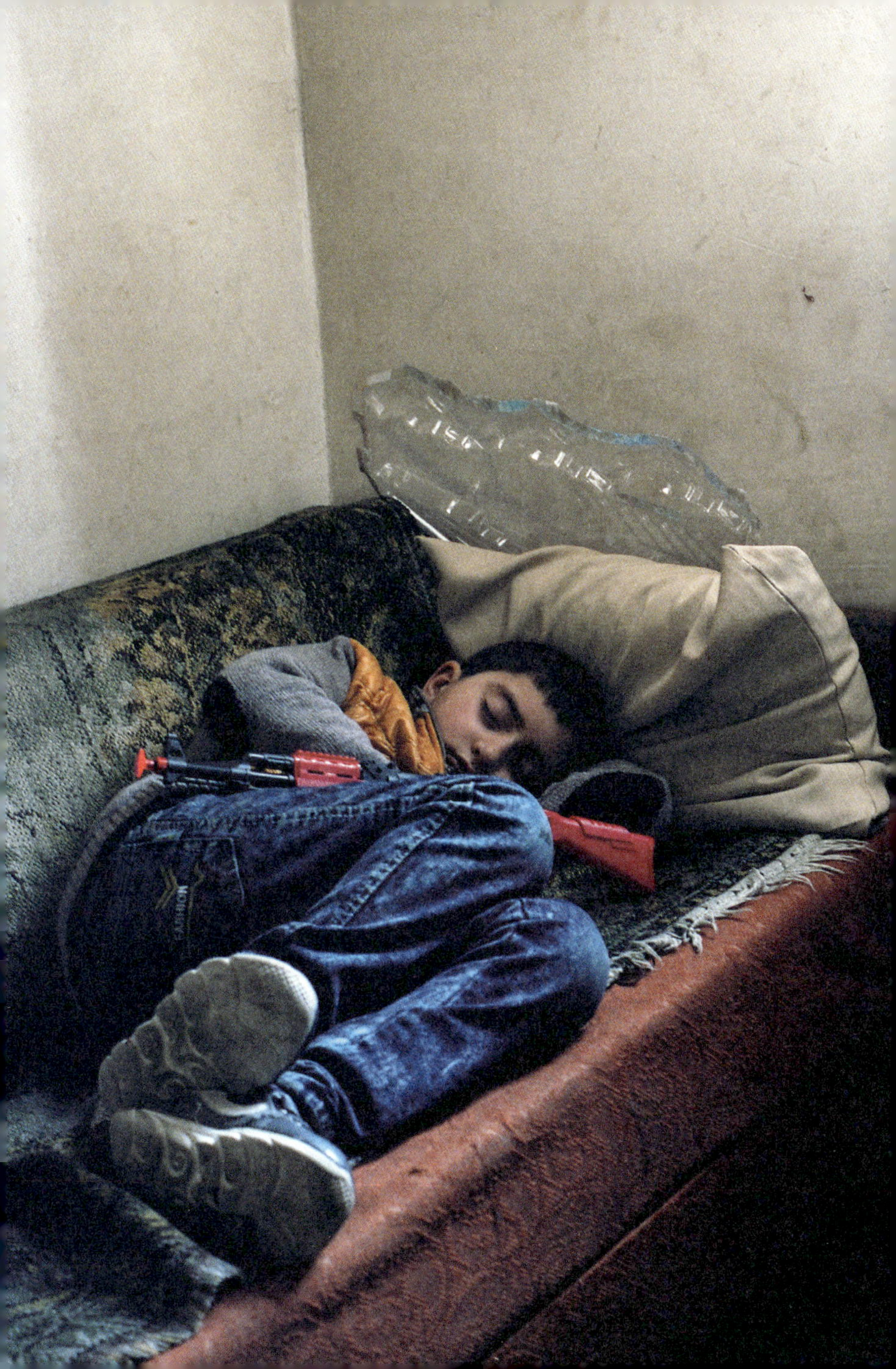

20

Gerd Kuck has been waiting for a donor's heart since 2008. He almost died, so the doctors gave him an artificial heart. His chances to receive a suitable organ are small, in Germany the number of donated organs have fallen to a historic low in 2017.

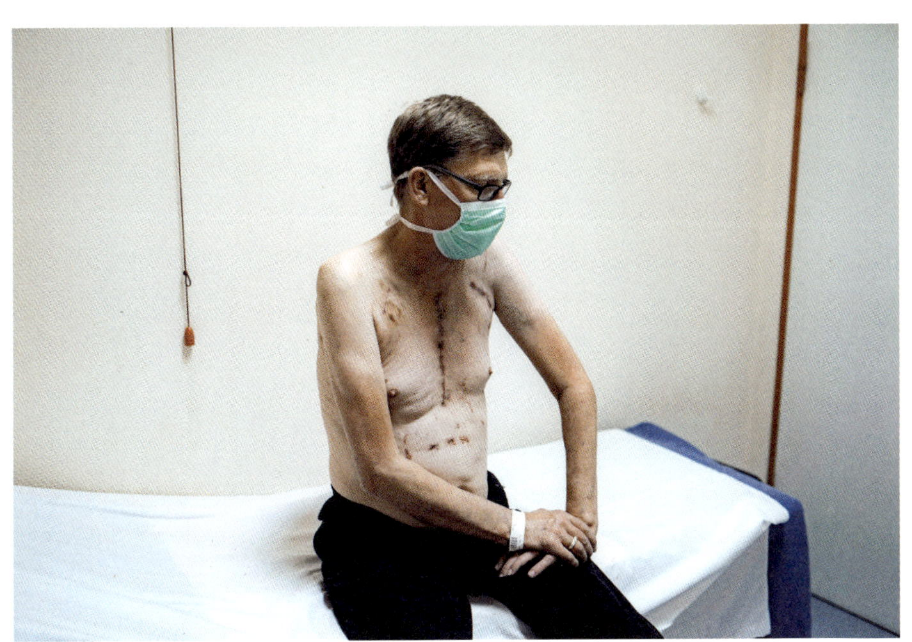

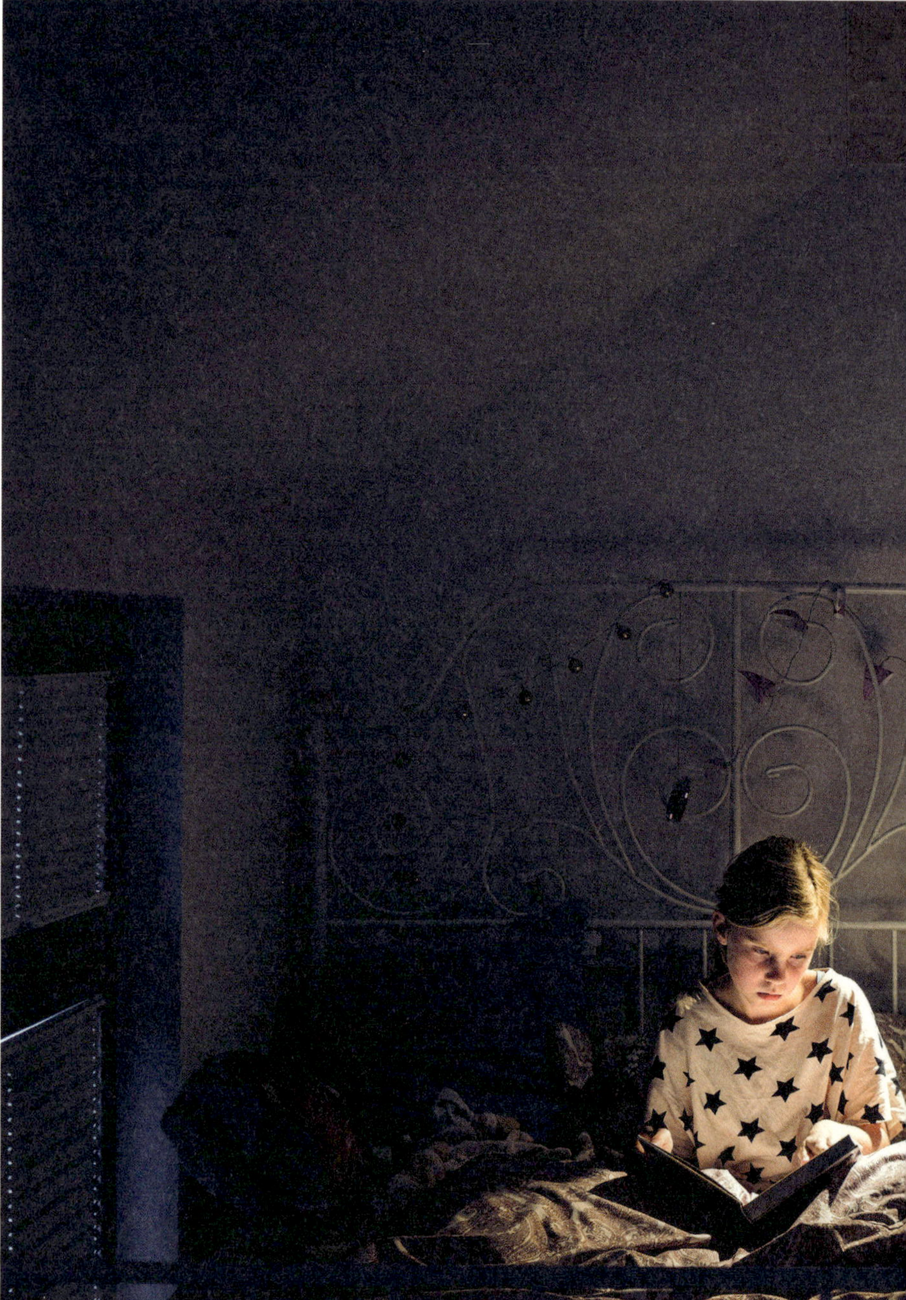

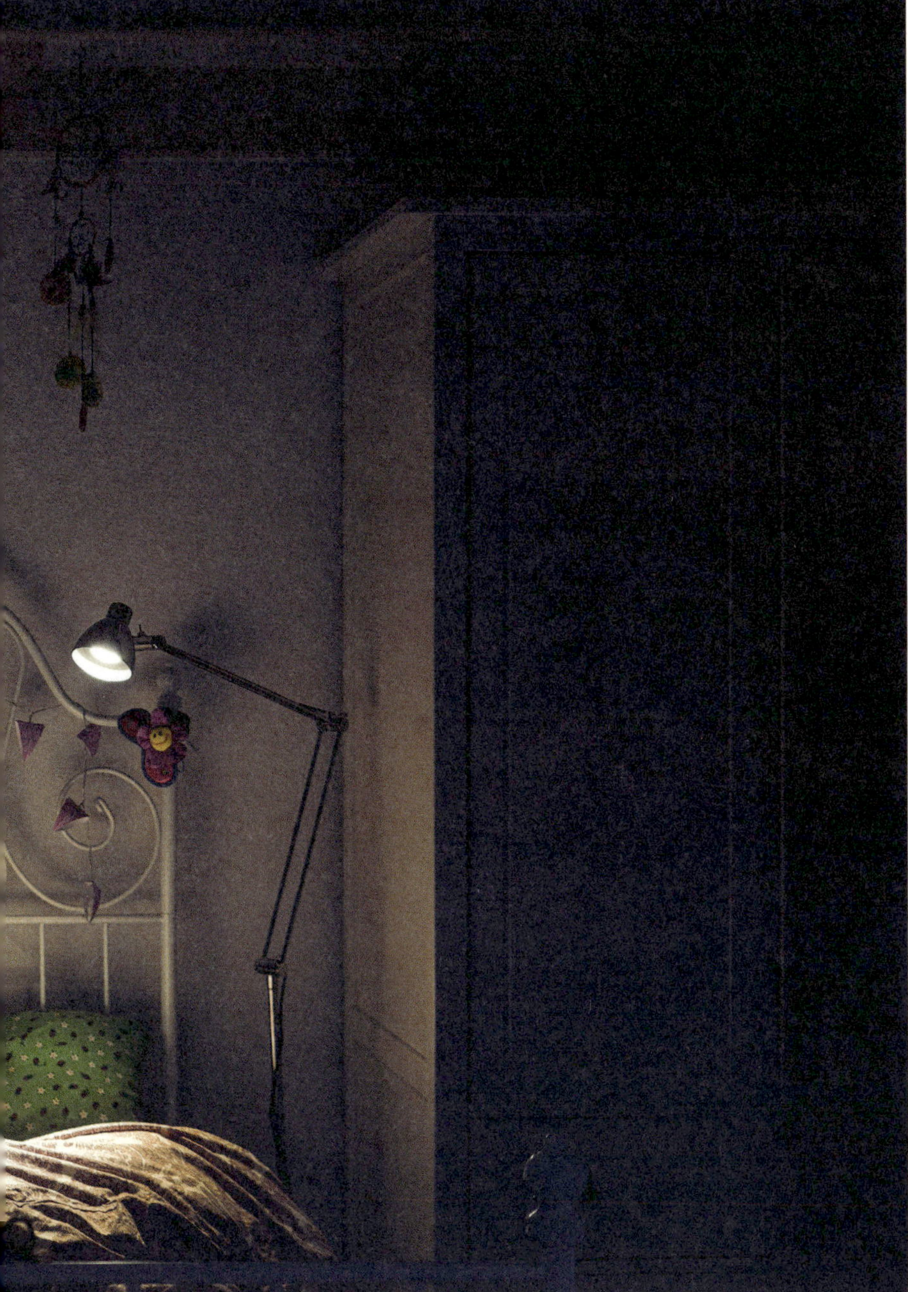

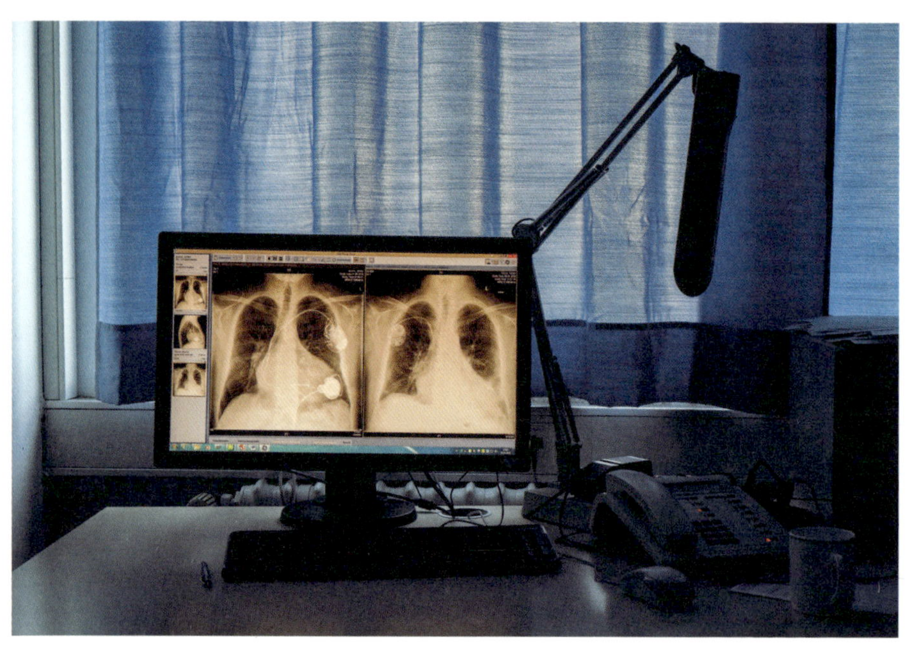

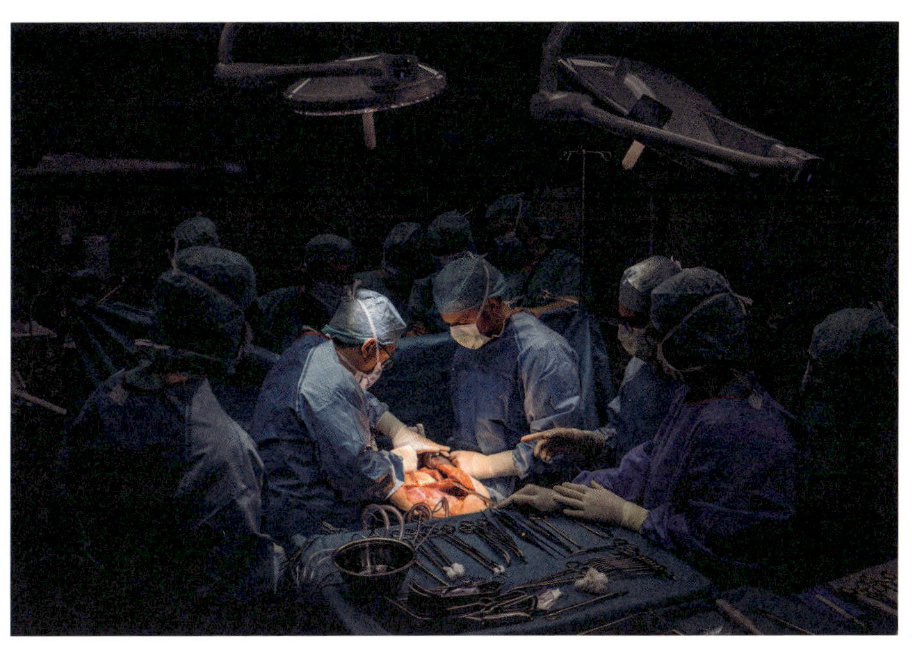

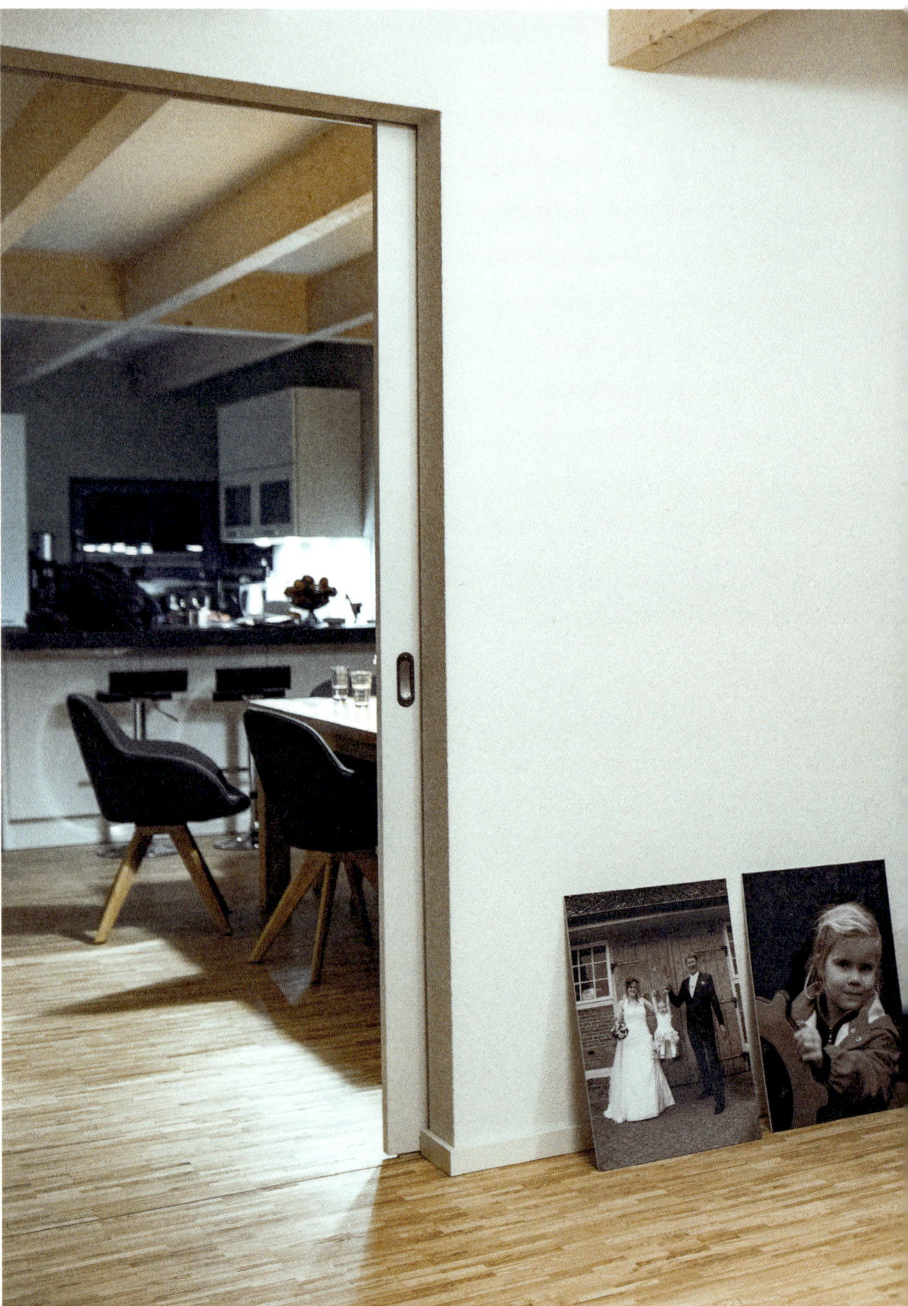

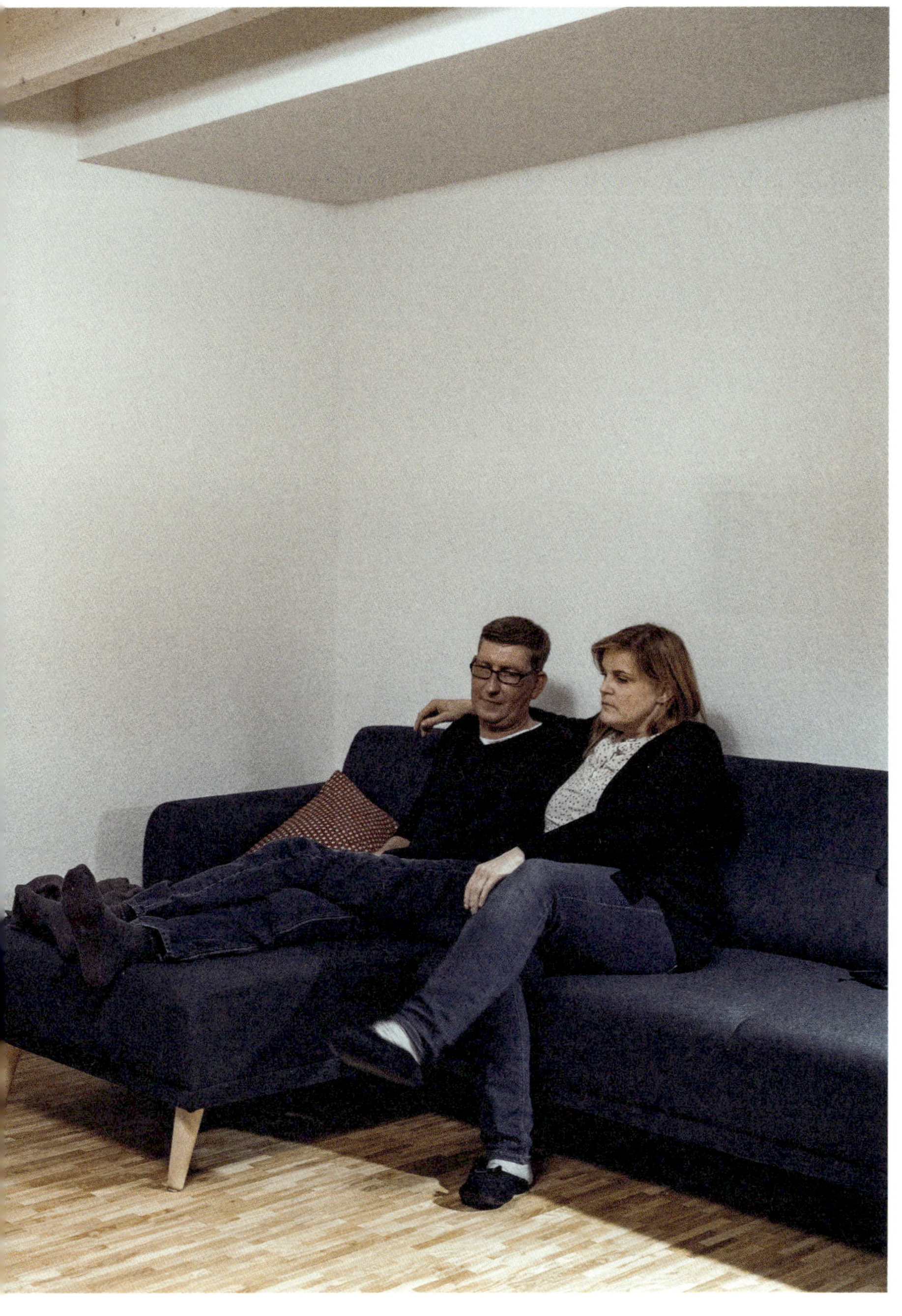

21

Arctic winters are getting warmer, the sea ice melts too early, and the Inuit have to adapt; the climate is changing and so is Uummannaq, an island town in Greenland, which is developing from a traditional community to a more modern society.

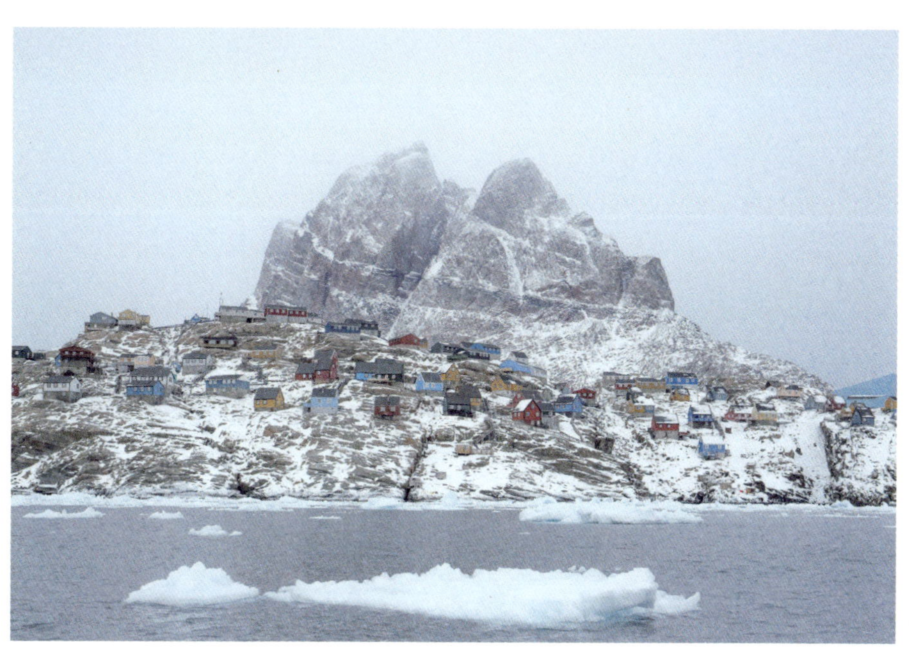

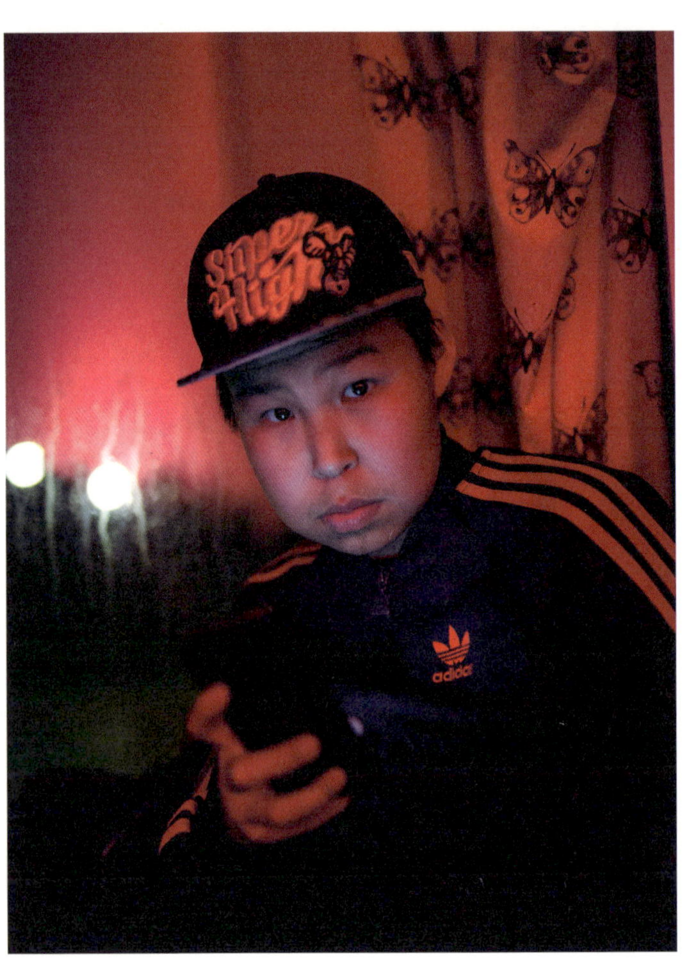
Super High
adidas

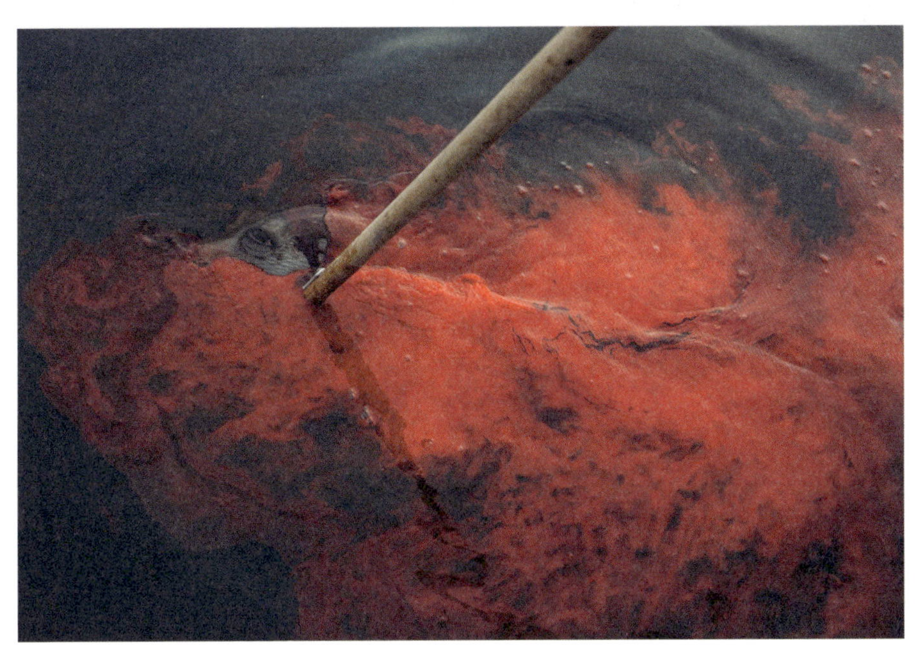

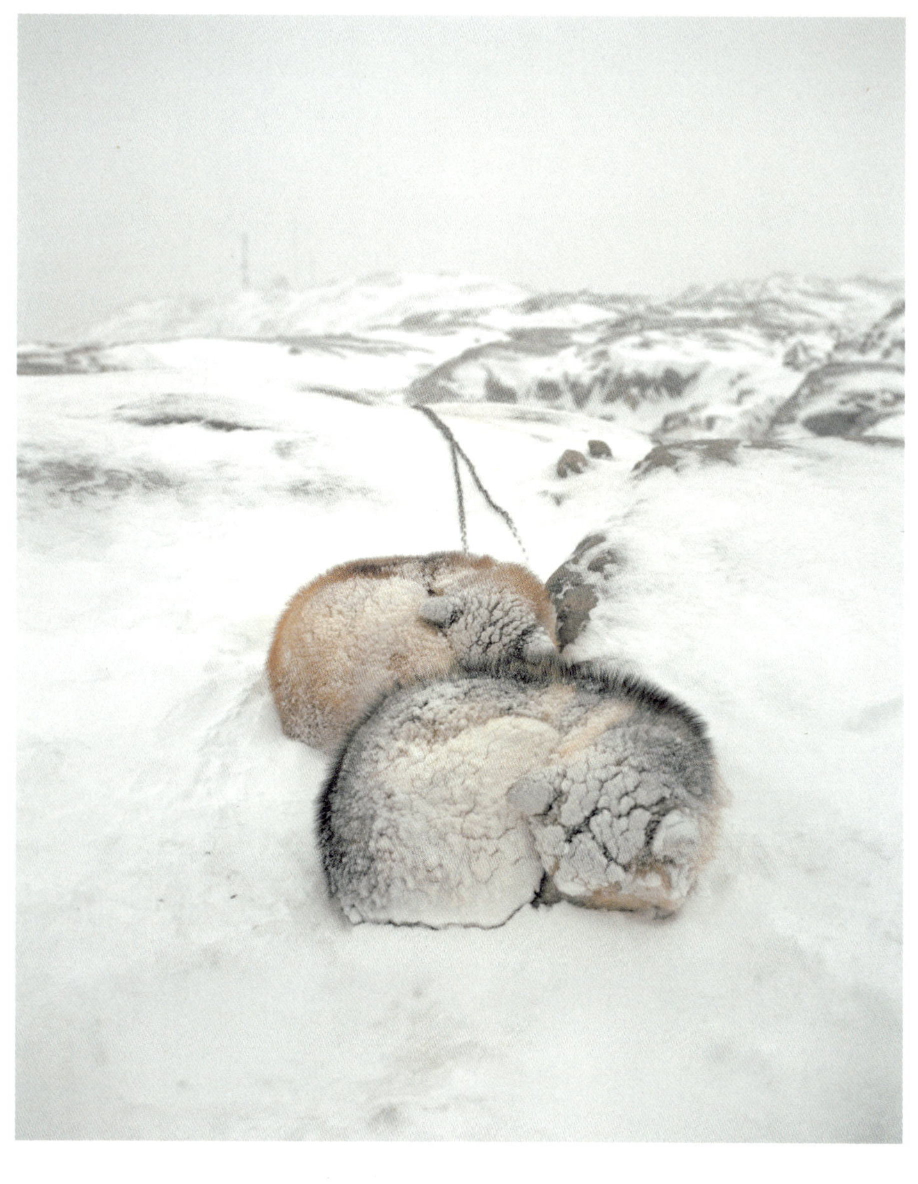

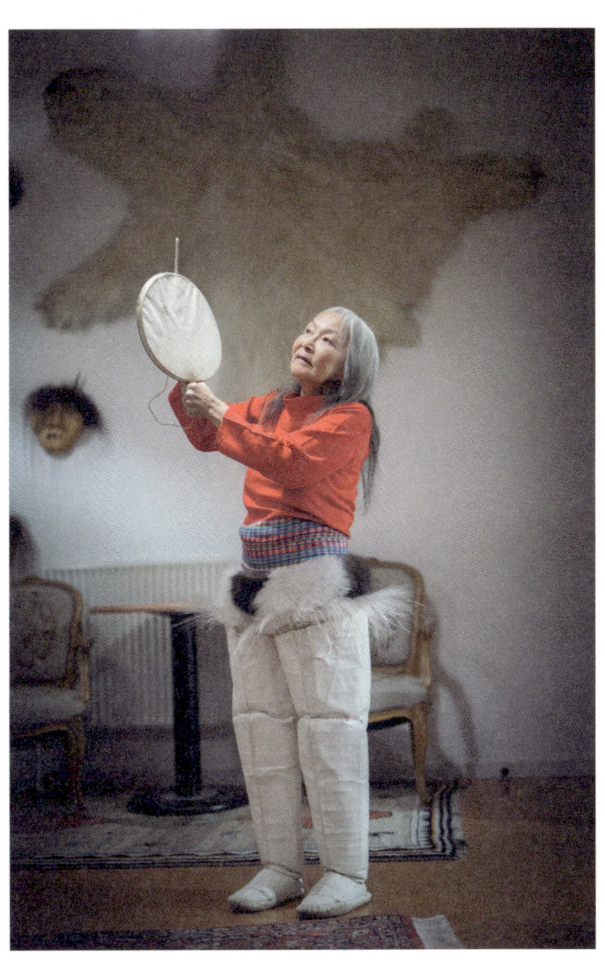

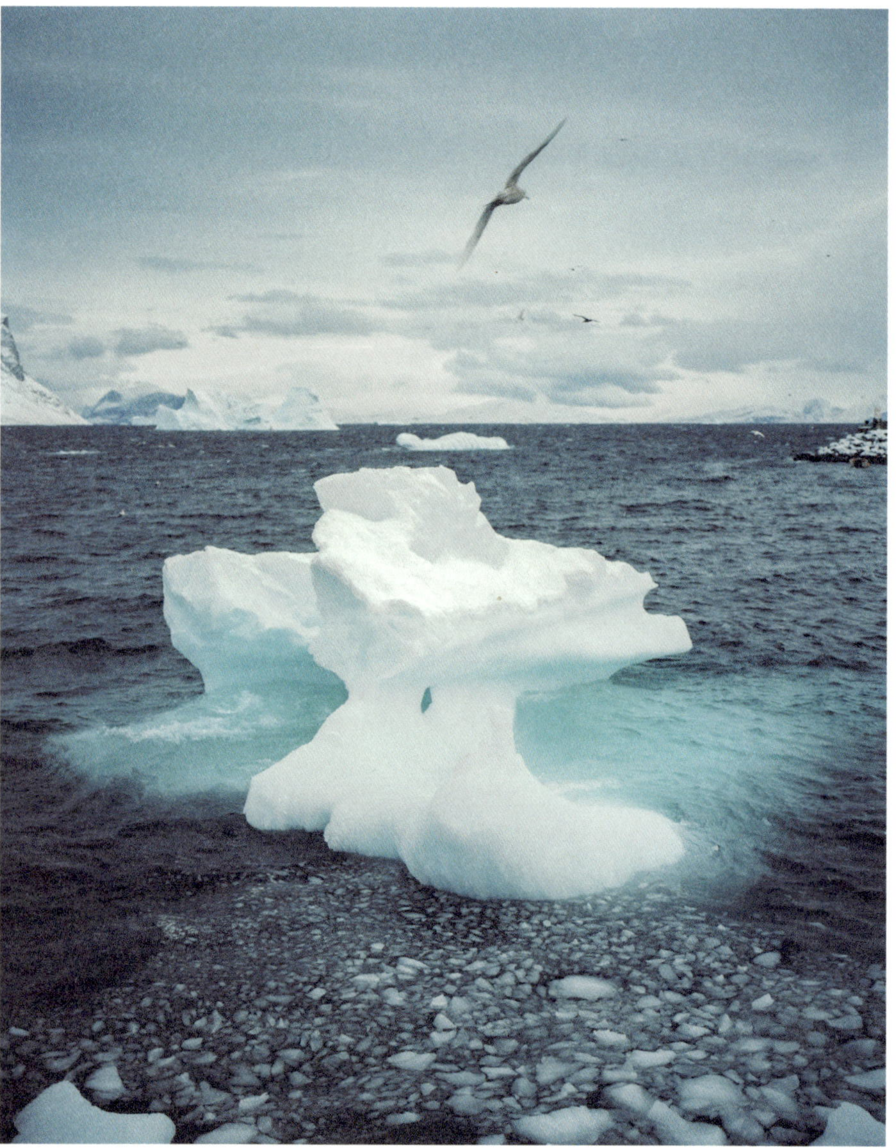

Sebi Berens

On The Anatomy Of Labour

22

In 2013, the Rana Plaza in Savar collapsed, killing at least 1,132 garment workers and focusing the world's attention on working conditions in Bangladesh for a while. But the situation of the cheap labor sector didn't improve at all.

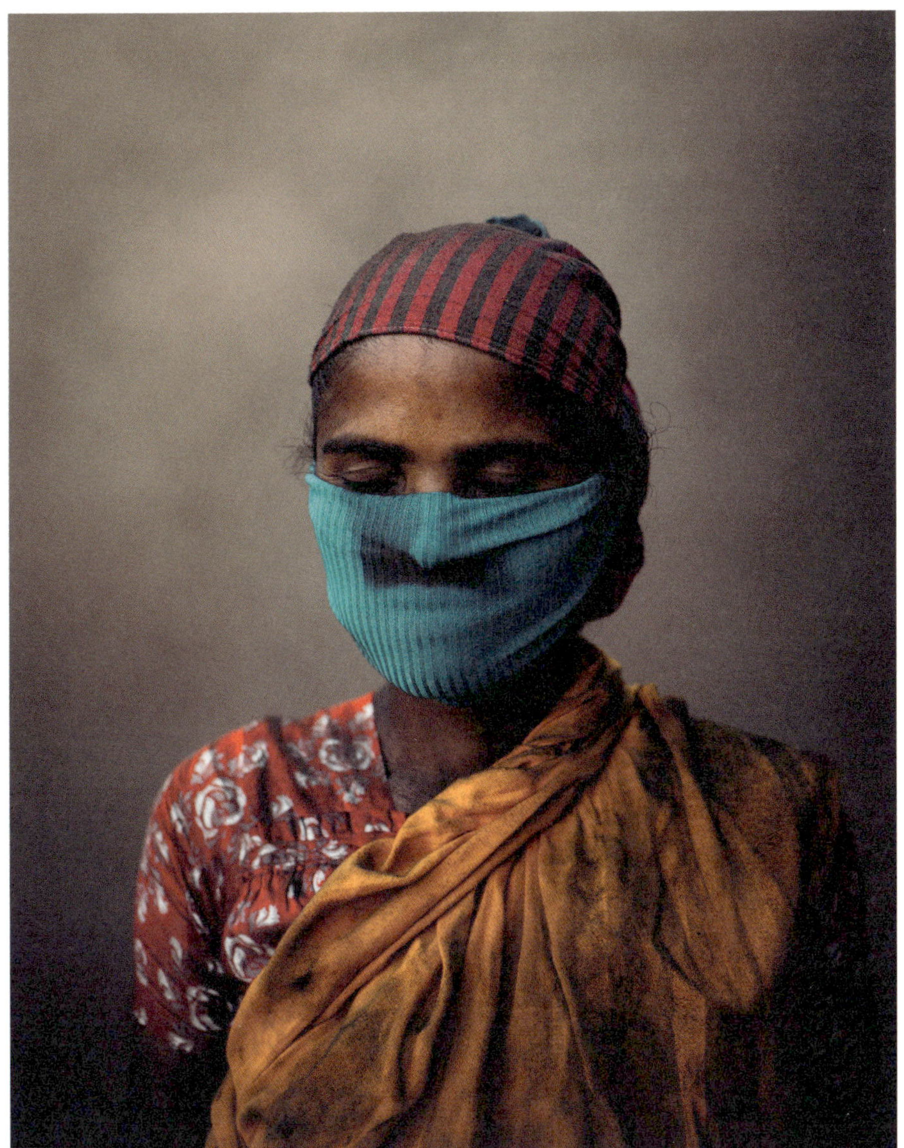

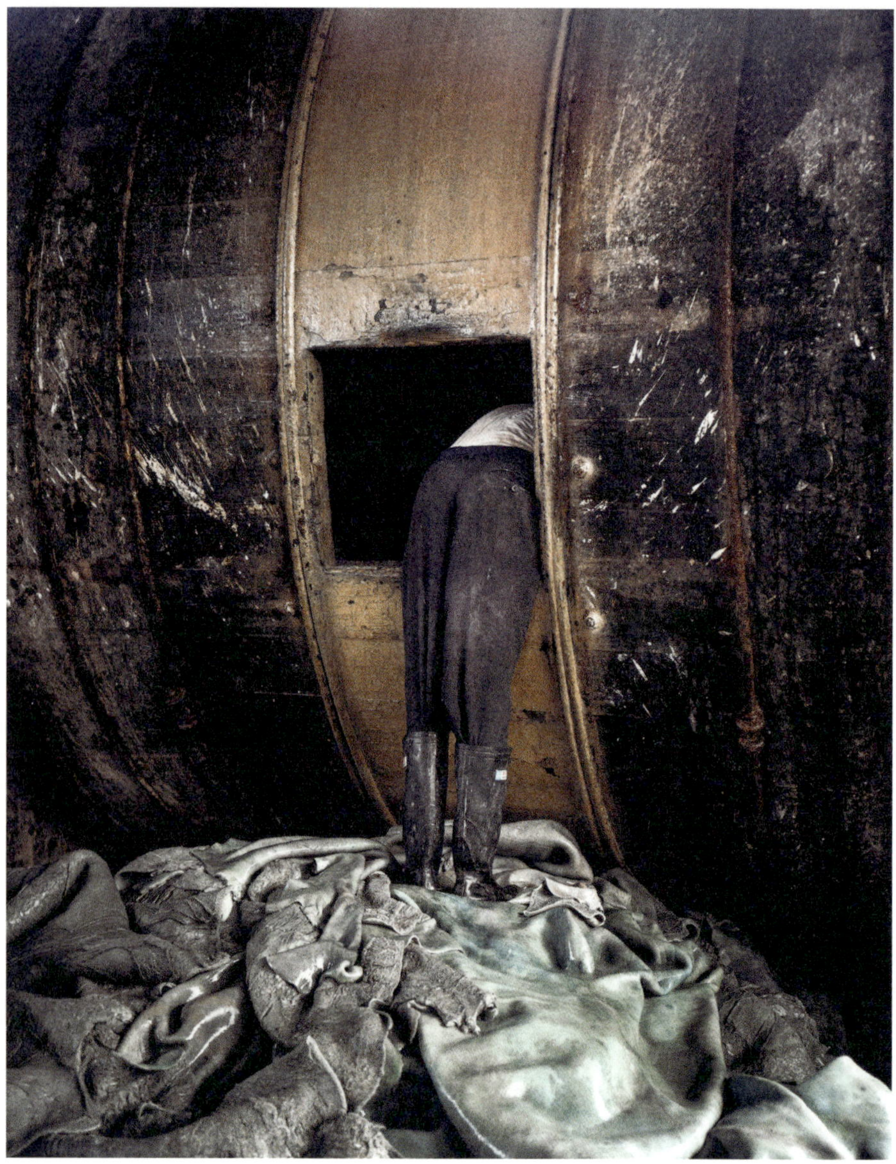

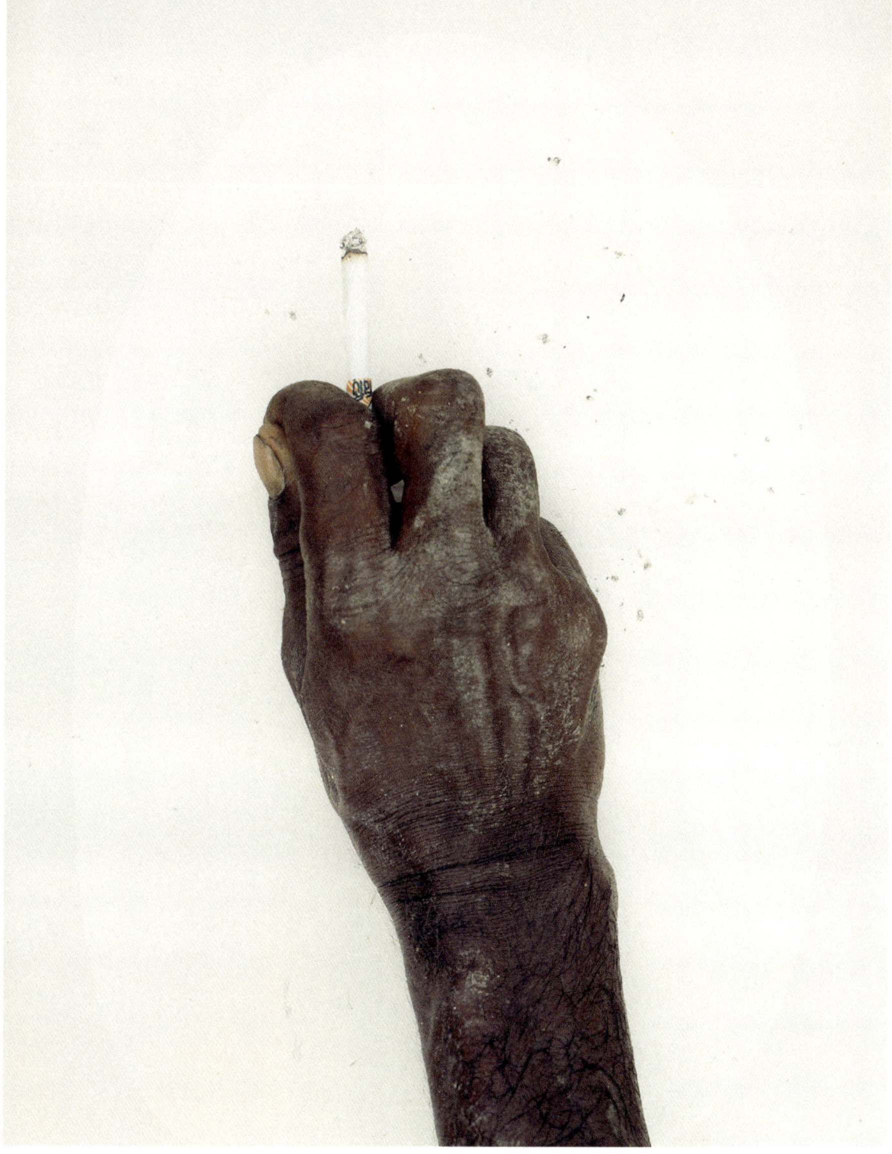

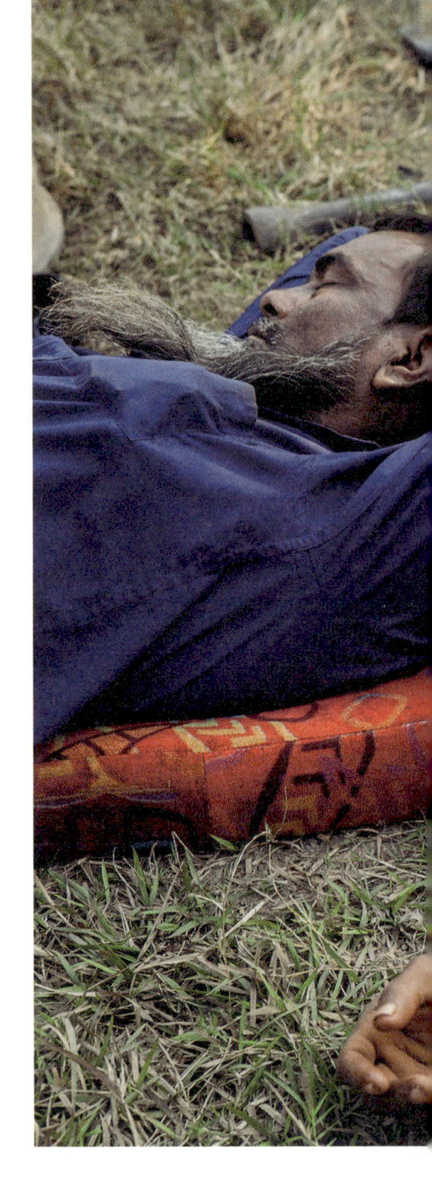

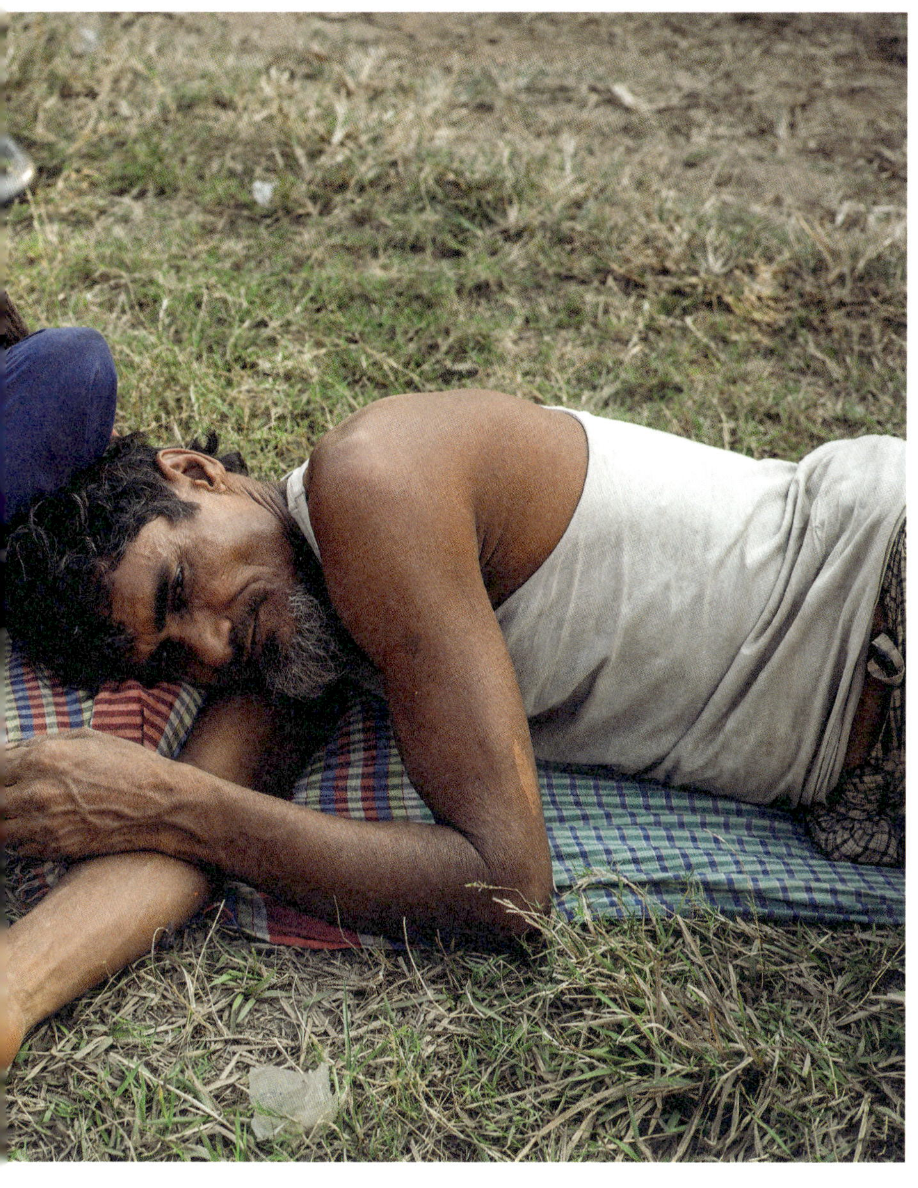

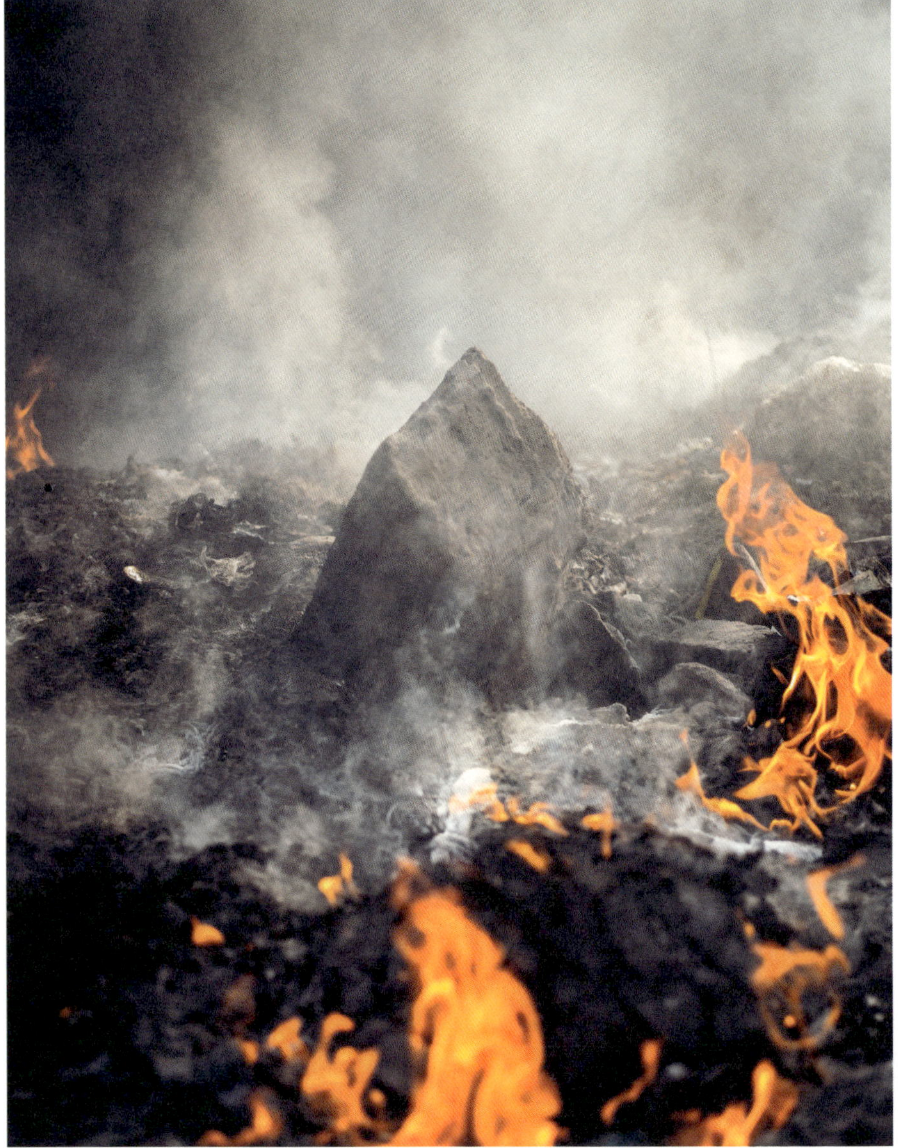

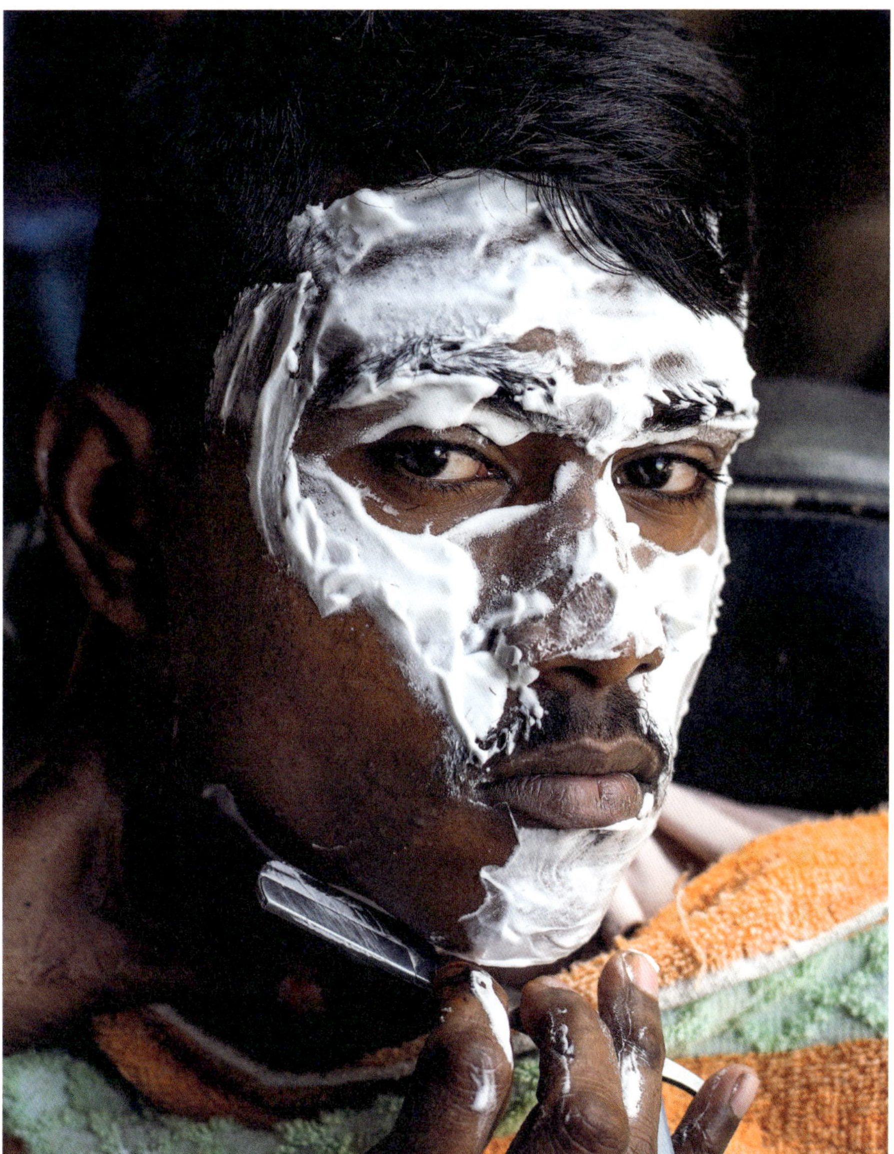

23

Where does war begin? The answer might be found away from battlefields: in video games, weapon fairs, and other places that make war consumable.

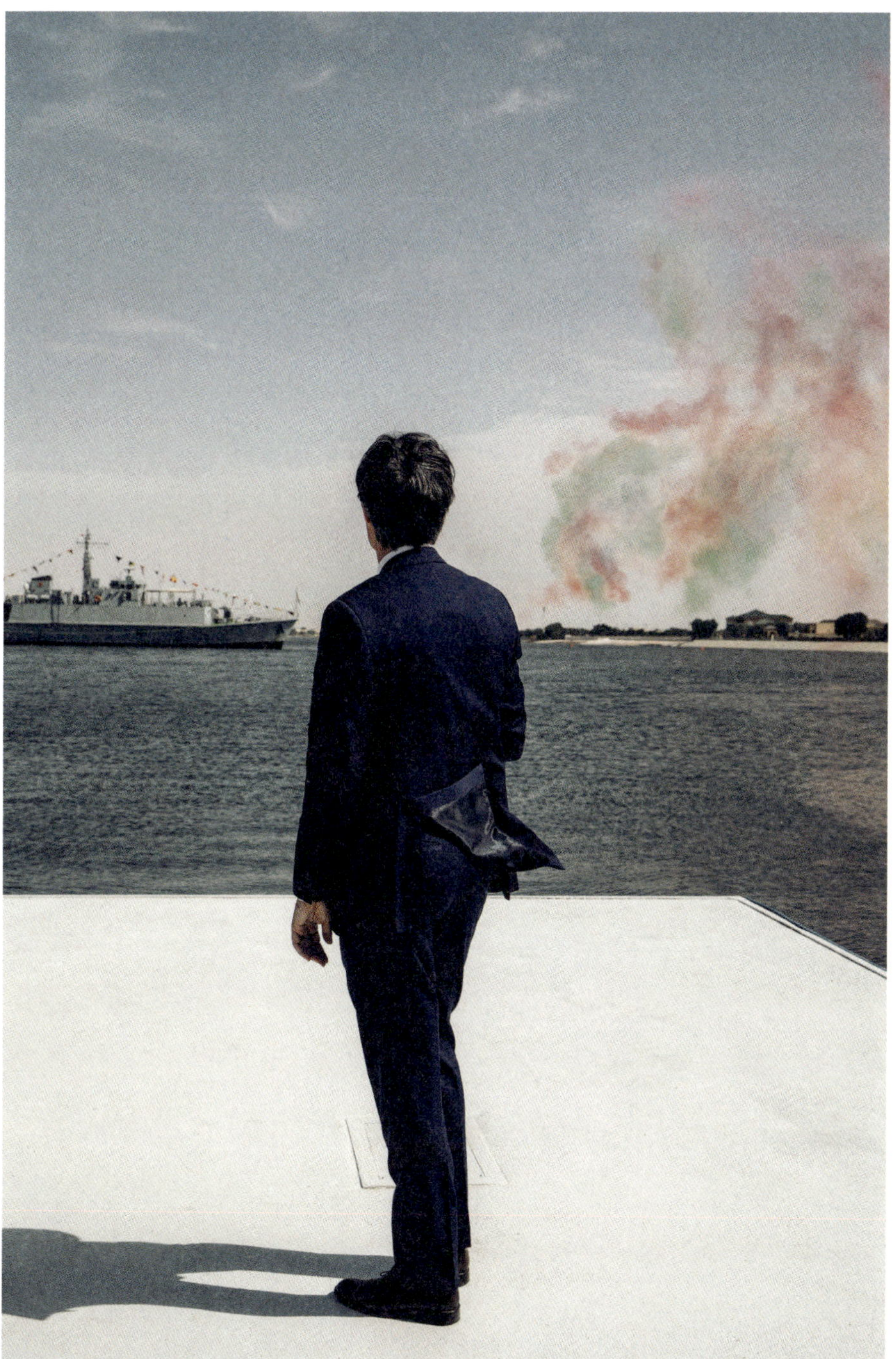

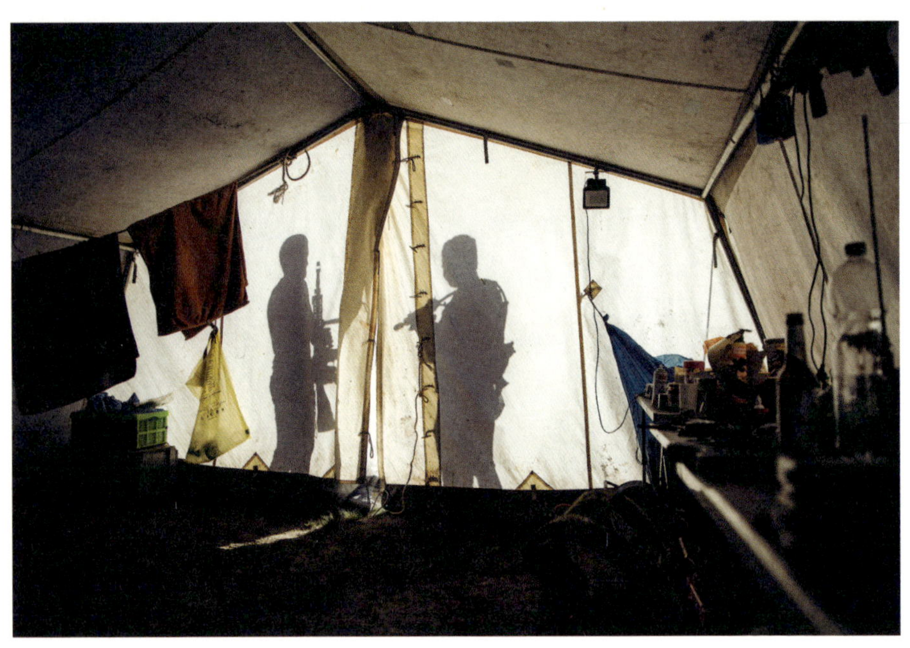

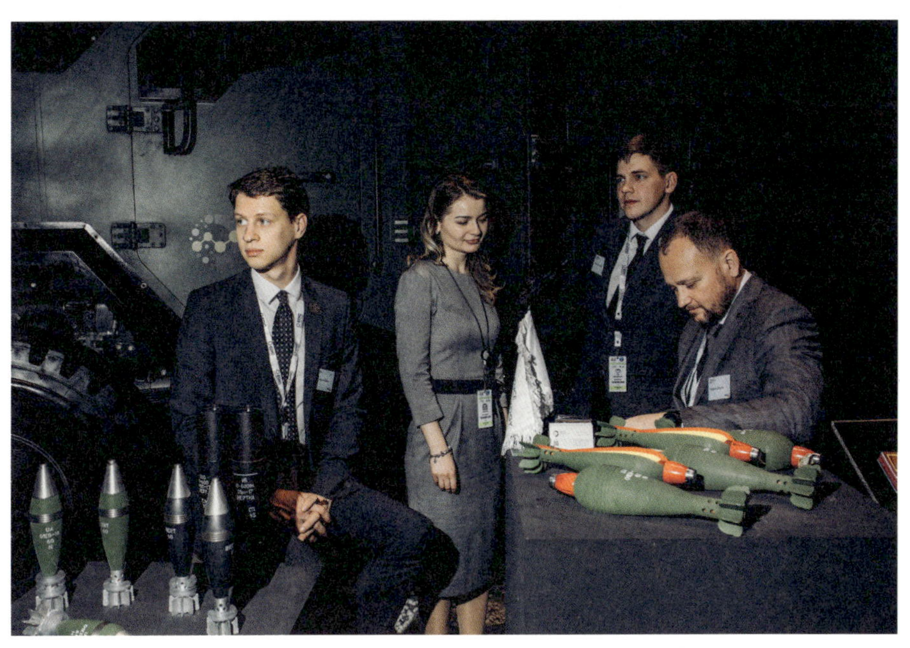

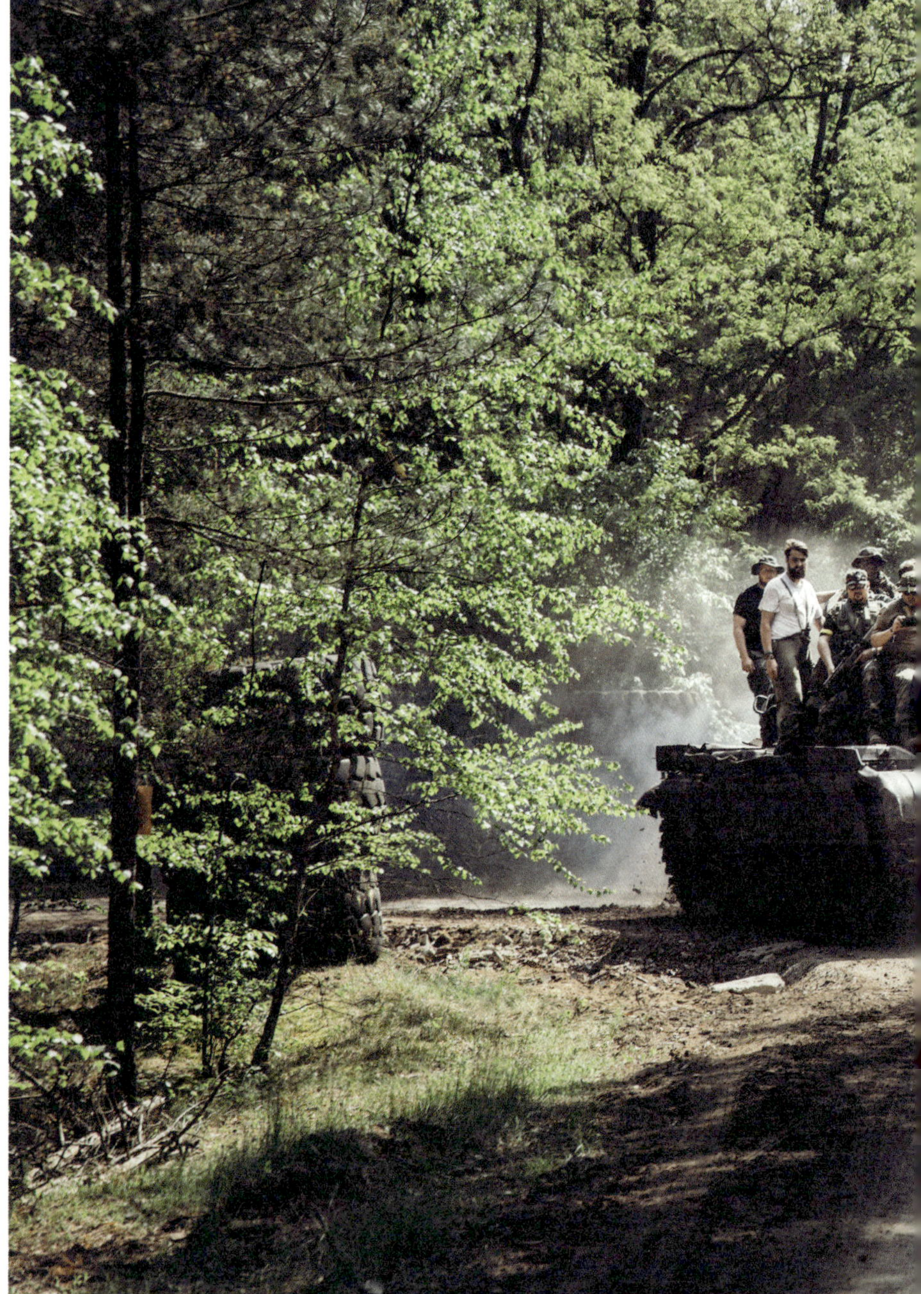

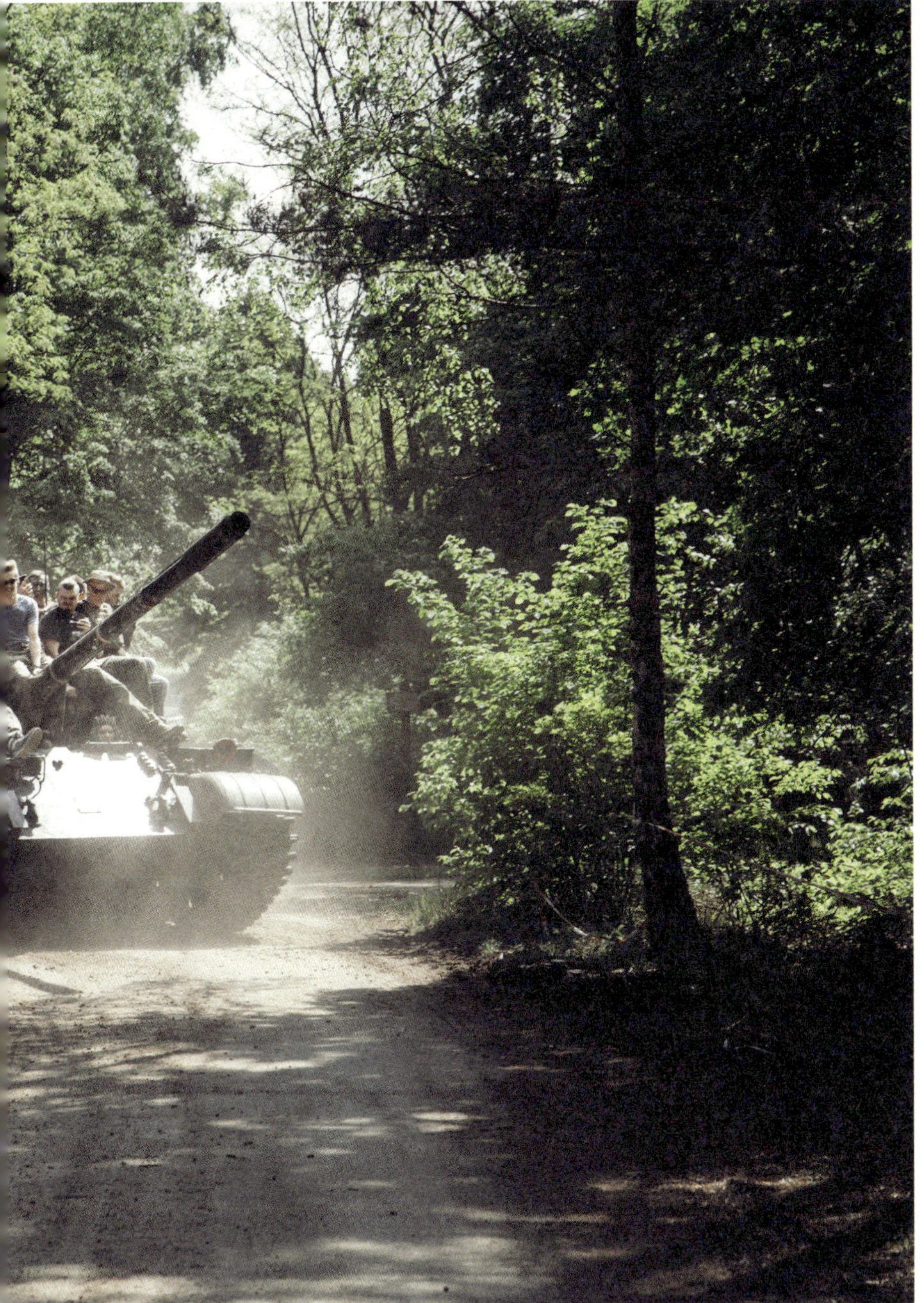

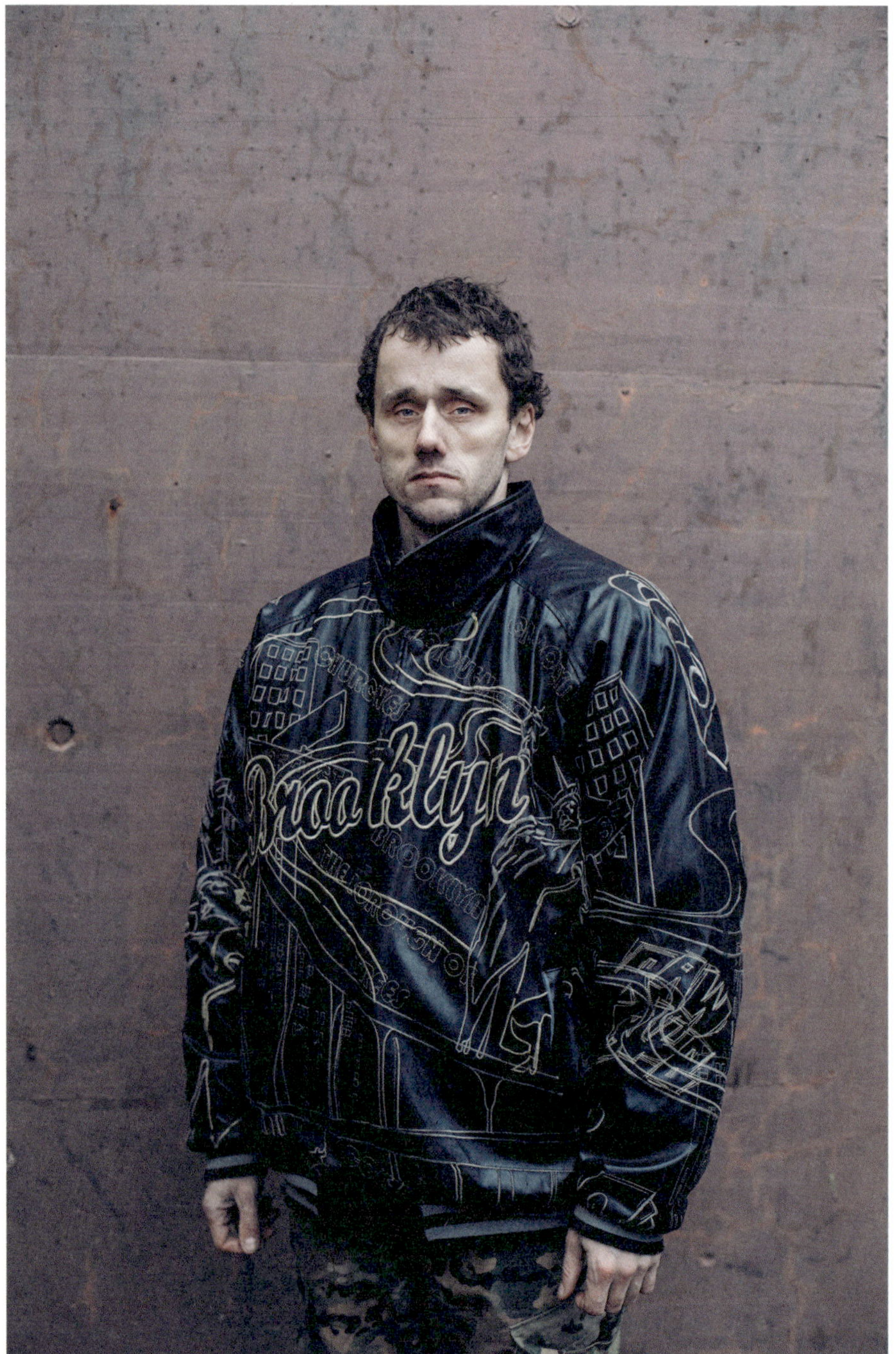
Brooklyn

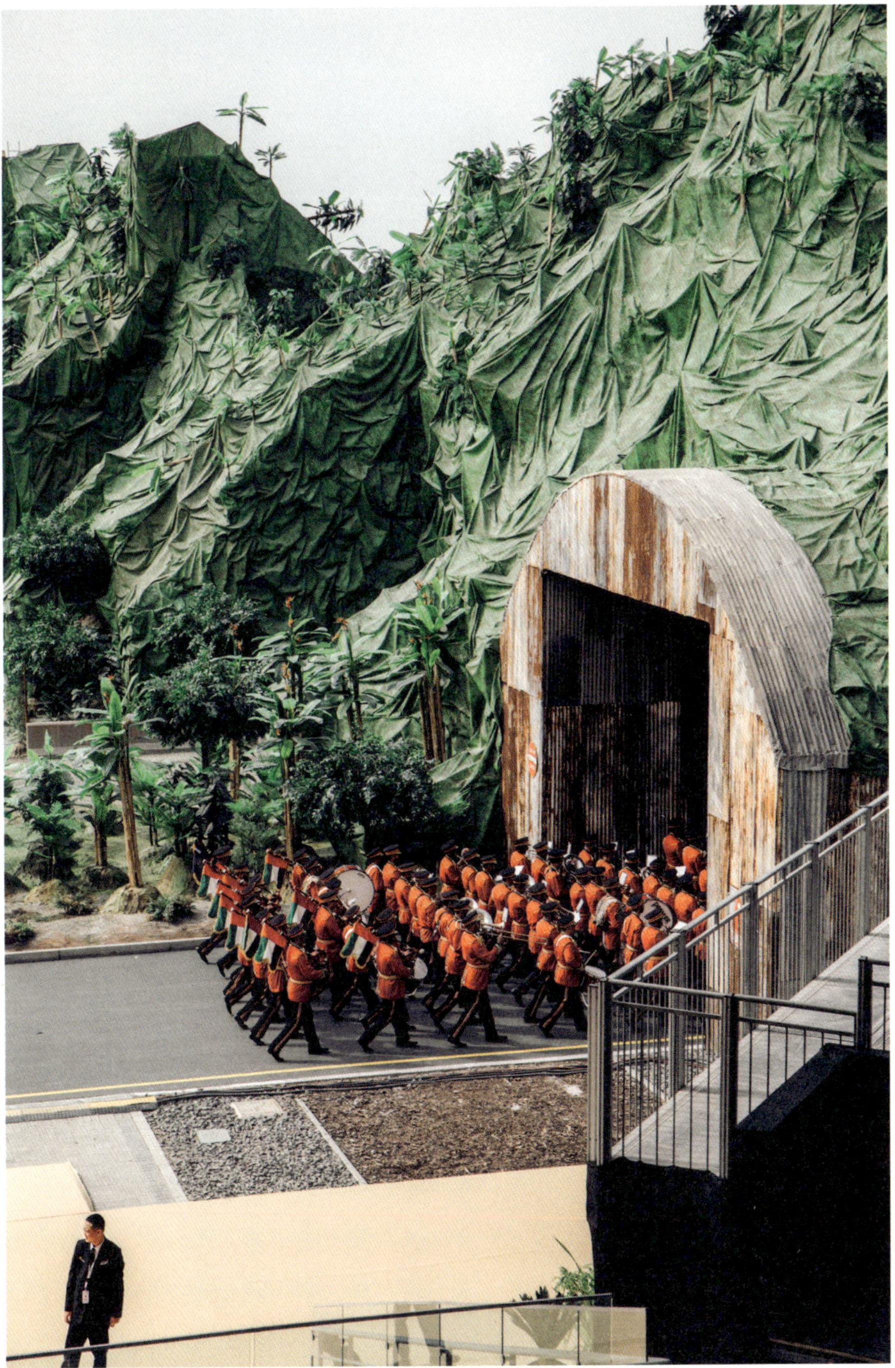

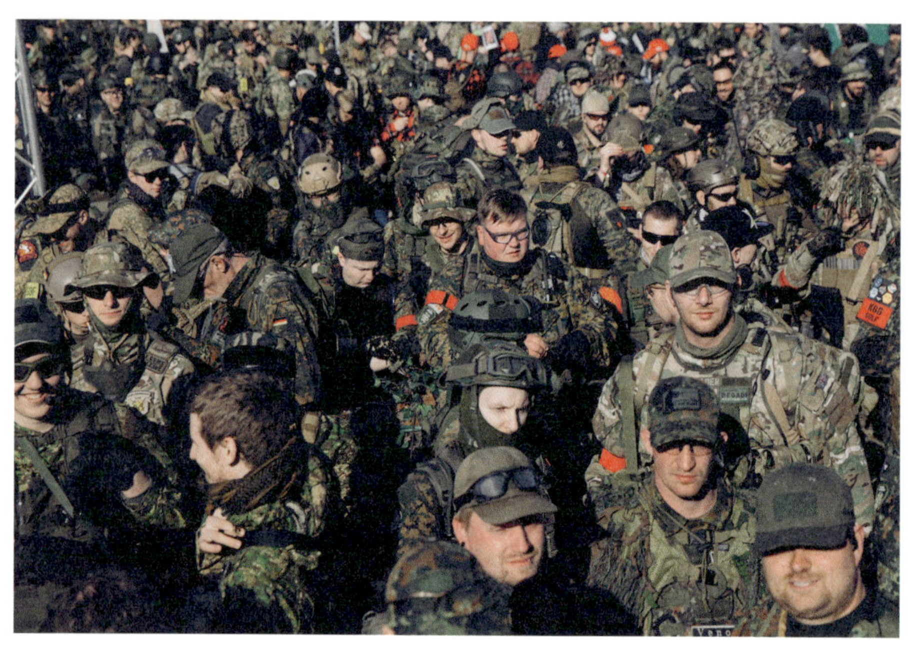

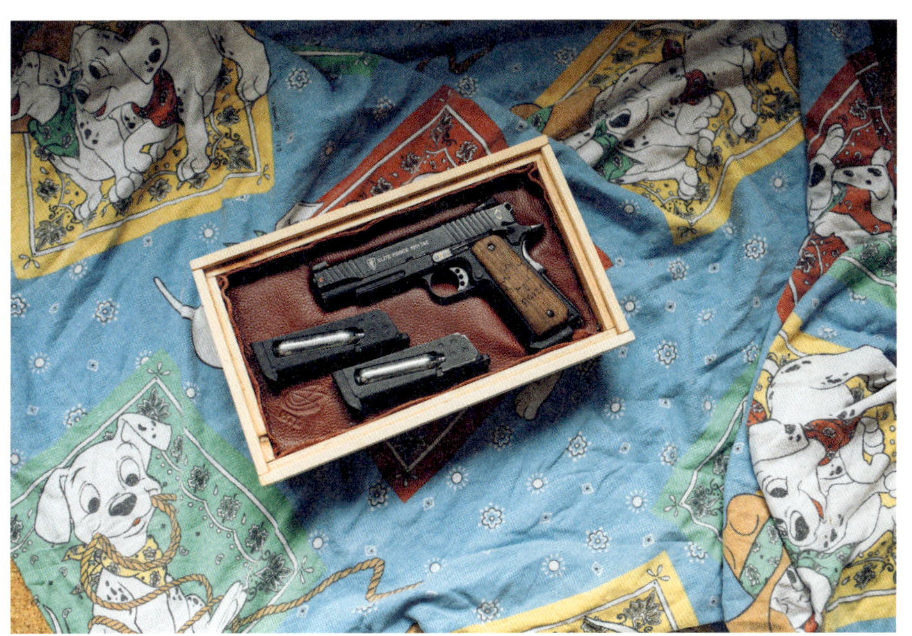

Jan Richard Heinicke

The City In The Forest

24

Singapore is growing. Land is scarce, agricultural areas and green spaces are being replaced with buildings for the rapidly growing population. Almost six million people and the effects of climate change continue to heat up the city. Green architecture and urban agriculture try to approach these problems and to create a greener and more liveable city.

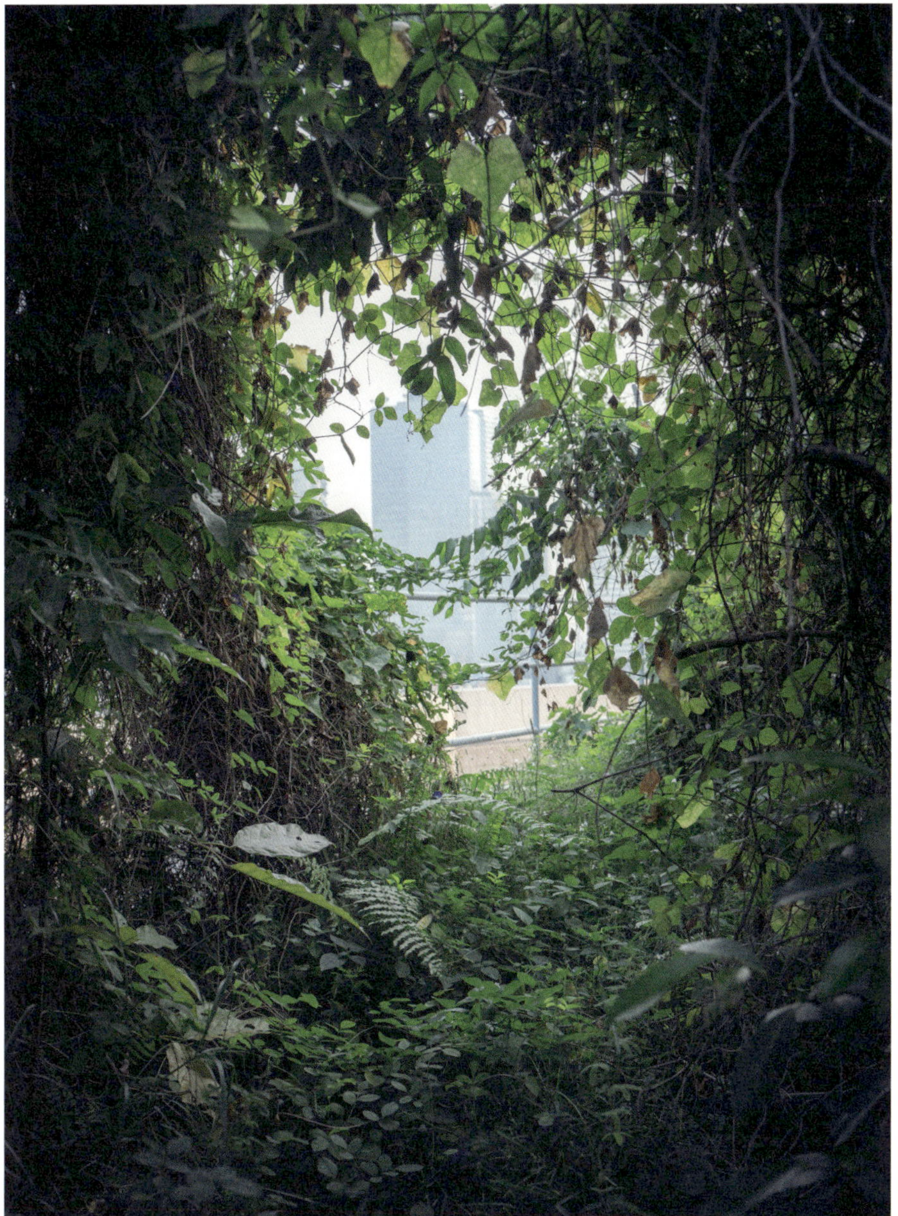

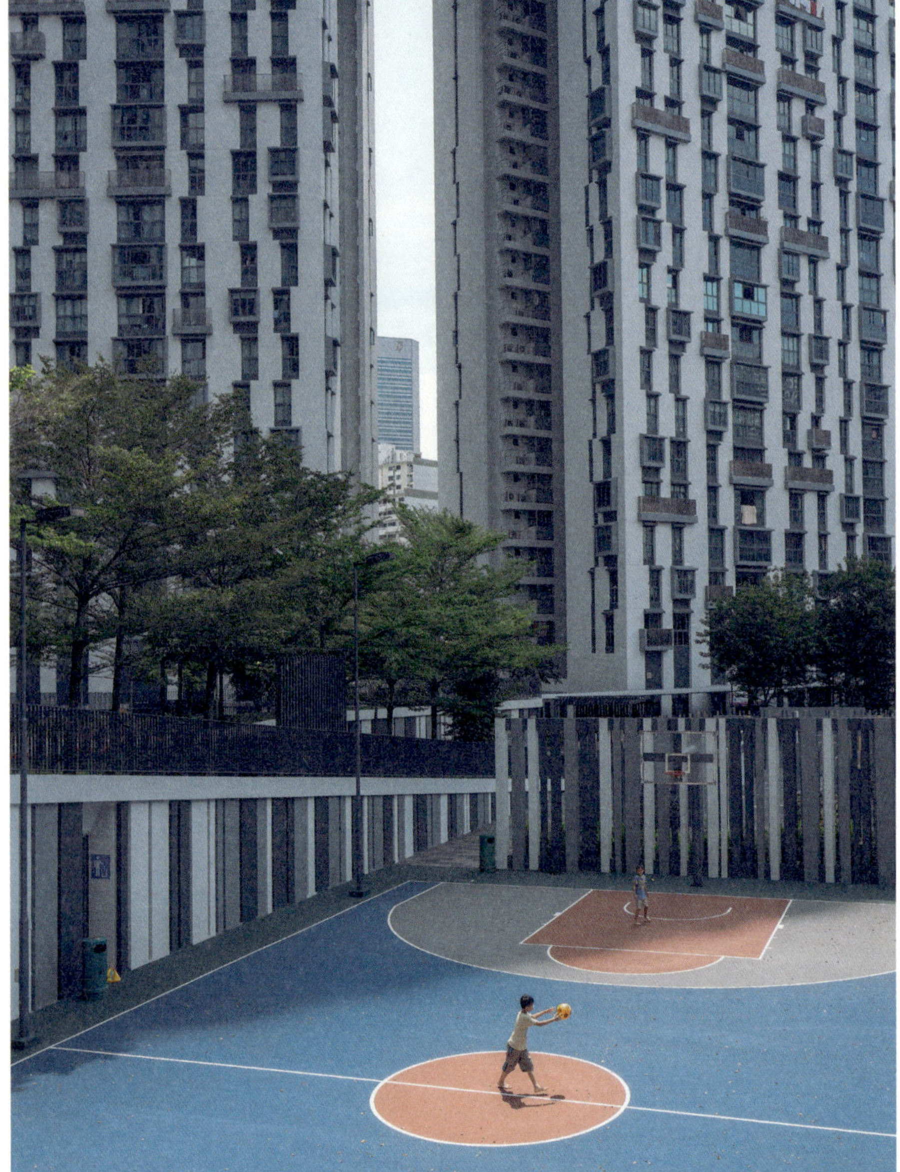

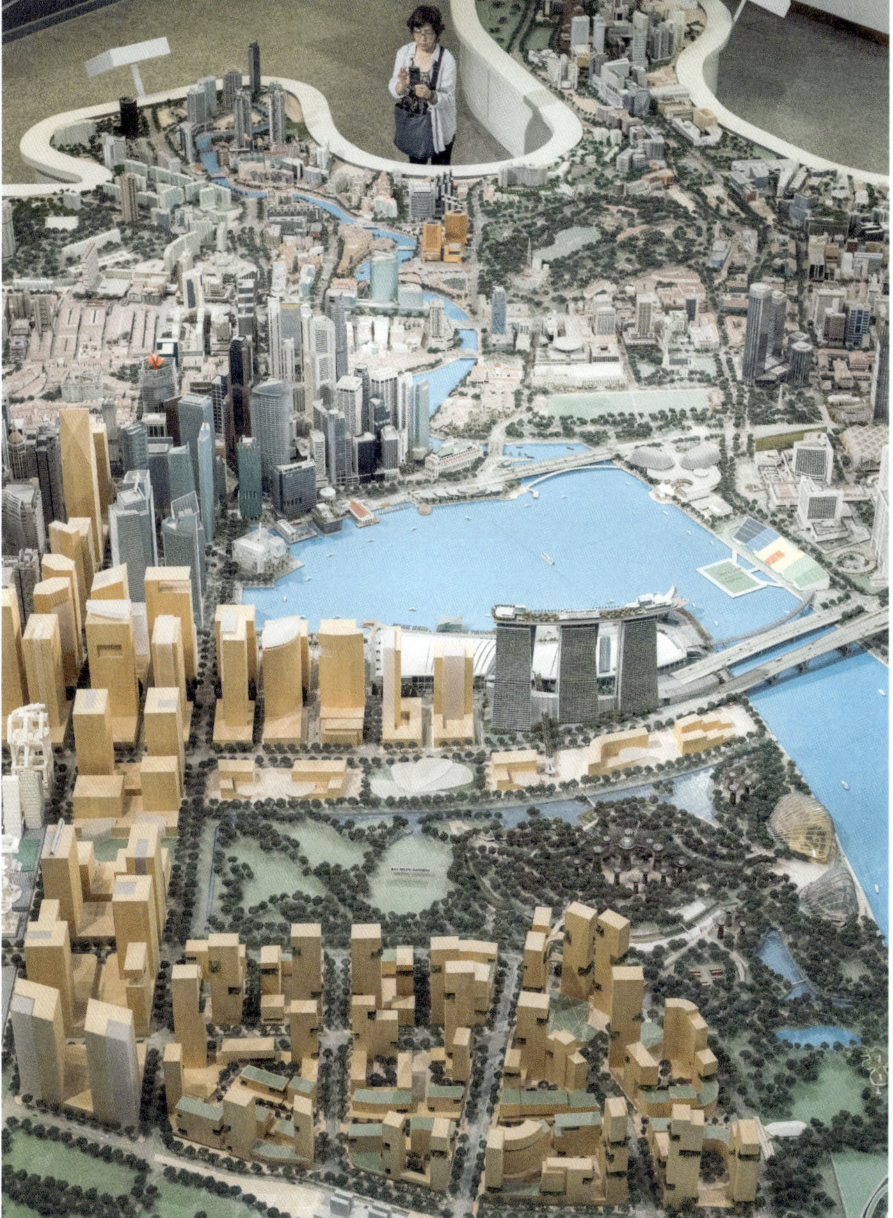

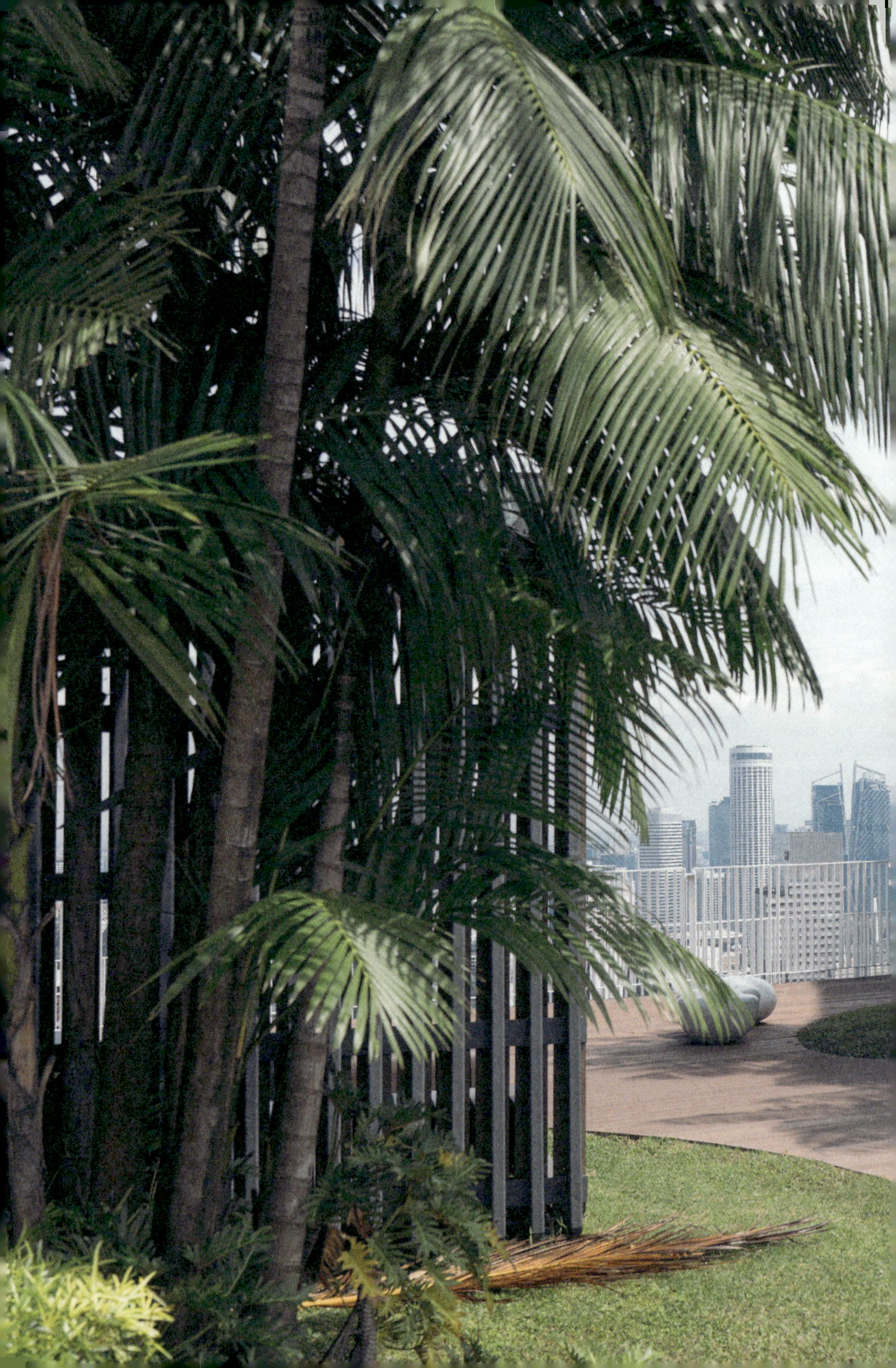

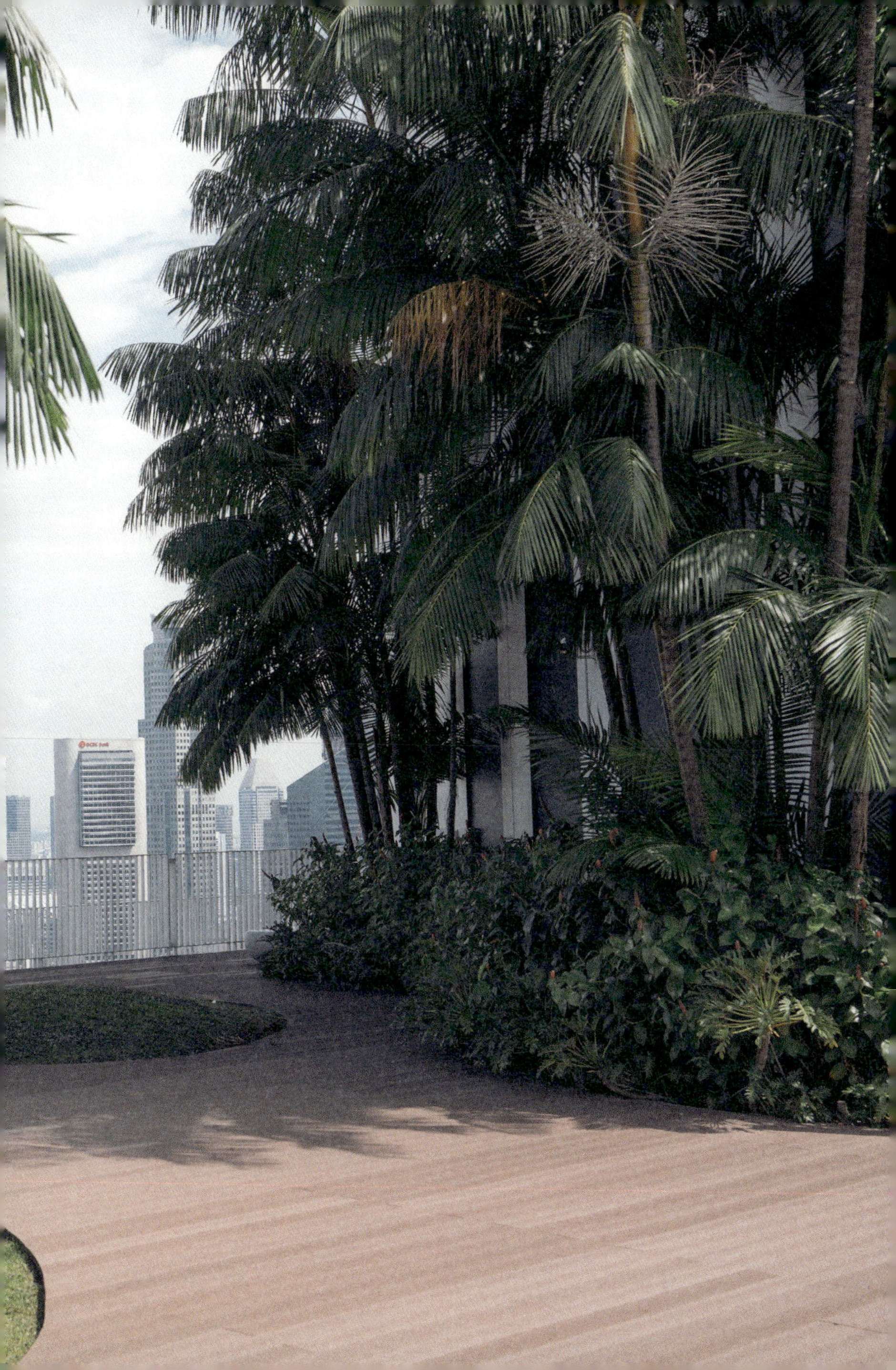

25

Lake Constance. A panorama of mountains in a rural idyll. Can this pensioner's paradise be home to a teenage subculture like "trap", a subgenre of hip hop with visual influences from punk and metal? Well, at their self-organized parties you can find uncontrolled pogo as well as offensive tight dancing. While searching for identity, big city vibes of US idols collide with ruffle curtains of the local tennis clubs.

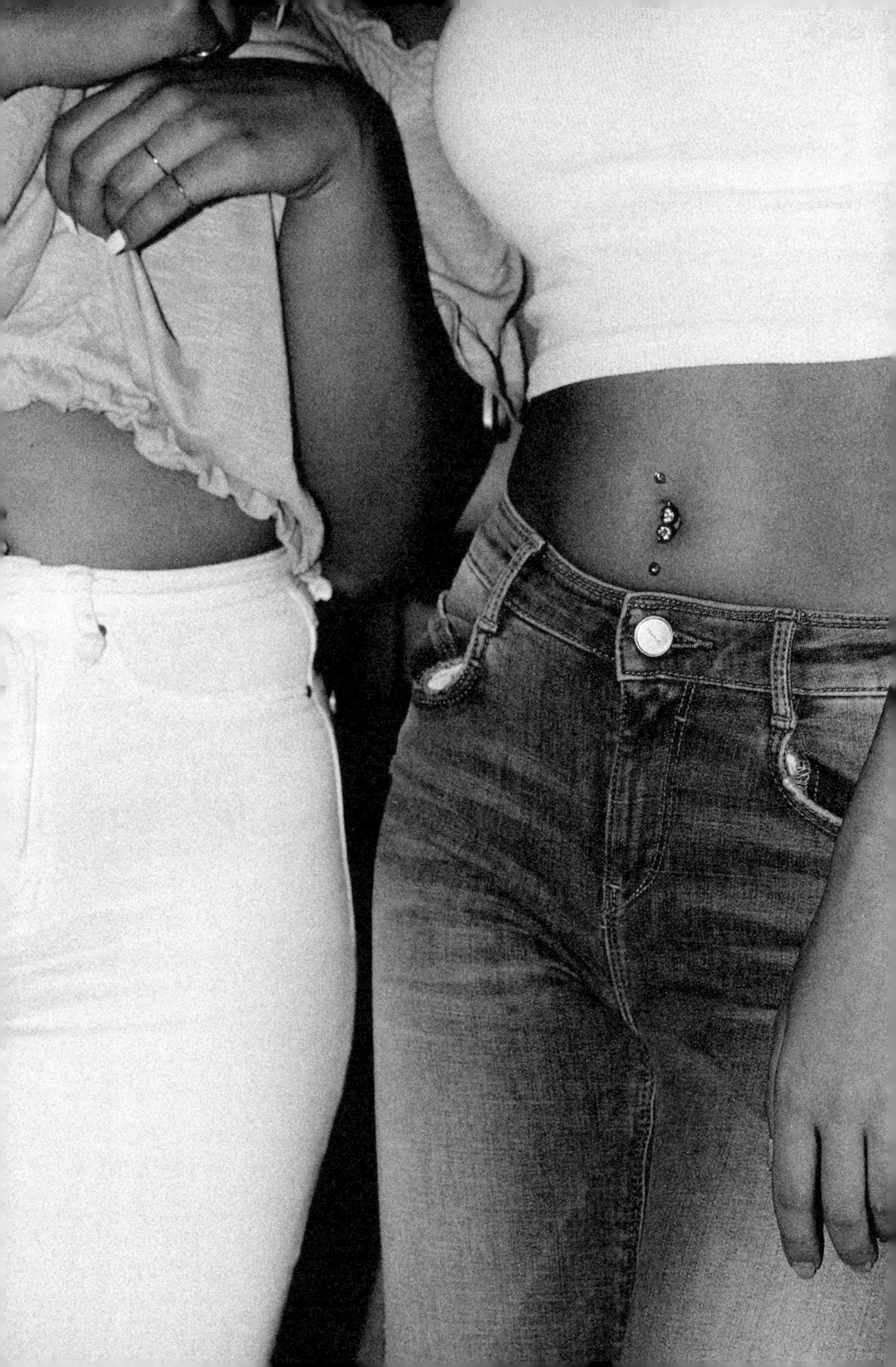

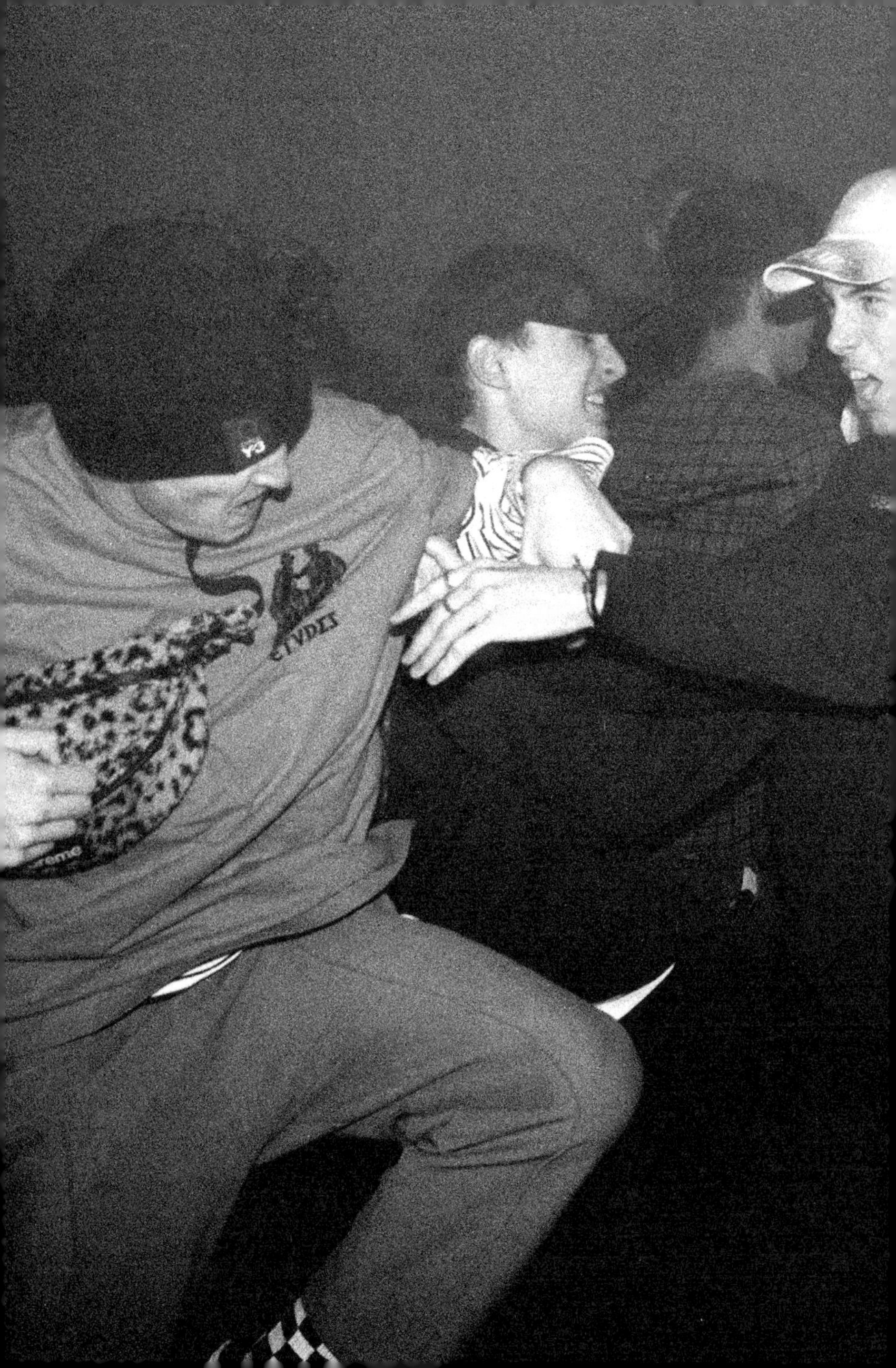
Y3

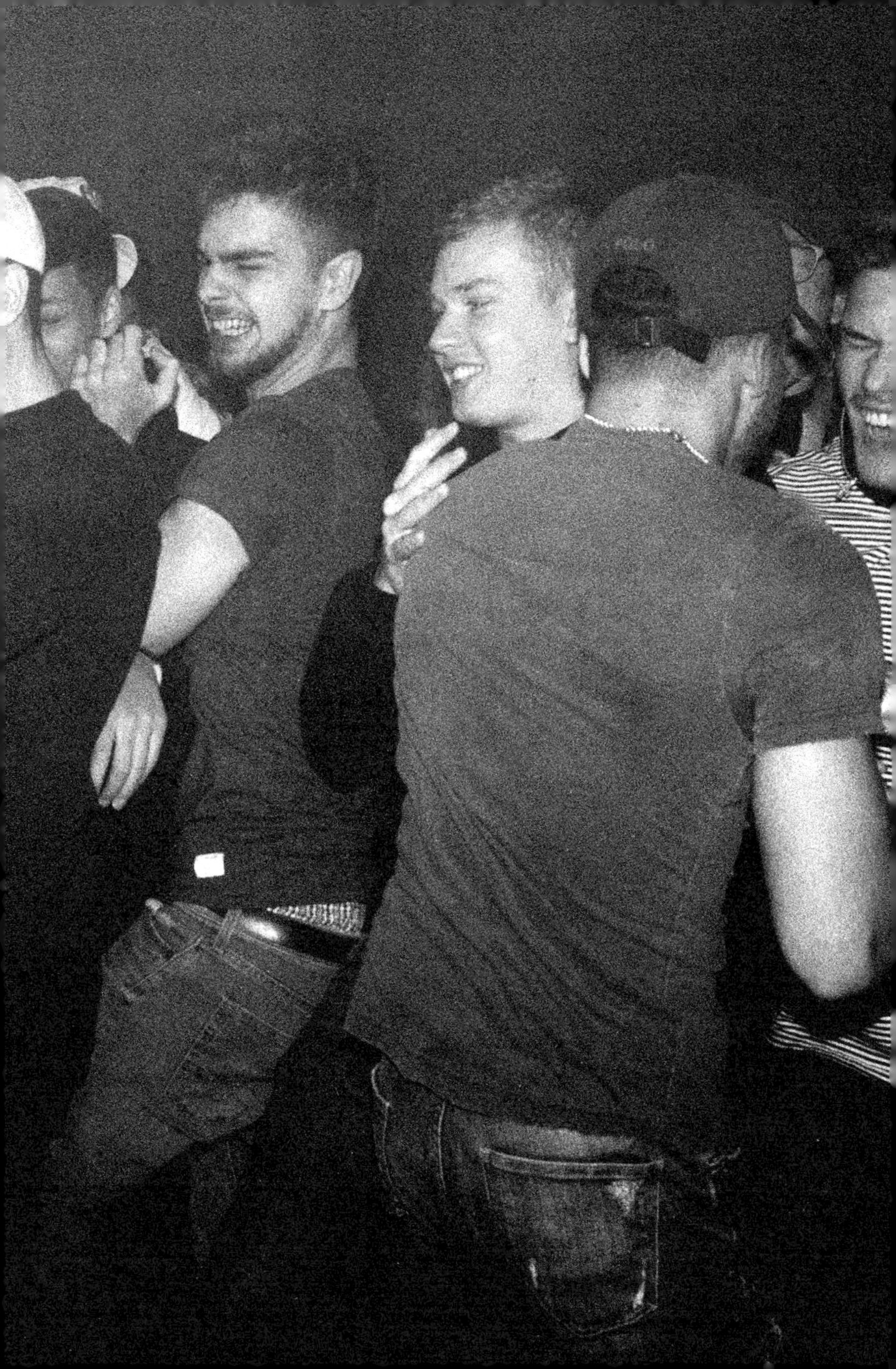

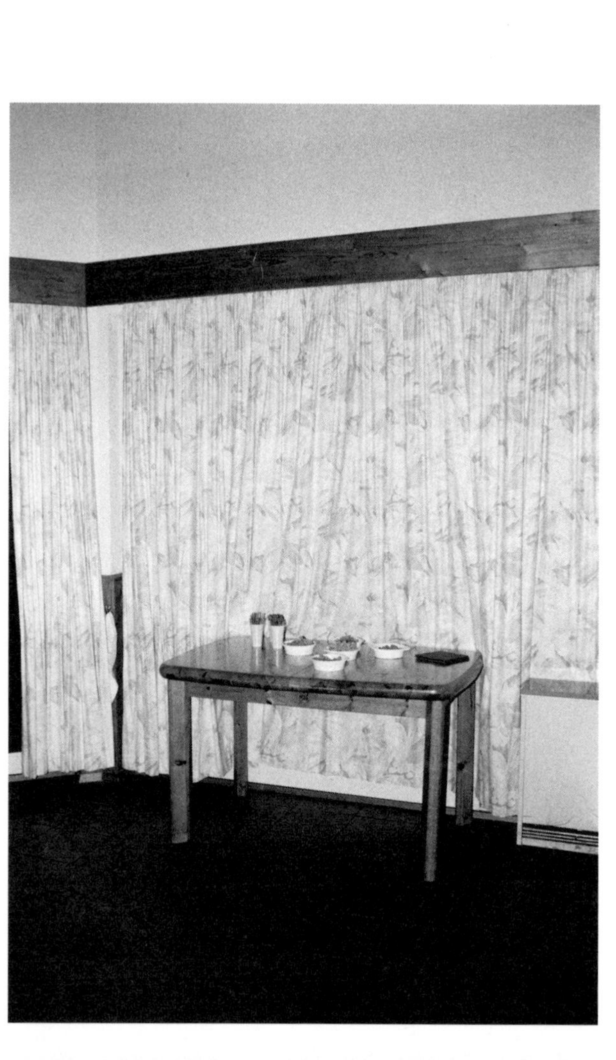

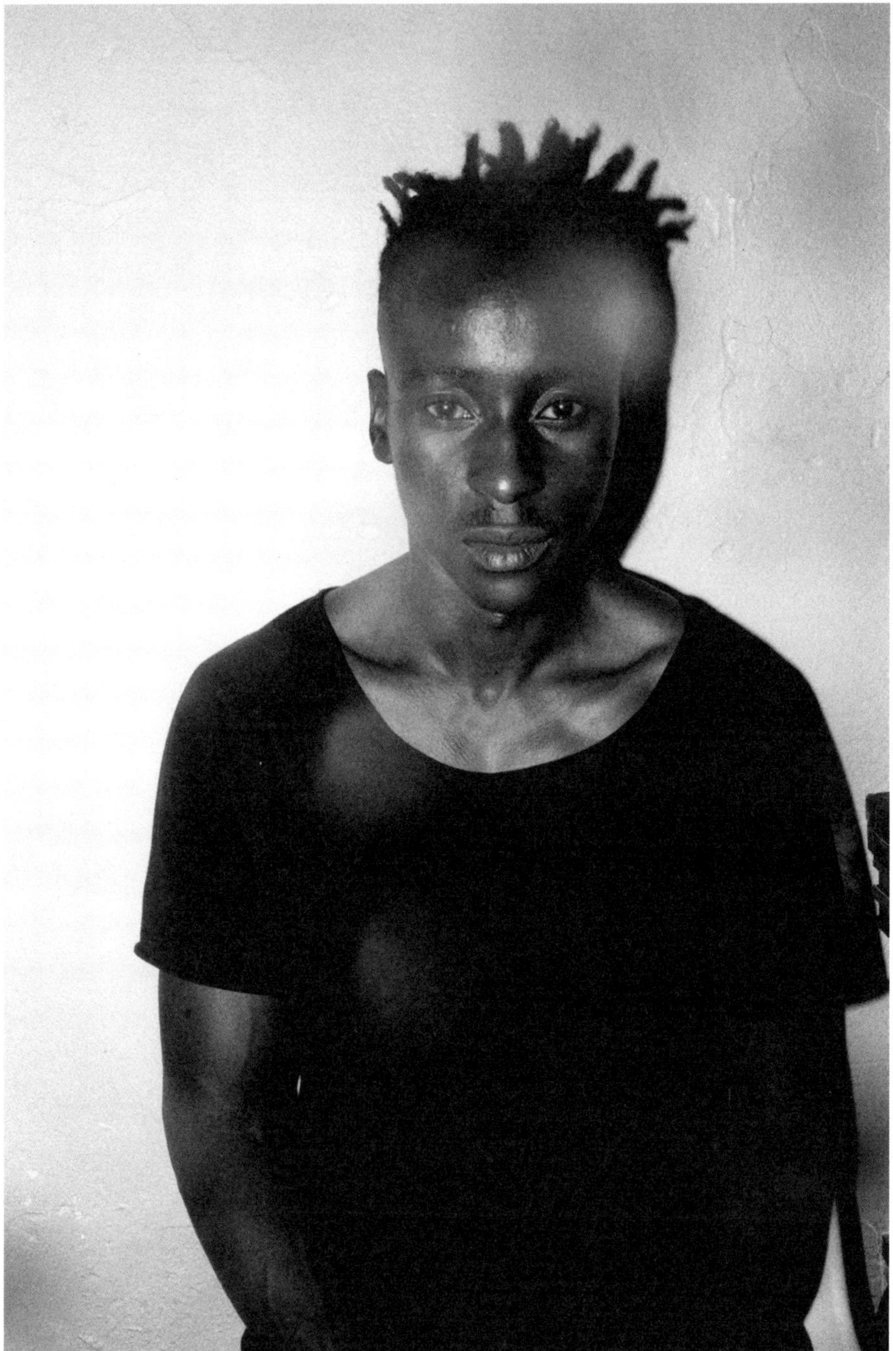

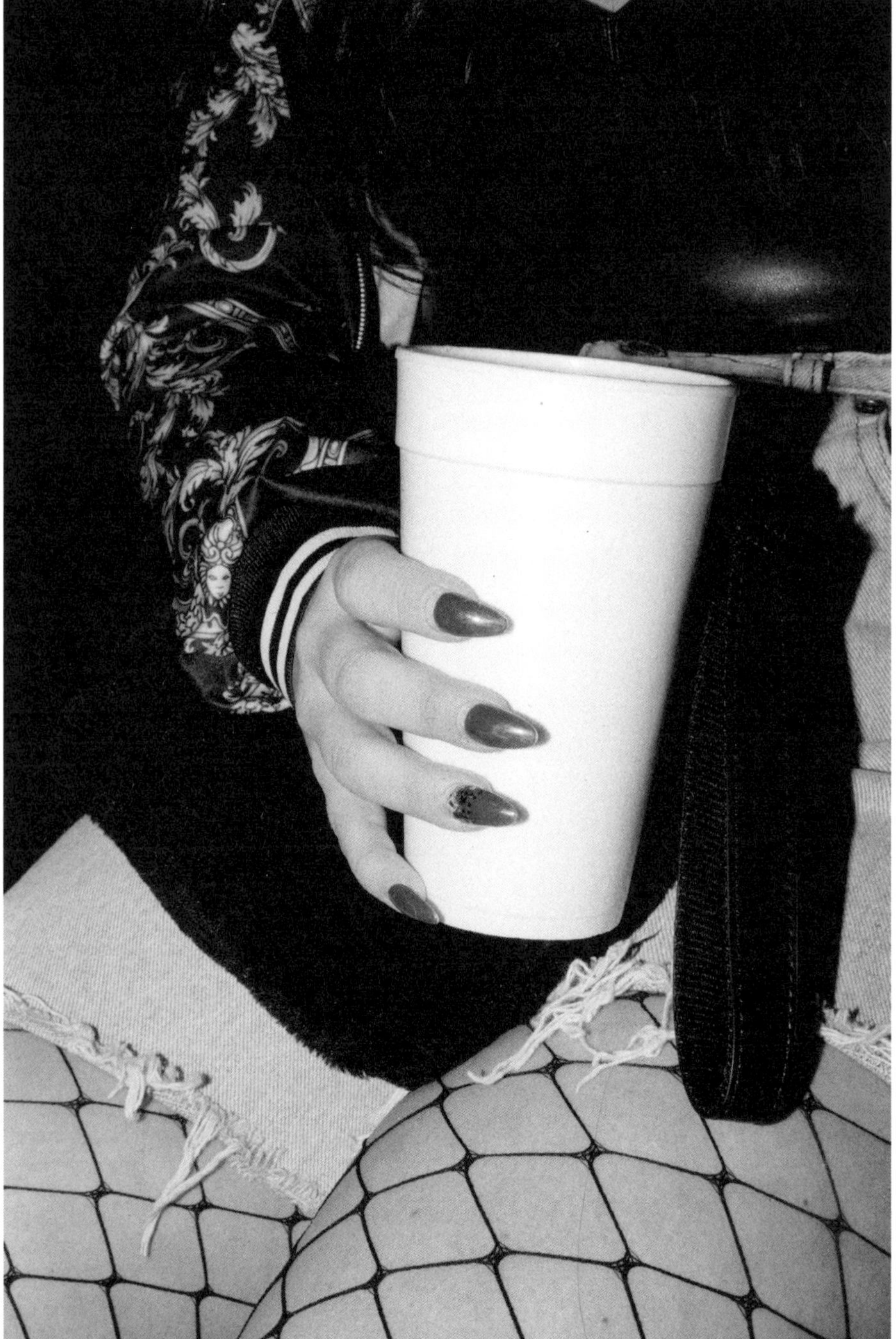

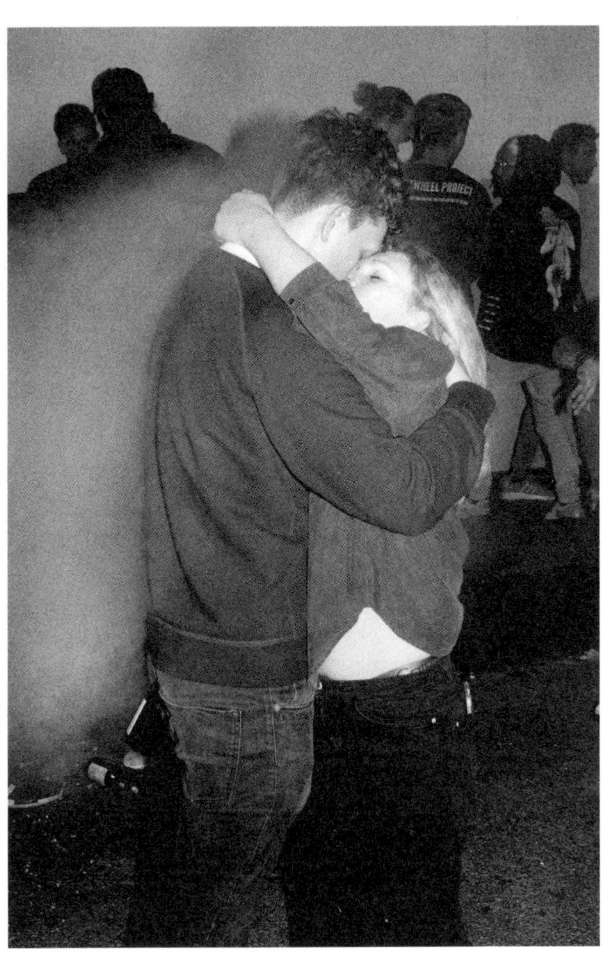
WHEEL PROJECT

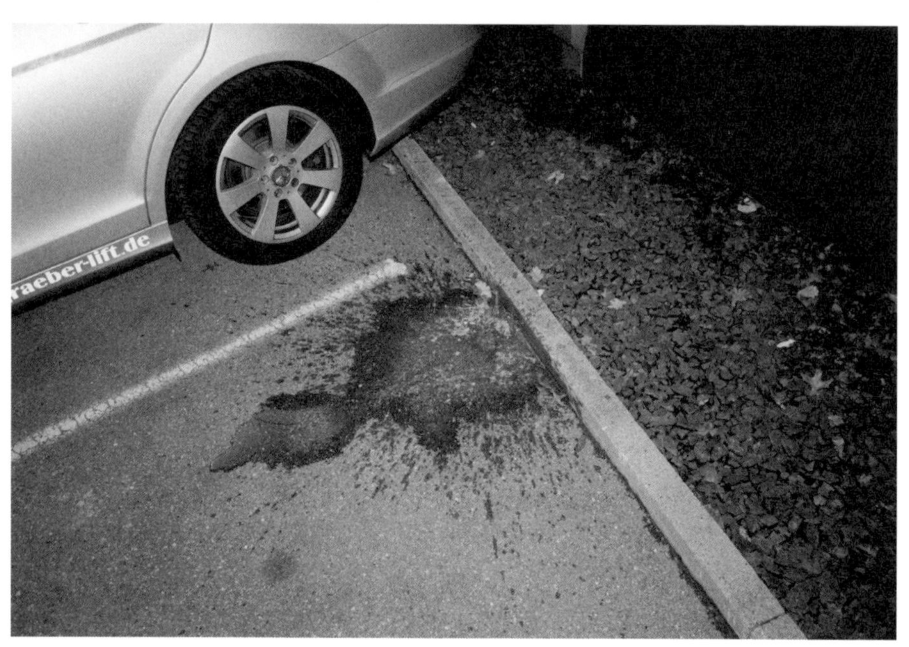
raeber-lift.de

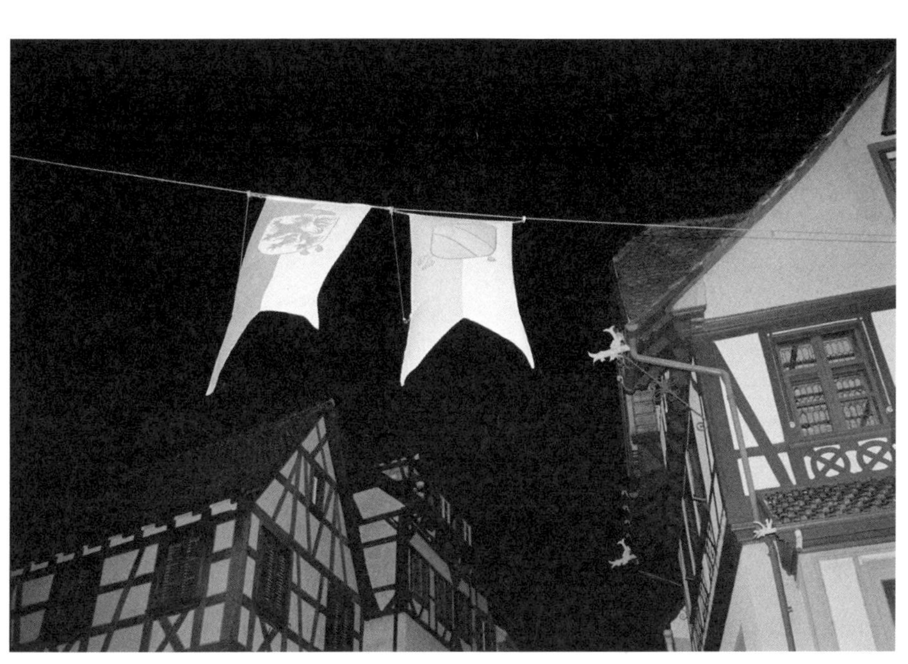

26

Perchtenlauf—a rare medieval folk custom was retained in the area around Salzburg, even though it was prohibited and fought by the church for centuries. Each New Year, the Perchten are said to bring good fortune and fertility to the farms of the village and banish demons. Each character has its own important role in starting the year under a happy omen.

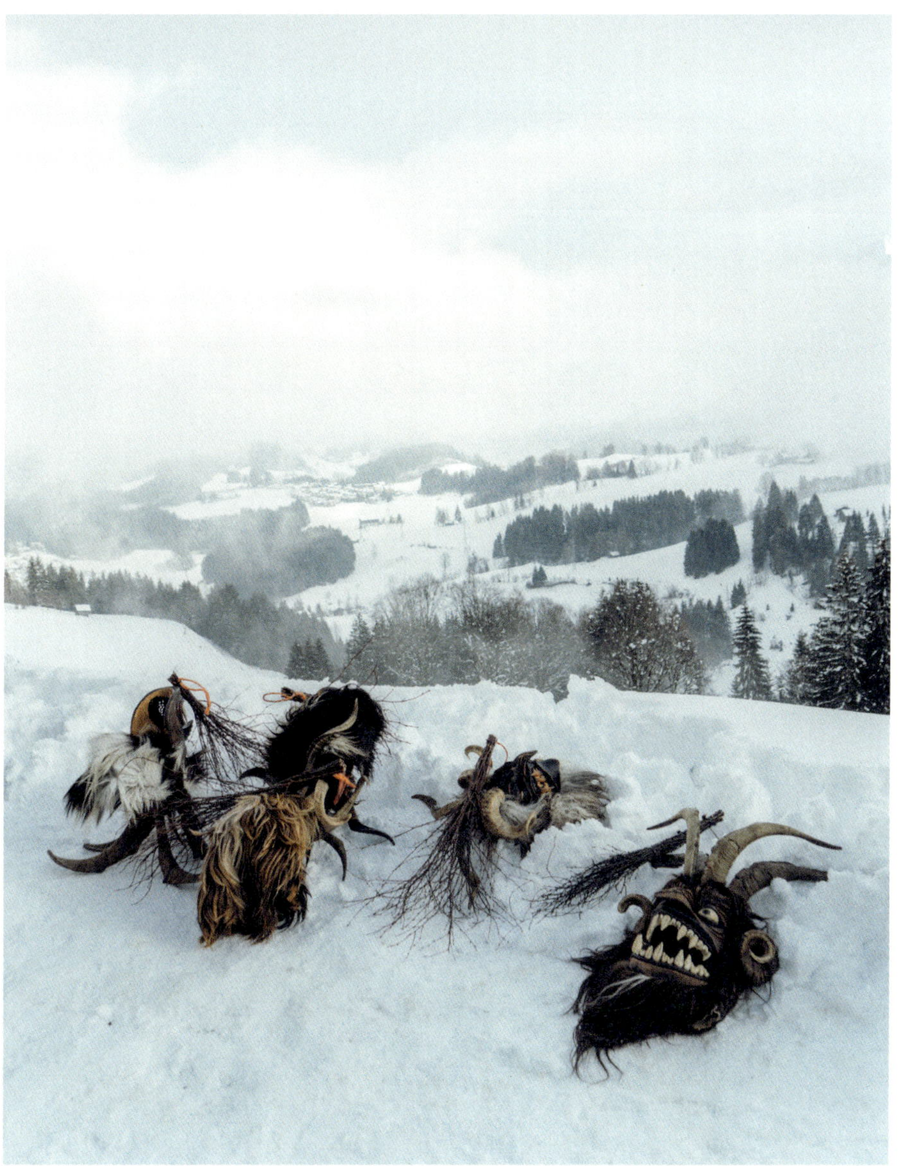

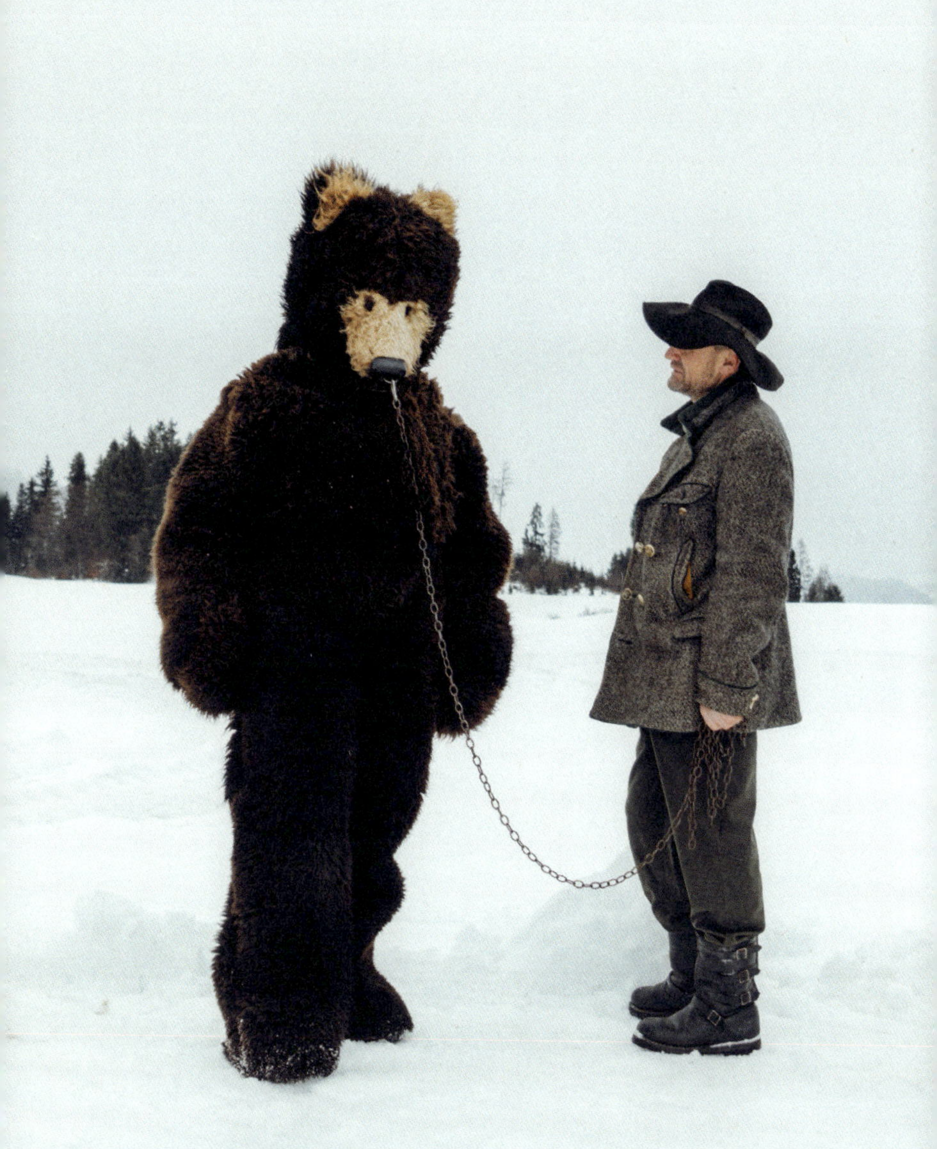

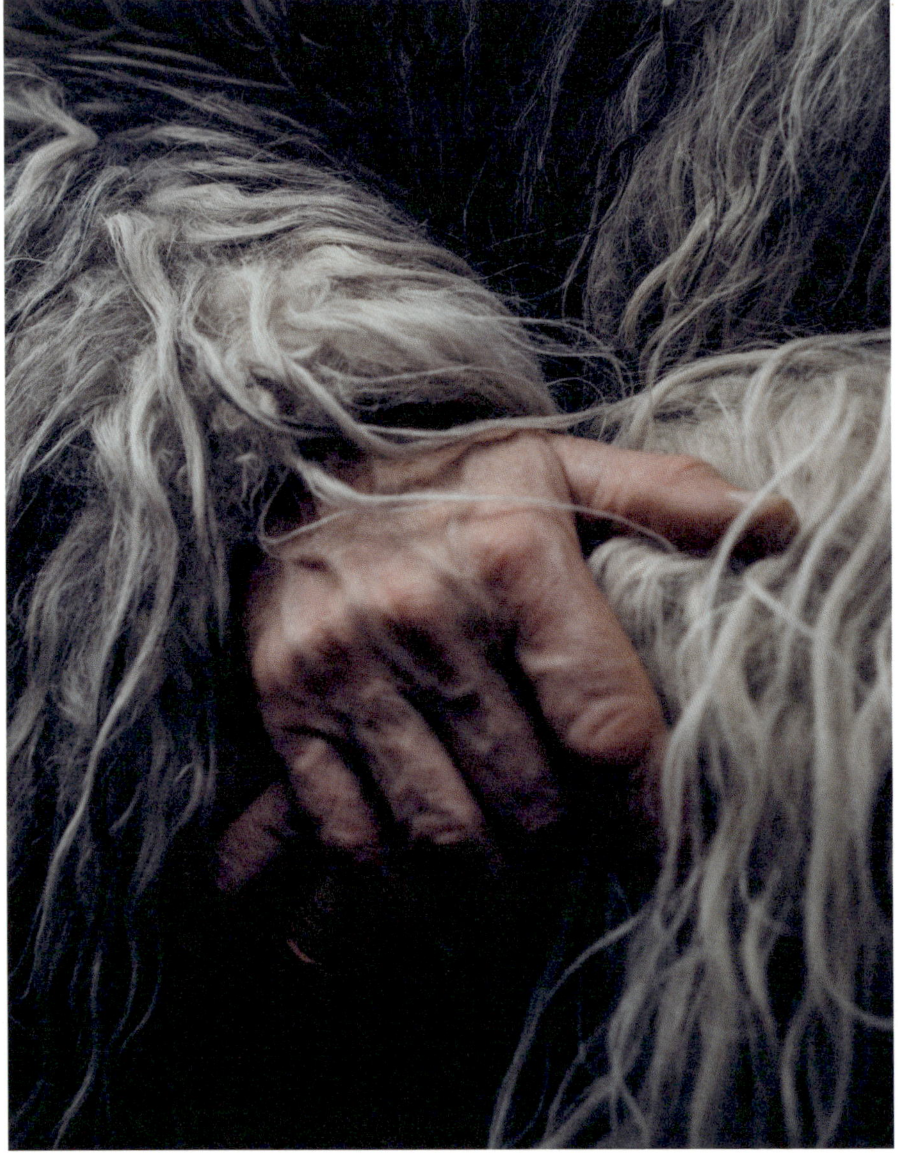

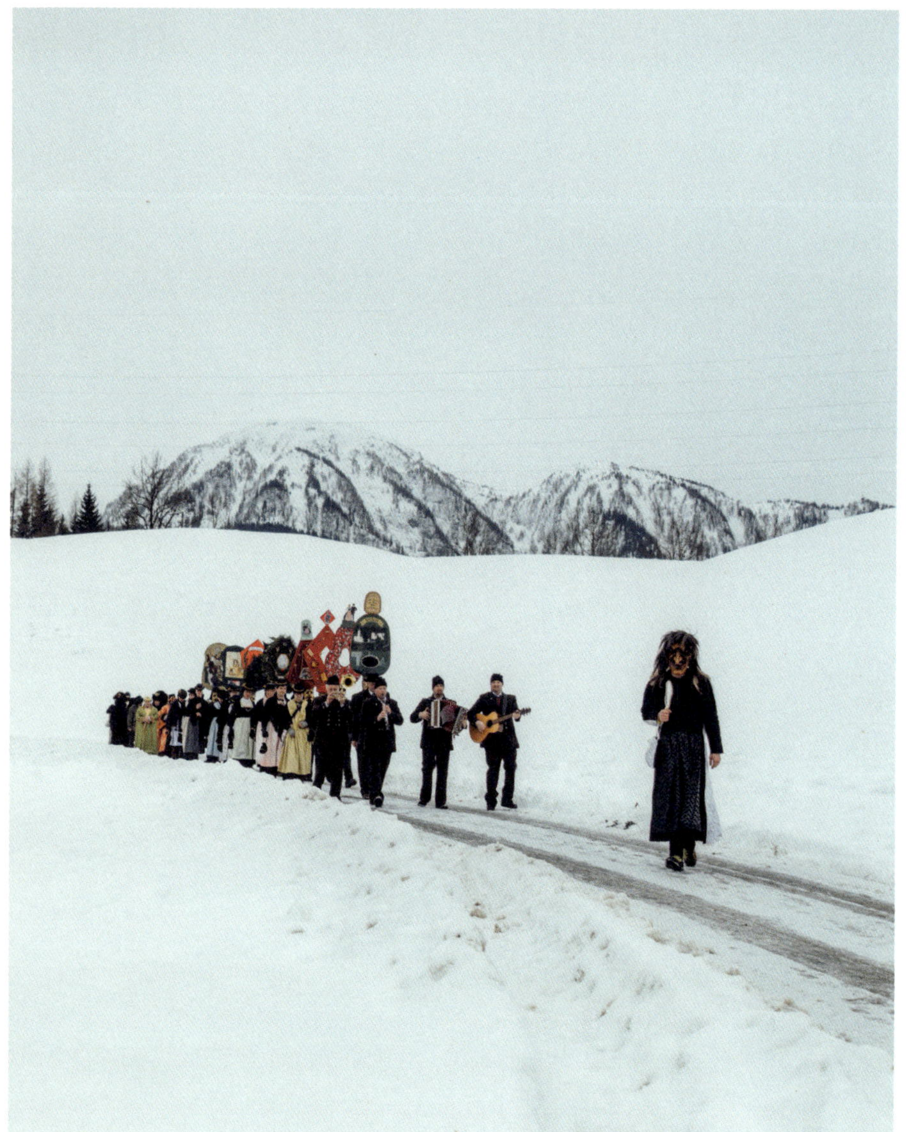

Magnus Terhorst
Thomas Morsch

Bukinje

27

There are about six hundred people living in Bukinje, a small town right next to Bosnia & Herzegovina's biggest coal power plant. Diseases like asthma and cancer are an immediate result caused by massive pollution and are part of everyday life.

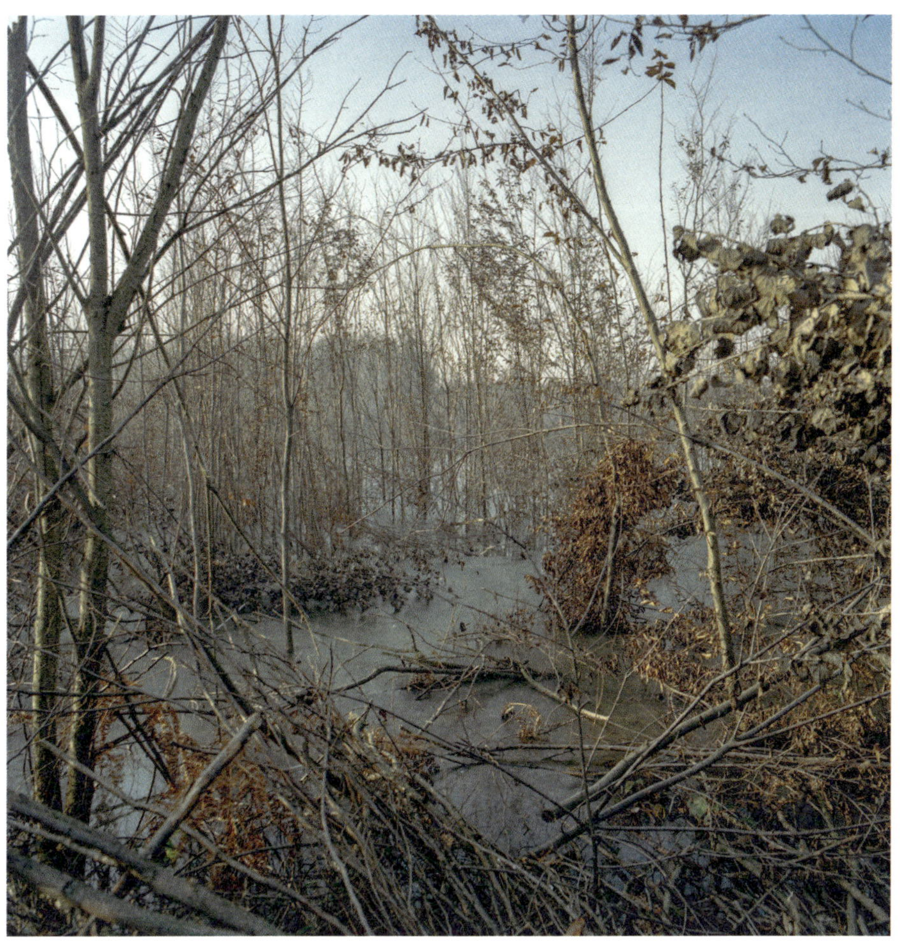

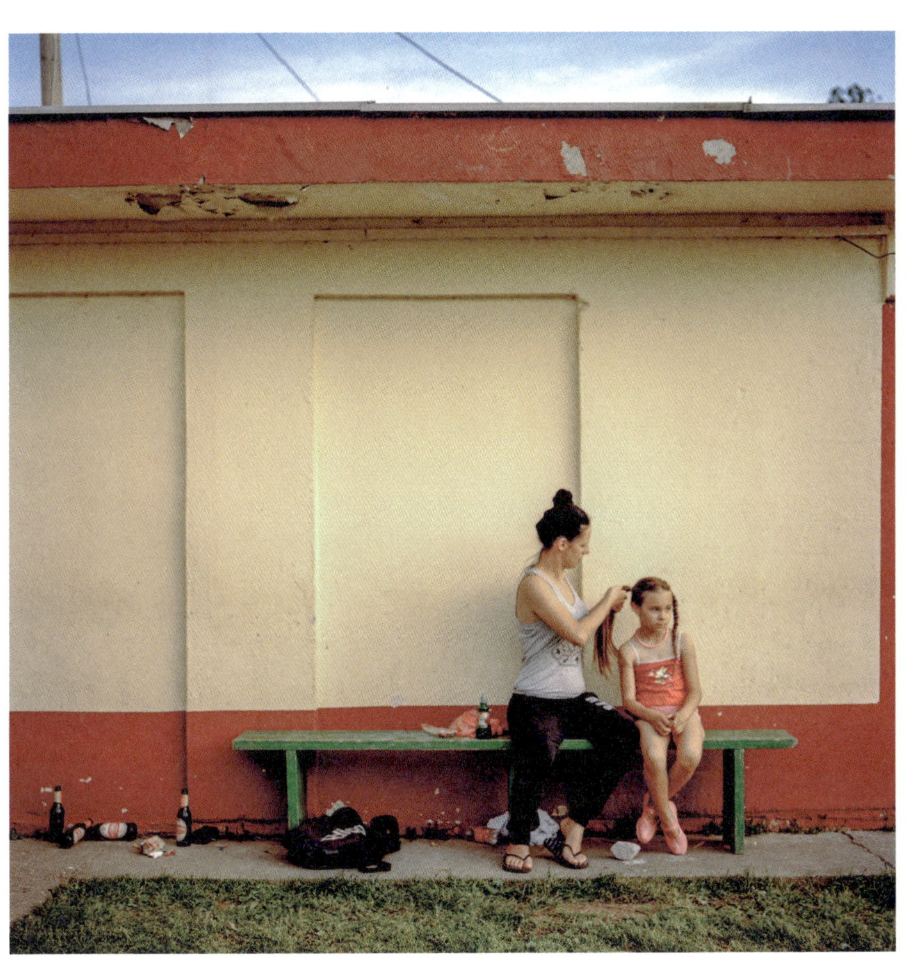

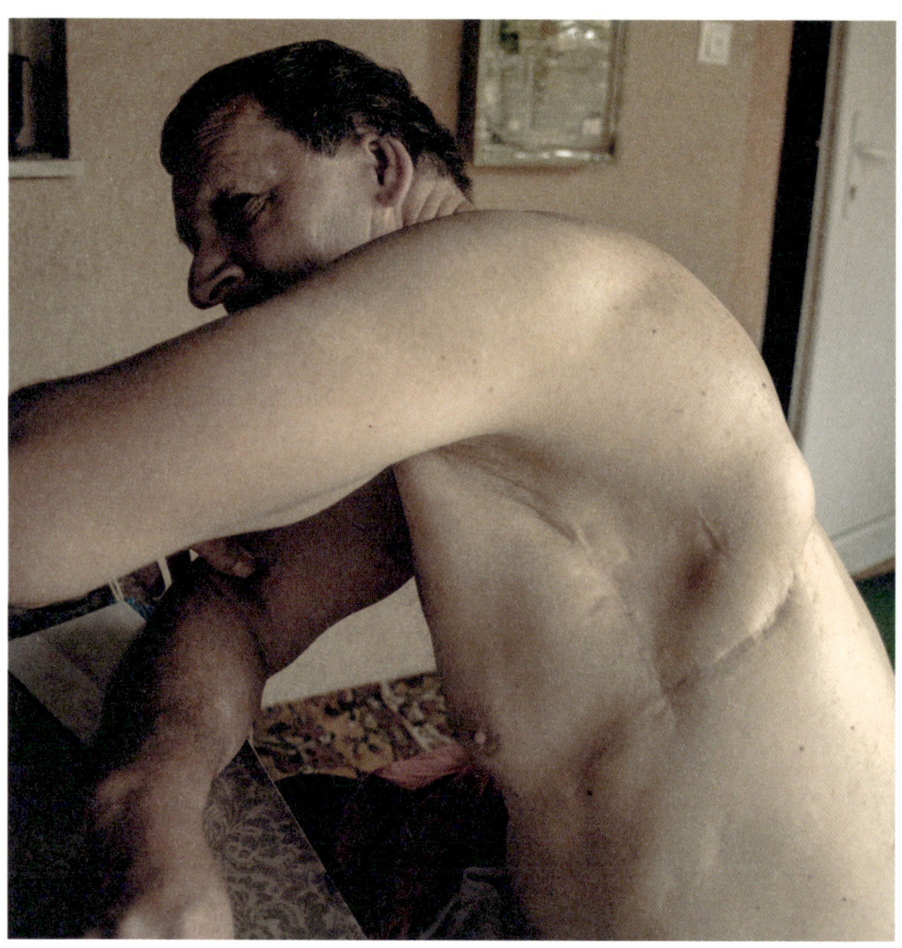

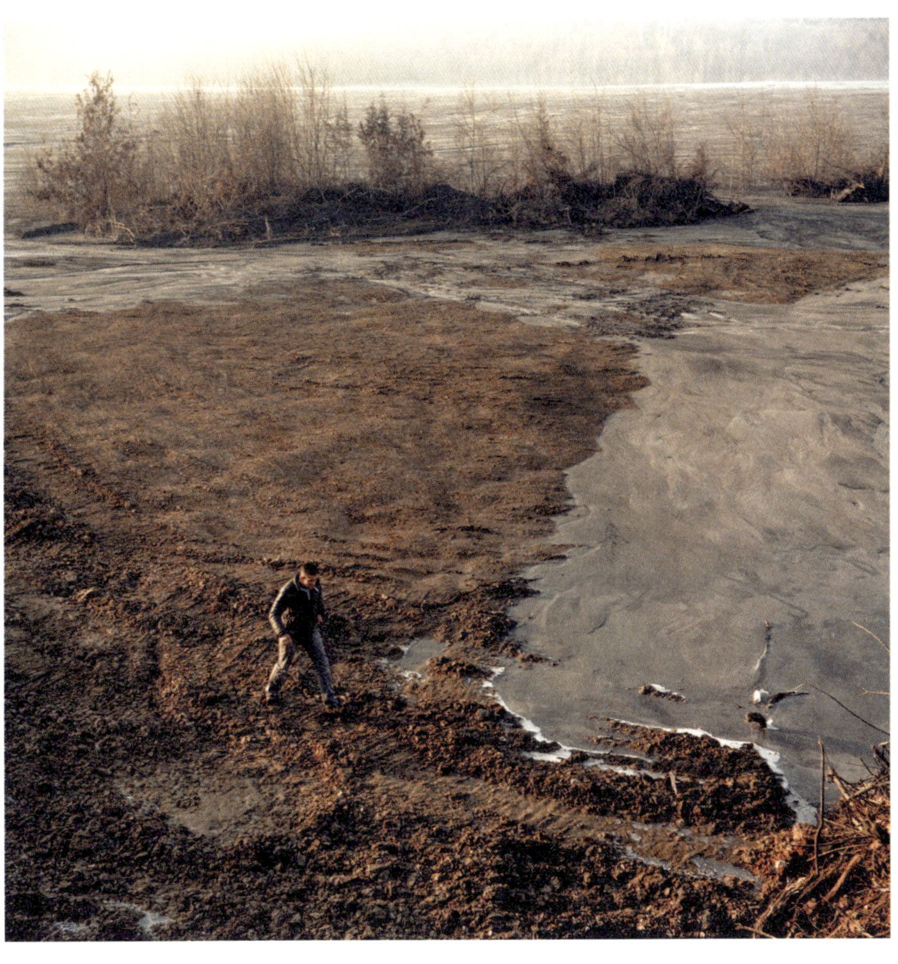

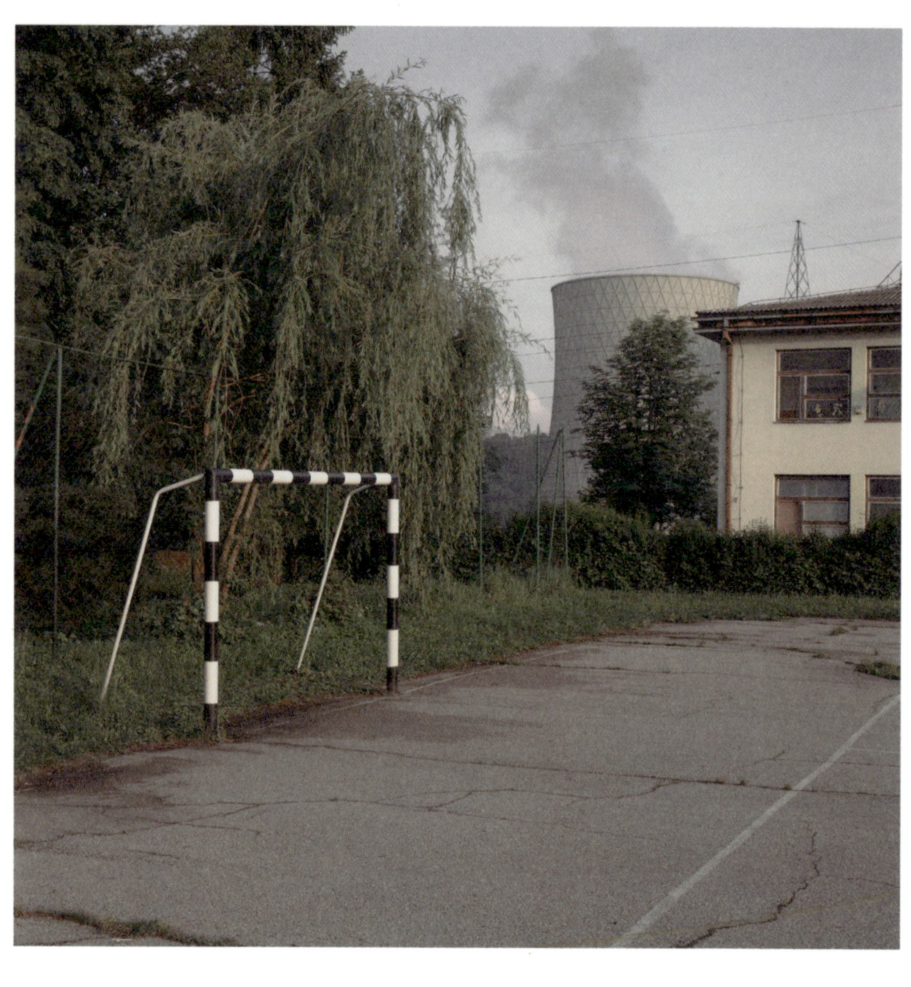

28

The tiny islands called “Halligen” are located in the North Sea and are home to 250 people. The inhabitants’ lives are shaped by the raving sea. About 30 times a year, the land is flooded and only the houses on man-made hills are above sea level.

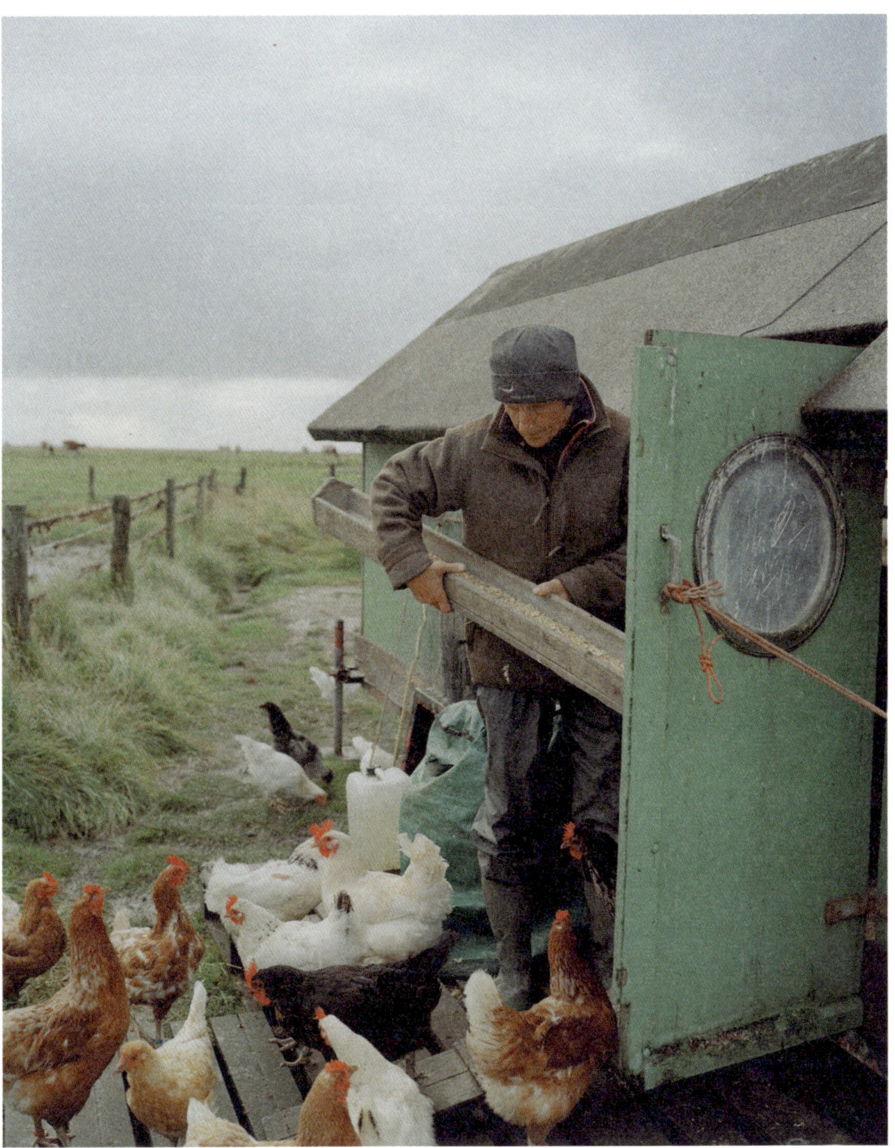

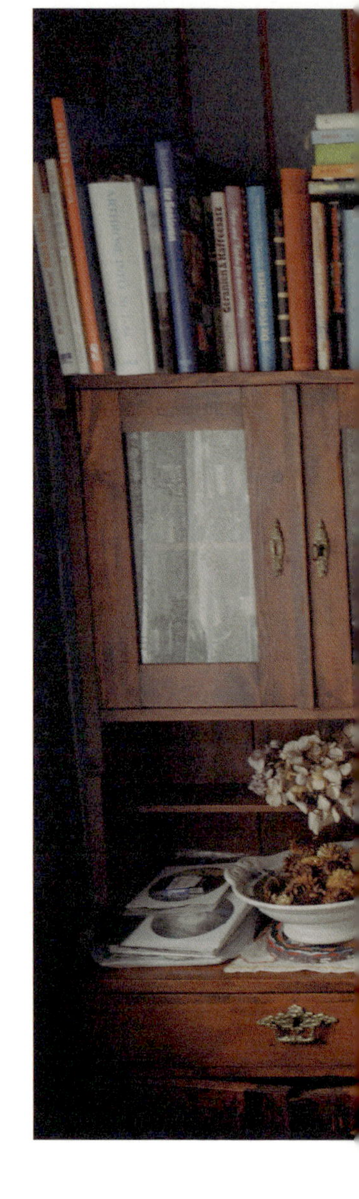

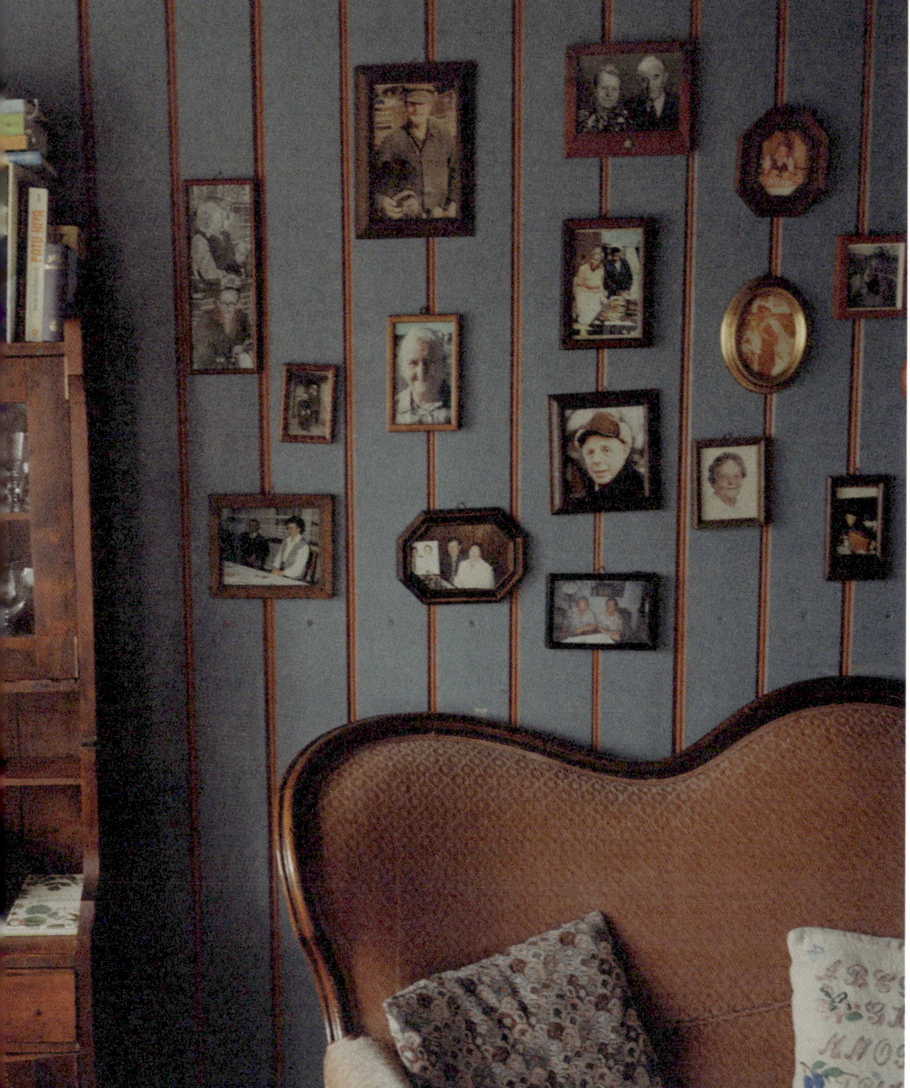

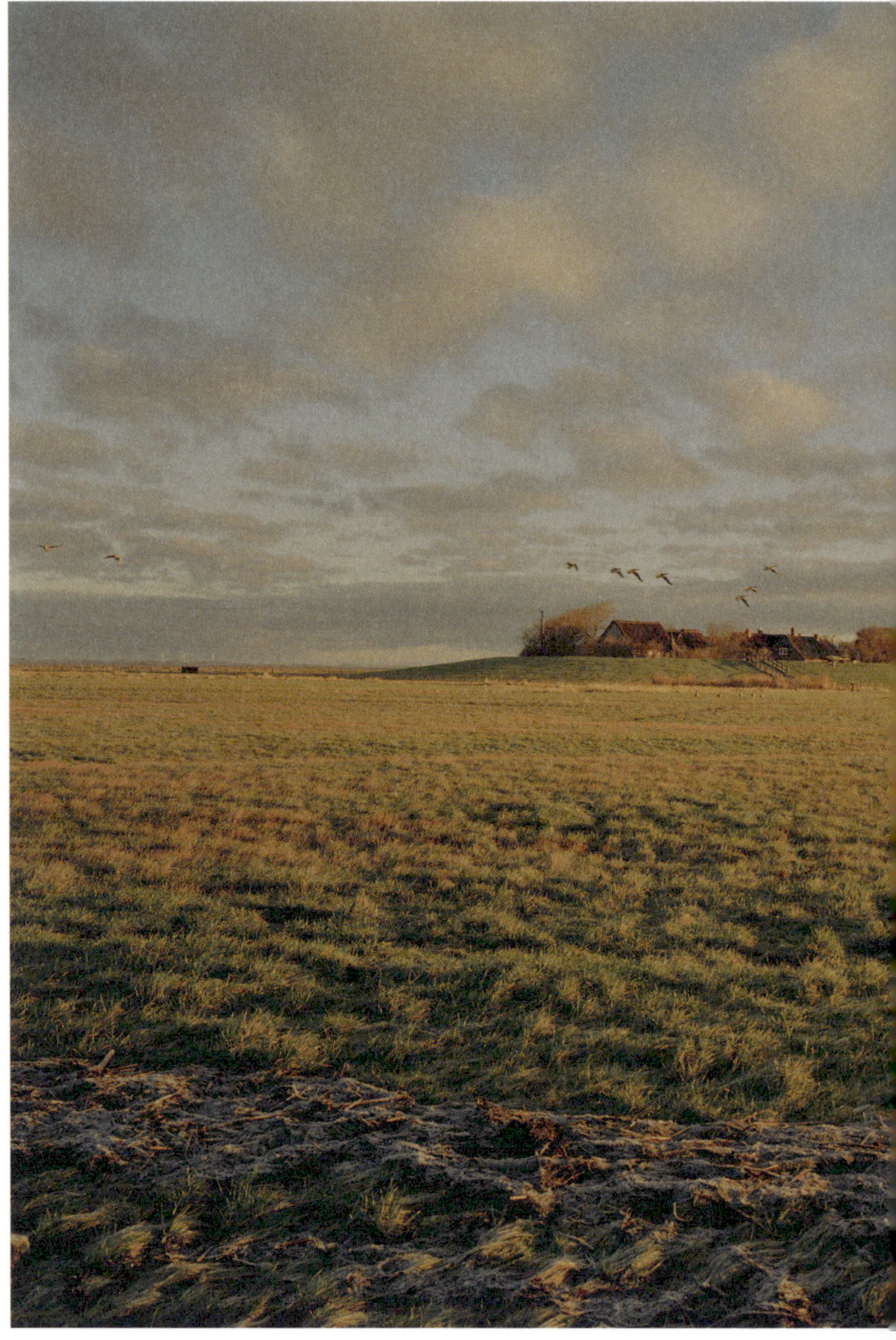

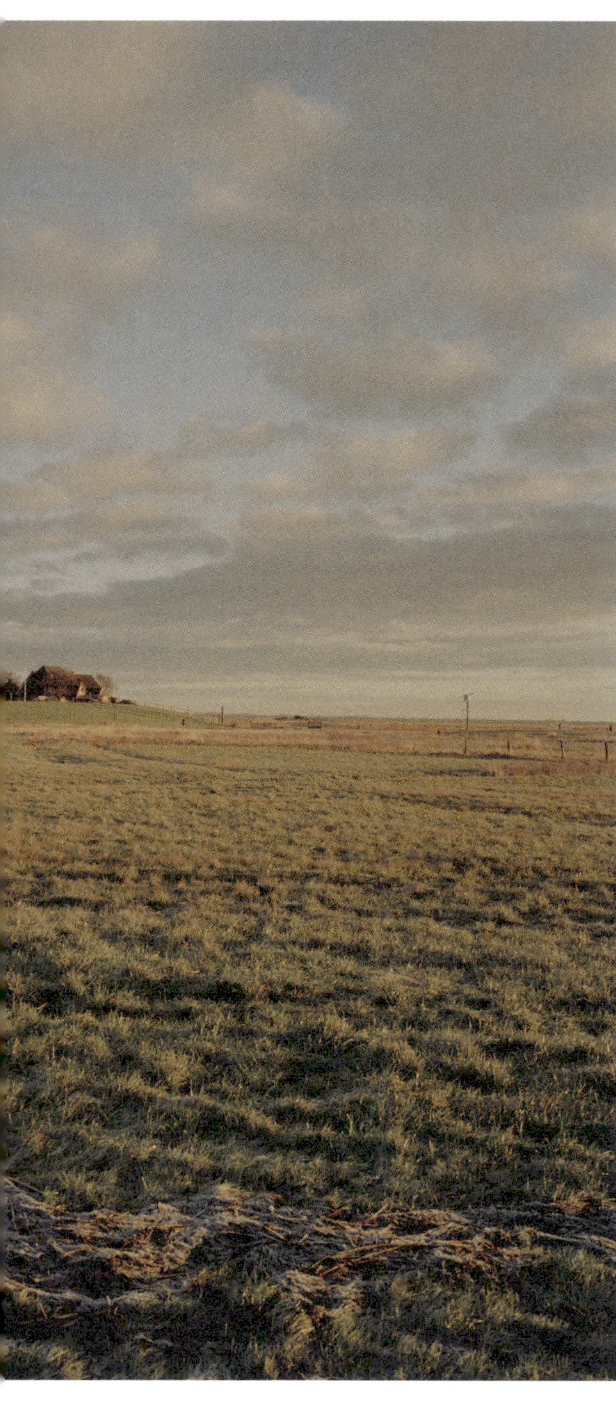

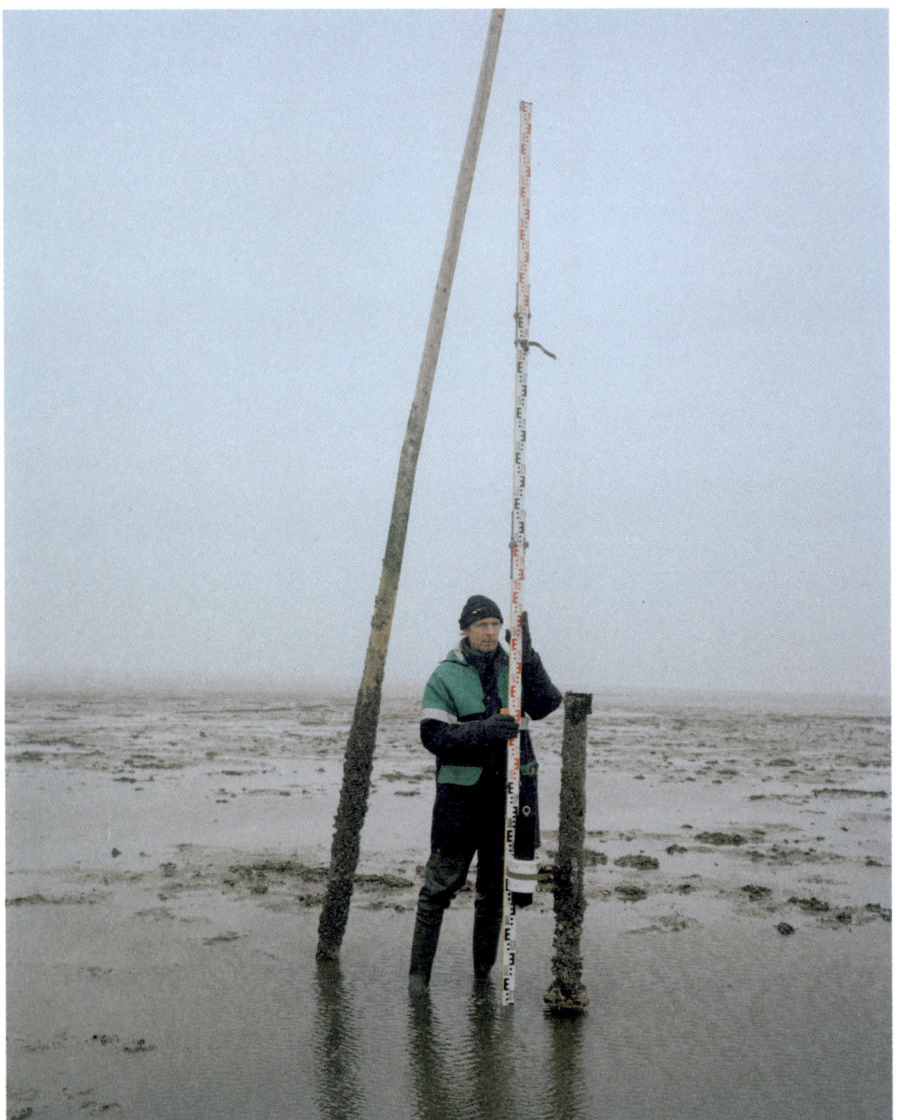

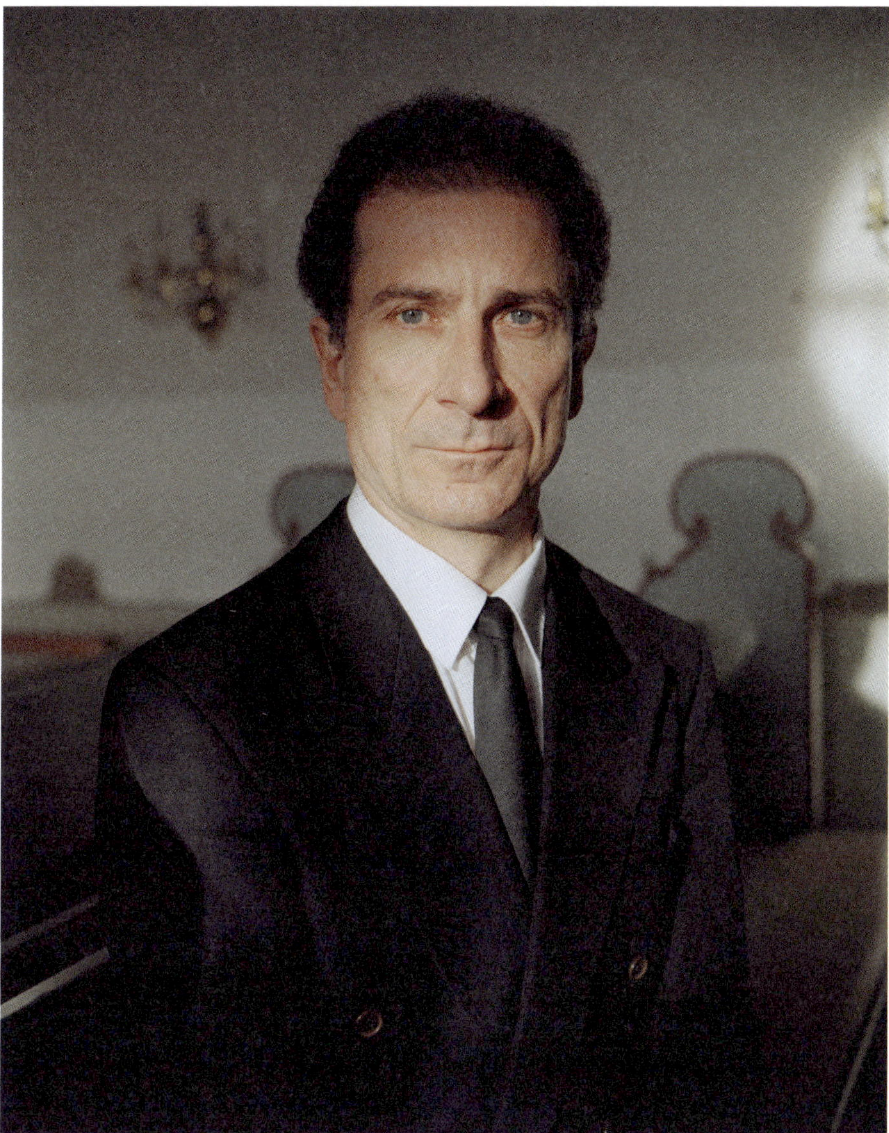

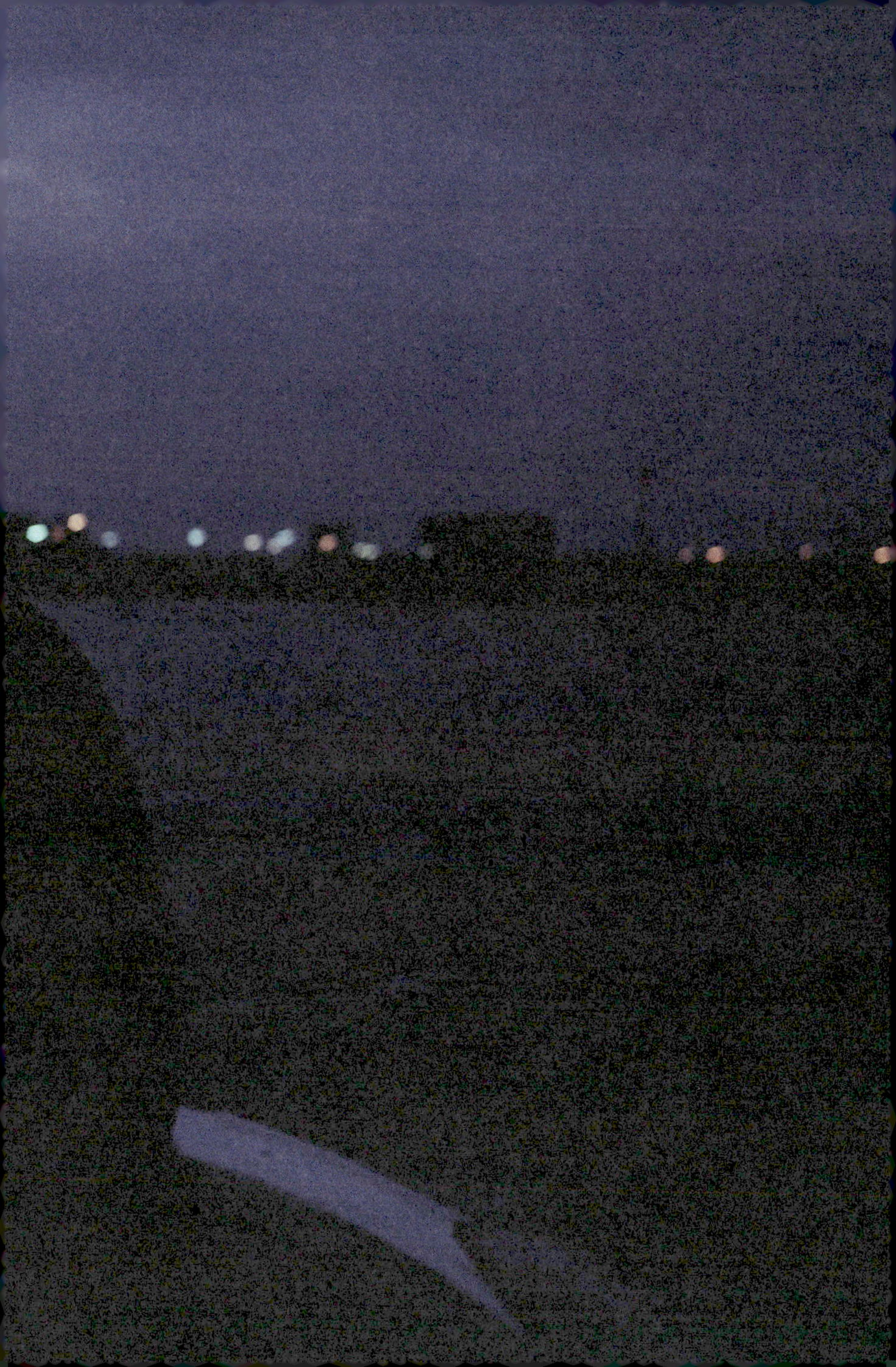

29

The outside temperature was about 45 degrees Celsius when the inferno started. Within 10 days, the Monchique wildfire destroyed 27,000 hectares of forest. There were no deaths because of the solidarity and support amongst the local population, but more than 50 residential houses were completely destroyed in Europe's largest forest fire of 2018.

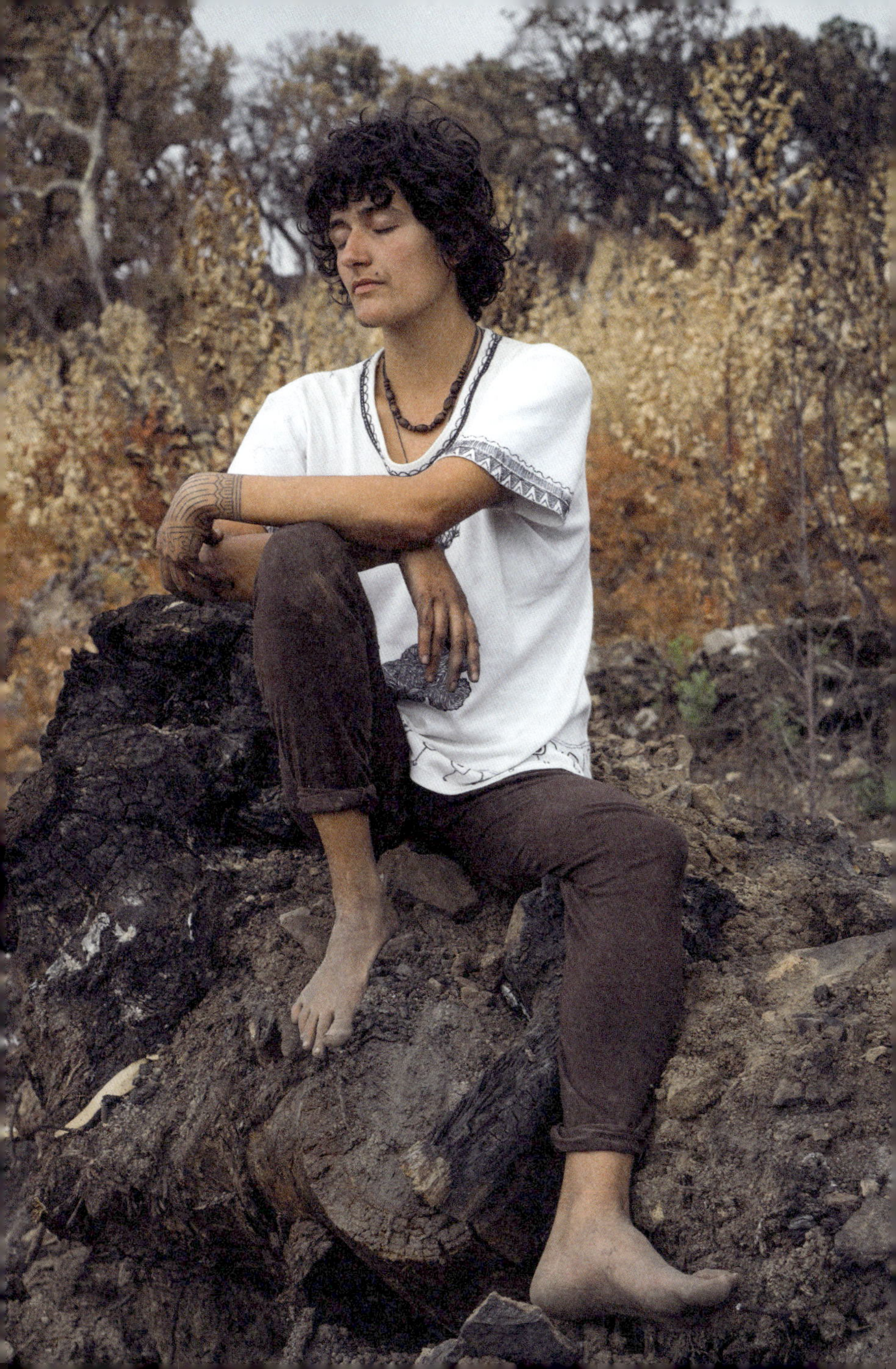

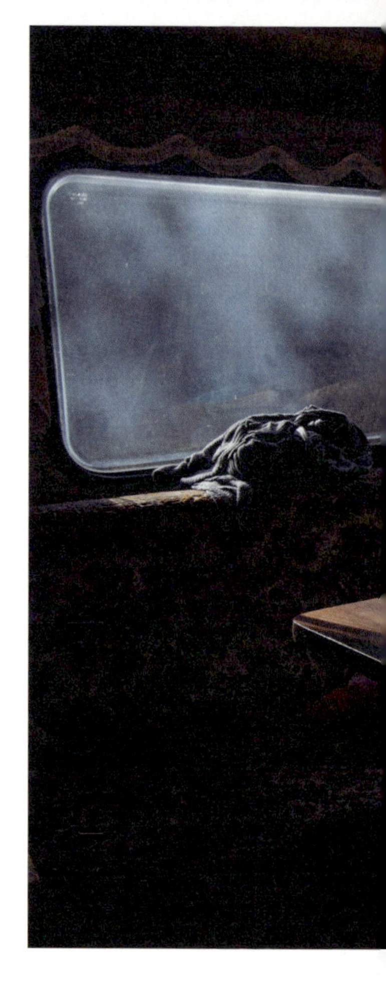

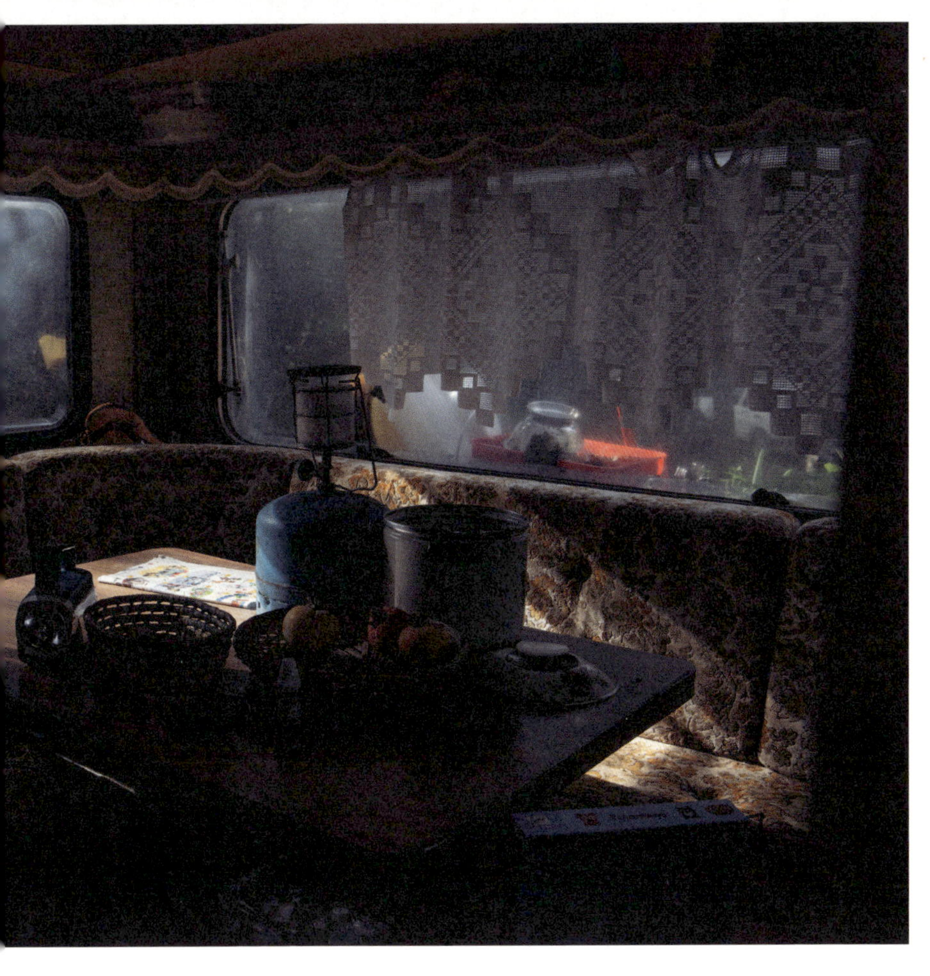

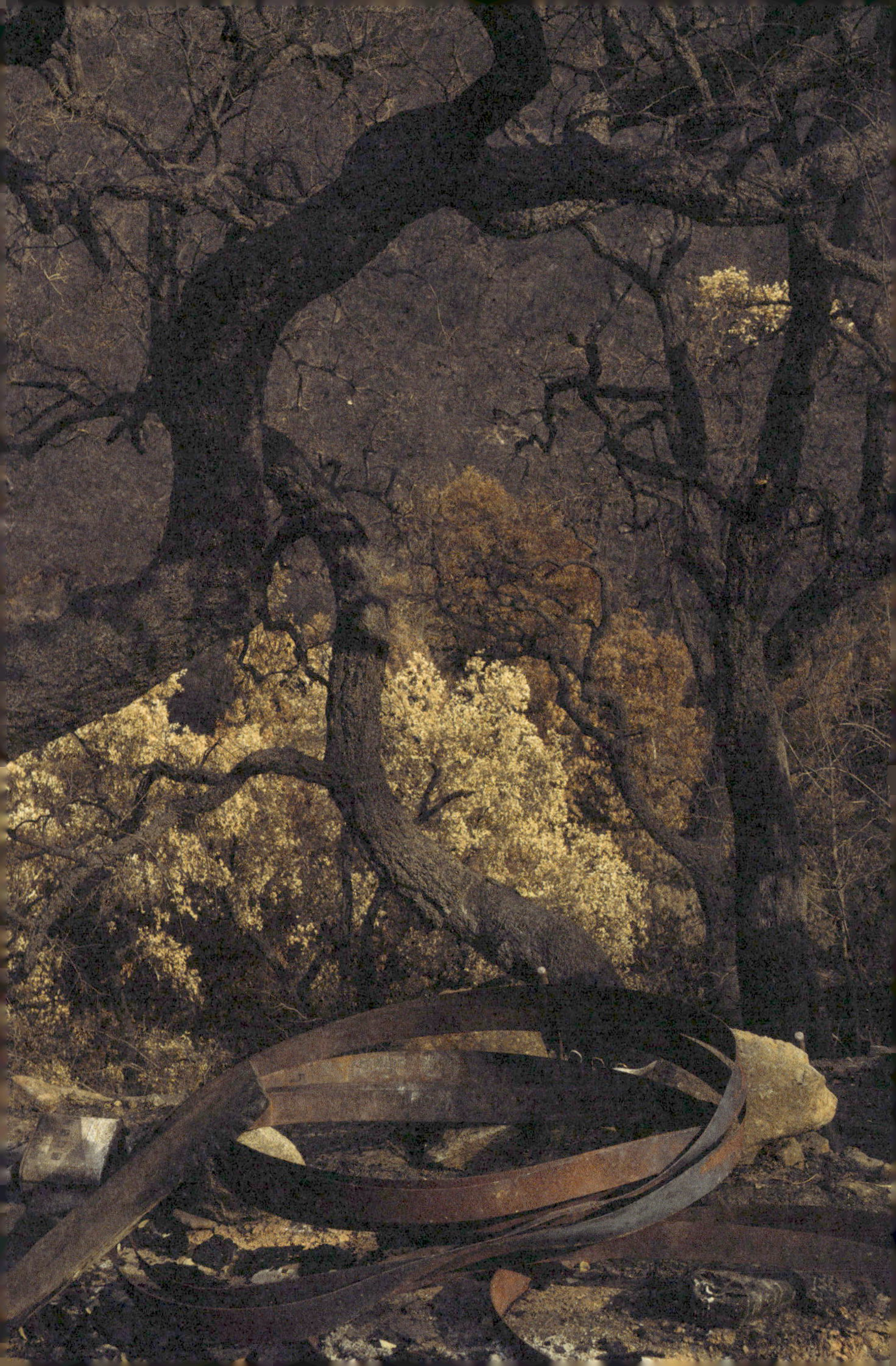

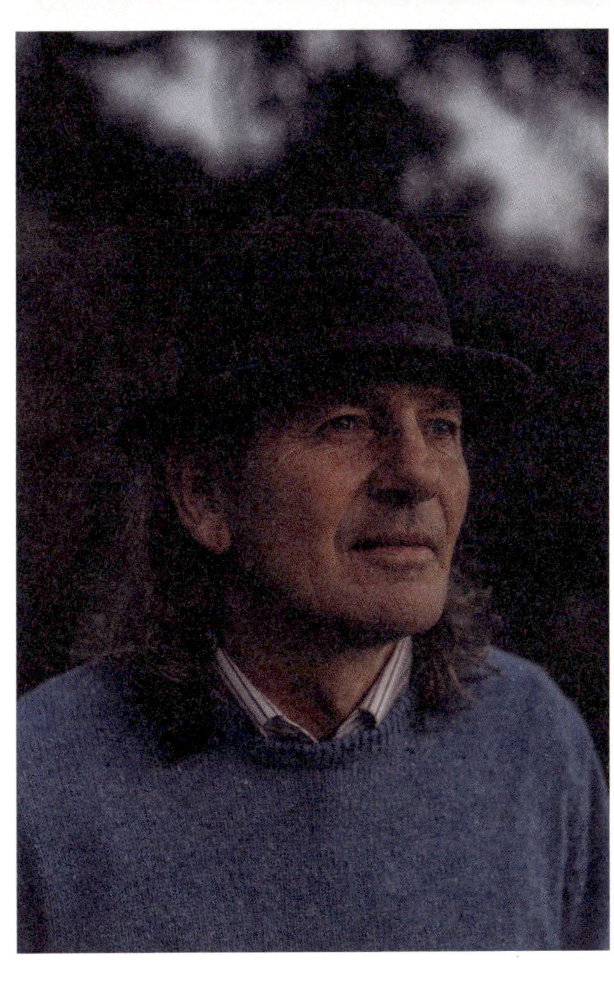

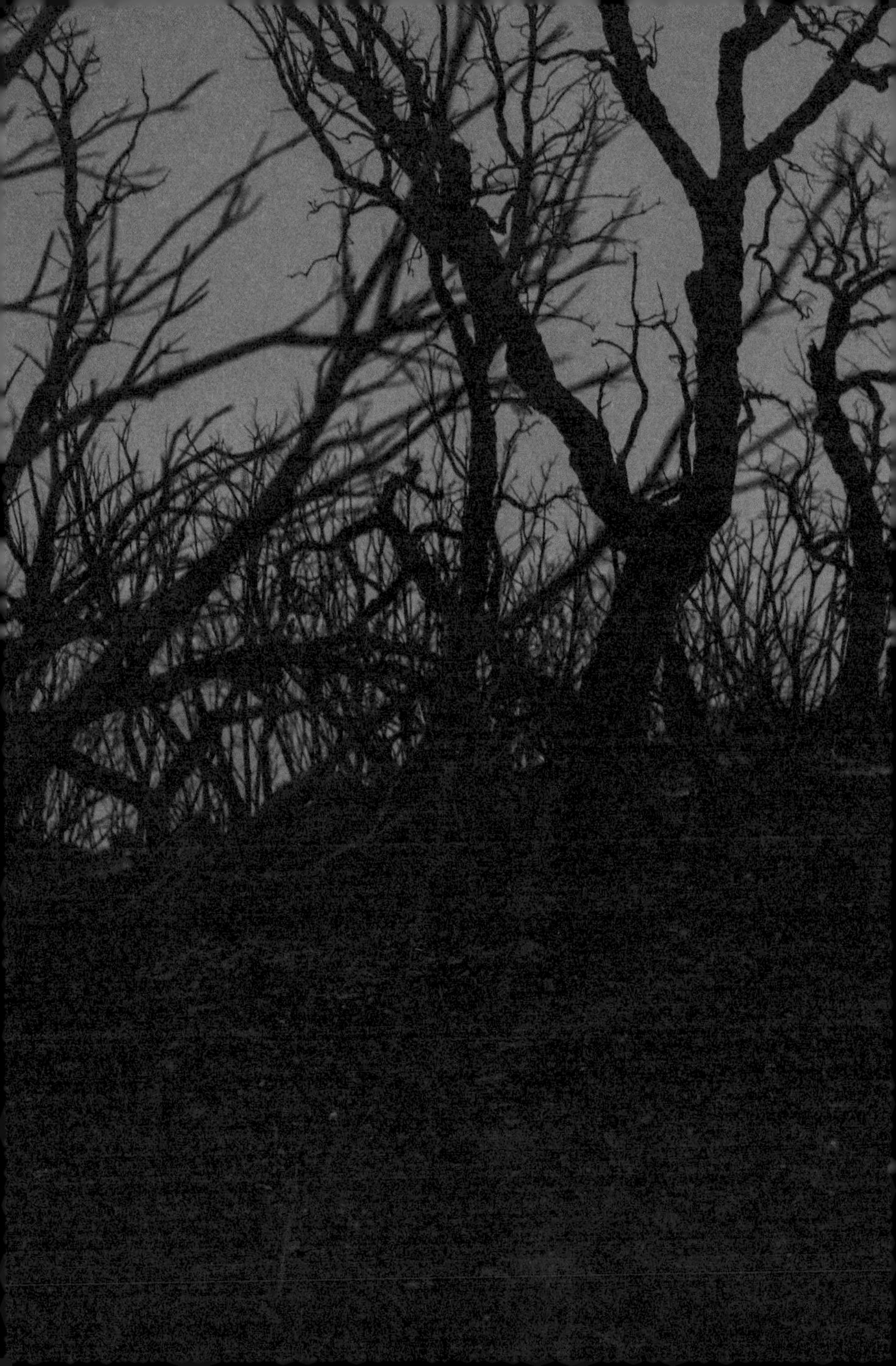

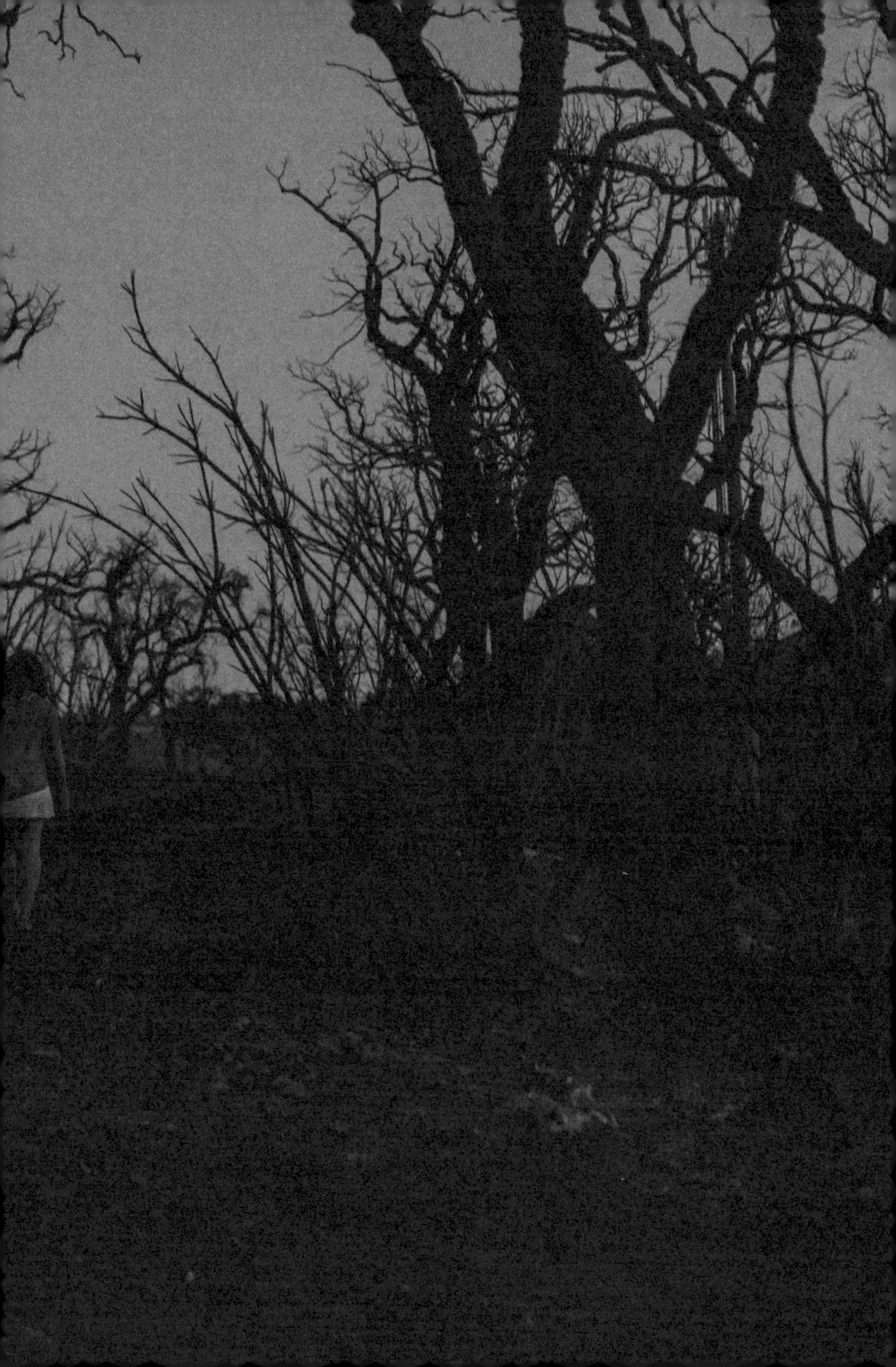

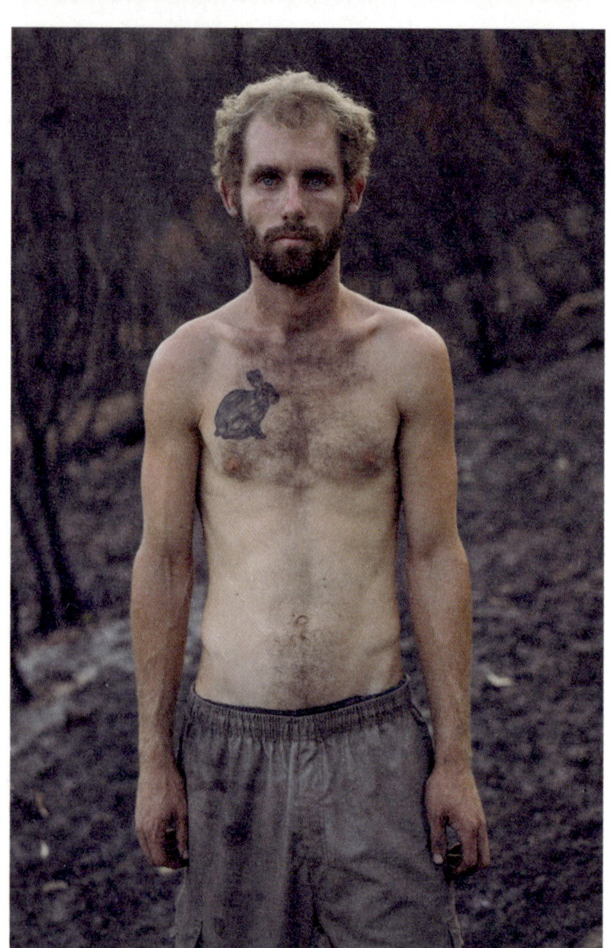

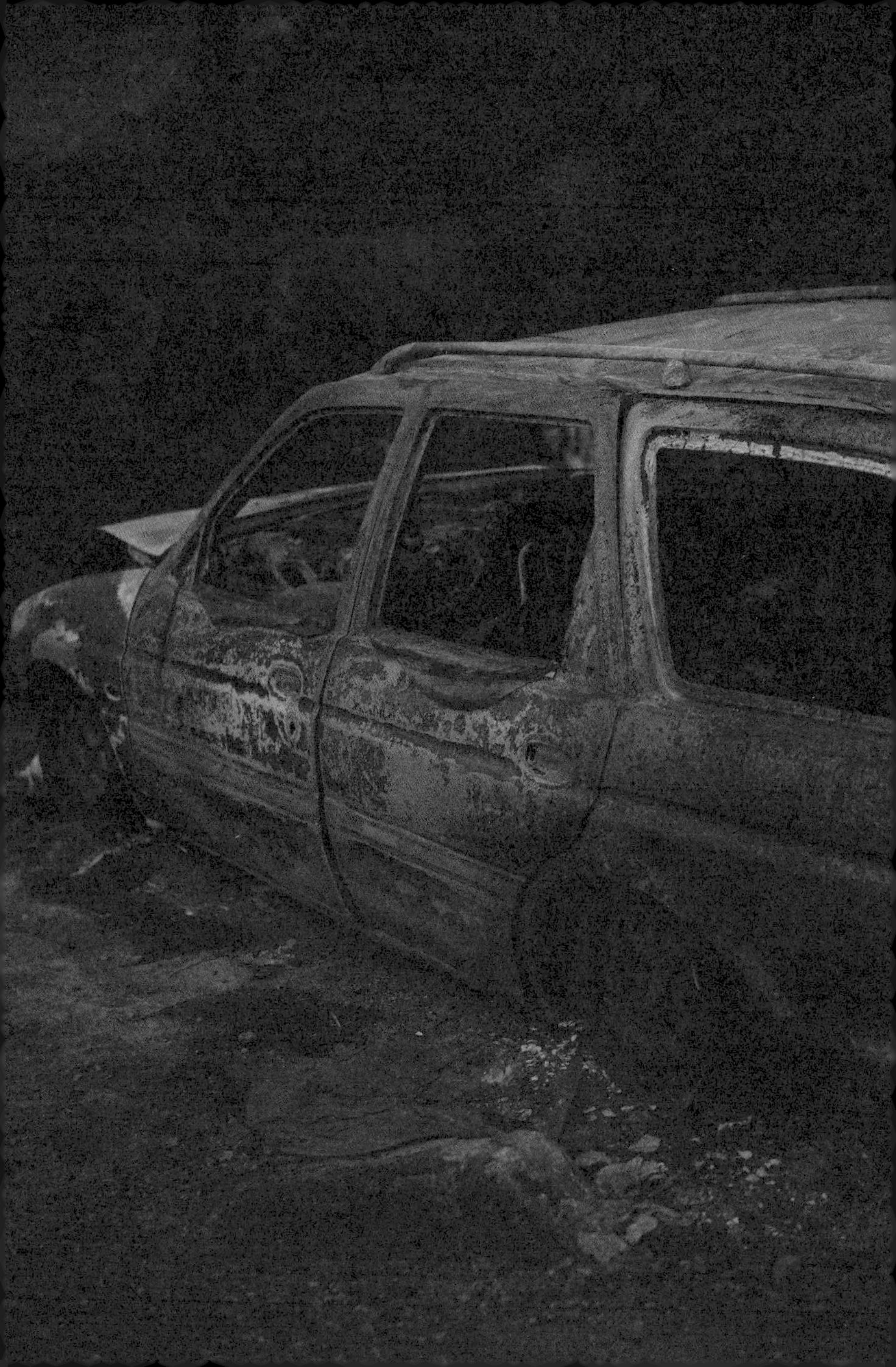

Katja Sterzik
Wolfgang Gähtgens
Ronja Hermann
Florian Genz

Walpurgisnacht

30

Each year during Walpurgis night, witches and demons meet on top of the Blocksberg, worshiping Satan by dancing and feasting till dawn. This Christian conspiracy theory claimed countless victims during the witch hunts of the early modern ages—and became one of the region's top tourist attractions.

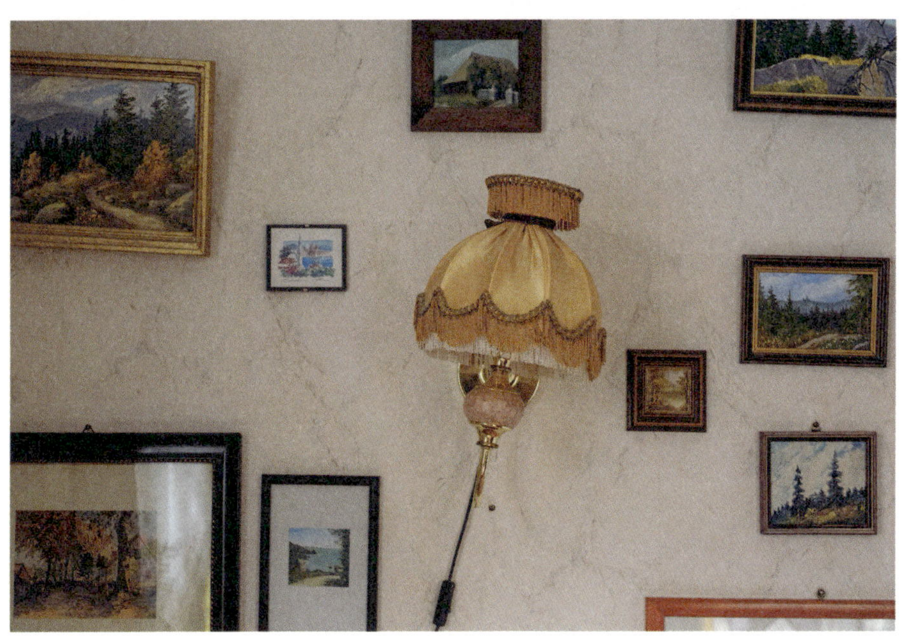

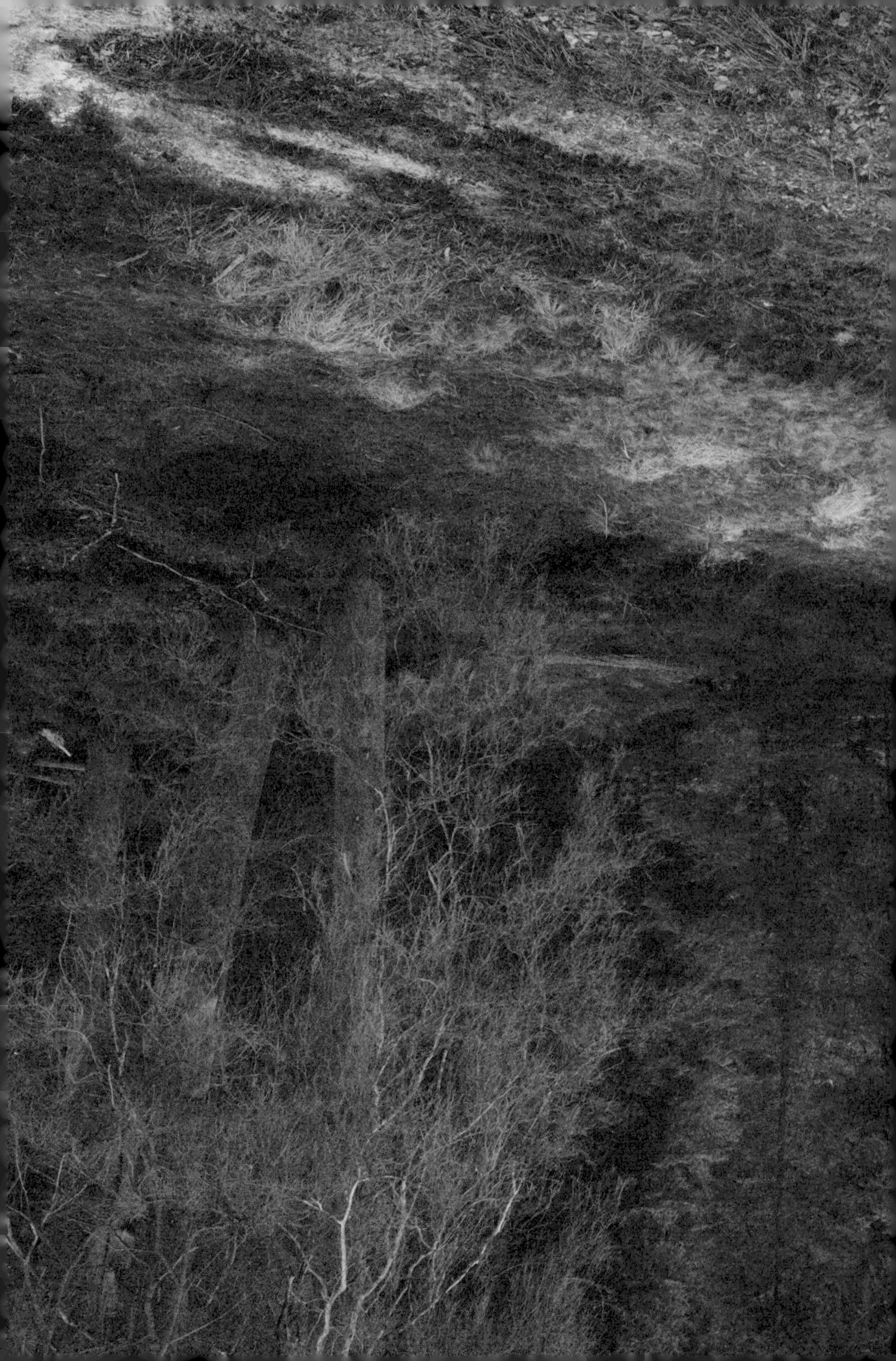

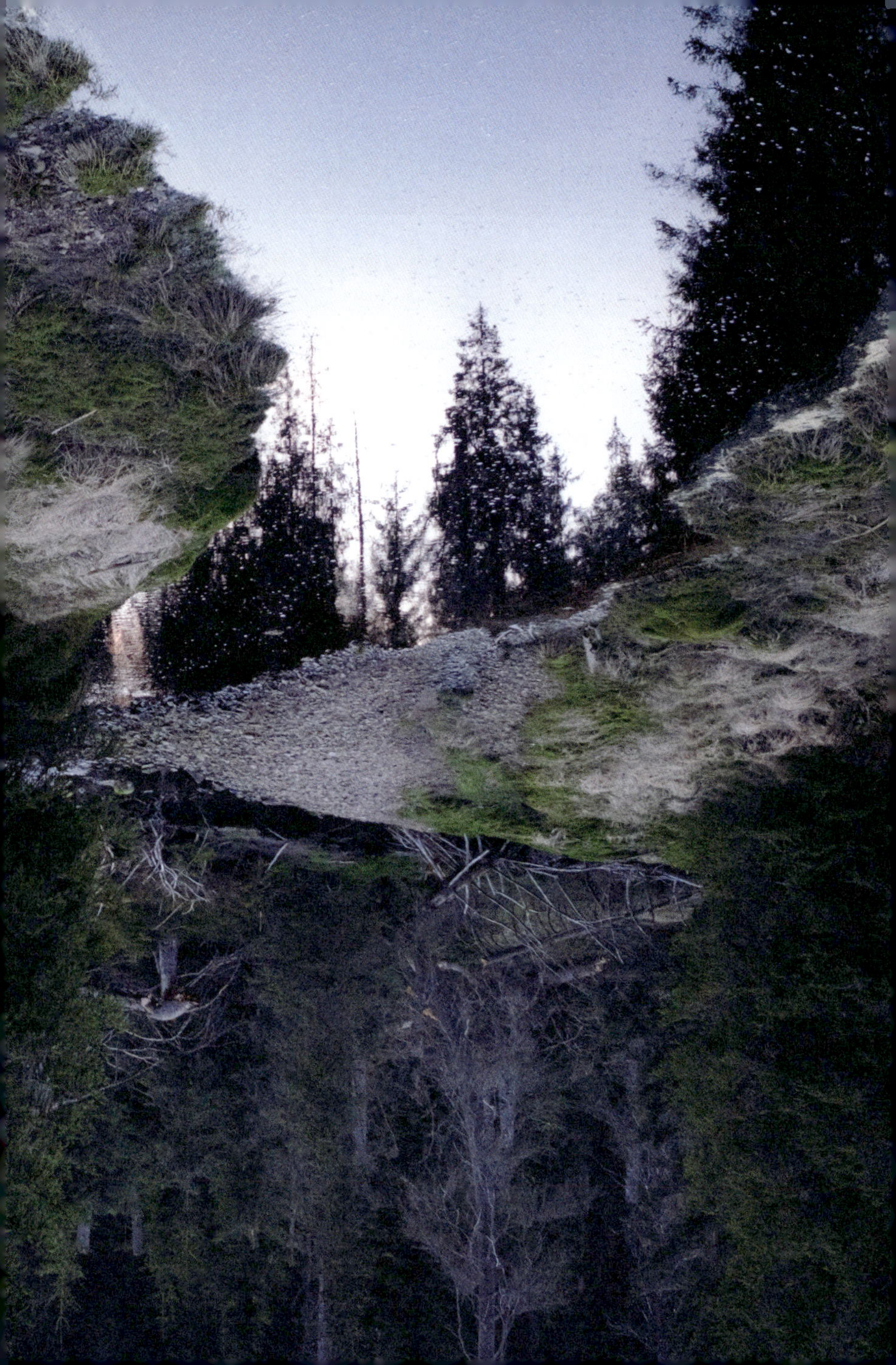

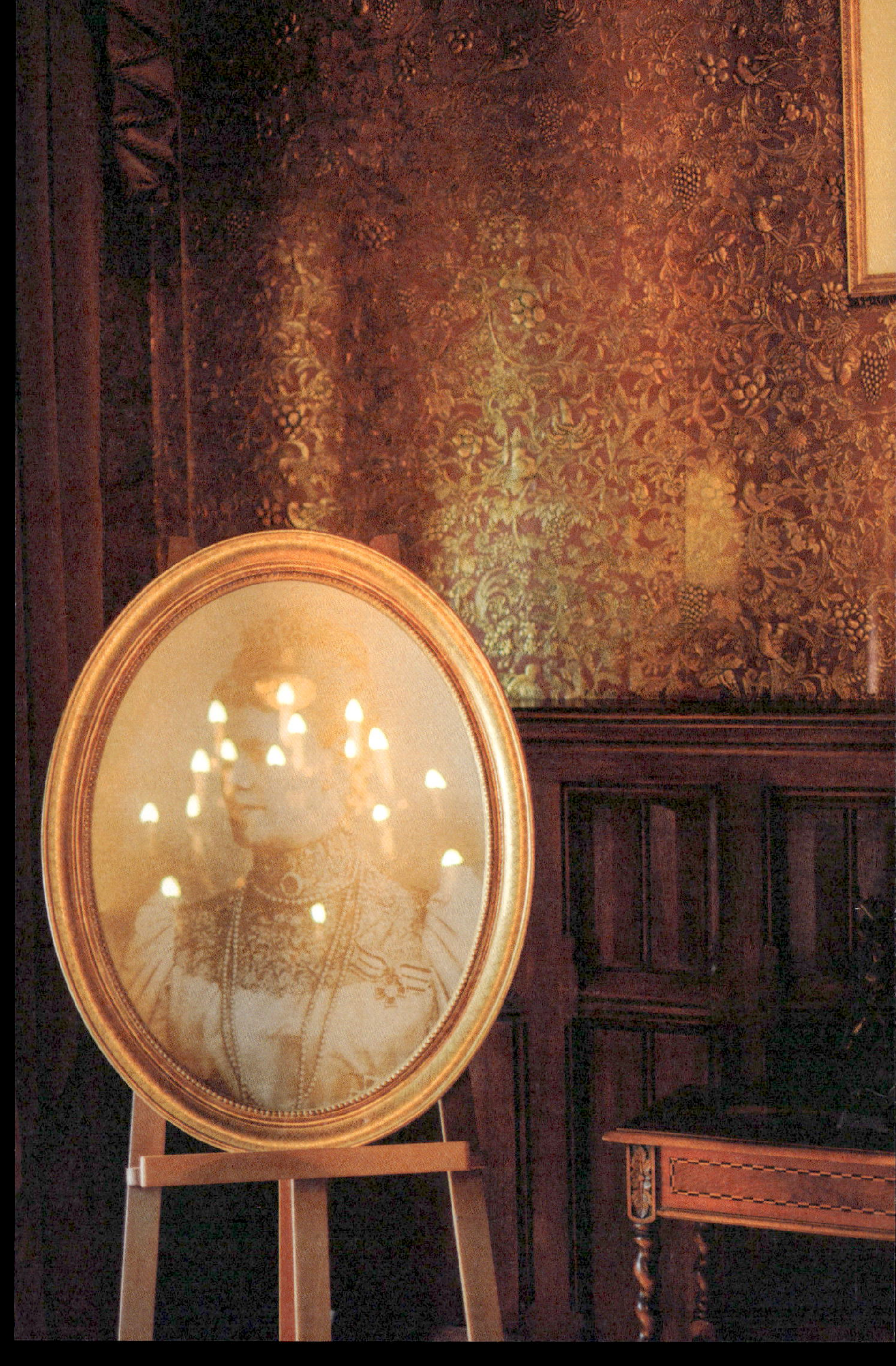

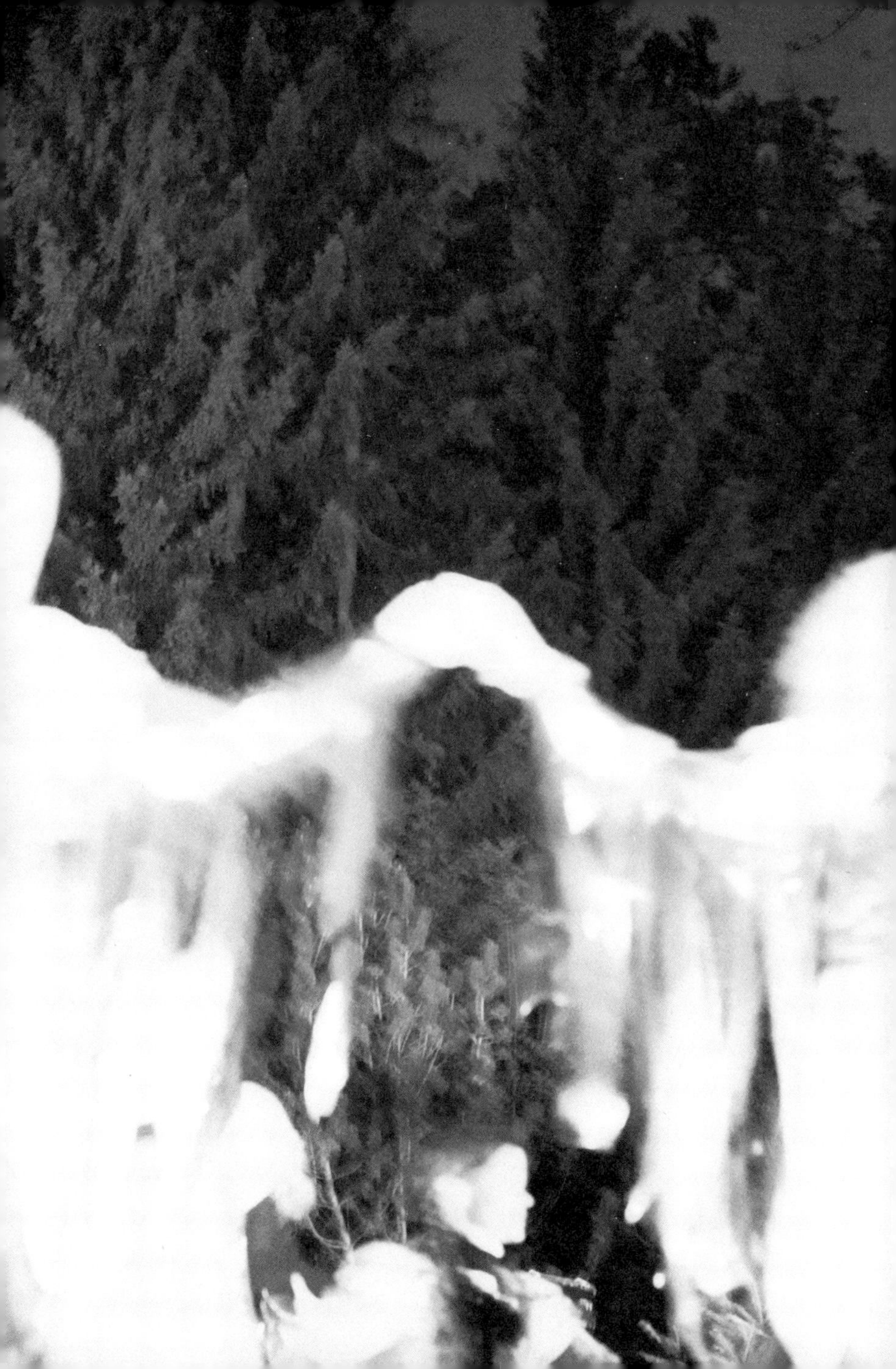

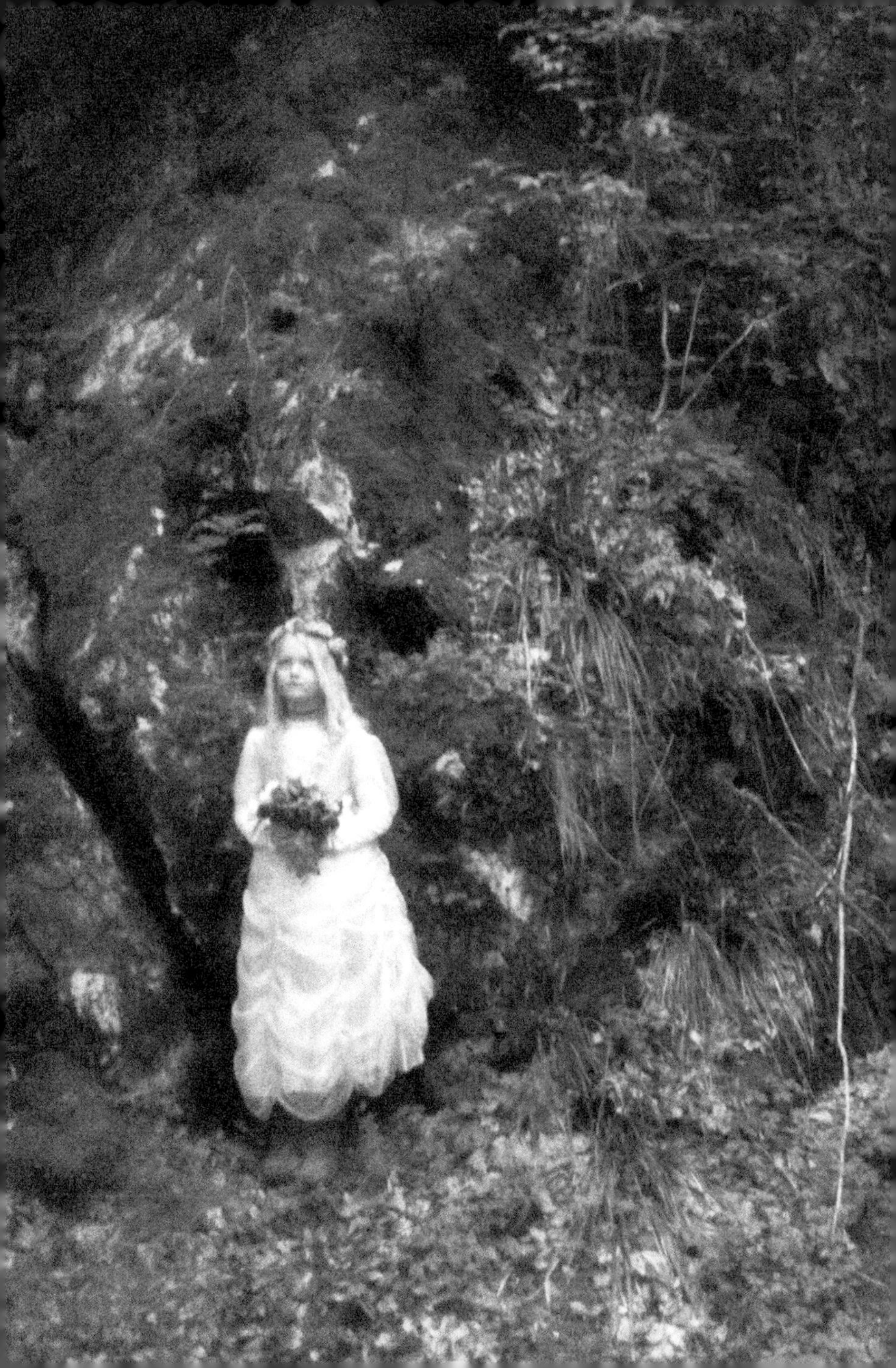

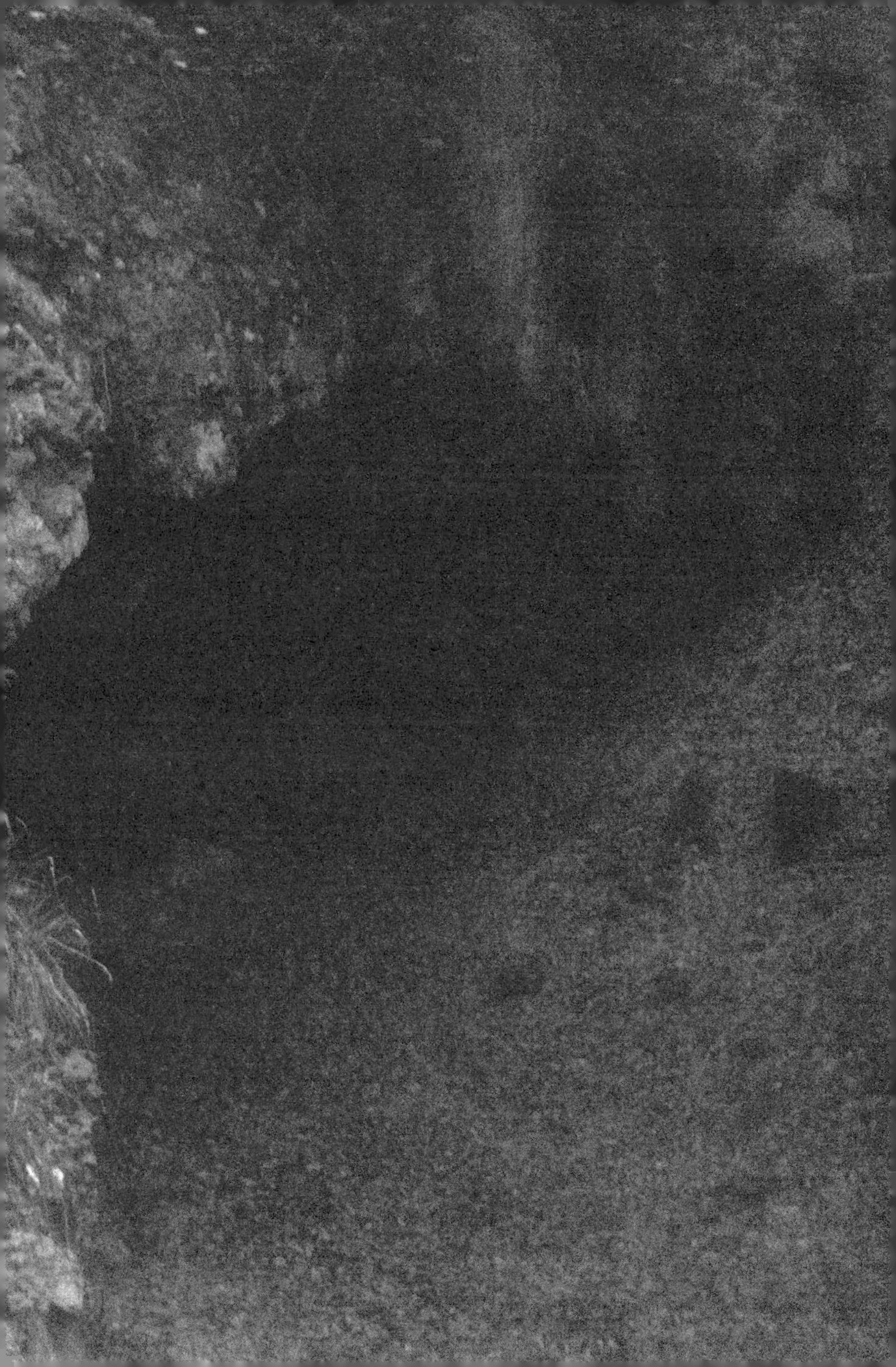

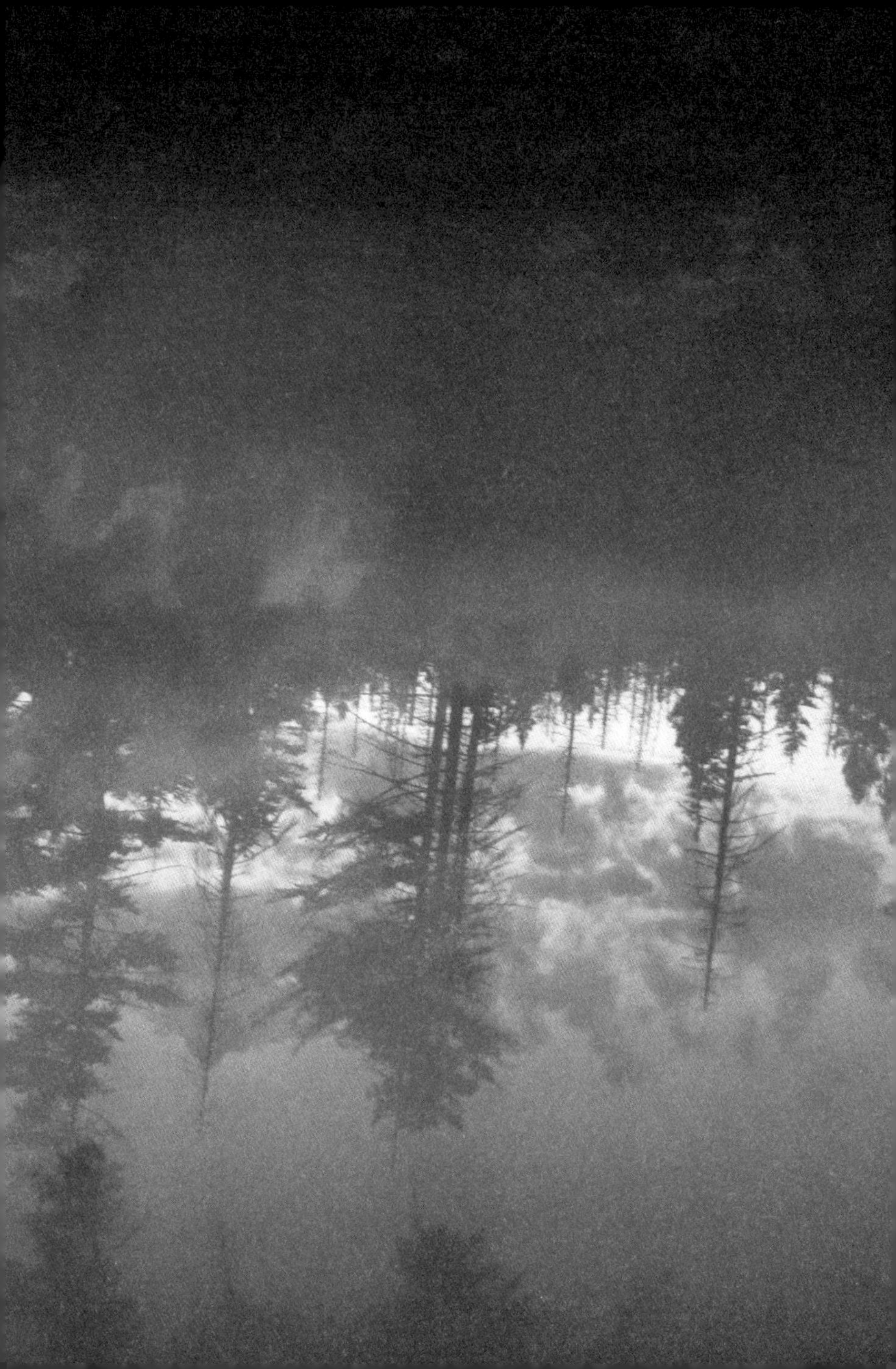

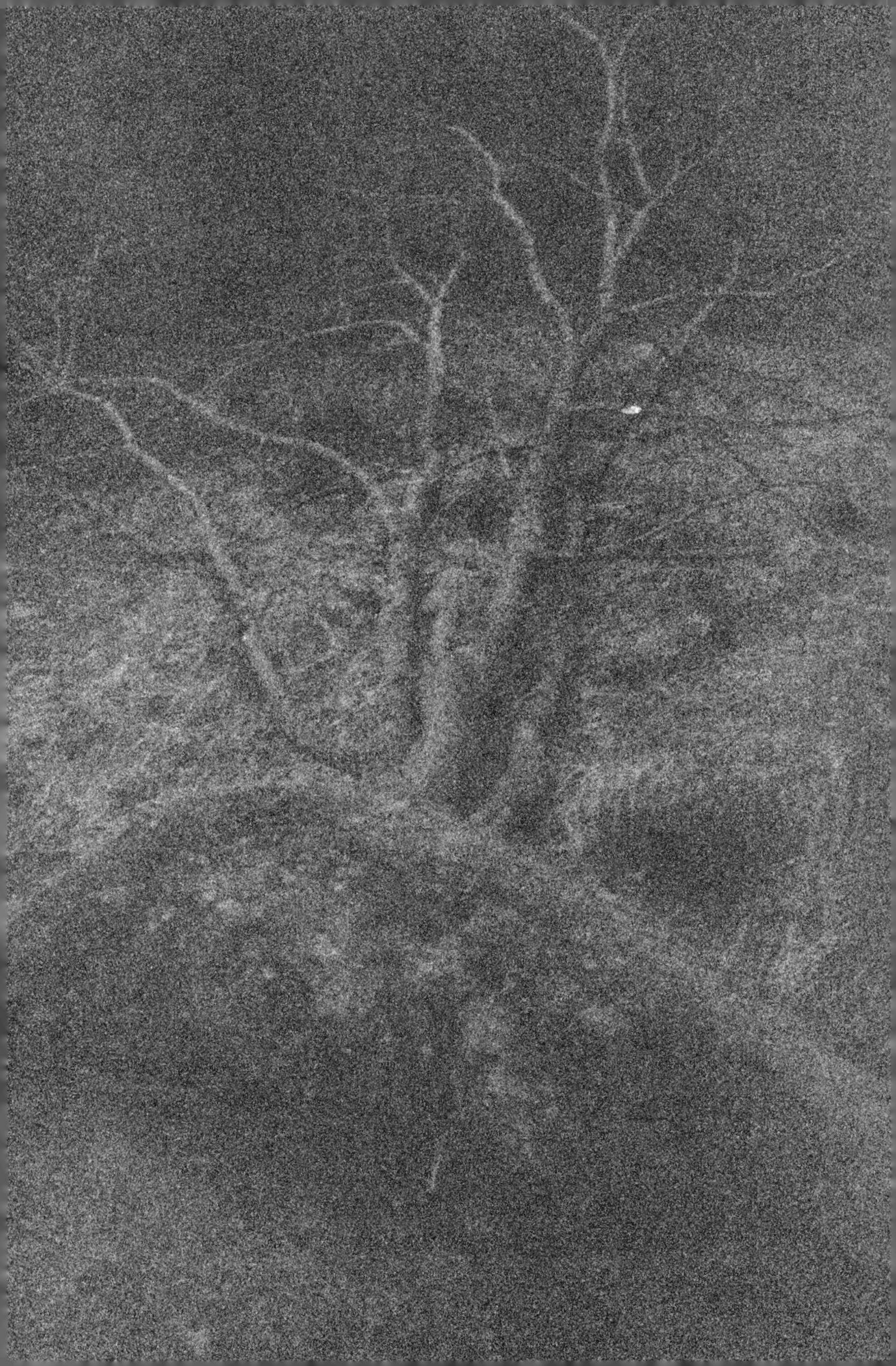

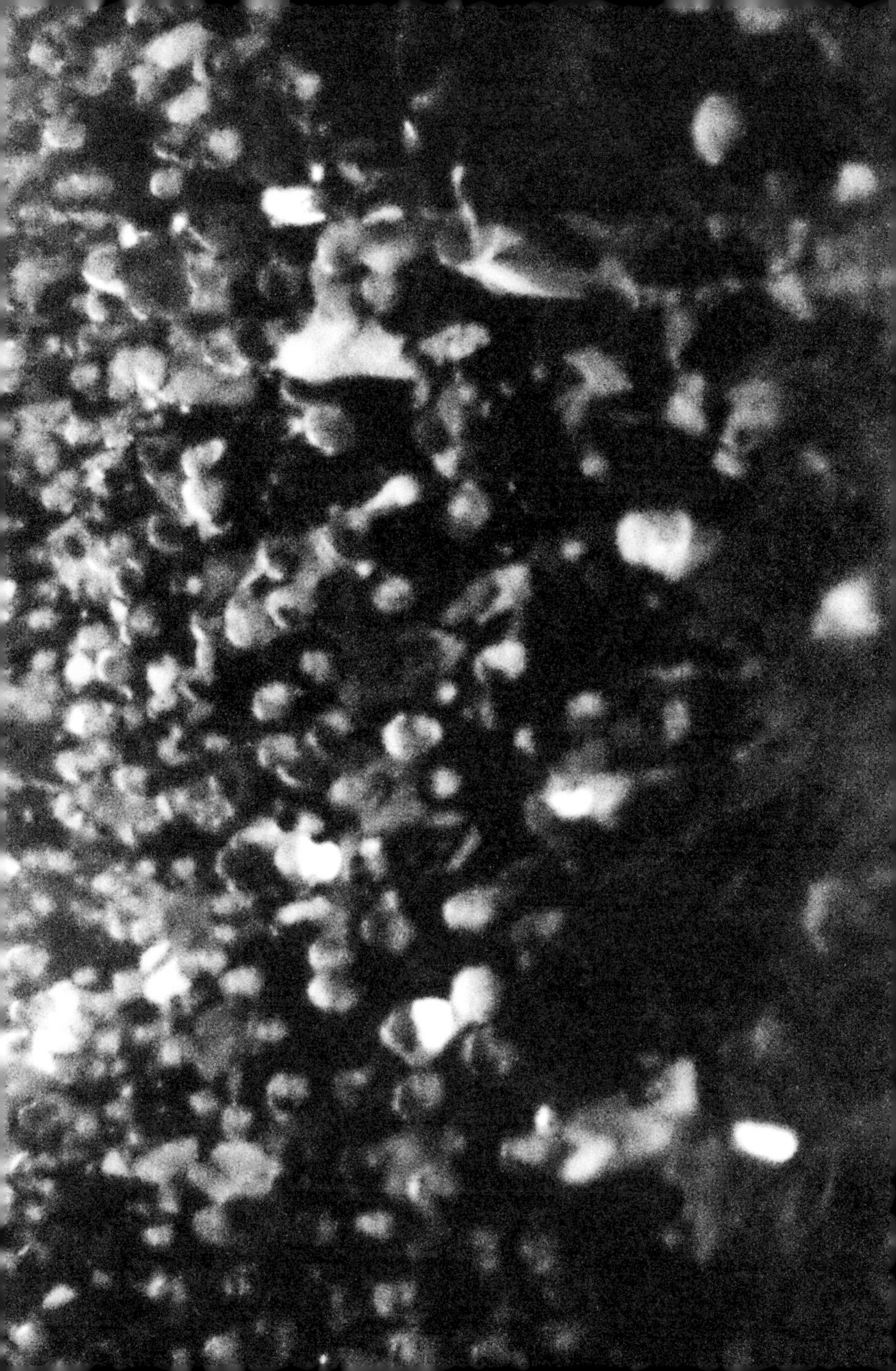

Monika Hanfland

Püppi Arrived.

31

Can dolls replace a human partner? The modular doll system lets you decide what your future partner will look like. Will we develop new types of relationships, in which we do not have to strive for affection anymore?

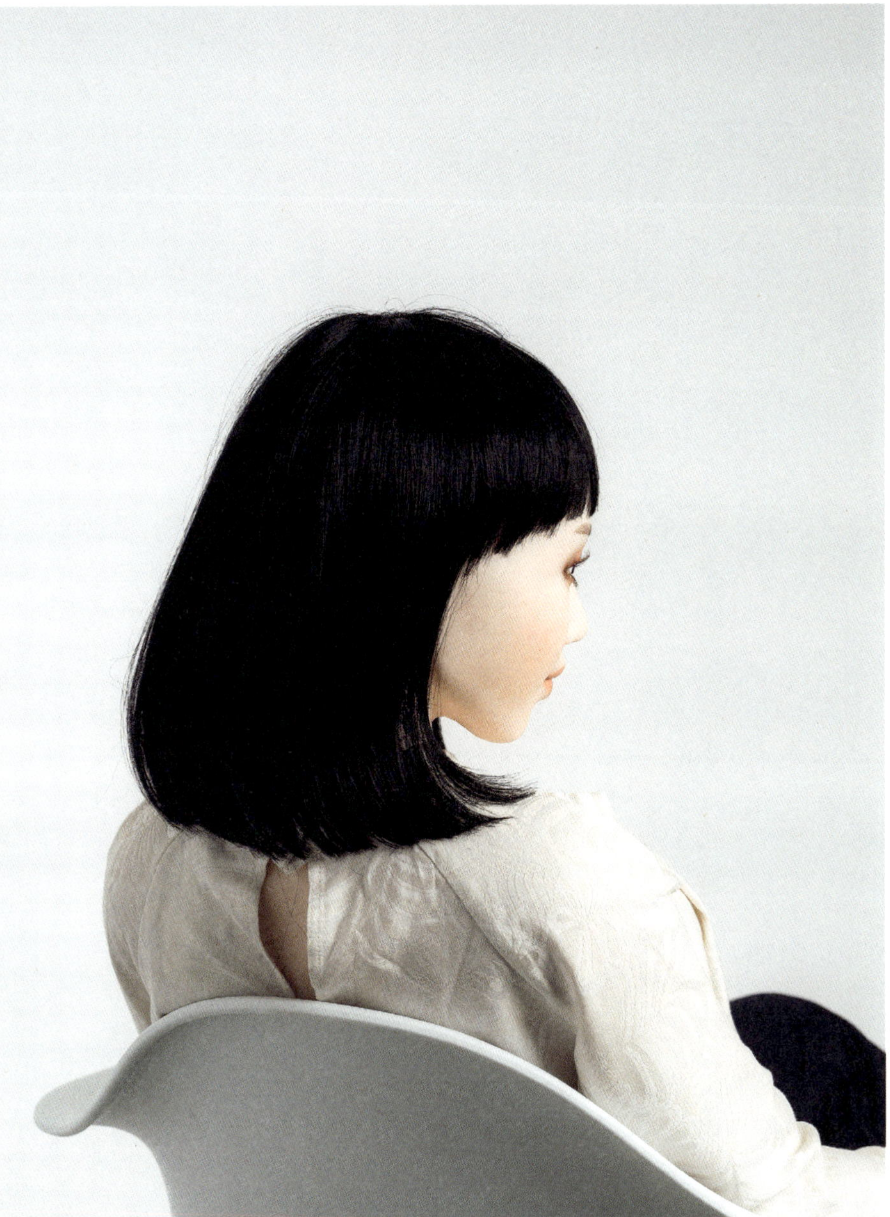

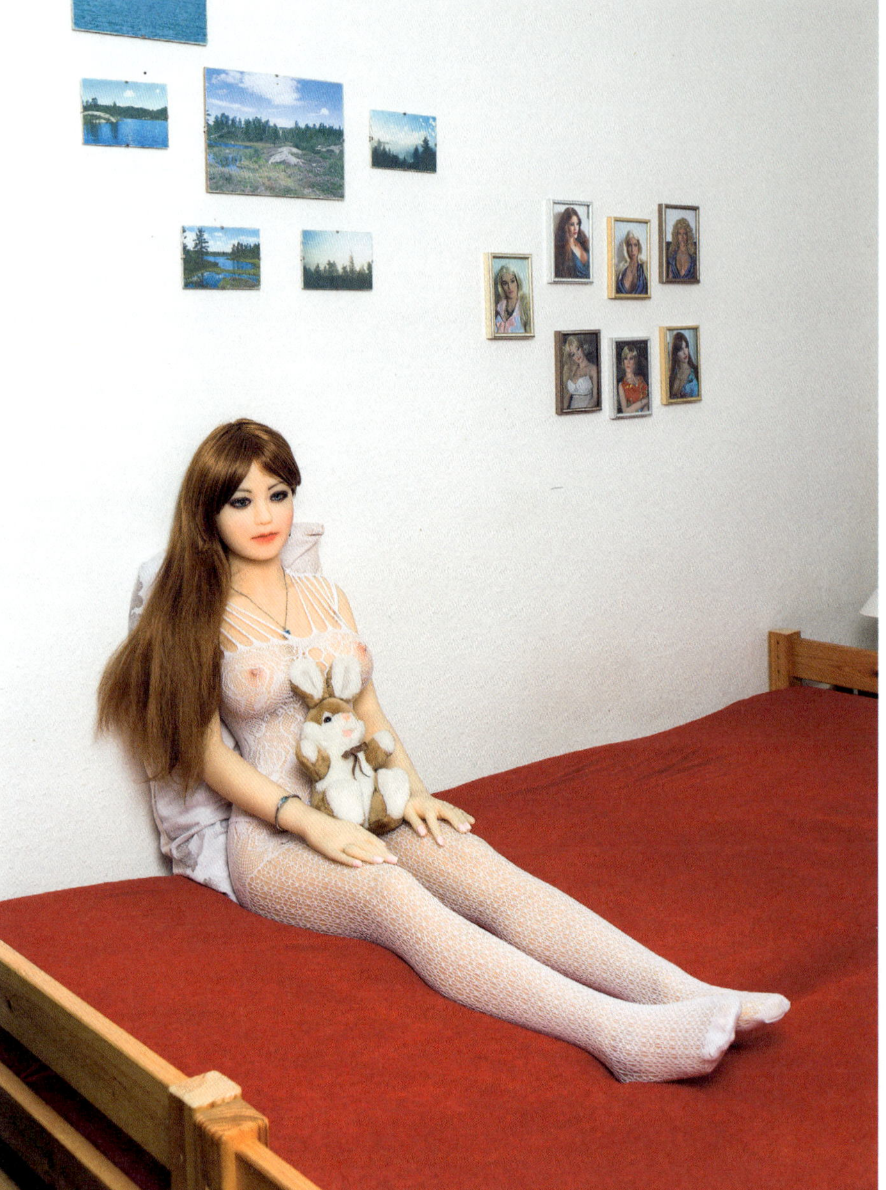

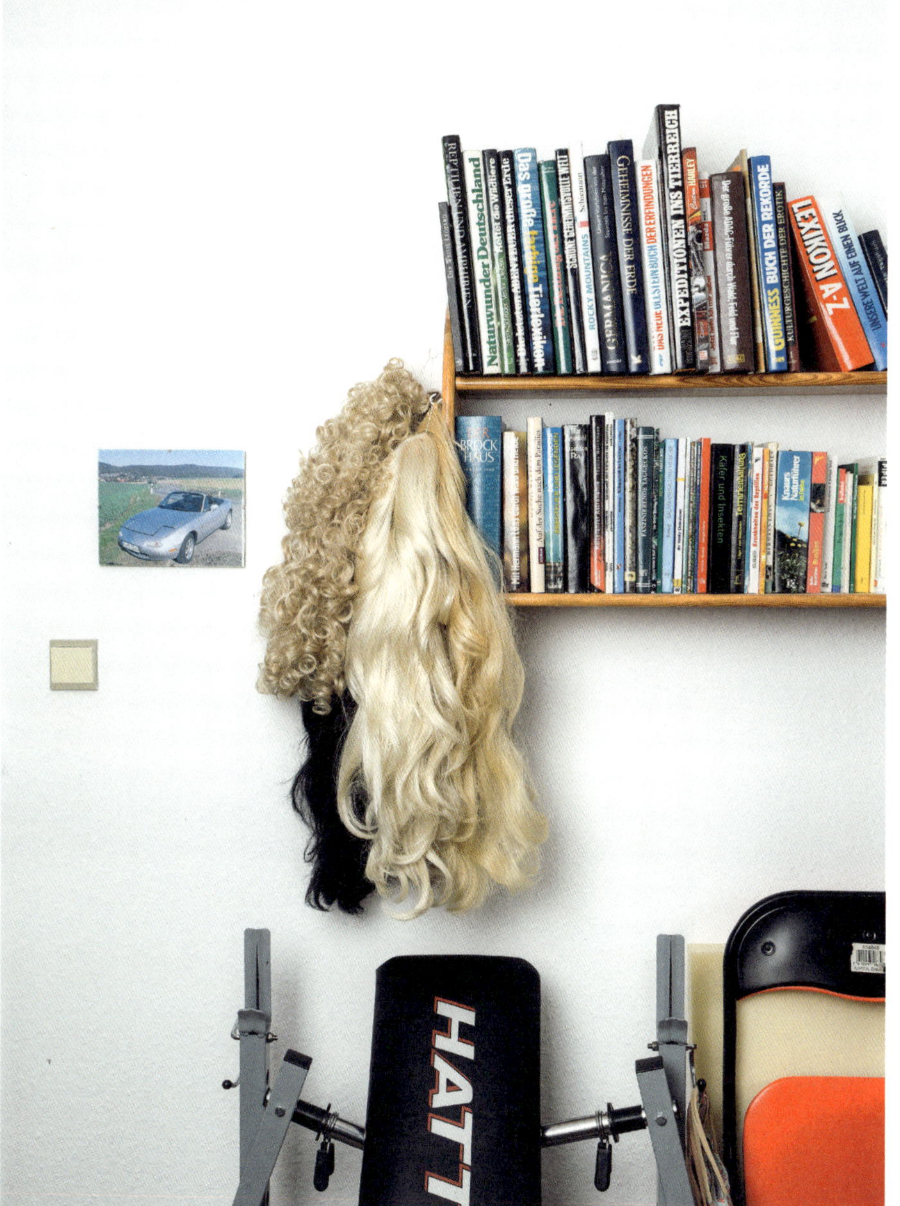
REPTILIEN UND AMPHIBIEN
Naturwunder Deutschland
Das große farbige Tierlexikon
ROCKY MOUNTAINS
GERMANICA
GEHEIMNISSE DER ERDE
DAS NEUE ULLSTEIN BUCH DER ERFINDUNGEN
EXPEDITIONEN INS TIERREICH
GUINNESS BUCH DER REKORDE
KULTURGESCHICHTE DER EROTIK
LEXIKON A-Z
UNSERE WELT AUF EINEN BLICK
DER BROCKHAUS
Auf der Suche nach dem Paradies
Käfer und Insekten
Knaurs Naturführer
HAT

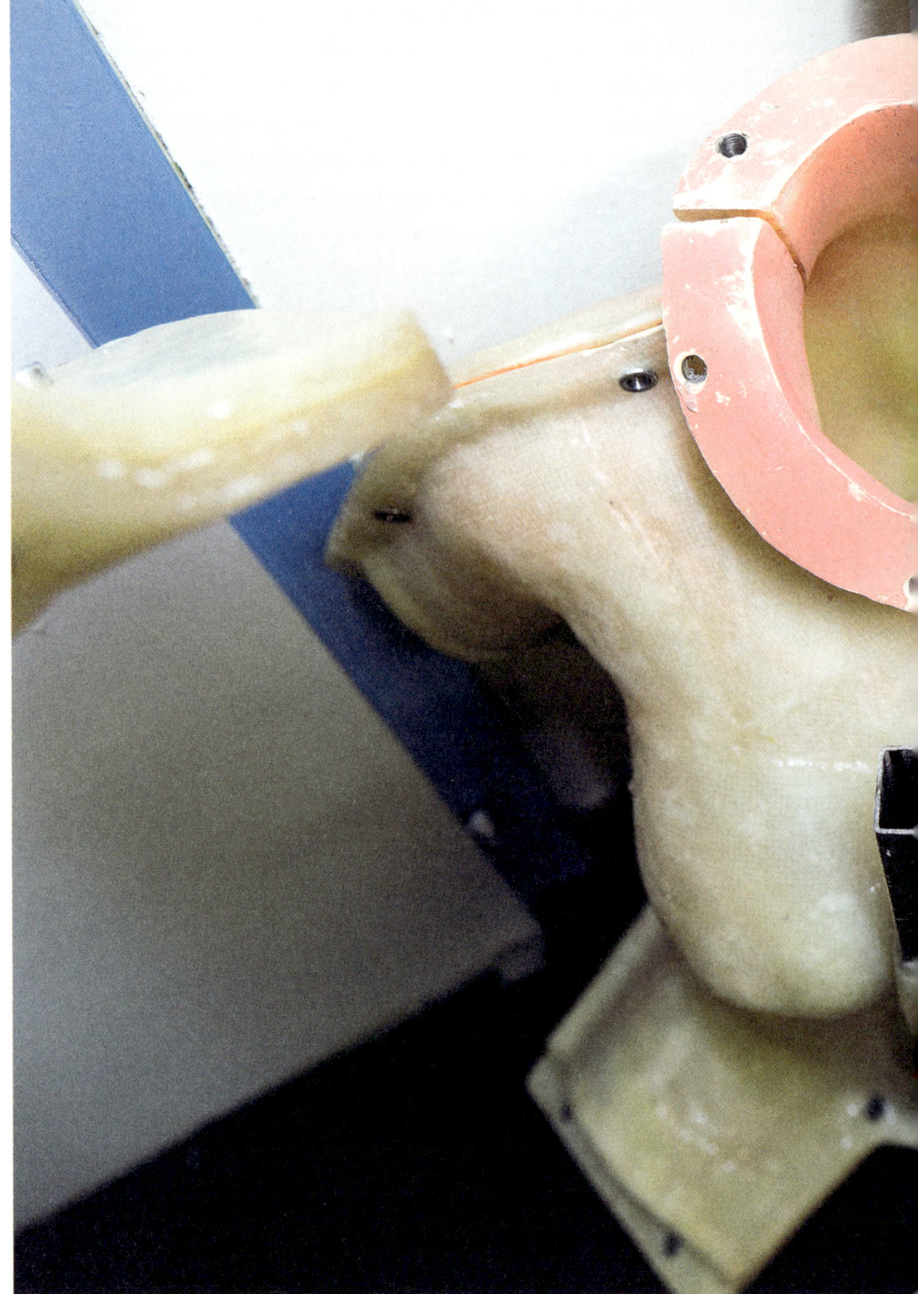

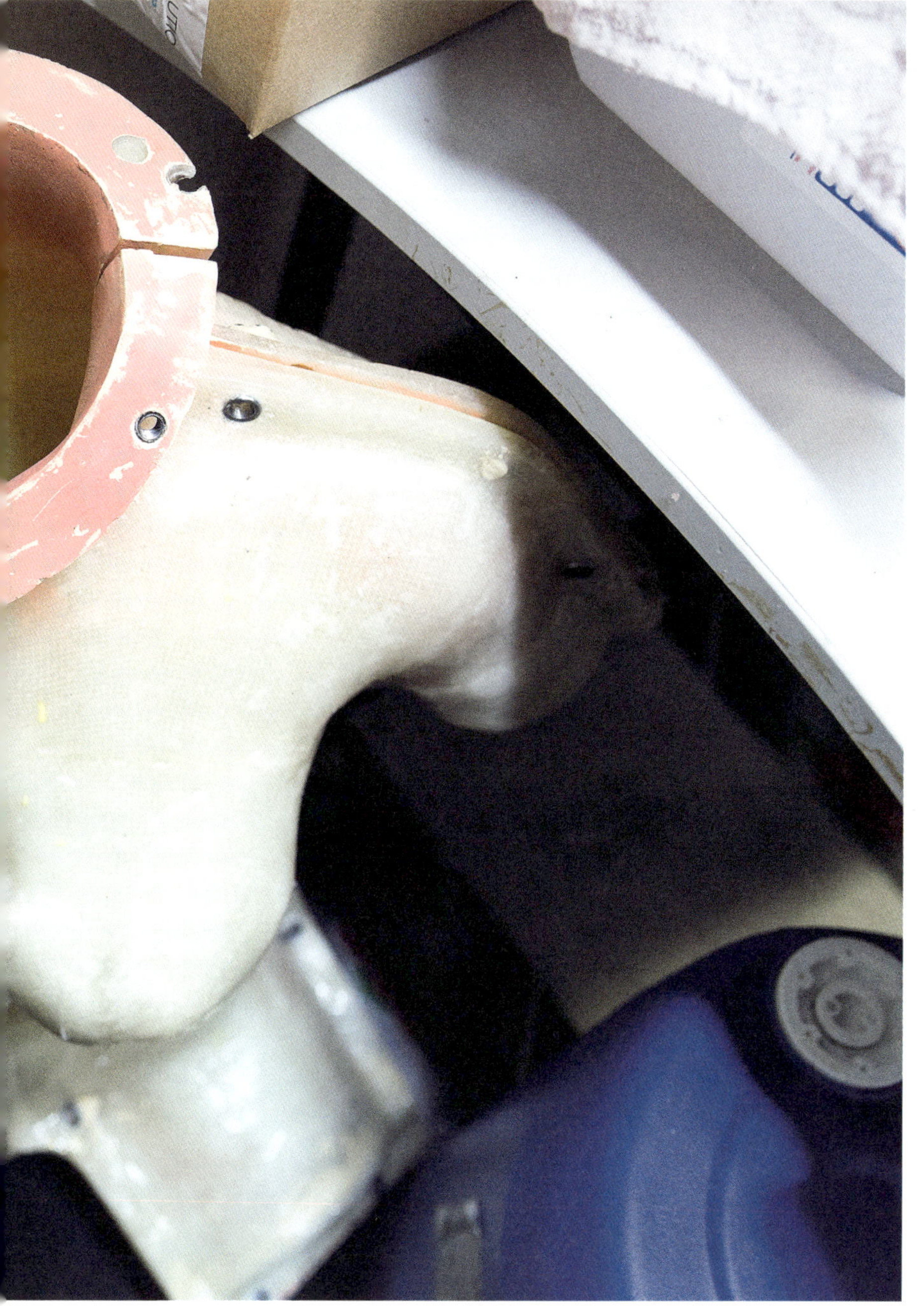

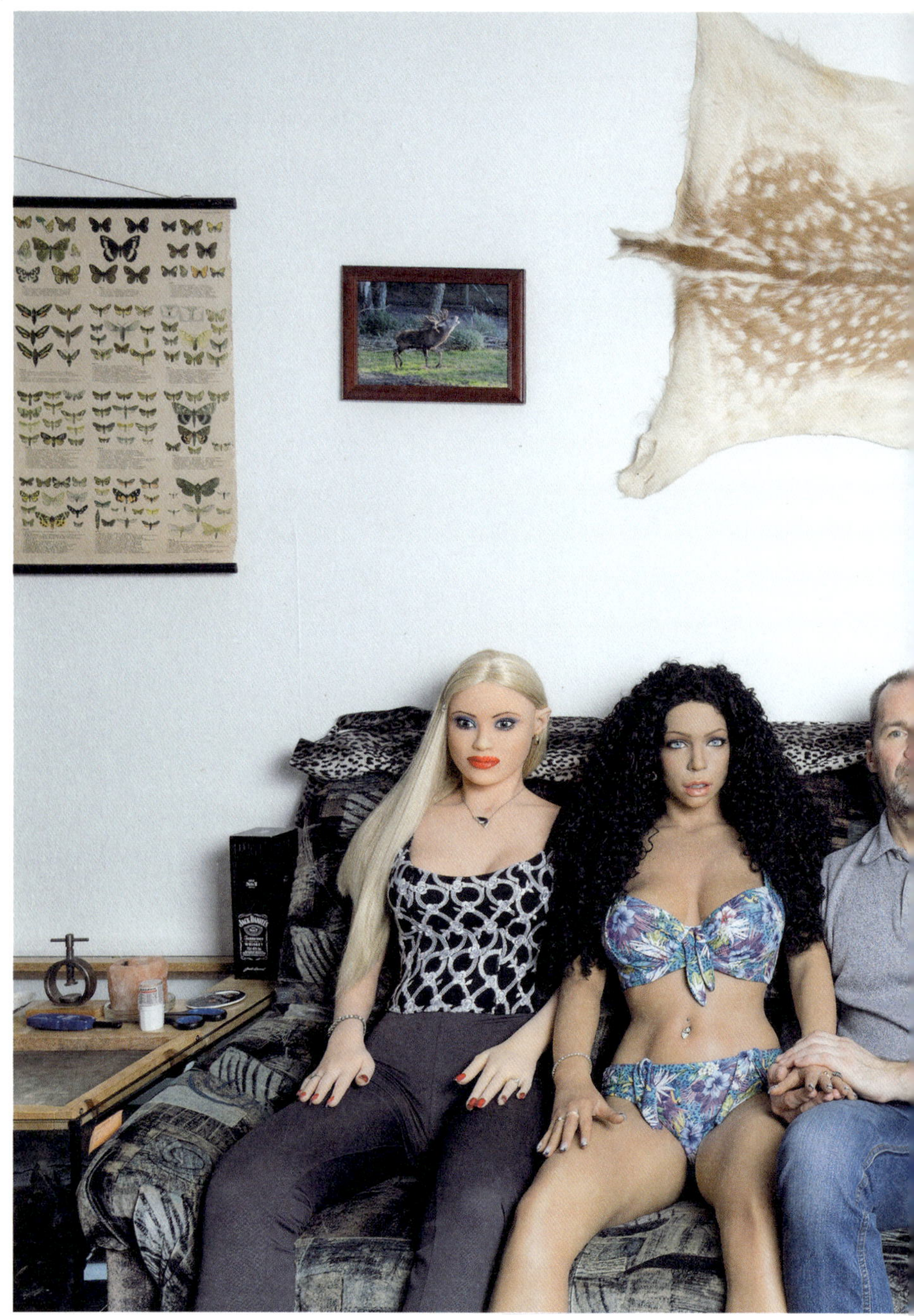
JACK DANIEL'S
WHISKEY

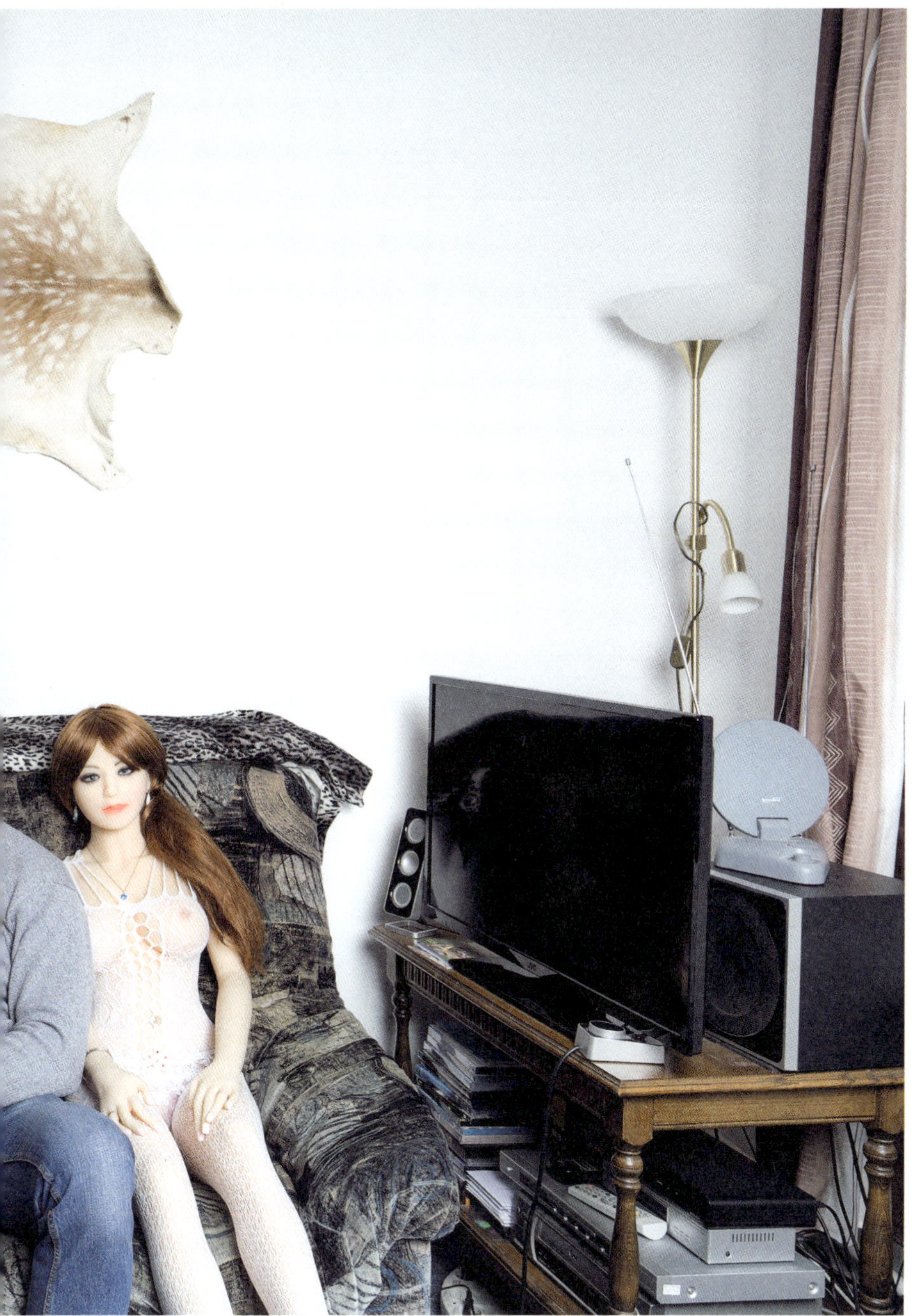

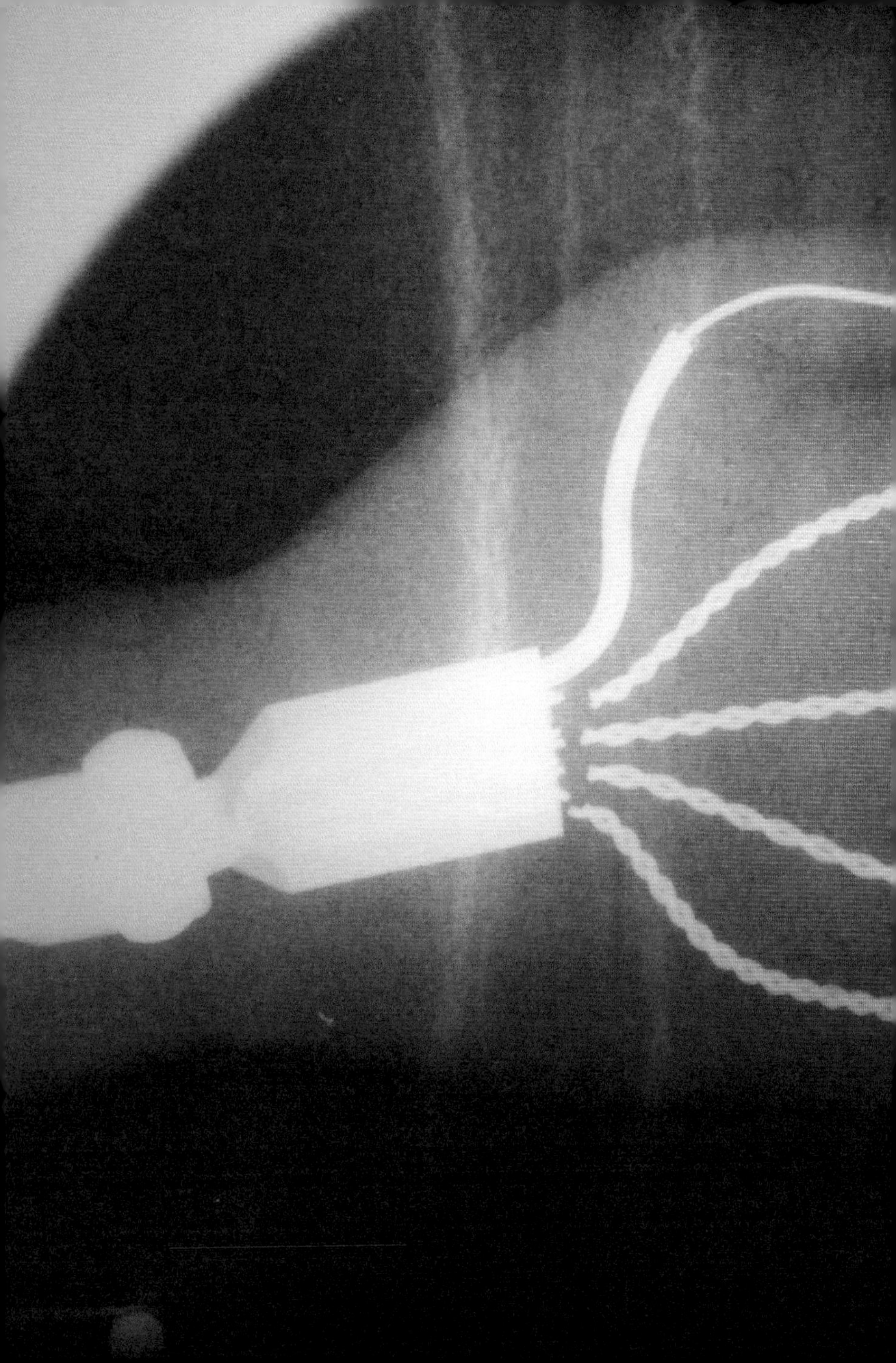

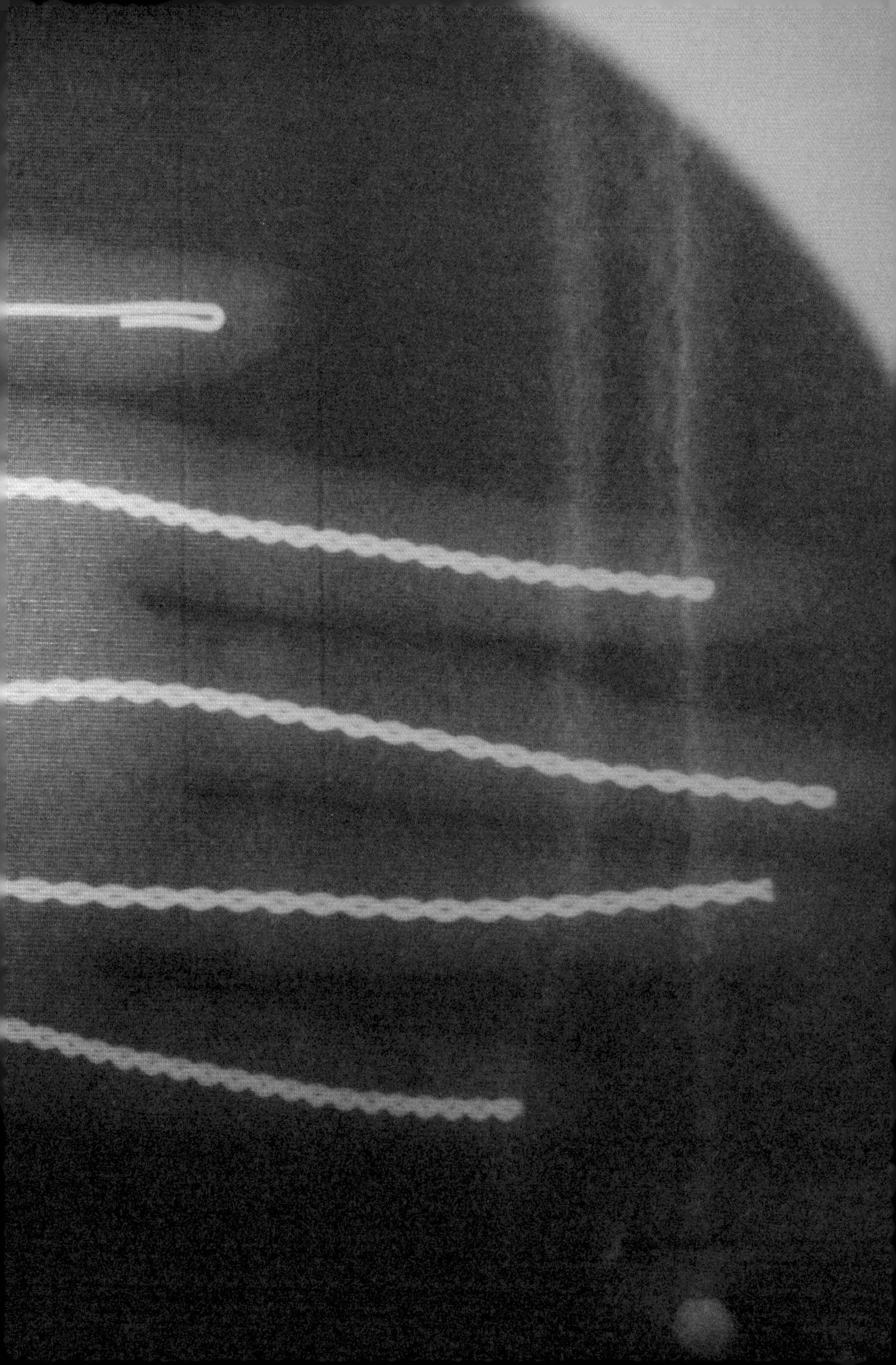

Marvin Böhm

You’re Not As ___ As You Think

32

Photography can be more than a document or a tool to create an artistic vision. Instinctively, I turned to photography when my mother was diagnosed with cancer. Taking pictures served as an outlet for my thoughts and feelings. Talking about the pictures forced me to talk about and confront my situation.

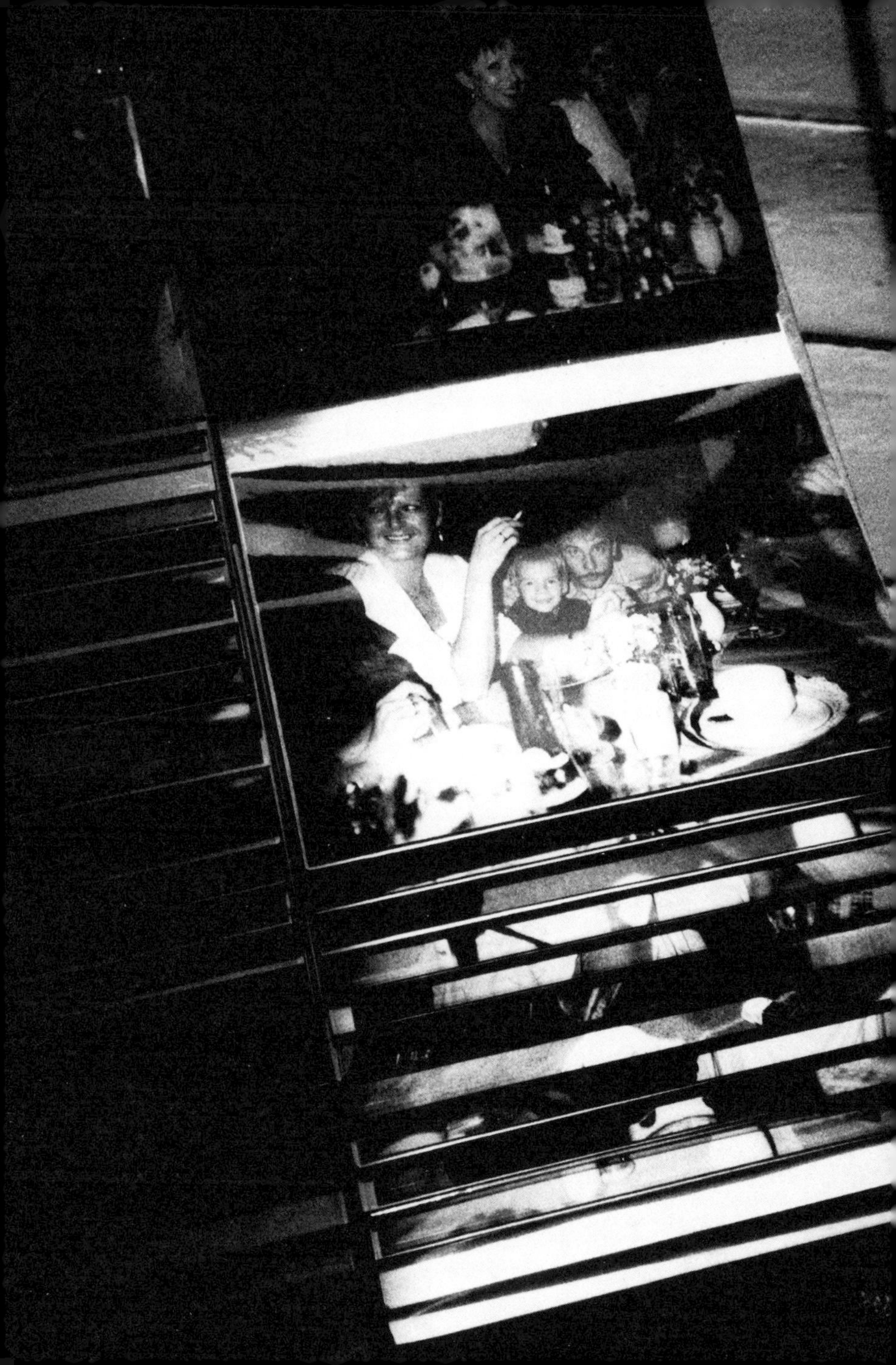

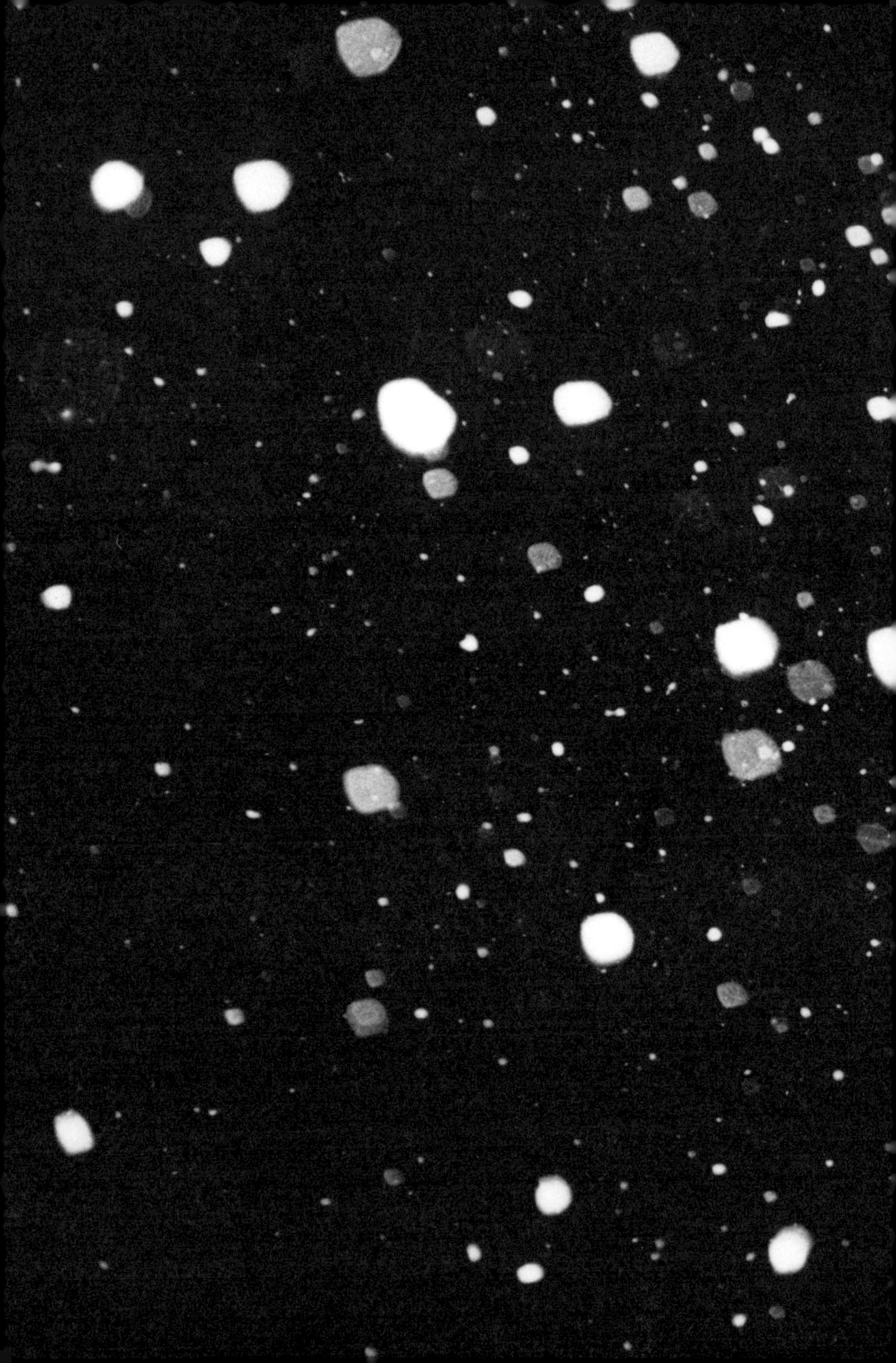

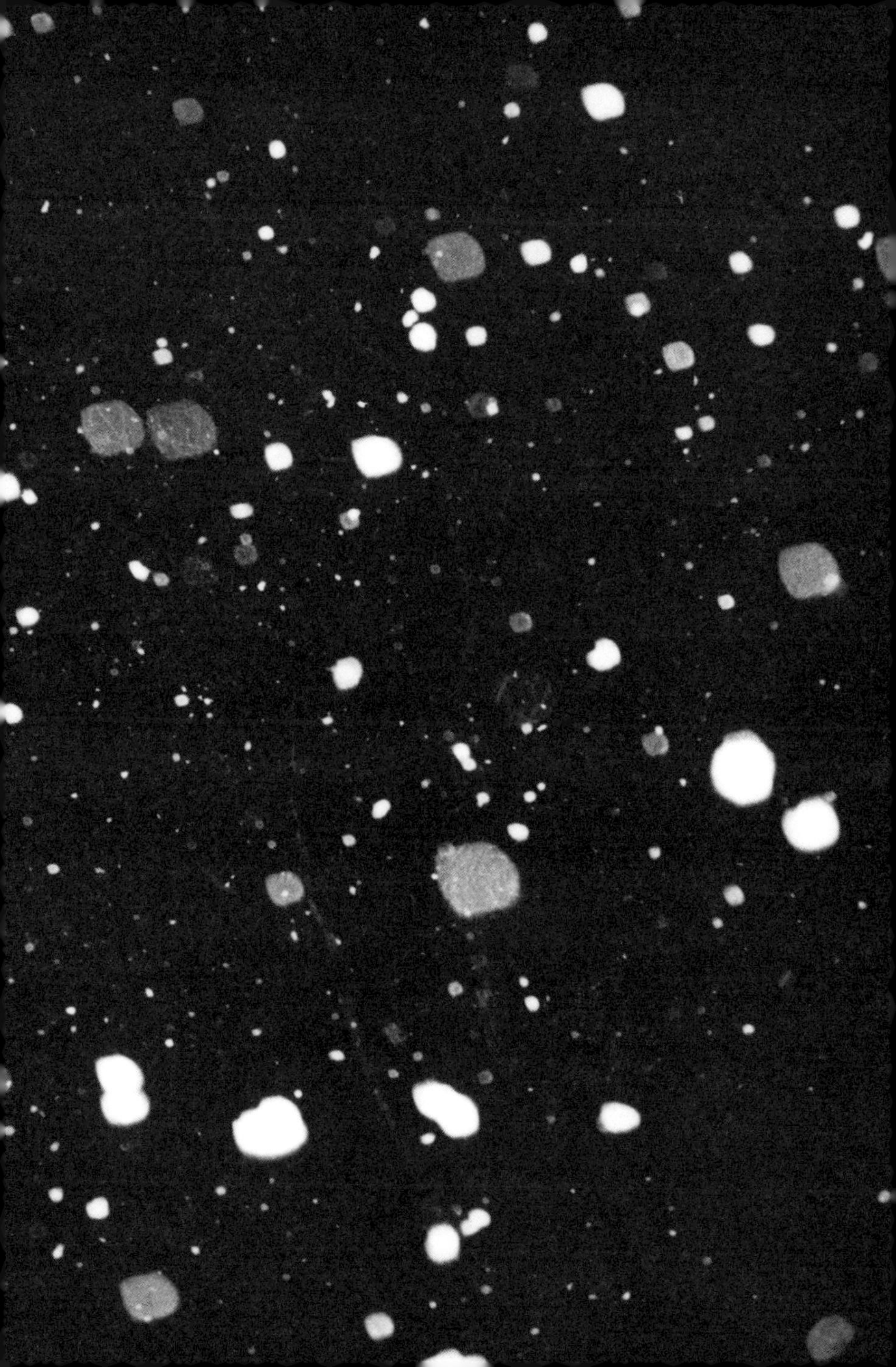

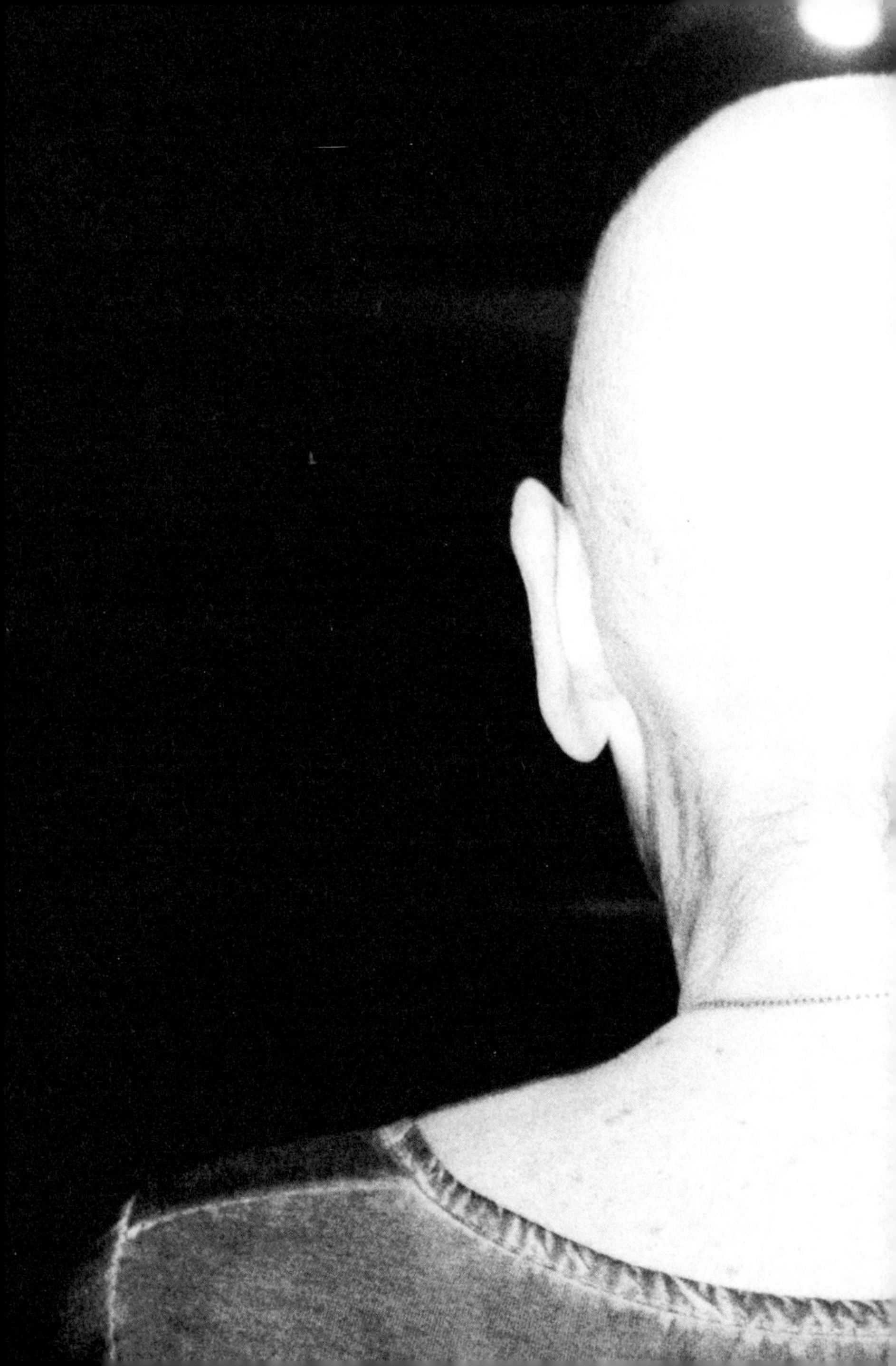

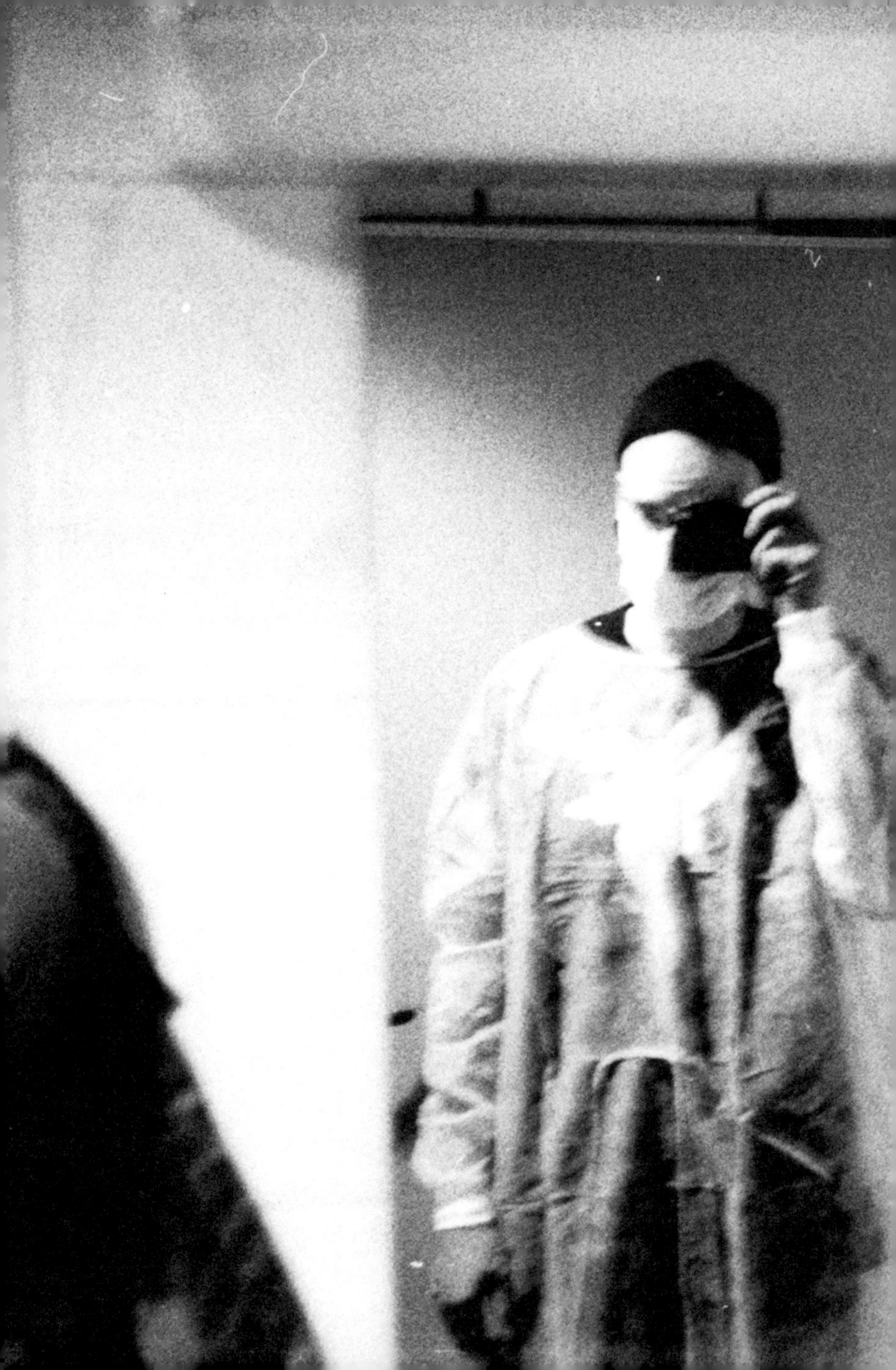

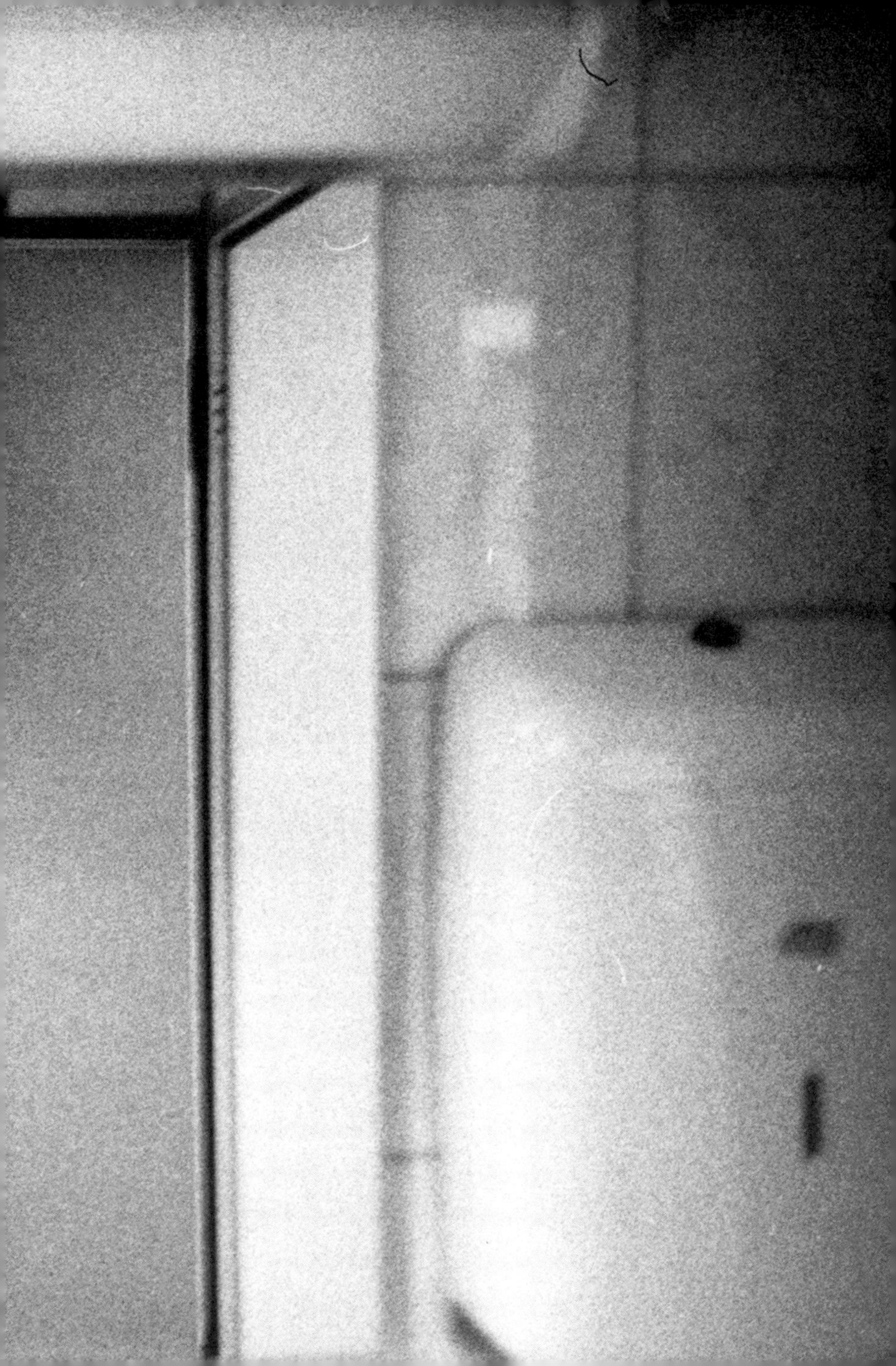

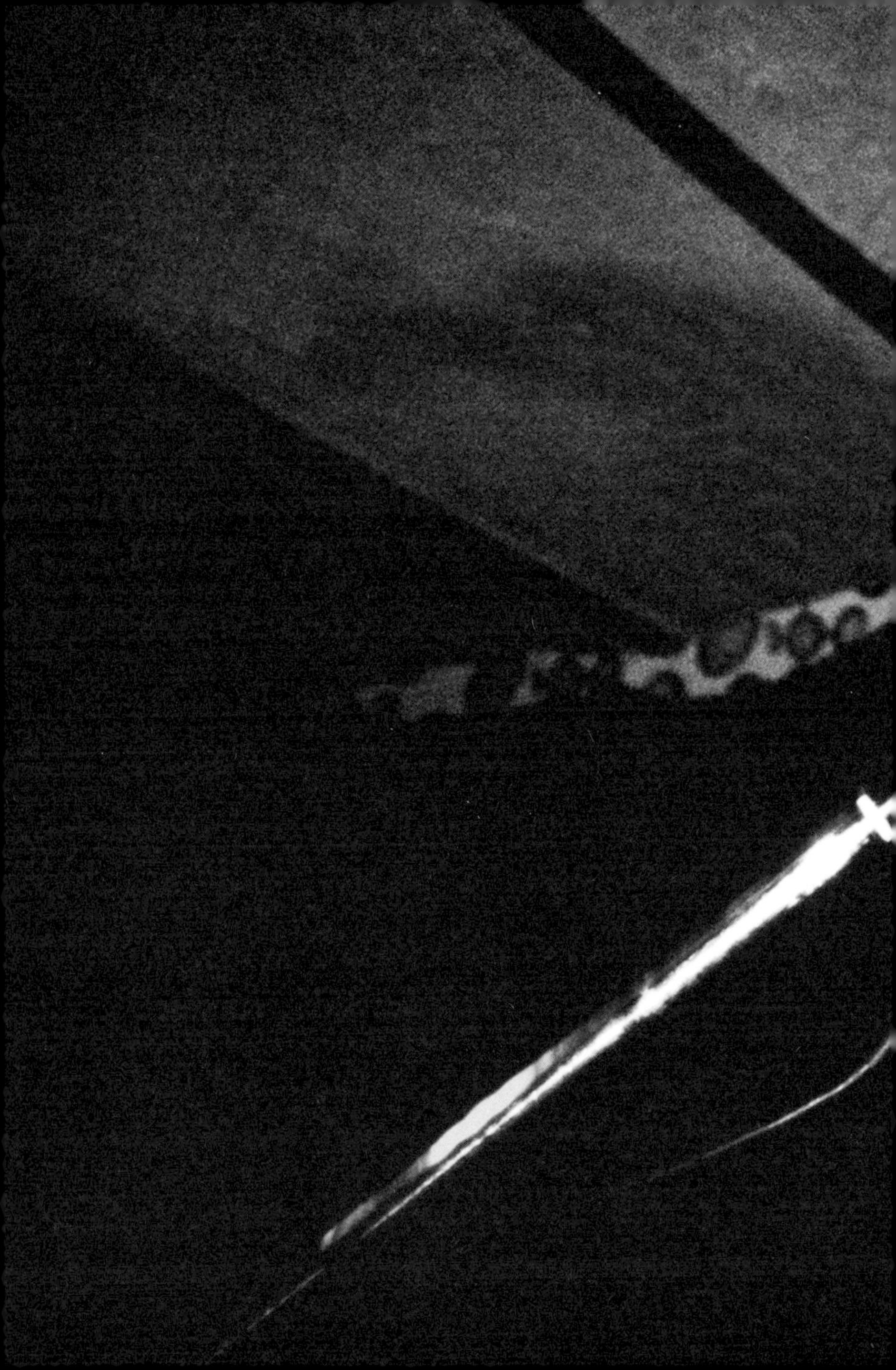

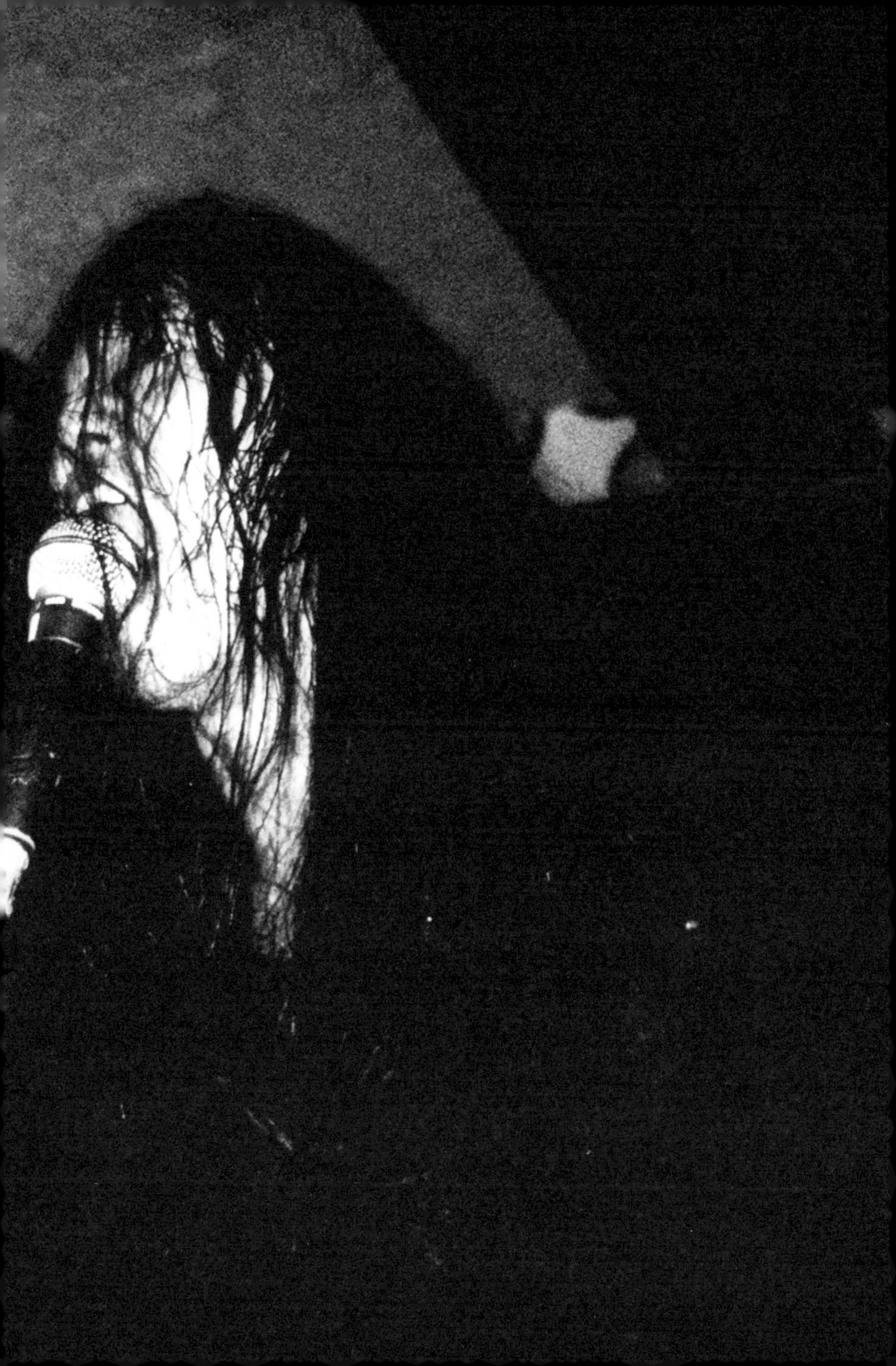

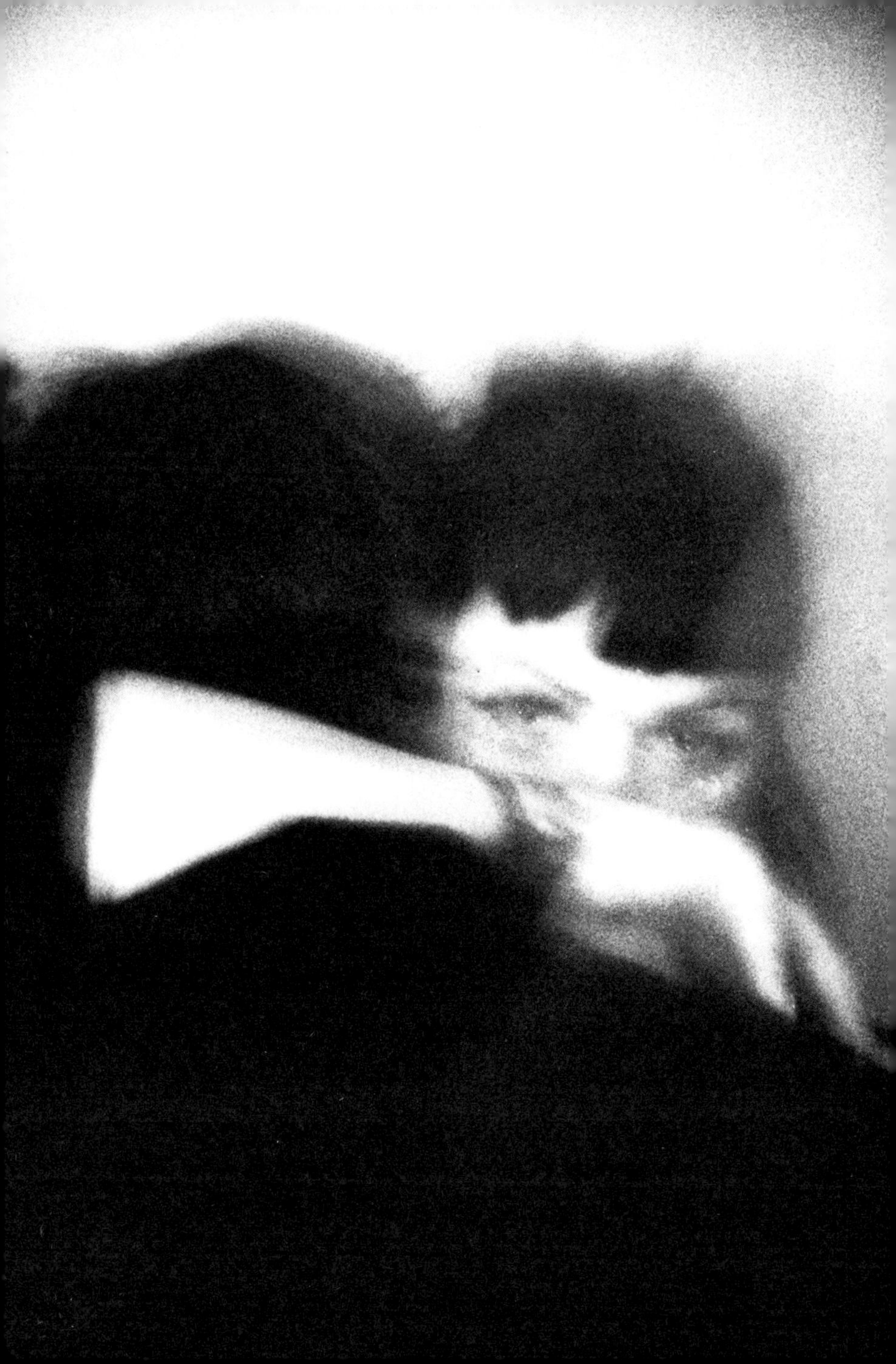

Josh Kern

Fuck Me

33

Youth—love, disappointment, being lost and finding oneself. Wild days, long nights.

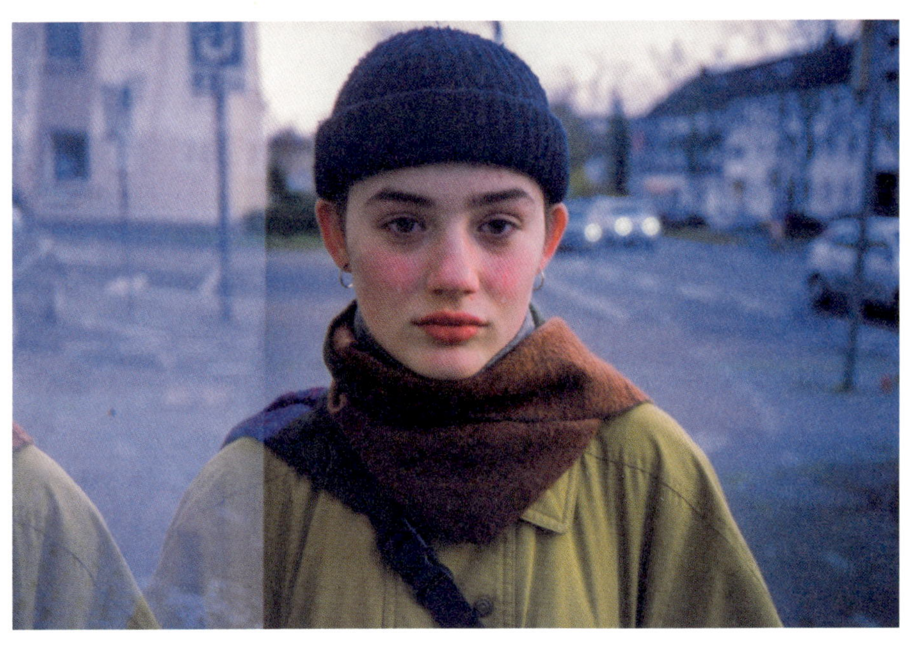

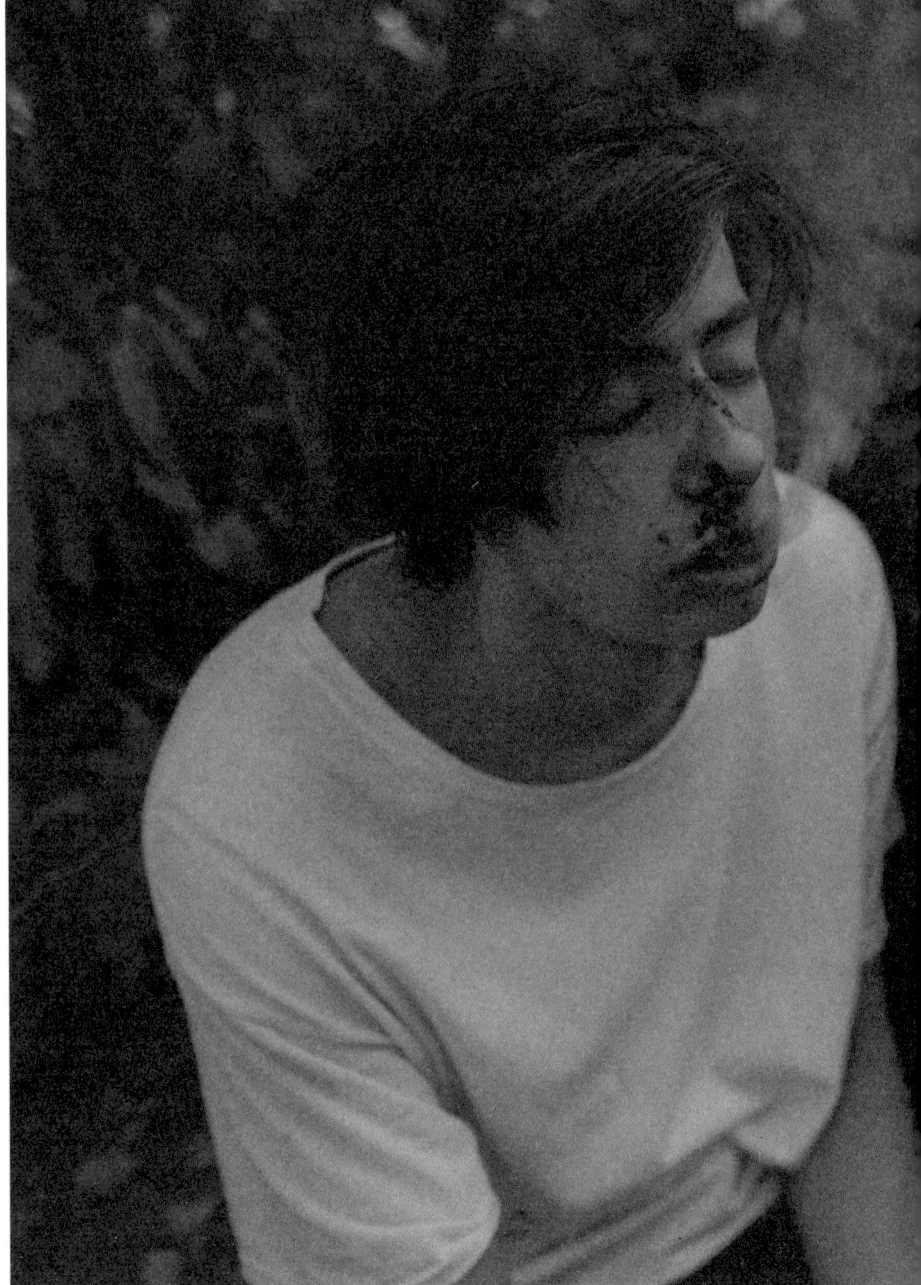

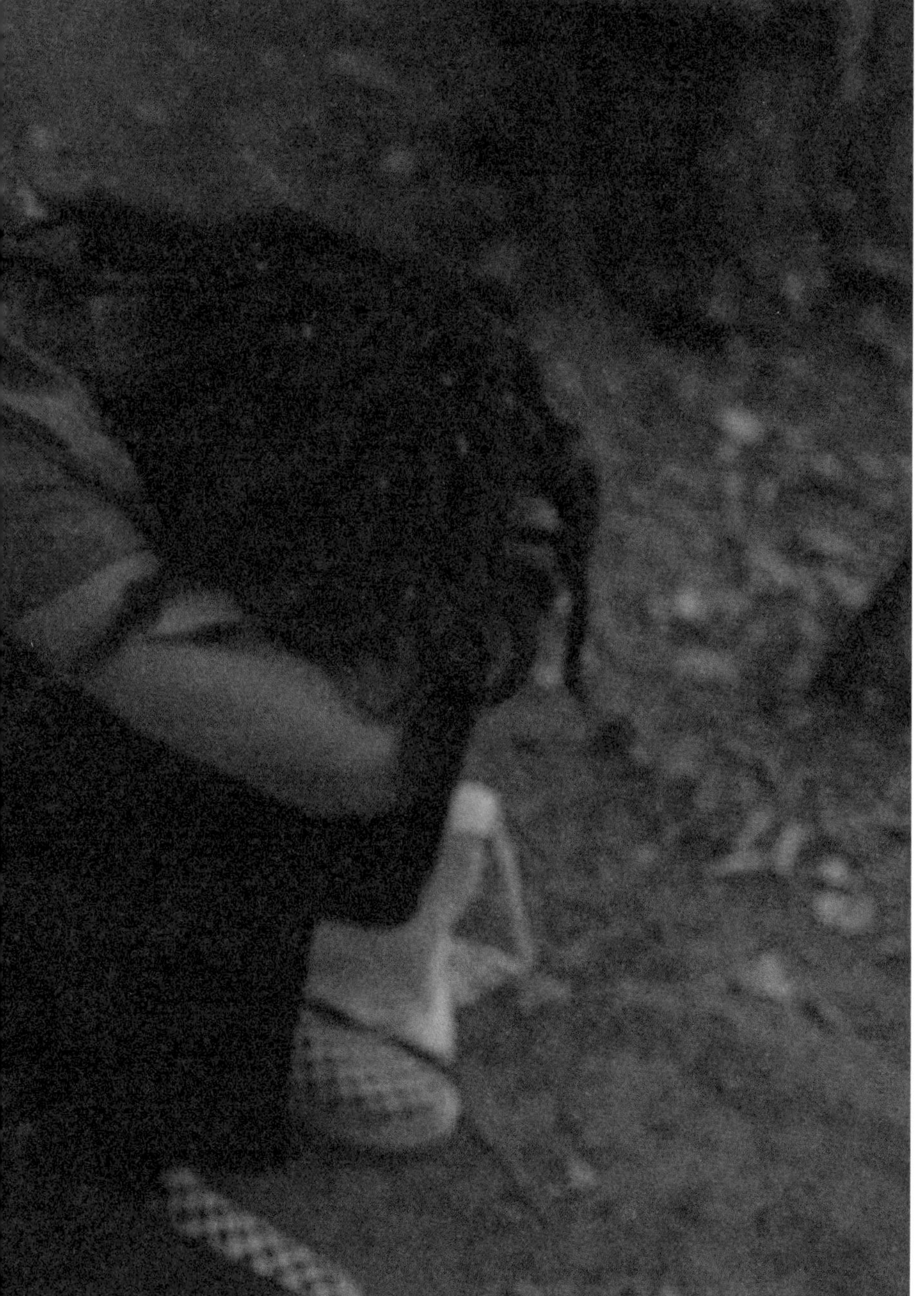

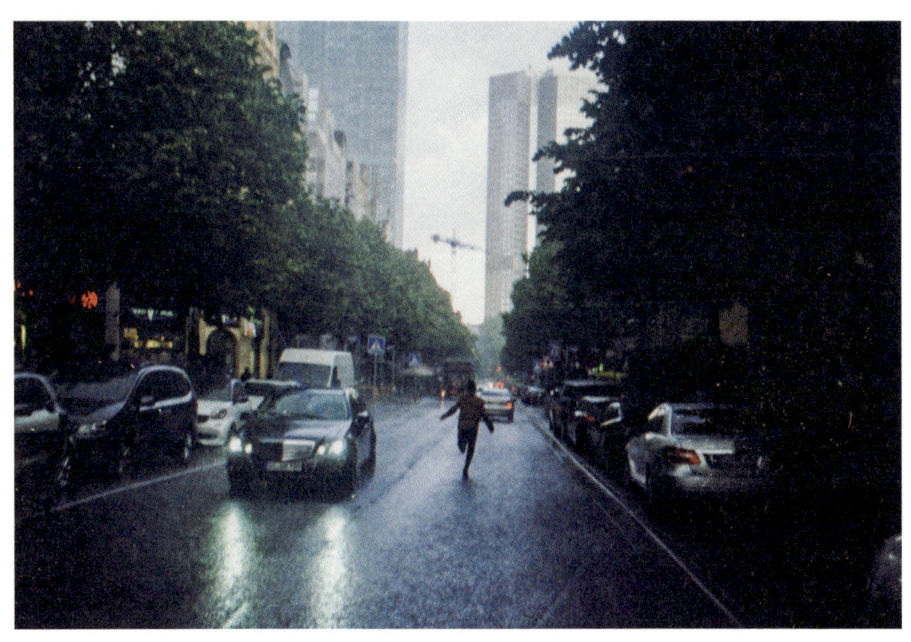

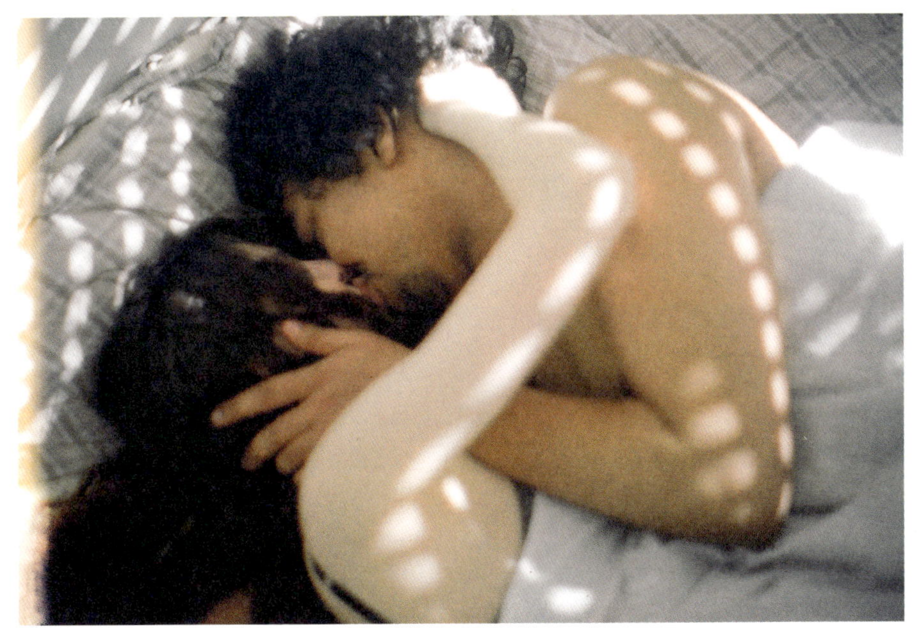

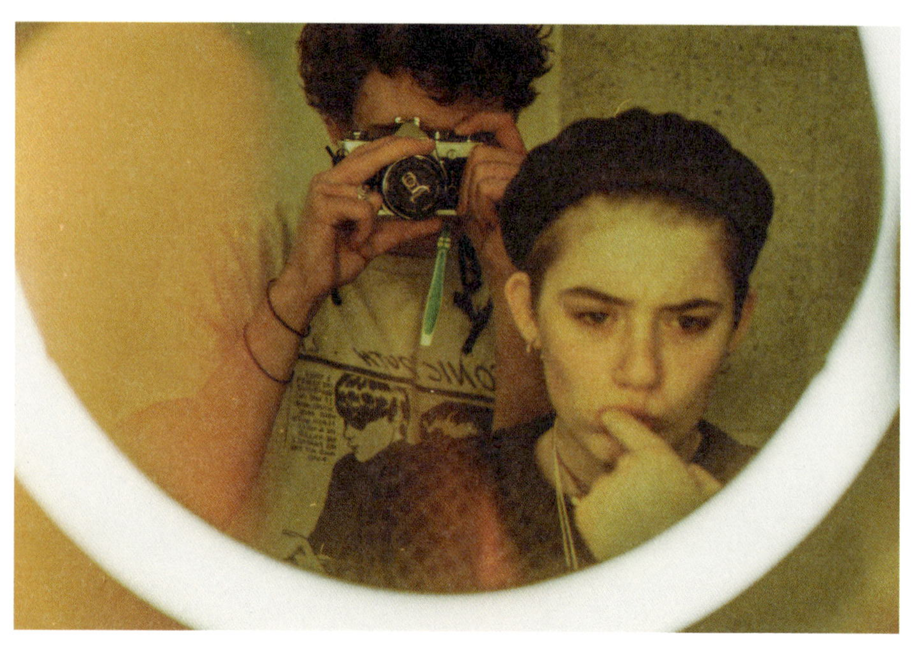

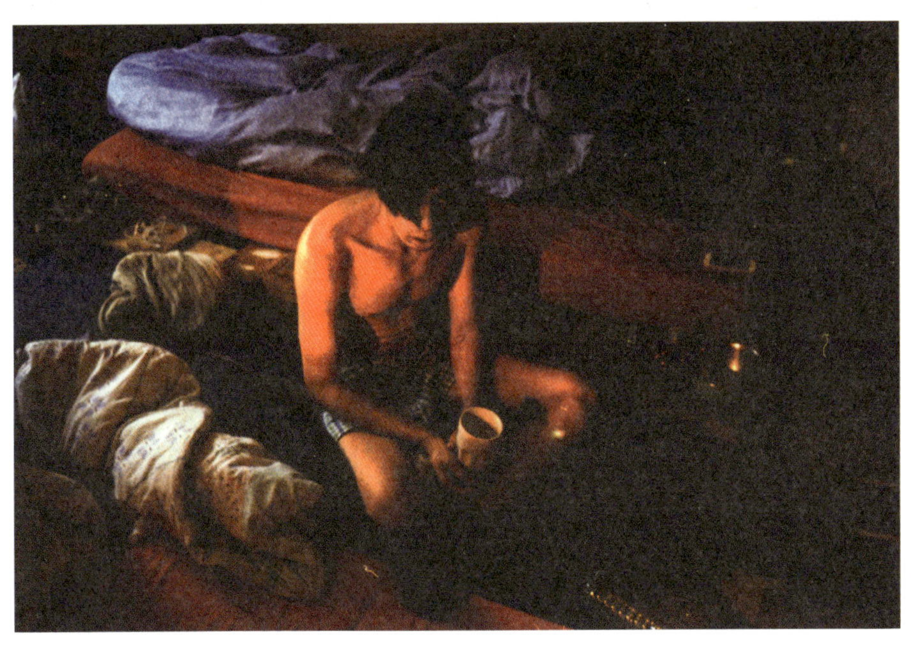

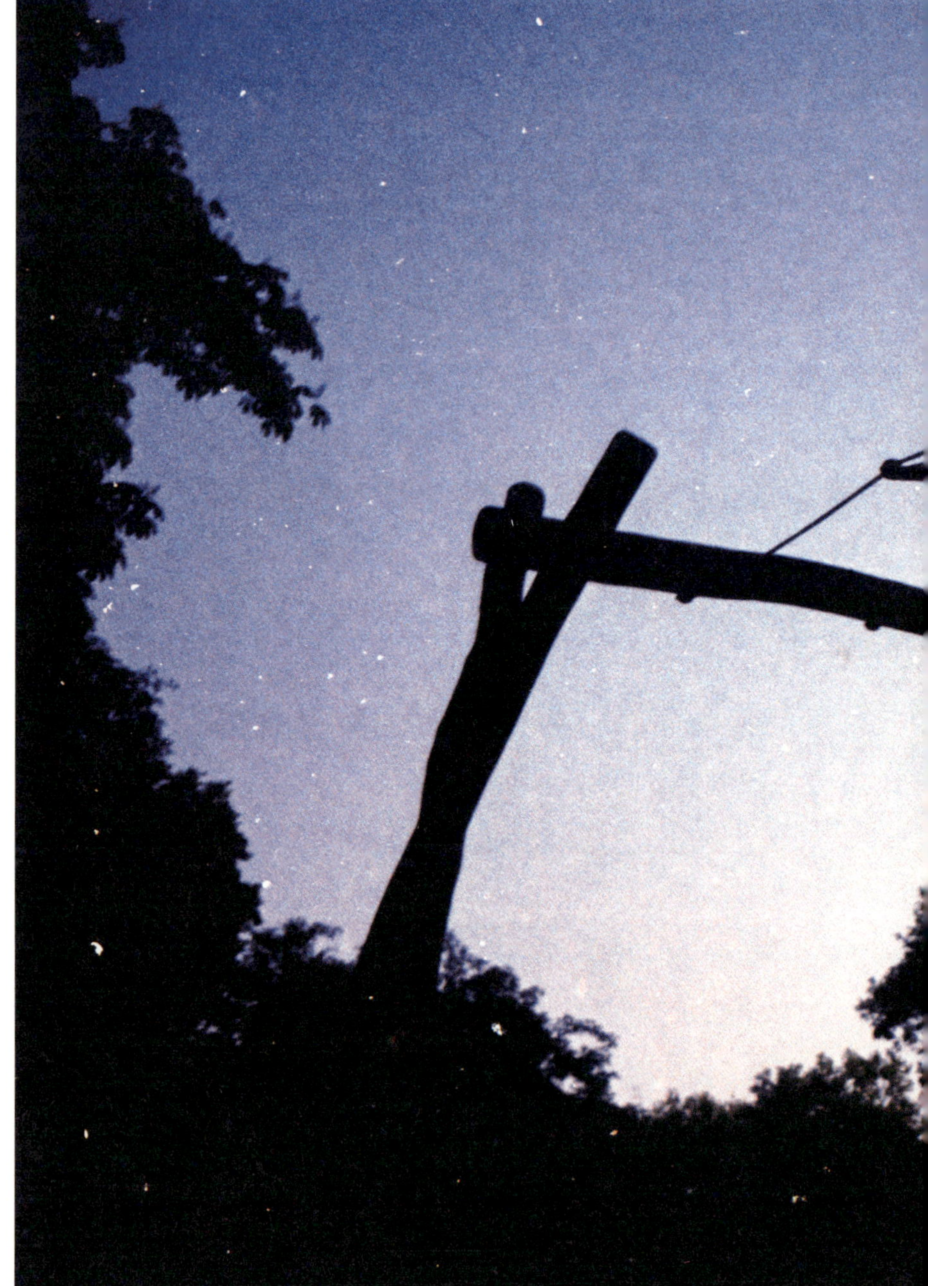

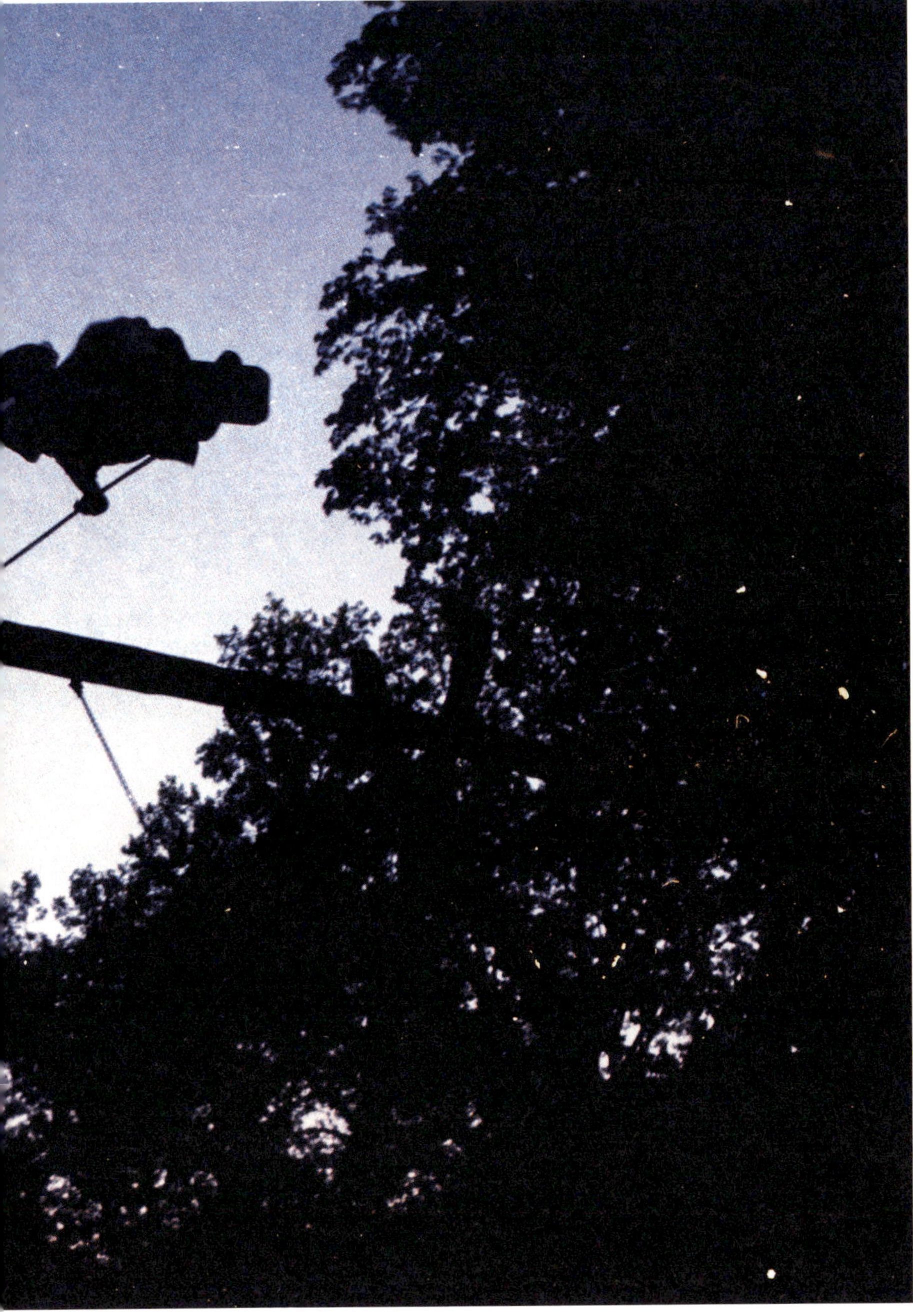

Benedikt Ziegler

An jedem weiteren Tag

34

The joints of adolescents hurt, their range of motion is restricted. For reasons unknown, progressive inflammation appears and forms one of the most common chronic diseases that begins in childhood: juvenile arthritis.

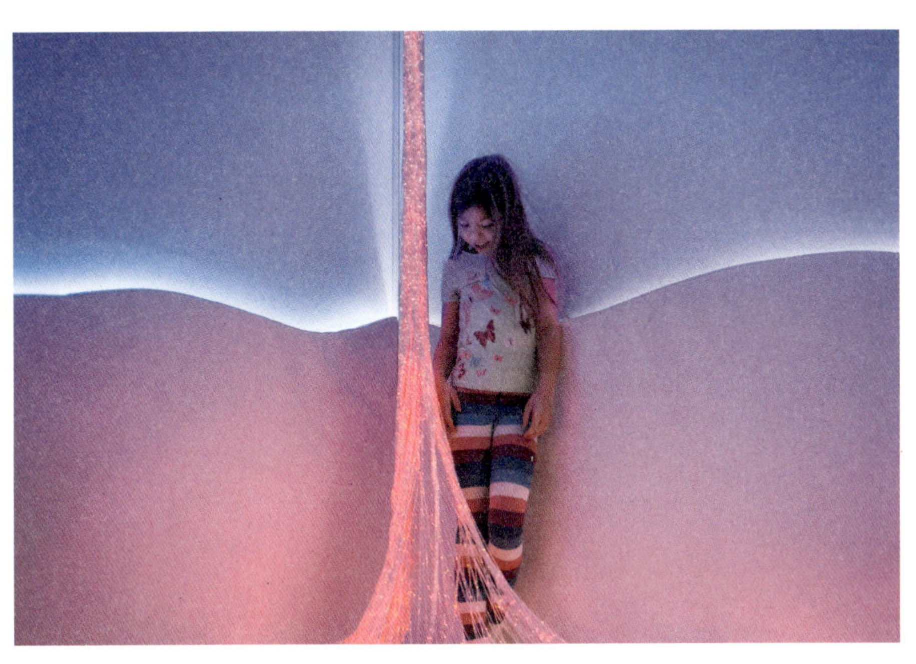

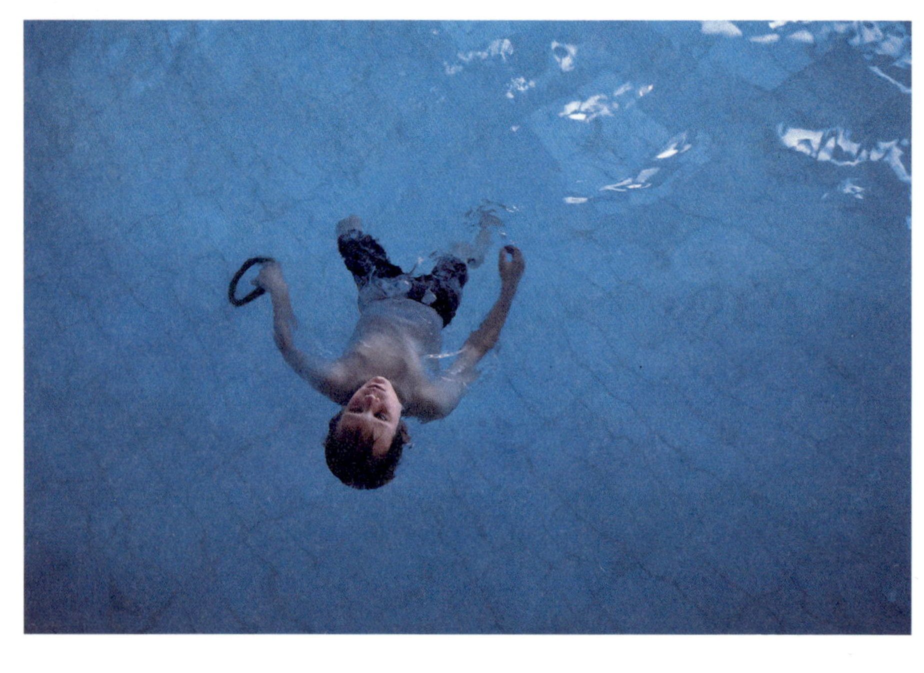

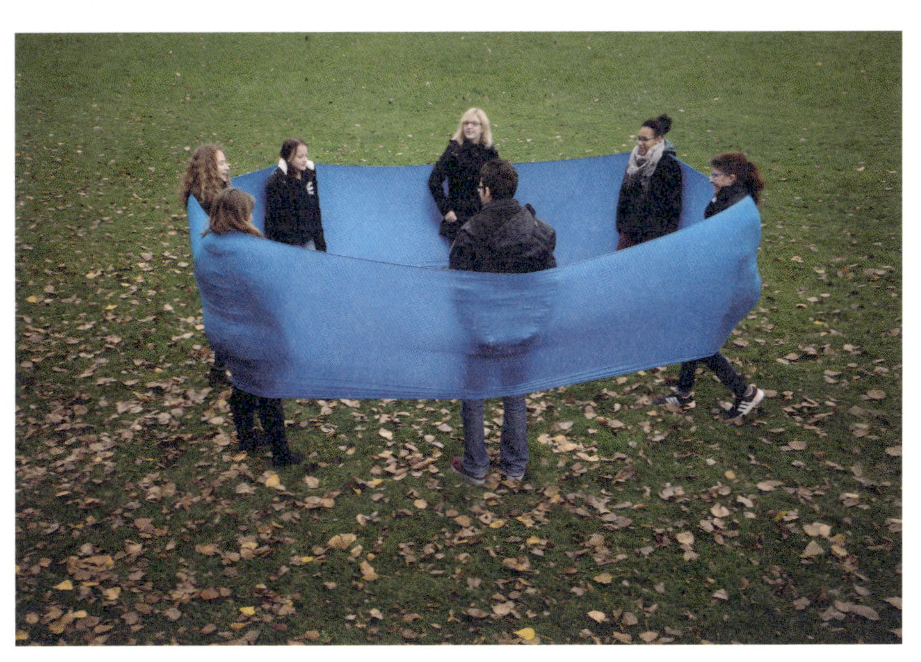

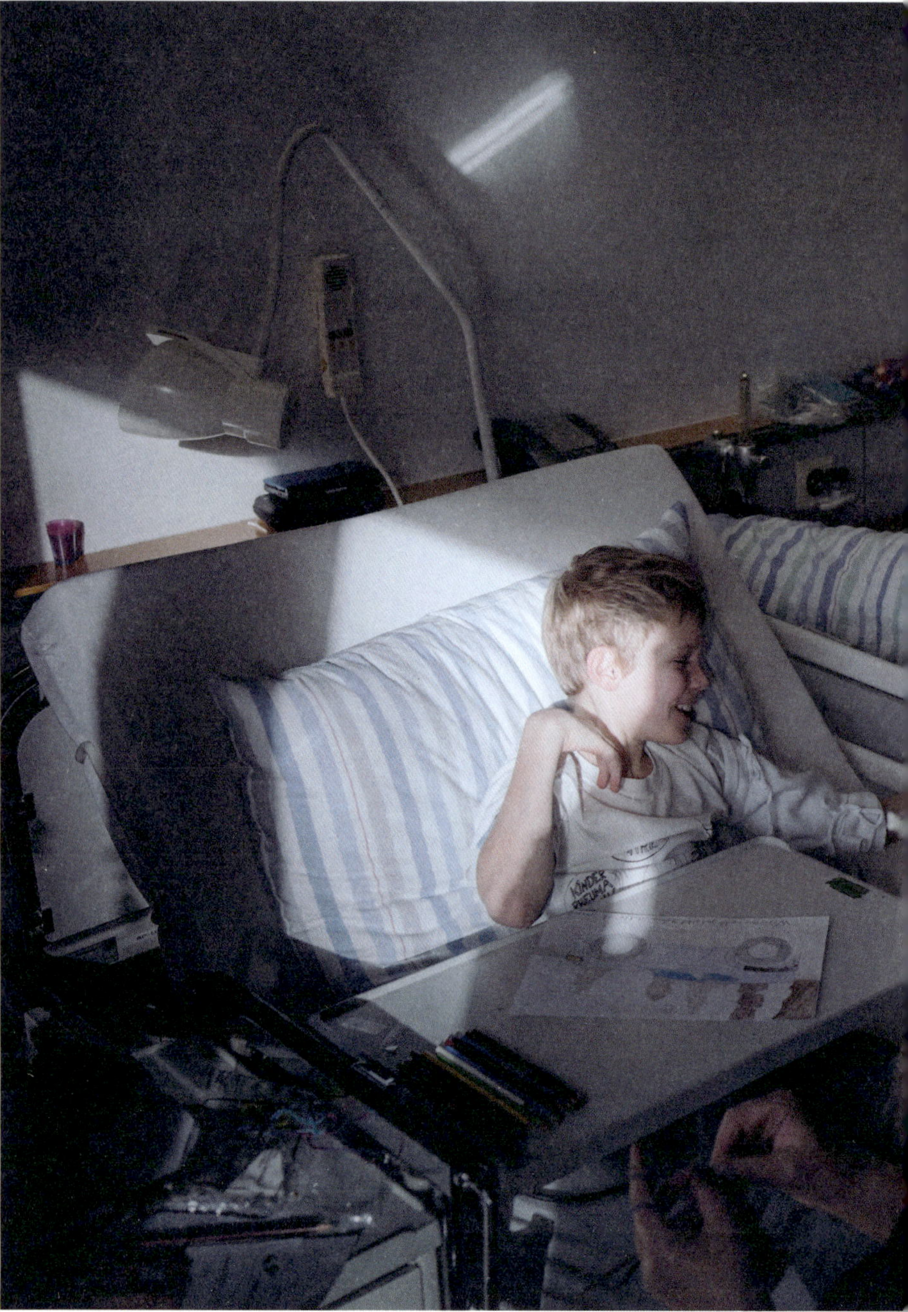

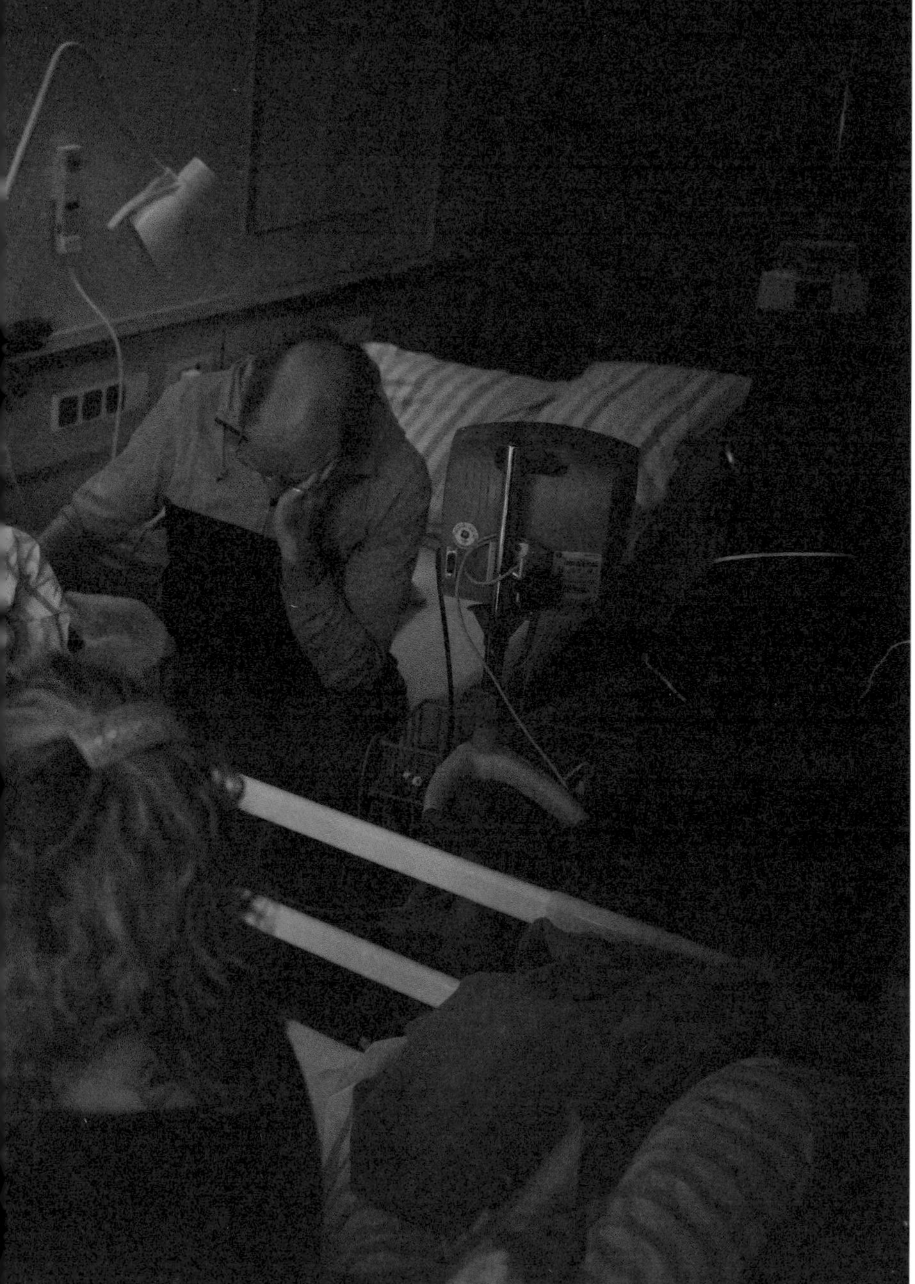

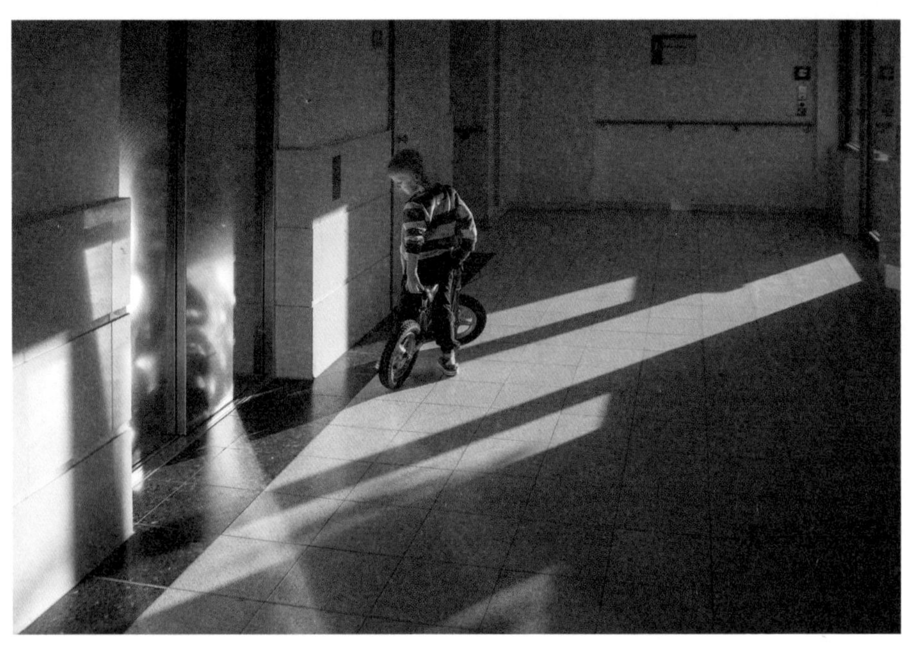

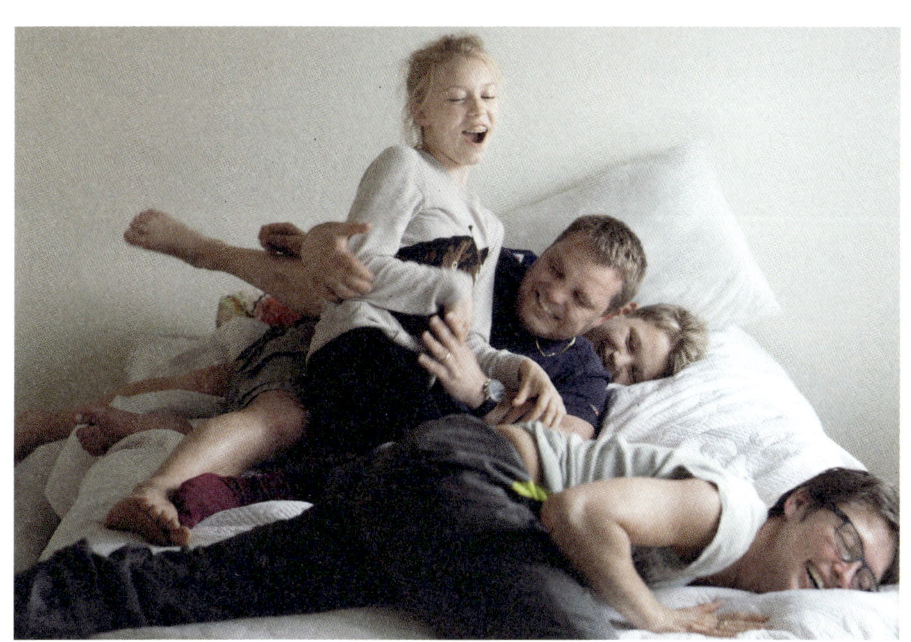

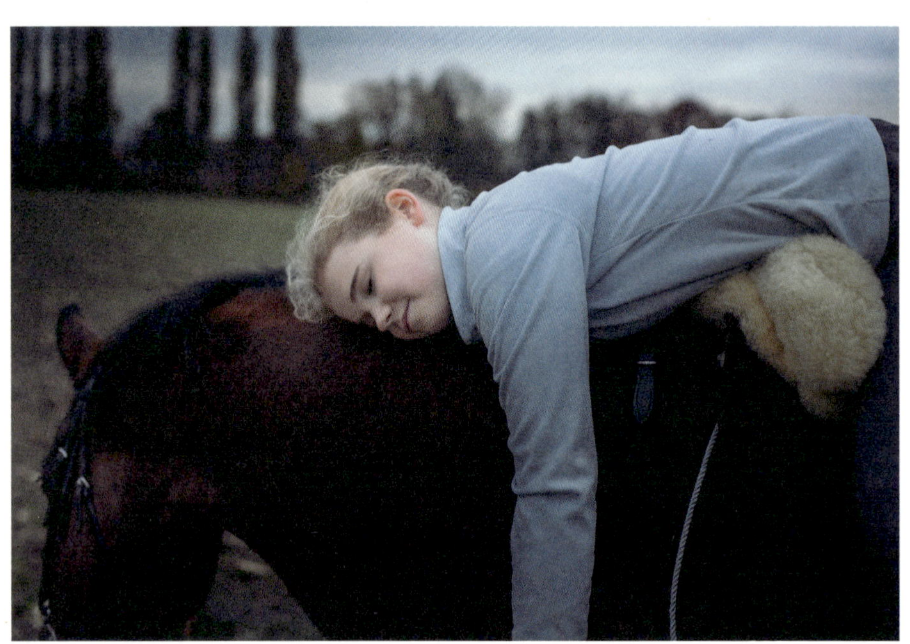

“We 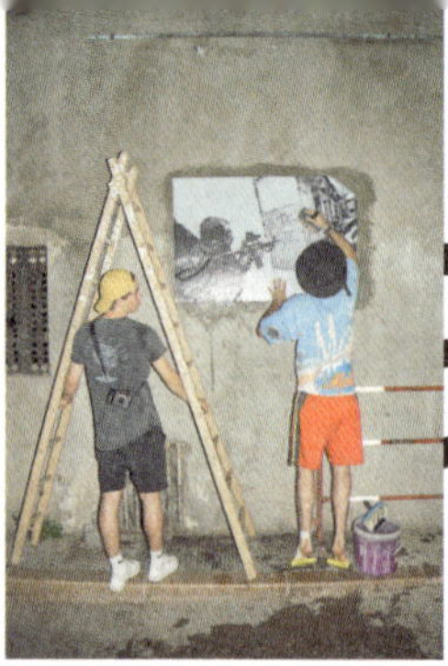 ag
love eac 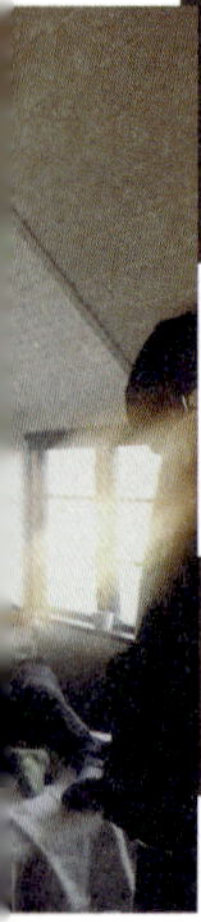
madly.”

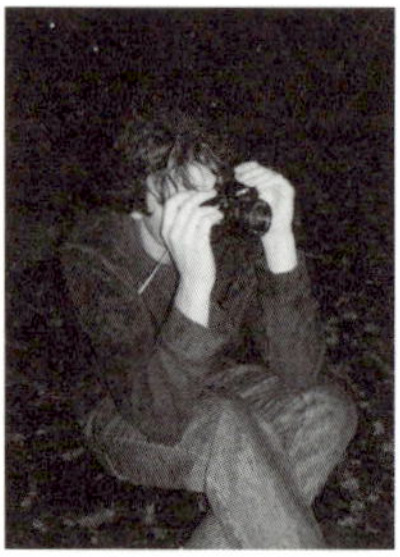

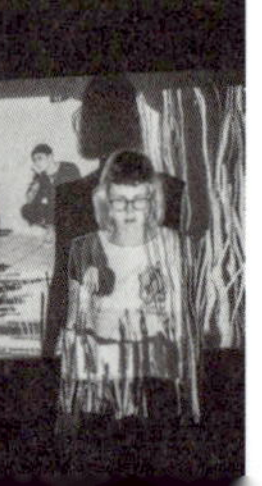

eed to

ch other

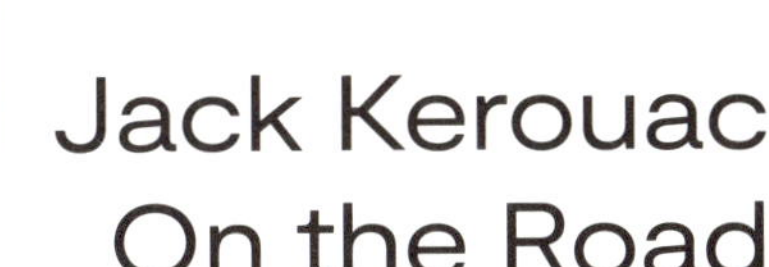

Jack Kerouac
On the Road

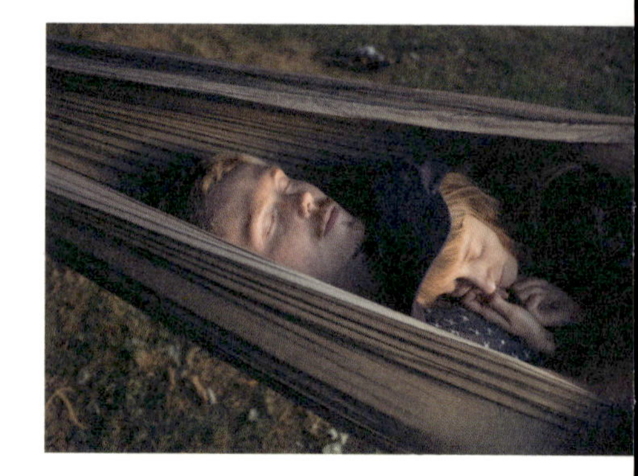

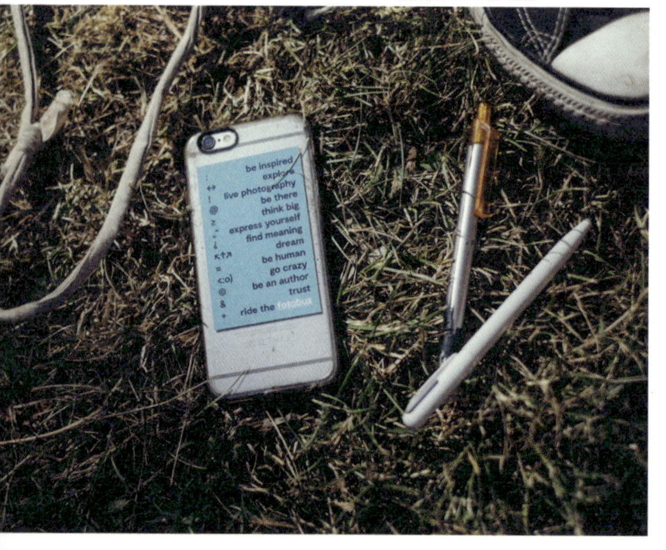
be inspired
explore
live photography
be there
think big
express yourself
find meaning
dream
be human
go crazy
be an author
trust
ride the fotobus

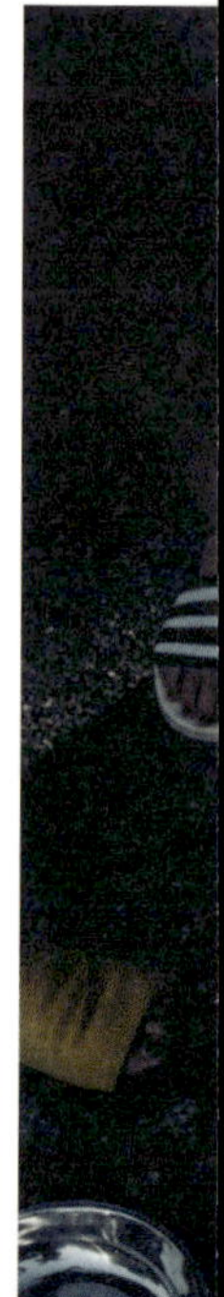

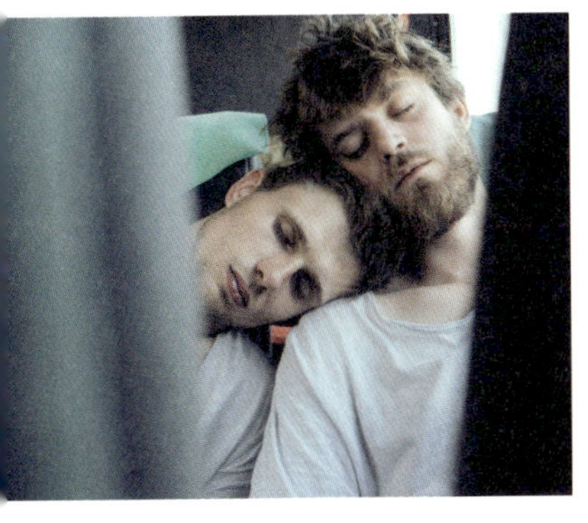

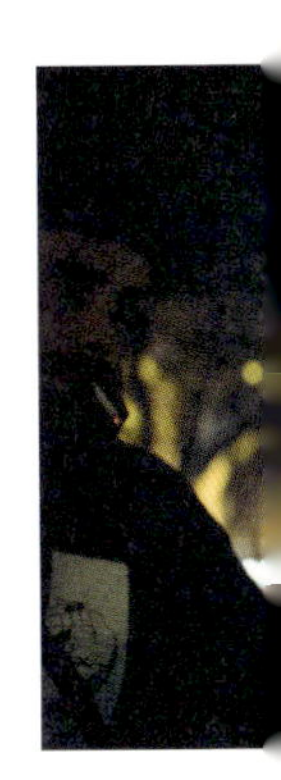

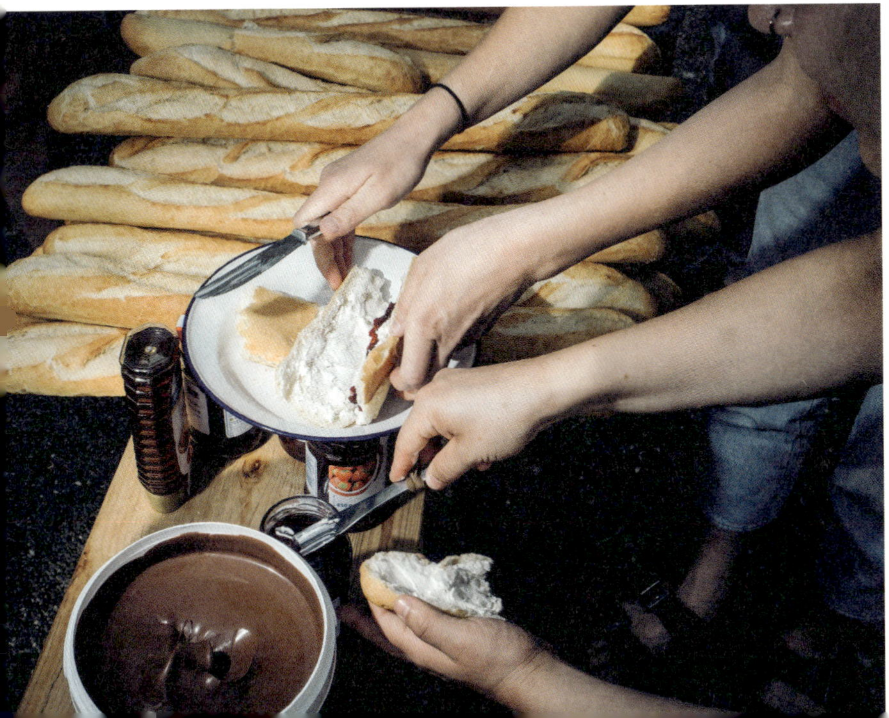

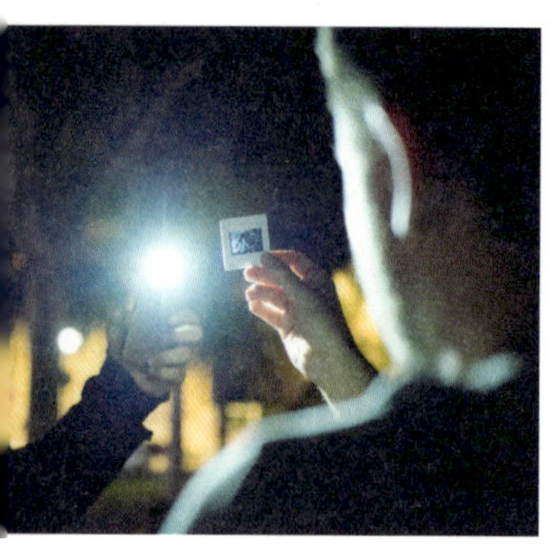

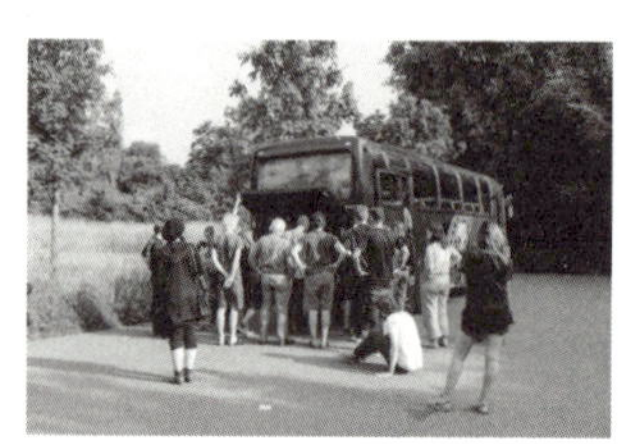

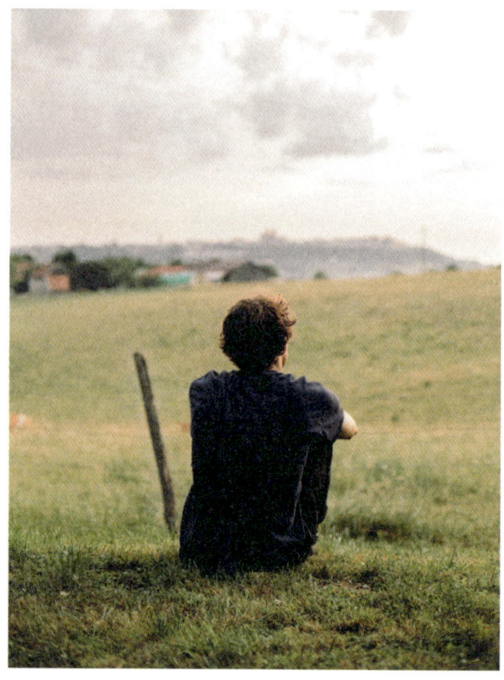

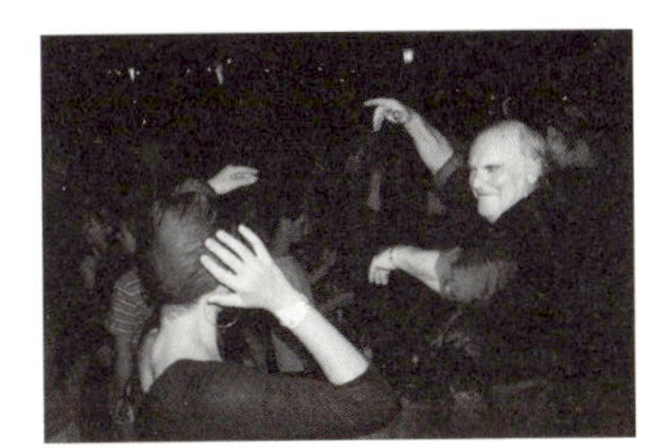

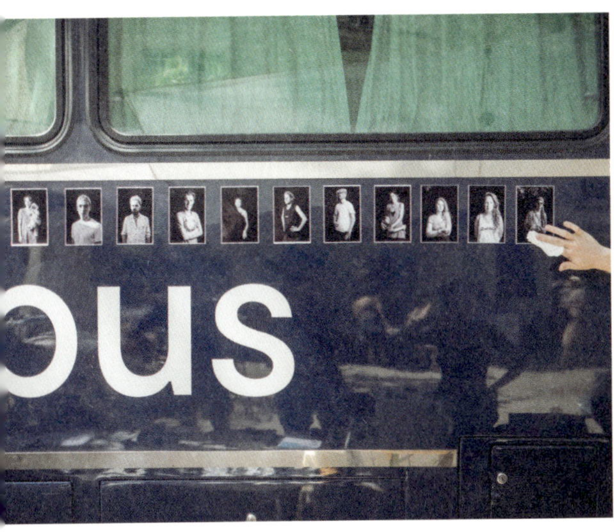
ous

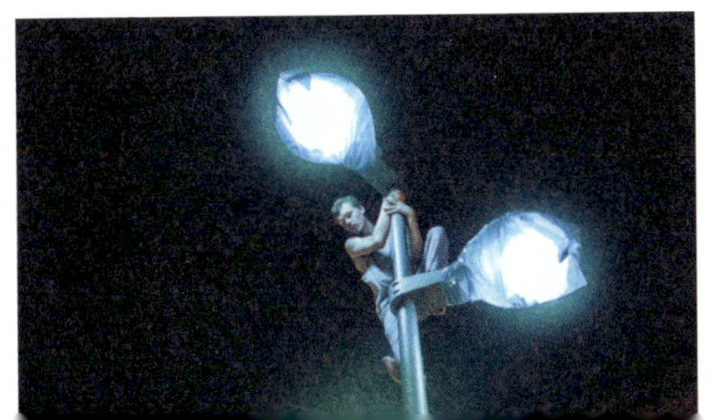

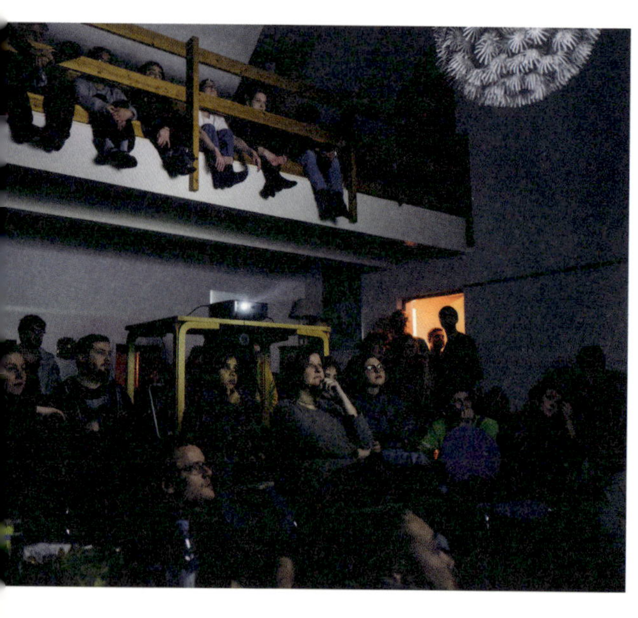

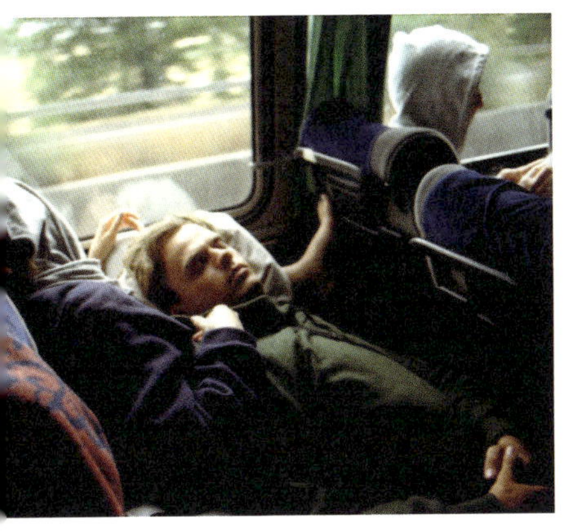

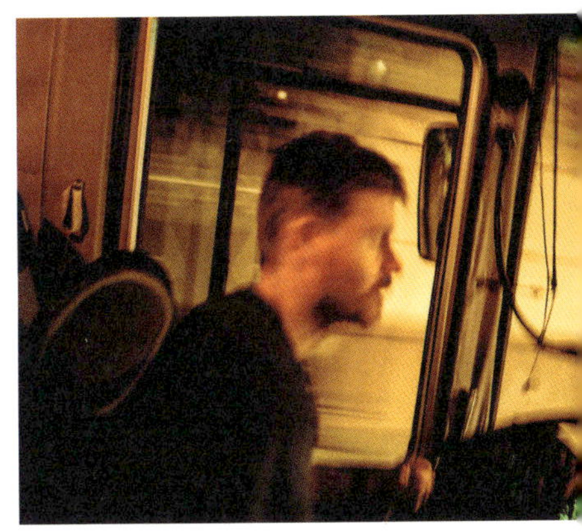

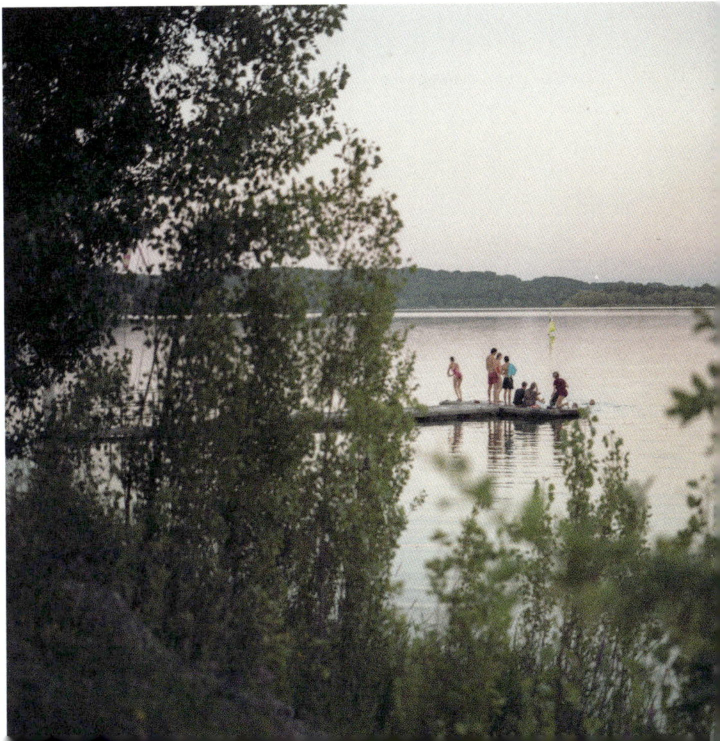

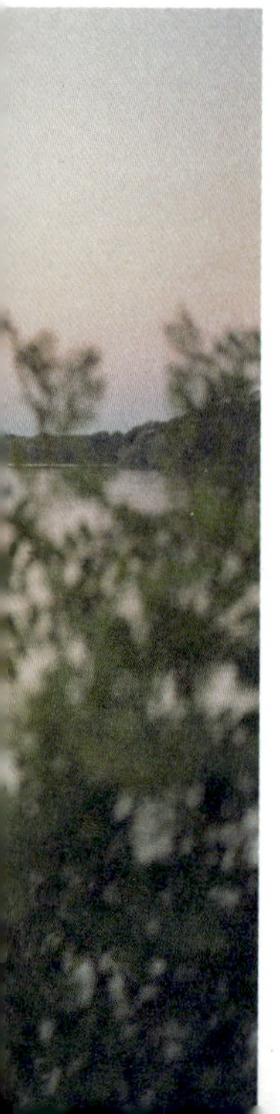
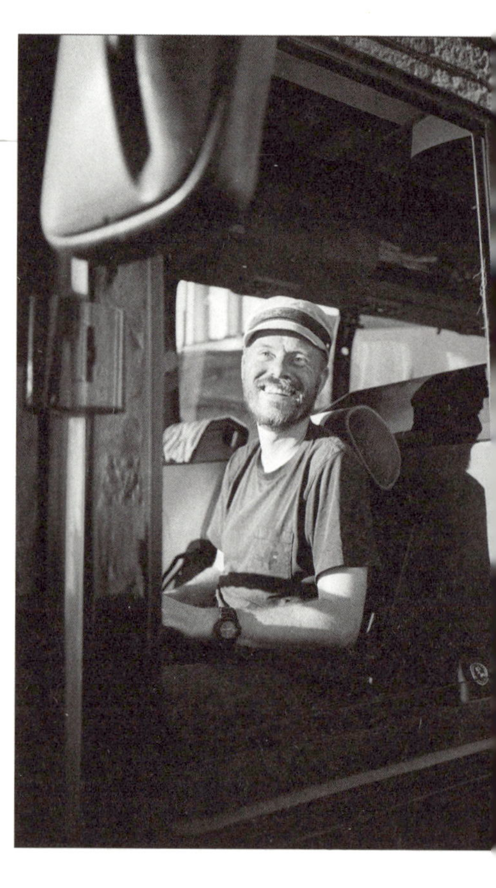